PUBLIC RELATIONS AS ACTIVISM

Postmodern Approaches to Theory & Practice

Derina R. Holtzhausen

Routledge
Taylor & Francis Group

NEW YORK AND LONDON

First published 2012
by Routledge
711 Third Ave, New York, NY 10017

Simultaneously published in the UK
by Routledge
2 Park Square, Milton Park, Abingdon, Oxon OX14 4RN

Routledge is an imprint of the Taylor & Francis Group, an informa business

Library of Congress Cataloging in Publication Data
Holtzhausen, Derina Rhoda.
    Public relations as activism : postmodern approaches to theory & practice / by Derina R. Holtzhausen.
    p. cm.
    1. Public relations. 2. Social movements. I. Title.
    HD59.H597 2011
    659.2—dc22
    2010042514

ISBN 13: 978-0-8058-5523-4 (hbk)
ISBN 13: 978-0-203-81909-8 (ebk)

Typeset in Bembo and Stone Sans by
EvS Communication Networx, Inc.

WITH THANKS TO MY FAMILY:

Paul Sr., Paul Jr., Helen, Marla, Lize,
Ben, Dries, Marie and Mandy

This book is dedicated to my granddaughter,
Lola Holtzhausen

Special recognition and thanks go to Helen Greene
of Greenhaus GFX for the cover design.

CONTENTS

PREFACE

I would not have been able to write this book if I had not been born and raised in South Africa. Due to a unique set of circumstances my consciousness took shape at the intersection of race, class, gender, ethnicity, and culture.

As an Afrikaner woman I had a unique vantage point to see and experience discrimination, both as perpetrator and recipient. I believe my and my parents' generations of Afrikaners have a collective responsibility for the years of discrimination of Blacks in that country. All White South Africans have that responsibility, including those from British and more recent European descent; however, I cannot speak for or on behalf of them. I can only speak from my reality as being raised an Afrikaner. There is no denying it; there can be no denying of the facts. We can blame it on the British, Dutch, and Blacks for their transgressions against the Afrikaner people but Afrikaners need to take responsibility for the institutionalized racism practiced in South Africa from 1948 to 1994. At the same time, we also should be proud of the way in which we ultimately did face up to it and became partners in the new South Africa, even though there are many Afrikaners who will never change their hearts and minds. Fortunately, there is now a young generation of Afrikaners who have no or little experience of the old South Africa and who are happily integrated into the new South Africa.

For me, the reality is that I was born and raised in exactly the time frame mentioned above and as a result that was the only reality I ever knew. I saw discrimination in every way imaginable: White against Black, men against women, father against daughter, English against Afrikaner, higher class against middle and lower class—it all existed in my immediate environment. Each of these experiences shaped my desire to understand why people who live in one country can have such different understandings of their world. I also wanted to know why people who understand discrimination well because they experienced it, could continue the hurt and discriminate against others. And ultimately I wanted to understand why people who have everything still want more and discriminate against those who are less privileged.

It was a long journey to get to the point where this book was possible. I was born in a remote part of South Africa, the Little Karoo, a semi-desert area in the southwest of South Africa. I was the youngest of four children and the only girl. My father was born and raised in the Orange Free State and my paternal grandparents experienced the devastation of the second Anglo-Boer War that took place from 1899–1902. I mention this because Afrikaner nationalism was largely born from this event, which had a profound influence on how my father saw the world and subsequently how I was raised. My maternal grandparents were from the southwestern Cape Province and were to a large extent not influenced by the Anglo-Boer War. However, both were descendants of the French Huguenots, who moved to South Africa via the Netherlands in 1688. This heritage in turn shaped my extremely conservative and Protestant upbringing, with its very strict expectations of how women should behave in the home and in society.

I remember a happy and carefree early childhood. My parents loved the Little Karoo, where I spent the first five years of my life. My father, a very smart and educated person, owned two general stores in the small town of De Rust (translated it means *The Rest*) at the mouth of one of the most gorgeous and unknown places in the world—Meiringspoort (*Meiring's Gorge*). De Rust was not a place for politics and I was not even aware of different races at that stage. That all changed when my father decided to return to teaching and by the time I turned six, he became the principal of P. J. Olivier High School in Grahamstown in the country's Eastern Cape.

Grahamstown was a toxic mix of South African politics and it was not long before I started to understand the realities of my country. The Eastern Cape is where the Xhosa people and the Whites met, often with brutal consequences. For the first time I realized there were Black people and the history lessons in school taught me to fear them. However, at this time my parents were house parents for the school's girls' boarding home and the cook was a Xhosa woman, Mary Nkosi, who was from the Fingo tribe. Mary was my second mother and I loved her and still do, although she is long dead. I spent many hours in the kitchen of the boarding home with Mary. She encouraged my interest in food, which still is a major hobby. She was a big woman, as African women of that time often were, and I can still feel her round hips under my arms as I hugged her, which was often. Thus, while from a historical perspective I was raised to see Black people as separate from us and inferior, I also experienced love for a Black woman as if she was my mother.

But that was only one layer of the artificially created segmentation of my society. Another one that had a profound influence on my understanding of the classification systems used to put each of us in our place was that of class. Grahamstown at that time had six or seven English private schools. Private schools as an institution were very foreign to Afrikaners, mostly because Afrikaners were poor and underprivileged at that time, and private schools were the epitome of the best South African society could offer. From a very early age I understood that only the very wealthy could send their children to these schools, which were associated with the upper class of the descendants of the British settlers in South Africa. Also, they always were English only, which made it inaccessible to Afrikaans speaking children, who had a big struggle learning that language. Except for one, all these private schools were for boys only; I must admit it made a huge impression on me to see how the neatly clad English school boys were served by Black waiters with white gloves when we drove by the dining room of St. Andrew's College every morning on our way to school. I, and I am sure all other Afrikaner children, felt inferior to this class of people. These feelings of inferiority were important to my later understanding and rejection of Afrikaner nationalism.

Then there was the school of which my father was the principal. It was the first and only school for Afrikaner children in Grahamstown and large parts of the Eastern Cape, which is why it was built. The English speaking community of Grahamstown was adamantly against having such a school in their midst and in a show of one-upmanship the Afrikaner-dominated administration of the Cape Province built the school on the highest hill in the town, overlooking the whole of Grahamstown. That most certainly did nothing for community relationships and virtually from the moment we set foot in Grahamstown I became aware of the tensions between Afrikaans and English speaking South Africans. With the Afrikaners firmly in the saddle of the South African government there was not much the English speaking people could do except resent the presence of such a dominant symbol of Afrikaner power and my father was very much the target of that resentment. The English community also made clear their disdain for Afrikaners in general and did not hide the fact that they thought we were inferior. This now also opened my eyes to the concept of cultural differences within the White community.

But the most profound classification that affected me personally and more than anything else shaped my consciousness of the effects of discrimination was that of gender. My father profoundly disliked women as a class of people and I grew up with the knowledge that my father thought I was a second class citizen. He never missed an opportunity to say how stupid and ignorant women were and of course the main targets were my mother and, as I grew older, myself. It was only when I lost my second brother to pancreatic cancer in 2001 that I found out how this affected my brothers. On his deathbed my brother admitted that even at that stage of his life he was unable to forgive our father for the way he treated our mother, who never complained and took everything on the chin because that was how women were expected to behave. Unfortunately I never accepted that, which led to years of friction with my family. I have always believed that one cannot understand the devastating effects of discrimination unless you have experienced it. The problem was that it was not only our father who felt that way but Afrikaner men in general, who have a strong misogynistic streak. And even if it was not as severe as in the case of my father, Afrikaner men of my generation and those who came before us believed women had a place and that place was only in the home. I prefer to forget how many times I was treated disrespectfully and dismissively in business meetings and business environments, not allowed into certain places, or left out of business events important to my career because I was a woman. Black women had the same experience. A Black woman friend with whom I worked once told me she experienced more discrimination as a woman than as a Black person in South African society. That just about sums it up for all South African women.

I was saved by a liberal education that my parents never understood anything about. My father was a scientist and my interest was literature, which was a very acceptable area of study for young women. It was supposed to educate us while not preparing us for a career, since we only were expected to become someone's wife. What my parents did not know was that while I was reading Afrikaans, Dutch, English, and German literature I was exposed to views of society other than my own and although I was far too young to really have a deep understanding of Kafka, Goethe, Schiller, Joyce, Breytenbach, Roux, Brink, and Dutch author, boon, to mention but a few, these readings enormously enriched my thinking. I also had a natural skill for critical thinking, which was nurtured in my university education. It also was the late sixties and early seventies and all over the Western hemisphere students started to question authority. Afrikaner culture was no exception and a new generation of authors called *die Sestigers* (the Sixtyers) started to seriously question segregation, racism, and Afrikaner nationalism. Several of them lived in self-exile in Europe, particularly France, and many of their works were banned in South Africa. That most certainly did not prevent these works from being printed and circulated in the country because they mostly only were banned after their first print editions were released and the Censor Board got to read them.

Thus, although most Afrikaners were brainwashed to support the Nationalist government, particularly because many media were state owned and we were fed very specific information to increase our fear of Blacks, my consciousness already was raised. Together with the intense discrimination I experienced as a woman I seriously started to question the hegemony of the White Afrikaner (and English) male and became very outspoken and rebellious within my own community. The turning point came when South Africa got television around 1975. Until that time the Nationalist government did not allow television because they believed it would corrupt the morals of the people. With television we all saw for the first time what was really happening in South Africa. We saw images of how viciously and violently Black people were suppressed when they resisted the apartheid system; how they were forcibly removed and relocated; and the dismal circumstances in which they lived.

By the time of the 1988 general election in South Africa (Blacks were still excluded from voting at that time) I had thoroughly rejected my Afrikaner heritage. I want to believe my 10-year-old son was proud of his mother, although it could not have been easy to have such an outspokenly liberal mother in a predominantly Afrikaner neighborhood. I rejoiced with the rest of the country when Nelson Mandela was freed from prison and was extremely proud of my fellow White South Africans when we overwhelmingly voted in a national referendum for Whites only to continue on the road to a new democratic society. The referendum was called as a result of a rightwing challenge to the constitutional process, with claims "the people" did not support it. This was the first (and only) election for Whites only that Black South Africans supported because they knew it was pivotal to the future of the country. This election led to the country's first general election in 1994 in which all South Africans participated equally and which led to the current dispensation in the country.

Before that election, in 1992, I received a grant from the South African Human Sciences Research Council to conduct international research for my doctorate, which I just started at that time. I enrolled in the Rand Afrikaans University in Johannesburg because they had the strongest and most dynamic program in communication science at that time. In fact, my initial adviser was Professor Willem de Klerk, the brother of F. W. de Klerk, who was the last White president of the country and who spearheaded the dismantling of apartheid. A few years later F. W. de Klerk was the joint winner of the Nobel Peace Prize with Nelson Mandela. It was general knowledge at that time that Professor de Klerk was the power behind the throne and played a big role in convincing his brother to dismantle the existing political system. I undertook my international trip before I started on my dissertation. I had a vague idea of what I wanted to do, as is the case with most doctoral students.

It took me many years to get to that point. Shortly after completing my honors degree in Afrikaans-Dutch literature at University of Pretoria in 1971 I became a journalist at the ripe age of 21. From there I moved into public relations counseling, serving mostly financial clients. After a three-year stint teaching at Technikon Pretoria at the beginning of the 1990s I became head of corporate communication of the South African Tourism Board and became very involved in preparing the organization for the now inevitable political transition. I became the first person to meet with representatives of the ANC to start talking about the role of tourism in the future government and enthusiastically supported my staff when they started a trade union for employees of the board. I also spearheaded a program to address the glaring inequalities between male and female employees and became very outspoken on issues of discrimination. During this time I realized that communication workers were uniquely positioned to become activists in organizations and in their societies and were able to facilitate change by bringing together people who have very opposing views and worldviews to at least discuss their different positions.

Using my grant I decided to spend a semester at the University of Maryland at College Park working with the two foremost academics in the field of public relations—Professor James Grunig and Professor Larissa Grunig, the two most gracious and giving academics I have ever met. For most lay people public relations is a frivolous endeavor, an activity mainly used to polish the image of fat cat corporate executives and egomaniac celebrities. Unfortunately this often is true but my experience in South Africa showed me another part of the practice —a part that is meaningful and life-changing. Under the guidance of the two Professors Grunig I started to understand the existing theoretical foundation of public relations, that it was a serious area of study, and that there was a community of international scholars who studied the subject intensely. The academic field was alive with discussions about ethics and about communication in the public sphere.

At the same time I knew I wanted to find a theoretical foundation and a philosophical home for this form of public relations practice I became so passionate about. I increasingly became interested in the concept of worldview, suspecting it played an important role in South Africa's history. Even though I did not have a formal education in philosophy I imagined there was some philosophical explanation for what happened in South Africa: why we as Afrikaners allowed our government to continue on the apartheid road for 50 years; why women were so marginalized in our society; why the English looked down their noses at Afrikaners; why White people thought they were better than other people of color; why culture often became a way to control people in unspoken ways; why the Afrikaans churches preached the gospel of Jesus while justifying apartheid from the pulpit; why Black men who were discriminated against continued to discriminate against each other and against Black women; why mothers who were discriminated against submitted their daughters to the same fate.

While taking a class with Professor Larissa Grunig in the preparation of my dissertation proposal, I came across a book that changed my life—*Postmodern theory, Critical interrogations* by Steven Best and Douglas Kellner (1991). Eighteen years later this book is a direct result of the work of these two authors. I have only recently met Douglas Kellner but I have read every word they wrote on the topic and I am deeply indebted to their thoughtful writing on the subject of the postmodern. This book is my interpretation of postmodern theory and its application to public relations. I am sure there will be people who say I am not well informed; that my interpretation of Foucault, Lyotard, and Deleuze and Guattari is wrong. That might be so, but my interpretation is from the original works of these philosophers. It is my interpretation based on the life-experiences told above, with a lot of help from other authors such as Best and Kellner.

In this process I mostly found the answers to my questions listed above. A lot of what happened in South Africa had to do with power and control and at the basis of that power and control laid a Western philosophy that has found it beneficial to transfer the natural sciences seamlessly to the social sciences. This led to the extreme segmentation and categorization of our societies, treating people like scientific objects and not human beings and as a result losing any empathy for those in categories invariably deemed as stupid, untrainable, deviant, less talented and therefore inferior human beings. That is why a husband and father could treat his wife and daughter with extreme disrespect; why Afrikaners could treat Blacks as inferior human beings; why the British could treat Afrikaners as lower class citizens; why men in general could treat women as *less than*. In that process culture, church, school, legal system, and language became silent and subversive methods of control.

The most joyous part of this journey was the realization that the individual is not powerless. You are only powerless if you internalize that powerlessness. There are ways to resist, even in the most insignificant ways. Those little resistances in everyday life not only empower the individual but also eventually lead to social change. From there the concept of activism in public relations practice was born. One of the most frequently made comments on my work is that it is impossible to be an activist, that my work is unrealistic and Utopian, as Lyotard (1984) predicted, as if activism means setting buildings on fire and destroying society. No. Activism is resistance in the small things and the big things. Activism means caring for the Other without asking anything in return. Activism means living life meaningfully, consciously, actively, honestly, responsibly, calling things the way you see them, intolerant of practices that marginalize, dehumanize, and discriminate, speaking truth to power. Activism also means continuously learning and gaining knowledge of how society functions. Knowledge remains the most powerful tool in leading a life of activism.

Postmodern theory is not for people who like their lives neatly packaged and controlled. To live life in postmodernity requires a tolerance for chaos and complexity and a resistance to unfair philosophies and practices. Now living in the United States I unfortunately find many things to question and resist. However much I love my new country and celebrate the grace and generosity of the American people I am increasingly seeing things that remind me of apartheid South Africa. The resistance to a Black president is nothing more than a code for racism. The so-called *Birthers*, Tea Party activists, and militia groups all have one thing in common: they cannot tolerate that the once unquestionable power of the White male is under siege, that more and more people are seeing what havoc they wrought on their societies and the globe, and that more and more people are joining a movement to resist. This movement includes White males who, like Afrikaners, have become critical of their heritage and are trying to change things for the better.

Now more than ever before there are reasons to become public relations activists. The new punitive and intrusive abortion legislation in Oklahoma, the immigration laws in Arizona, the rewriting of history in school text books in Texas, and the predatory capitalism that led to the environmental destruction in the Gulf of Mexico all are emerging from exactly the same worldview that drove apartheid. These are localized signs of a regressive movement and should be resisted locally. Let us as a profession stand up and be counted. Let us become involved in our local communities with local activist groups using our knowledge of and experience with public communication to bring about change. Working in capitalist institutions, we are the people who can and should question the devastation wrought on people and the environment in the name of profit. Perhaps we can finally shed the mantle of spin doctors, manipulators, persuaders, and empty heads who are the blind servants of those in power. Let us become "the next generation of radical intellectuals and activists who ... will use the insights of postmodern theory and other critical discourses to develop new theories and politics to meet the challenges of the current decade and next century" (Best & Kellner, 1991, p. xi).

DERINA HOLTZHAUSEN

1

POSTMODERNITY, POSTMODERNISM, AND PUBLIC RELATIONS

> *[I]t is not really a matter of arriving at the truth of the content of the theses of the book, but rather a question of coming to grips with the new effects produced by the new situation of a joint discussion ... it will be rather an attempt to produce a new book. The effects that have been produced upon us will be constitutive elements of the new book (the book of our conversations), and the latter will not be the clarification, the correct version, of the previous ones, but one of their effects upon two addressees, you and me, who are in no way privileged.*
>
> (Lyotard, in Lyotard and Thébaud, 1985)

The aim of this book, among others, is to provide a different lens to look at the impact of public relations theory and practice on society and is a continuation of the project I started in my dissertation and in subsequent publications (Holtzhausen, 1995, 2000, 2002, 2002a, 2002b; Holtzhausen & Voto, 2002). I hope that this book will contribute to a discussion, to producing a "new book," as Lyotard (Lyotard & Thébaud, 1985) suggests, on the nature of public relations in the Western world and the possibilities of practice to bring about a more just and egalitarian society. That is the first aim of this book. The aim is not to provide a direct critique of specific public relations theories, although I do occasionally use some theories to show how the underlying worldview and philosophical assumptions lead to theory building and related practice. This is a second aim of this book: to show that no public relations theory or practice is neutral or objective but, particularly in the social and human sciences, deeply influenced by the cultures and societies in which they are formulated. In turn these theories and practices contribute to shaping those societies and cultures.

As such this text might very well raise more questions than answers. It investigates the possibilities of postmodern theory for public relations theory and practice in more depth than any of my previous work. I believe that many postmodern perspectives already have become a natural part of the discourse in our societies. The genie is out of the bottle and because so many people found their voices through postmodern perspectives, the postmodern genie will not go back. As Ermarth (2001b) says,

> Once across the threshold of postmodernity—and most of us already have crossed it here and there whether we like it or not—history in its traditional sense, along with its founding unitary subject, [is] no longer possible simply because the postmodern world is not one system but many.

(pp. 207–208)

In the United States the fact that Barack Obama was elected president indicated that some of the old barriers of race and class are breaking down and that there is a much bigger appreciation of diversity in society. Other phenomena of postmodernity are the fragmentation of media and their audiences, facilitated by new technologies; an increased understanding of the complexities of the postmodern world; and more general acceptance of the reality that life and society are not neatly ordered but quite chaotic. At the same time this event has threatened many whose hegemony and norms have never been challenged in such a fundamental way and who do believe the world works in one way only.

This relates to two issues the book will focus on in terms of their application to public relations theory and practice: the postmodernization of society and the possibilities postmodern theories offer to explain, understand, and deal with a changing society. This does not per definition mean that existing public relations theories are redundant. However, it is important to understand that theories are created by people who themselves have specific understandings. Theories are not objective and all-knowing but rather represent one way of looking and explaining. Theories are the products of specific contexts. If contexts change, so do theories. In public relations there still is a dominant modernist and positivist approach to theory building. Much of practice is situated in the context of market economic principles of organizing and in finding linear causal relationships between distinct variables. In a recent bibliographic analysis of public relations theory Pasadeos, Berger, and Renfro (2010) found that the field of public relations is maturing but this also presents a challenge because much of the cited work resides in a specific scholarly (and one might argue self-referential) community. They believe it will be necessary to take note of Broom's (2006) warning that public relations theorists cannot work in a closed system and that public relations scholars need to see their work cited by scholars from other disciplines. In conducting the research for this book I found very little evidence of any citations of public relations theorists in other domains.

Fortunately, Pasadeos et al. (2010) also found that there is a very strong tradition of critical theory in the field and I hope this book will contribute to that genre. Many phenomena in our field today are undertheorized or explained in naïve ways, such as the role of media in society and their impact on public relations practice, the implications of globalization, and practice in the context of new organizational structures. Unfortunately, in public relations as in many other social and human sciences many "theorists went on with 'business as usual,' ignoring the massive alterations taking place and the controversies over their significance" (Best & Kellner, 2001, p. 4).

Rupture or Progression?

Some might argue that postmodernism is a passing fad and that modernism has won the day. And there are indeed many who wish it away because the questions and viewpoints postmodern-leaning scholars raise are uncomfortable. I wish to argue that postmodernity in many instances is an outflow of modernity, rather than a rupture with modernity; that pitting the modern against the post-modern is a form of intellectual blackmail that forces one to choose between the two (Foucault, 1984; Lyotard, 1984). They also are not binary opposites; as a result I do not support the interpretation that the two philosophies lie on a continuum with modernism on the one extreme and postmodernism on the other, as Mumby (1997) contends. These two philosophies do differ in impor-tant ways. At the same time I would argue with Best and Kellner (1991, 1997, 2001) that there need to be some criteria on which a life of activism can be built, even if those criteria are always contested and might change from situa-tion to situation.

Some postmodern theorists argue the process of postmodernization gave rise to a form of society that is so radically different from that given within modernity that a continuation is impossible. This book, however, will take the approach Lyotard (1992) offers when he proposes that postmodernism is a con-dition that *precedes* modernism: "A work can become modern only if it is first postmodern" (p. 147). He criticized the notion of a rupture with modernity as "a way of forgetting or repressing the past ... repeating it and not surpassing it" (Lyotard, 1993b, p. 48). As I have argued previously (Holtzhausen, 2000), post-modernity provides an opportunity to look at public relations differently and to find alternative solutions for a more just and democratic society by entering into a postmodern condition, to borrow Lyotard's phrase.

Lyotard's definition would challenge those who argue that postmodernism is a passing fad. If the postmodern is considered a phase through which para-digms are challenged and new ways of thinking are sought, all modern phases will be preceded by postmodern phases, even though they might not be called such. The specifics of this postmodern phase will then most certainly pass as it is absorbed into a new modern phase, which will eventually be challenged by another postmodern phase, and so forth. I also strongly support Foucault's (1984) argument that his work, and I would argue the work of others who we identify as postmodernists, is not a "doctrine, nor even ... a permanent body of knowledge that is accumulating; it has to be conceived as an attitude, an ethos, a philosophical life" (p. 50).

This is similar to what Eagan (2009, p. 141) calls "a method or strategy" to deal with postmodernity. His arguments shed more light on the relationship between modernity and postmodernity when he says postmodernists do not pretend that "there is anything genuinely new under the sun" (p. 141) but rather view postmodernism as a tool to interpret actual and linguistic events differently. It is a dialogue with tradition and does this in a flexible way that challenges fixed modernist interpretations. The purpose of this dialogue with modernity is an attempt "to heal some of the wounds inflicted by the excesses of modernity, such as imperialism, patriarchy, racism, fascism, etc." (p. 142). Thus postmodernism "[stings] us into acknowledging that our intellectual grids are deficient" (Farmer, 1997, p. 119, as cited in Vickers, 2005, p. 84).

At the same time postmodernism is not only about philosophy but also about the real changes in society that go hand-in-hand with different ways of looking at the current time. Ignoring postmodernism "would fly in the face of some significant evidence for seismic socio-cultural shifts" (Lyon, 1999, p. 92). An exploration of the postmodern would enable us to "discern what sorts of questions—of knowing and being, of ethics and politics—are raised" (p. 92) and "obliges us to lift our eyes above narrowly technical and discrete issues and to grapple with historical change on a grand scale" (p. 7). Many scholars indeed view postmodernism as an "epochal shift" from modernity that involves the "emergence of a new social totality with its own distinct organizing principles" (Featherstone, 1991, p. 1), mostly facilitated by new communication technologies.

Some scholars identify different types of postmodernisms, such as "epochal postmodernism" (Boje, Fitzgibbons, & Steingard, 1996, p. 63), "epistemological postmodernism" (p. 63), and "critical postmodernism" (p. 64). In epistemological postmodernism Derrida's deconstruction methods are applied to, among others, organizational discourse. Mickey's (2003) work is an example of this application in public relations. Such analyses focus on showing how so-called rational decision-making in organizations are procedures used to mask the underlying power strategies of those already in power (Cooper & Burrell, 1988, p. 110). Epistemological postmodernism reflects a sceptical postmodern perspective, whereas critical postmodernism takes an affirmative position (Rosenau, 1992). Critical postmodernism is a mid-range position that moves seamlessly between applying postmodern perspectives to modernist organizations. Although there is a transition from modern to postmodern organizing, it "is in its infancy. Modernism, modernist organization, and positivist science rule the day" (Boje et al., 1996, p. 62). I believe this also is the case in public relations and this type of approach is by far the preferred methodology for publication in journals such as *Journalism*

& Mass Communication Quarterly, which is the flagship journal of the Association for Education in Journalism and Mass Communication in the United States. But labeling an organizational dimension as postmodern does not guarantee the disappearance of exploitative practices in organizations. The approach that will be used in this book is a combination of epistemological postmodernism and critical postmodernism. These two approaches allow for a cross-over approach between otherwise incompatible theorists such as Bourdieu, Gramsci, Foucault, and Lyotard (Deetz, 2001).

Reading the works of those philosophers who generally are viewed as postmodern, or somewhat postmodern, such as Foucault, Lyotard, and Deleuze and Guattari, it will be hard to argue for postmodernism as a rupture. The works of these theorists even sometimes hark back to ancient philosophers such as Socrates and Plato in the sense that the works of these philosophers often are cited as laying the foundation for those principles of modernism postmodernists critique. Seeds for major changes in society were invariably planted in preceding ideologies and philosophies (Lyon, 1999).[1] Postmodern phenomena should be situated in time and eras such as the Baroque crisis in the 17th century or the turbulence at the transition from the 19th to the 20th centuries. These periods should guide us during our own time to ask the right questions, Lyon argues.

Since that time, and to this day, I am most informed and influenced about postmodernism and postmodernity through the work of Best (1995) and Best and Kellner (1991, 1997, 2001). Having read, and reread, everything they have written on this topic, their work has hugely informed my own work in and perspectives on public relations. With full recognition to these two authors, who set me on my "postmodern adventure," to borrow from the title of their 2001 text, I follow their direction and distance myself from the extreme postmodern notion that there is a rupture between modernity and postmodernity. Therefore, this book does not intend to become a propaganda piece for postmodernism, but rather a text that, in the words of Best and Kellner, "combines the most useful of modern and postmodern perspectives" (2001, p. 5) in an effort to advance theory in the field of public relations.

At the same time I feel my work is somewhat more radical than theirs because of my extreme wariness of metanarratives, most likely because of my personal history as related in the Preface to this book. The results of the metanarrative of *apartheid* are now familiar to us all. From this follows my insistence on the importance of theory building and practice at a local and regional level and as a technique for empowerment because I believe change from resistance at the local level is what facilitates positive change. This also might be a consequence of my focus on public relations, a field I have now been involved in as a practitioner and academic for close on forty years. Most likely also because of my many years as a public relations practitioner the biggest influence on my work is that of Lyotard, whose perspectives in my view are particularly relevant to public relations practice. In the end one can only critique what you know. As Foucault

(1989b, p. 65) says, "It's up to you, who are directly involved with what goes on in [your terrain of expertise], faced with all the conflicts of power which traverse it, to confront them and construct the instruments which will enable you to fight in that terrain." The theories one would use to critique your terrain of knowledge will therefore also depend on their applicability to that field.

While I might have a stronger anti-foundationalist stance than Best and Kellner (n.d.) I do support their belief that theories can be compared on the basis of their logic and ability to promote an argument that "are reasonable to hold" (¶ 10), e.g. arguments against racism have stronger merits than those for racism. As they say, "Our court of appeal is reason, facts, verified bodies of knowledge, and our experience of the world itself, which is not infinitely malleable to any and all descriptions, such as the one which says the world is flat" (¶ 11). Similarly Ermarth (2001b) argues that instead of being "loonies unable to kick a stone" (p. 212) postmodernists are more respectful of detail than modernists. The reason why postmodernists argue for complexity and chaos is that they do not disregard certain facts just to fit their empiricist paradigm; "in the same way quantum theory is more precise just as it becomes less secure in the familiar empiricist way" (p. 212).

A related argument about theorizing and choosing the best theories is the one of theorizing as a "wrangle in the marketplace" (Heath, 2009, location 790). In an excellent overview of the rhetorical tradition in public relations Heath repeats the argument that theoretical approaches to public relations are similar to a marketplace because their usefulness is debated through rhetorical strategies. Theories that have the best explanatory abilities will be the ones with longevity. I find this seamless transition from metaphor to practice problematic, as I generally do when metaphors are treated as facts. First, treating theory building as capitalism has an ideological base that those who use it should be clear about. Capitalism is not the only possible explanation for the phenomenon of public relations. As I argue repeatedly, democracy offers a better explanation. Ermarth (2001b, p. 196) refers to the market as an "often dysfunctional fiction" (p. 196) and Westwood and Clegg (2003, p. 12) describe such an approach as "an overt pragmatic politics promulgated as the means to redirect and give impetus to the field" in the case of organization theory. Even Pfeffer (1997), that stalwart of positivist approaches to the field of organization theory, rejects such an approach as

> tautological reasoning. Practices are presumed to be efficient because of their very existence—if they were inefficient they would disappear—and thus the logic of economic science as it is practiced is, given a particular empirical observation, to derive a proof that demonstrates the efficiency properties of what has been observed. (p. 49)

Perceived usefulness of theories also can be a symptom of intellectual laziness or resistance to acknowledge other ways of seeing. This argument also would presume that everybody knows every theory and that everybody has the same basis of knowledge and access to argue about the usefulness of all theories.

Some scholars, such as Deetz (2001), while acknowledging the basic tenets of postmodernism, proposed the alternative name of "dialogic studies" (p. 31) for this new movement, particularly because of the extreme viewpoints so often associated with it. Although I believe postmodernism goes far beyond a rhetorical approach, I do support Deetz's notion that a broader approach allows scholars to include theorists not normally associated with the postmodern movement, again resonating the views of Best and Kellner. Yet another approach is that of Cornell (1992) who prefers to call it a "philosophy of the limit" because it does not refer to a "periodization" (p. 10) of the term but rather points to the philosophical differences between the two traditions. Nonetheless, I believe that the term postmodern now has generated enough debate to become a fixed term and that other terminology created with the aim of deflecting the accusations of "presumed relativism, amorality, and rampant subjectivity" (Westwood & Clegg, 2003, p. 13) are no longer necessary.

The rest of this chapter is devoted to an explication of the differences between the modern and the postmodern. I also give a brief and introductory overview of the major tenets of postmodern theory at the hands of the major philosophers associated with this movement: Derrida, Foucault, Lyotard, Deleuze, and Guattari. Lastly, I provide a brief overview of the chapters of this book.

But first it might be beneficial to set the scene briefly for further theory development by elaborating on the postmodernization of society, or postmodernity, and to explain the difference in the terms postmodernity and postmodernism. Scholars generally discern between postmodernism, which is the theoretical and philosophical school of thought that flowed from the *Zeitgeist* of the time; and postmodernity, which referred to social, cultural, and political changes in society itself (Boyne & Rattansi, 1990; Crook, Pakulski, & Waters, 1992; Friedberg, 1990; Lyon, 1999; Lyotard, 1989). These changes manifest themselves in different forms of culture, state, inequalities in society, politics, work organization, science, and technology (Best & Kellner, 2001; Crook, et al., 1992). This also is the distinction made in this book. While postmodernity will refer to societal changes, postmodernism will refer to the theoretical and philosophical thoughts underlying postmodernity. Postmodernism thus is "an intellectual practice that problematizes philosophy and all matters of ontology and epistemology" (Westwood & Clegg, 2003, p. 8).

The (Post)Modernization of Society

To understand the postmodern it is important to understand what modernism means because postmodernism largely represents a critique of and resistance to modernism per se.

The Impact of Modernity

Modernity generally refers to a variety of economic, political, social, and cultural transformations that took place in the historical epoch following on the Middle Ages or feudalism (Best & Kellner, 1991). Ermarth (2001b) traces it back to a "culture of representation" (p. 202) that emerged during the Renaissance and was defined in relation to the debate between the ancient and the modern (Featherstone, 1991). Modernity devised a way to describe both natural and human phenomena through a systematic process of representation or description, which laid the foundation for the management of society. At the end of the 19th century the term came to be contrasted to the traditional order and implied progressive economic and administrative processes that resulted in the modern capitalist-industrial state.

While the term *modern* actually means *today*, the term *modernity* refers to a kind of society different from those preceding it and is recognized by developments in science, technology, industrialization, and an improvement in living standards, including life expectance (Cahoone, 2003). A philosophy that promoted "free markets, a largely secular culture, liberal democracy, individualism, rationalism, humanism, etc." (p. 8) facilitated these developments. The exact starting point of modernism is in question. Cahoone's philosophical starting point is Descarte's *Meditations* written in the 17th century but he acknowledges that the religious reformist movements in Europe and the scientific revolutions in the 17th century among others could also be regarded as such. With him I would argue that it really does not matter because it is what it meant that is important for us to understand the postmodern.

Modernity also is linked to a philosophical movement called the Enlightenment, which Cahoone (2003) refers to as a "positive self-image" of Western culture "which places the highest premium on individual life and freedom, and believes that such freedom and rationality will lead to social progress through virtuous, self-controlled work, creating a better material, political, and intellectual life for all" (p. 9). As he rightly remarks, despite the evidence to the contrary, this philosophy persists. The continuous insinuations that Blacks and women (McNutt, 2011) do not want to work but merely want to rely on the state is a typical example of this belief. One of the great benefits of modernity, Cahoone argues, is the explosion of art forms, which he refers to as "aesthetic modernism" (p. 9).

What is important is that modernism is associated with liberalism and humanism, which still today remain important in some significant ways, also in public relations. I wish to suggest that these also are the underlying values of the work of James Grunig (Grunig & White, 1992) and his contemporaries and the subsequent focus on two-way symmetry as a communication approach in the field. This is a state of the field that scholars from other fields do not realize because they prefer to not read these works and would rather revert to naïve and simplistic descriptions of public relations as "spin." Inherent in symmetry is the *desire* to live and practice the values of liberalism, which Good (2001, p. 3, citing Gray, 1995) describes as

> individualist, in that it asserts the moral primacy of the person against any collectivity; egalitarian, in that it confers on all human beings the same basic moral status; universalist, affirming the moral unity of the species; and meliorist, in that it asserts the open-ended improvability, by use of critical reason, of human life.

This definition, however, also brings to light the major issues with modernism, such as the individual as solely responsible for his destiny; the claims of universality; and the concept of reason. Modernism regarded reason as the source of progress in knowledge and society, the locus of truth, and the foundation of systematic knowledge. I use the word *his* here deliberately because to suggest that women and others on the margins of society were included in this perspective is simply untruthful. As an aside, this is a strategy often used, namely to seamlessly slip in *women* when cited philosophers used the term *men*. To do this is disingenuous, to say the least, because with a simple stroke of the keyboard millennia of the suffering and abuse of women and men who were not from the privileged classes are swept under the rug, while simultaneously suggesting that a new utopia of equality has been reached. A recent example is Heath's (2009) review of the rhetorical tradition in public relations. It is indeed a wonderful piece but I do wish to critique his insertion of "[and women]" and "[or women]" when citing Aristotle (locations 907–916) for the above reasons.

It is exactly scientific reasoning that many argue led to many of the problems of modernity, such as the extreme differentiation of labor and the life world, the breakdown of community and communalism through urbanization, social control through the rise of bureaucracy, self-discipline and self-surveillance, and the rise of secularity at the cost of religion, to mention but a few (Lyon, 1999, pp. 25–45). This produced a new industrialized and colonial world that resulted in untold suffering, genocide, and repression, of among other women and people who were viewed as different—the Other. It produced disciplinary institutions, practices, and discourses that legitimized domination and control, also over men (Best & Kellner, 1991).

The United States is generally viewed as the ultimate modern society because of its pervasive bureaucratization of society, which is made increasingly possible through technology, supervision, control, and standardization. The engine that drives this kind of society is capitalism, which manifests in a continuous quest for new products and new consumers, portrayed as progress. In modernism not only the life world is differentiated in terms of work, home, church, recreation, and so forth, but also society, where men and women are given different roles, and *normal* people are differentiated from the *deviant*, particularly through the use of psychology, psychiatry, and empiricism that is used to create categories of people. The accessibility of information about individual behavior of people further strengthens this process. Differentiation in turn creates problems of integration, which necessitates surveillance, also made possible by new technologies. The "rational" increasingly displaces the traditional, particularly through the advancement of science, mathematics, and other forms of calculation, such as accounting practices.

At the basis of modernist philosophy lies the belief that "there is *a* human nature" [italics added], which Rabinow (1984, p. 3) views as fundamental to modernist perspectives on true scientific knowledge. Modernists believe human nature is a bio-physical structure that allows humans to develop a unified language, which will eventually lead to a universal understanding of all life. This, for instance, was the life goal of Noam Chomsky, namely, to develop "a testable mathematical theory of mind" (p. 3). It is the unified, single language that describes all of human existence that is known as *reason*. Reason is central to the Enlightenment, which promotes the idea that all humanity has the faculty of reason to find a universal understanding of life. Reason then becomes the unified way of improving and reconstructing human society. From the very beginning some 18th and 19th-century philosophers were critical of reason and argued that it per definition implied the replacement of one form of life for another, which in reality resulted in "a very real loss: community, tradition, religion, familiar political authority, customs and manners" (Cahoone, 2003, p. 17).

It is against this background that this book will offer a critique of public relations theory to see to what extent existing theoretical approaches still are based in modernist principles of rationality. Some of the assumptions of modernism are evident in public relations theory in terms of the focus of public relations as a management (control) function, the need to measure our outcomes, the different roles we perform, differentiation between men and women's work, the increasing emphasis on our ability to conquer and apply new technologies, and the quest for the standardization of public relations practice on a global (universal) scale.

Ringing in Postmodernity

The rise of postmodernism is generally associated with a political and social mood that points to deep and permanent changes in society. This manifested openly at the end of the 1960s and the beginning of the 1970s. Postmodernity is largely a reaction to the many "discontents" with modernity (Lyon, 1999, p. 25).

However, modernity now has led to postmodernity, which is typified by globalization with its resultant power conflicts, new modes of work, uneven economic development, rampant consumerism, environmental exploitation, and bioengineering. Thus postmodernity is the consequence of foundations laid in modernity. At the same time, paradigmatic changes did redefine theory and knowledge in the arts, sciences, and the socio-cultural environment in general (Best & Kellner, 2001, pp. 1–5). The question is, how can postmodernism help us to develop public relations theories appropriate for the times we live in? To what extent are existing theories with their roots in modernism still relevant to today's practice? If postmodernism does not represent a rupture with modernism, can one assume a continued relevance of these theories, albeit in a revised version, to public relations?

Some postmodern scholars of the doomsday type, in particular Baudrillard (1975, 1983a, 1983b),[2] argue that postmodernity was created through the new, high tech media society and emergent processes of change and transformation, which resulted in a novel stage of history where the sign is more real than reality. Computers, media and other technologies, new forms of knowledge, and changes in socio-economic systems produce and are producing postmodern social reform. This is resulting in increased cultural fragmentation, changes in experience of time and space, and new modes of experience, subjectivity, and culture.

The Root of the Problem

Several scholars explore the roots of the term. Lyotard (1989, pp. 7–10), one of the few postmodernists who openly identifies with the movement, points to the many debates around the term postmodern, many of which he believes interpret the term incorrectly. He, for example, contests the popular belief that the term *postmodern* originated in architecture. Although there is no clear indication when the term *postmodernism* was used for the first time, some suggest it started in the mid-fifties and early sixties (Boyne & Rattansi, 1990, p. 13; Huyssen, 1986, p. 184). In a very thorough overview of the development of the postmodern movement, Best and Kellner (1991, pp. 5–31) cite Toynbee, who said it was first used in 1875, referring to a state of anarchy and total relativism. They believe the term further developed in 1957 when Rosenberg and White used it in terms of mass culture and the economist Peter Drucker used it in terms of postindustrial society. The postmodern has for decades invoked strong feelings on both the positive and negative sides of the fence. Some believe postmodernism attacks the inner connection between reason and freedom and therefore rings in the end of the Enlightenment and the destruction of Western civilization. Others welcome its challenge to rationalism and how it is used to create meaning and order.

The argument can be made, however, that modernity already carried the seed of its downfall, as Nietzsche predicted in 1888 (Vattimo, 1988). Nietzsche's concept of nihilism laid the foundation for our current understanding that meanings are not fixed but situated in personal belief systems that are created to dominate society. Modernity inevitably led to extreme forms of individualism, the kind of militant individualism that is emerging in our societies, and the rejection of religion and other dominant forms of control. It is this set of circumstances that led to the emergence of postmodernism and that provides the theoretical and philosophical foundations for understanding the rejection of modernity and the emergence of postmodernity.

Major Tenets of Postmodern Theory

Although general agreement exists that the structuralist and poststructuralist schools do not form part of postmodernism, there also is consensus that the arguments that emanated from these schools played an important role in creating the *Zeitgeist* that gave rise to the student revolution in May 1968 and prompted postmodern theorists such as Foucault to investigate the links between power and knowledge (Best & Kellner, 1991; Harland, 1987; Macdonnel, 1986). The structuralist revolution describes phenomena in terms of linguistic structures, rules, codes, and systems. It rejects the Enlightenment focus on the self as the center of knowledge and was the first to argue that the self is structured through language and socialization (Cahoone, 2003). Although this might sound familiar to critical and postmodern scholars they also argue that the self can be studied purely through the scientific analysis of linguistic and sign systems.

Poststructuralists reject the "scientific pretentions" of structuralists (Cahoone, 2003, p. 4) and argue that humans cannot objectively study themselves, much like Lyotard (1984) would later argue. I believe much of critical theory today, also in public relations, is related to poststructuralism, with its rejection of the unified self, and the way in which the poststructuralists theorized the "oppressive nature of Western institutions" (Cahoone, 2003, p. 4). The tradition in public relations that critiques societal institutions and their use of language reflects poststructuralism.

Poststructuralism broke with conventional representational schemes of meaning and rejected totalizing, centered theories of meaning and systems. This led to a collapse of boundaries between philosophy, cultural critique, social theory, literature, and other academic fields (Best & Kellner, 1991, pp.19–25). Poststructuralism therefore forms part of the matrix of postmodern theory and is a subset of a broader range of theoretical, cultural, and social tendencies that constitute postmodern discourses.

Next I will review a number of recurring themes in postmodern theory that I apply to public relations theory throughout this book. My review will be quite cursory because these tenets of postmodern theory are discussed in depth in their application to specific themes in public relations theory.

The General Debate in Postmodern Theory

Before a formal analysis of postmodern theory is undertaken, it might be useful to broadly sketch the *Zeitgeist* within which postmodernism developed and to highlight the major issues, without specific reference to the main contributors to postmodern theory. These theorists will be discussed in detail in subsequent chapters and in specific contexts.

There is no unified postmodern theory; it is diverse and pluralistic and often conflicting (Best & Kellner, 1991, p. 2). The overriding issue in postmodernism is a questioning of modernist philosophies and their quest for a single truth that tries to mould the thinking of Western civilization into a single direction. This is what Ermarth (2001b, p. 202) refers to as the "One World Hypothesis." Postmodern philosophers insist that it is a philosophy specifically pertaining to Western thinking and that it cannot speak on behalf of or be applied to Afrocentric or Orient-centric philosophies.

A major area of postmodern focus is the way in which Western societies dominated and still try to dominate other cultures through colonization and the institution of power structures in those communities and cultures. Postmodernism attacks the way in which modern philosophy contributes to the marginalization of Blacks, women, men outside of the existing power structures, and people who function outside "normal" society, such as homosexuals and criminals. As mentioned, capitalism is viewed as a manifestation of modernist philosophies and although many postmodern philosophers started their criticism of capitalism from a Marxist perspective most, with the notable exception of Jameson (1984), reject Marxism as inadequate to criticize capitalism. Most regard Marxism as just another manifestation of modernist capitalist structures. They generally view Marxism as just another ideology that is part of invisible power structures that subject humankind to limited thinking patterns and domination.

The concept of power and how it subjects people at both the macro and micro levels of society is a major focus of postmodernists. In terms of a macro perspective, postmodernism shows how people are dominated and subjected, not only by the state, but also by all the institutions and bureaucracies inherent in a capitalist society. The role history plays in this process is also highlighted.

At the micro level people willingly subject themselves to power by inhibiting their libido, subconscious, and creativity through ordered and structured ways of thinking to fit in with what they believe are the norms of society. Postmodernists argue for a release of the natural and uninhibited power sources within the individual and argue for an aesthetic of the self that will allow people to create themselves outside of the bondages of a normalized society. They are particularly sympathetic to people who are incarcerated in asylums and prisons because their psyches do not fit into the orderly world of modernist thinking with its prefixed categories of behavior. Postmodernists attack the normalization that comes with modernism, which rejects any form of behavior that does not fall within the norms promoted in modernity.

Language is not only a part of life but is the basis of society. Because there is no single truth or way to understand life, language has no representational value outside of itself, and its original meaning only can be determined at the moment of its use. Language also is a manifestation of how culture, society, history, knowledge, and power, among others, shape the individual. An analysis of language would therefore also shed light on the broader social and political discourses that take place in society. The discourse of the postmodern is furthermore full of metaphors, imagery, and new ways of writing, aimed at explaining its multi-faceted approach and defying structured ways of thinking, writing, and applying knowledge.

Postmodern philosophers also critique the way in which knowledge and meaning are formed and proliferated through the many educational institutions in society. In fact, the postmodern approach defies structure and promotes difference, multiplicity, and non-hierarchical tradition. It attacks the hegemony of the many obvious and also invisible power structures in society. Postmodernism views the guiding motivation as to respect differences (Foucault, 1973b, p. xii).

The postmodern concept of micropolitics further suggests that a different kind of political movement will evolve. Political struggle will no longer be fought in terms of ideology but in terms of value systems. This political struggle will particularly include people who have been marginalized and discriminated against in the past. It also suggests that individuals might attach themselves to more than one of these smaller political groupings, depending on what the issue of struggle is at a particular point and might belong to different political groups at any single moment. From there comes the concept of the fragmented nature of the postmodern individual.

From this very brief and evidently simplistic introduction the work of major postmodern philosophers might be more accessible for the uninitiated reader.

Postmodern Discourse

As discussed in the previous section, one of the mainstays of modernity was its belief that rationality, objectivity, and a single, unified understanding of how the world works would lead to the emancipation of humankind. Therefore, probably the most important aspect of postmodern discourse is the rejection of the modernist belief in logic and truth. Although the subject of theories and knowledge will be discussed in greater depth in later chapters, it becomes clear that postmodernists reject any form of totalizing discourse. From their perspective, theory and science can never be held as the ultimate truth, but only as the interpretation of the person who proposed it. All knowledge, particularly in the human and social sciences, is based on narrative and therefore value-based.

Discourse as Conversation

The concept of *discourse* is directly related to this argument. Discourse refers to "all that is written and spoken and all that invites dialogue or conversation" (Rosenau, 1992, p. xi). For instance, the whole postmodern debate is a discourse, consisting of many different discourses (debates). The concept of discourse emanated from new ways of looking at how meaning is formed. Dialogue is the primary condition for discourse, which is always socially related, although postmodernists rather promote a dialectic approach to discourse. Discourses differ "with the kinds of institutions and social practices in which they took shape, and with the positions of those who speak and those whom they address" (Macdonnel, 1986, p. 1).

Discourse is Unstable

In addition to a discourse being related to institutions and speakers, it takes effect indirectly or directly through its relation to other discourses in which the speakers were involved, the speakers before them, and so forth. As a result it is impossible to determine the point from which discourse originated. Because meaning cannot be retraced to its original meaning or intention it topples forward and is always future-directed. Meaning does not only originate from spoken and written discourse but also from signs, which may be verbal or non-verbal.

Discourse Also is Created through Institutional Practice

Institutions have the power to shape the way we talk about issues. This leads to the argument that discourse is formed and meaning is created through institutional practice, particularly through the use of language and signs in institutional context. This places public relations practice squarely in the postmodern debate and I will explore later in the book how public relations practice is used in this regard. The way in which ideologies shape meaning and language is another important focus of postmodern discourse. This is a particularly poststructuralist position that argues that ideologies proliferate through society in various forms and institutions, all supporting the capitalist system. These ideologies subject humans in various ways to support the capitalist ideology. Thus, meaning is formed through ideologies promoted by institutions supporting capitalism.

Discourse as Strategy

Discourse often is associated with a strategy to examine contradictory positions (Gordon, 1979). The term discourse is normally used in two ways (Fairclough, 1992). The one is in terms of the use of language and signs in texts, samples of spoken words, and different contexts. The term can also be extended beyond language to symbolic forms such as visual images. The other is its use in social theory, where it refers to different ways of structuring areas of knowledge and social practice. Fairclough argues that with the move to a post-industrial society language is assuming greater importance as a means of production and social control, also in the workplace. With new styles of management and the democratization of the workplace, workers are expected to be more proficient in communication skills. There is general agreement that discourse analysis is a strategy or method to study social phenomena and that discourse can only be understood within a broader social context (Best & Kellner, 1991; Cook, 1989; Schiffrin, 1987; Stappers, 1986).

The Quest against the Ultimate Truth

To understand the development of discourse in its postmodern sense, it will be important to understand the historical context through which this argument was shaped. With the revolt among students and academics in 1968 in both Europe and the United States, presuppositions about knowledge and truth were called into doubt. Students in particular revolted against the institutional practices that subjected individuals to social norms. Foucault (1982, p. 212) argues these struggles were not aimed at class or racial struggles, but engaged with ideological practices. They were directed against "subjection, against forms of subjectivity and submission."

The contribution Althusser (1971) made to the postmodern interpretation of the term *discourse* should be seen against this background. Although Althusser cannot be regarded as a postmodernist, his 1970 essay on ideology and ideological state apparatuses (ISA's) made a radical breakthrough in the understanding of ideologies.[3] The argument that meaning is formed through a number of institutions that support the capitalist state originated from him. These "apparatuses" are largely ideological and encompass churches, education, the family, the law, political parties, trade unions, communication, and culture (pp. 136–137). He believes ideologies are systems of meaning that position everyone in imaginary relations different from the real relations in which they live. For instance, he would argue that in the institution of family the father as the head of the household is an imaginary position and not a real one in the sense that the position was created to serve a social and political purpose. Education acts as the key ISA in capitalist societies, a point that is repeatedly made in this book. One of the important points that emerged from Althusser's work is that the ideology dominant in an ISA comes from a point of struggle and that it is reshaped through struggle. Thus, an ideology can only exist with some opposing ideology that shows what it is not and therefore ideologies shape each other through struggle (Macdonnell, 1986).

In a further development of Althusser's work, Pêcheux (1982) suggests that discourses develop out of clashes with one another and as a result words and phrases in writing or in speech have a political dimension (Macdonnell, 1986). Similar to Althusser, Pêcheux holds that meaning does not exist in itself but antagonistically, from positions in struggle, so that words change their meaning according to the positions from which they are used. Pêcheux used the term *discourse* to stress the ideological nature of language use (Fairclough, 1992).

Thus, because ideology is shaped in the struggle between differing meanings, language is ideological. This perspective again poses a problem to existing public relations theory, questioning the underlying assumptions about symmetry in practice. Because meaning exists antagonistically and is formed through struggle, no public relations discourse can be truly symmetrical, and will always be political in nature. These arguments will be further explored in a later discussion on public relations as a form of activism.

The Double Bind of Binary Opposites

Postmodernism rejects the use of binary opposites in modernist discourse, which always implies the superiority of one meaning over another. Because there cannot be a single truth, the use of binary opposites cannot be validated. The work of Jacques Derrida is closely associated with postmodern theory and he is generally regarded as the first linguist to be termed as such, although he followed the route to postmodernism via poststructuralism (Best & Kellner, 1991; Featherstone, 1991; Harland, 1987). As Pêcheux, Derrida also takes issue with the binary opposites inherent in Western philosophy and discourse. He argues that it constitutes a hierarchy of values that attempts to guarantee truth and devalue inferior terms or positions, such as man's superiority over women, speech over writing, and reason over nature. He proposed the now famous term *deconstruction*, arguing that modern philosophy needed to be deconstructed to determine the way in which it constructed meaning (Derrida, 1976).

Garver, in his preface to the English translation by David Allison of Derrida's *Speech and phenomena* (1973), remarks that Derrida attacks the notion that language is conceived through logic, rather than rhetoric. Garver uses rhetoric as an analogy for discourse and argues that Derrida attacks the modernist concept that signs represent ideas that are timeless and thus not located spatiotemporally. In other words, Derrida attacks the concept of logic, which says that signs (ideas) stand in some logical relation to each other (p. xiv). Derrida further rejects the concept of "private understanding" (p. xvii), which means that logical understanding exists within a human being without prior learning. He regards the role of utterances in actual discourse as the essence of language and meaning, and therefore views logic as shaped through rhetoric. His development of the principle of *différance* is unique and radical in that it suggests that "definition rests not on the entity itself but in its positive and negative references to other texts. Meaning changes over time, and ultimately the attribution of meaning is put off, postponed, deferred, forever" (Derrida, 1981, pp. 39–40). This elaboration of the terms *discourse* and *deconstruction* are important because one of the aims of this book is the deconstruction of public relations discourse through an analysis of its underlying philosophies, theories, and practices to determine how they influence and are influenced by larger discourses in society. This process will mirror Allison's interpretation of the term *deconstruction* as "a project of critical thought whose task is to locate and 'take apart' those concepts which serve as the axioms or rules for a period of thought, those concepts which command the unfolding of an entire epoch of metaphysics" (Derrida, 1973, p. xxxii). Derrida maintains that linguistic meaning is the product of the arbitrary configuration of differences between signs. As such, there can never be an absolutely signified content or an absolutely identical or univocal meaning in language. Purity of language is impossible because "there can be no expression without indication, no signified without the signifier, no meaning or sense without the factually constituted complex of signifiers" (p. xl).[4] For Derrida, the belief that an absolute objective core of meaning is impossible means that a certain period of metaphysical thought has come to a close.

The Instability of Meaning

An outflow of Derrida's argument is the understanding that meaning and its formation are unstable. Based on Derrida's radical interpretation of language and meaning the signified does not exist and is merely an illusion invented by humans (Harland, 1987). Signifiers are always signifying, pointing away from themselves to other signifiers. This constant state of unfulfilled meaning that exists in the absence of the signified is called *dissemination*. The result is that language takes on its own energy and creativity, distinct from the creativity of the individual writer, much like Lyotard tells Thébaud in the introductory quote to this chapter. In the words of Harland "(L)anguage in the mode of dissemination is endlessly unbalanced and out of equilibrium ... [meanings] push successively, in causal chains, toppling one another over like lines of fallen dominoes" (p. 137).

This understanding of how meaning is formed questions the assumption that public relations practitioners are responsible for the outcomes of campaigns, and that message effects can be measured and controlled—another point of interrogation in this book. Because meaning is socially constructed, always changing, and always unstable, new ways of understanding meaning have to be found. Even when the social, historical, and political contexts within which communication takes place are considered understanding always will be limited because the person trying to understand can never go back to the original understanding. Meaning proliferates because the signifier keeps changing its meaning through a process of dissemination. This book will continuously return to this notion, and will explore how this changes our current understanding of public relations theory and practice.

The social context of meaning is a recurrent theme in postmodern theory. Foucault (1980b) comes close to the position that discourse constitutes all social phenomena. He defines the social body as "a thoroughly heterogeneous ensem-

ble consisting of discourses, institutions, architectural forms, regulatory decisions, laws, administrative measures, scientific statements, philosophical, moral
and philanthropic propositions – in short, the said as much as the unsaid" (p. 194).

Foucault continuously does battle with the discourse of modern rationality, which he believes dominates the individual through social institutions,
discourses, and practices. He argues modernism attempts to classify and regulate all forms of experience through a systematic construction of knowledge
and discourse, echoing Althusser and Pêcheux. In his earlier work (Foucault,
1972, 1973a, 1973b) he develops the concept of the archaeology of knowledge
in which he attempts to show that history and society are not unified and are
single entities that can be understood through reason. Instead of being a single
linear discourse, history for example is actually a narrative of disconnected
events strung together to create a single understanding of history to promote a
particular ideology that uses history for its own purposes of power. Discourse
is so complex a reality that it cannot be analyzed from one single truth, theory,
or method but should be analyzed at different levels with different methods
(Foucault, 1973b, pp. xii–xiv). Foucault's concept of the archaeology of knowledge will be more fully explored when postmodern theories on power and
knowledge are discussed.

Several other philosophers, such as Deleuze and Guattari (1983, 1987) and
Laclau and Mouffe (1987) reflect these thoughts of Foucault. Best and Kellner
(1991, p. 176) argue that although these philosophers did not want to be called
postmodern their continued efforts to dismantle modern concepts of unity,
hierarchy, identity, and subjectivity place them in the midst of the postmodern
discourse. Like Foucault, they developed counterprinciples of difference and
multiplicity in theory, politics, and everyday life.

Media Discourse as Hyperreality

Another issue that postmodernism takes up is the discourse of technology and
the mass media, which Baudrillard in particular believes results in a completely
new society that needs new ways to be understood. In this new society, class
and economic struggles are replaced by new forms of social reality, which have
nothing to do with the real and are therefore a hyperreality. In hyperreality
new forms of communication, such as marketing, advertising, and public relations, use the mass media to implode the barriers between reality and simulation in an effort to create a demand for commodities. This results in social
groupings around life styles rather than class and ideology.

Baudrillard and Lyotard are two of the few postmodernists who openly
identify themselves with the movement. Baudrillard's postmodern discourse is
mainly concerned with the way in which signs and sign systems dominated the
individual in the new world order, which he referred to as hypercivilization.
For Baudrillard the new order constitutes a momentous rupture in history and

with modernity (Baudrillard, 1975). He called this new era the era of simulation. This era is organized around simulation codes and models that replace production as the organizing principle of society. He coins the term "semiurgic" society (Baudrillard, 1981, p. 185) where signs take on a life of their own. This constitutes a new social order structured by models, codes, and signs. He believes the concept of *real* disappears in postmodern society as the boundaries between simulation and reality implode, creating a hyperreality (Baudrillard, 1981). Baudrillard (1983b) argues the media play a deciding role in this process by increasingly imploding boundaries between information, entertainment, images, and politics. He blames public relations experts and other media advisors for transforming politics into image contests or sign struggles. According to his theory of implosion, a process of social entropy develops that leads to a collapse of boundaries in which the social disappears and with it distinctions between classes, political ideologies, and cultural forms and between media semiurgy and reality (Baudrillard, 1983a, 1983b). Although many see Baudrillard's views as extreme, there also is general consensus that his interpretation of the current media environment needs consideration. Not only are his references to public relations directly relevant to the context of this book, but also to his interpretation of the media environment that creates the climate within which public relations practitioners have to operate.

Theory as Discourse

As is the case with other postmodern theorists, Lyotard (1984) also attacks the totalizing discourse of modernity and champions difference and plurality in theory and discourse. He supports Derrida's viewpoint that Western philosophy is organized around a set of binary opposites (Lyotard, 1971). He critiques metalanguage, or totalizing theories, and uses linguistics as a strategy to provide new ways of theorizing, talking, and writing (Best & Kellner, 1991, p. 159). All discourse is narrative and he makes a distinction between "grand narratives" as totalizing strategies, and "little narratives," which refer to the proliferation of narratives in culture (Lyotard, 1984). He argues that theories, particularly those in the social and human sciences, are narratives and that they are not valid for all time (Lyotard, 1989, p. 130). His conceptualization of postmodern knowledge will be further discussed in the section on postmodern views on power and knowledge and will be addressed at length in Chapter 6.

Power and Knowledge

A problem in an analysis of postmodernism is that the concepts discussed here are not clearly defined, but free-flowing, and its basic philosophical concepts do not wish to be structured and over-theorized. As a result there will be an overlap of themes in the various sections, which is inevitable. The aim in this section will be to investigate postmodern thinking on scientific and theoretical knowledge and how the modernist approach to knowledge impacts on the individual. It will also focus on the theoretical strategies of postmodernists to counteract modernist approaches.

A Critique of Knowledge

Postmodernism is critical of institutions of knowledge and of the processes by which philosophical thought and scientific knowledge develop. The general postmodern approach is that institutions of knowledge also are institutions of power and their aim is to normalize, control, and administer people. As a result of the struggle of students and workers in the late 1960s Foucault in particular began to theorize how the intimate connection between power and knowledge is used to control society. Students turned their attention to "the full range of hidden mechanisms through which a society conveys its knowledge and ensures its survival under the mask of knowledge: newspapers, television, technical schools, and the high school" (Foucault, 1977a, p. 25). It also was at this time that poststructuralism focused its attention on the production of the subject through language and systems of meaning and power.

The term *subject* in postmodern theory has different meanings but generally refers to the entity under study (Rosenau, 1992) and also to being human, as in contrast to the human as object. In the Foucaultian tradition 'subject' means humans who are subordinate. Through a number of works, Foucault creates his now famous principles of archaeology and genealogy, with the objective "to create a history of the different modes by which, in our culture, human beings are made subjects" (Foucault, 1982, p. 208). In his search for the relationship between power and knowledge, Foucault concentrates on the domination of the individual through social institutions, discourses, knowledge creation, and practices of discipline. Reason attempts to classify and regulate all forms of experience through a systematic construction of knowledge and discourse, which he understands as systems of language imbricated with social practice.

He argues that human experiences are discursively reconstituted within rationalist and modern science frames of reference, particularly in the form of categories and differentiation, which make people accessible for administration and control (Foucault, 1982, p. 38). This is a point I return to repeatedly in this book to show how this process has also permeated public relations theories and practice. Modern theories view knowledge and truth as neutral, objective, universal, and vehicles of progress and emancipation and is developed particularly through empirical methods. Foucault analyzes theories as integral components of power and domination. Postmodern theories in general reject totalizing or meta-theories as myths that obscure the complexity inherent in the social field to enforce conformity and homogeneity, similar to the argument Ermarth (2001b) made earlier.

The Historicity of Knowledge

As opposed to modernism, the aim of postmodernism is to fragment and break up and not to unify. History and philosophy in particular are the targets of postmodernists. For postmodernists theory and knowledge are always relative, never a given, and can never stand for all time. They aim to break up metanarratives by making people aware of how metanarratives are constructed, what their aims are, and how it is possible for the individual to resist these totalizing structures. This postmodern stance is another core principle of this book, which argues that if public relations is not practiced as a form of activism that resists dominating power structures, public relations practitioners will become subjects serving the power needs of others, such as corporate managers and other powerful communicative entities who have a lot to gain from public relations practice.

Foucault opposed conventional history in favor of historicity, which aims to break up the vast unities of historical thought to see whether they could be reaffirmed, or whether other groupings could be made (Foucault, 1972). Foucault seeks to destroy historical identities by creating many alternative historical perspectives and by critically analyzing modern reason through a history of the human sciences (Foucault, 1977a, p. 160). Chapter 3 in this book applies many of Foucault's approaches to historical analysis to public relations history.

Knowledge as Normalizing Practice

Postmodernists target capitalism and its normalizing strategies, especially medicine and psychology. Their special attention to psychology is not incidental, because they accuse the discipline of categorizing human behavior and creating norms for what is normal and what is deviant. The categories of normal and deviant are arbitrary and socially constructed. The main aim of psychology is to create a type of morality that will control the subject from within.

Although other theorists such as Deleuze and Guattari also support this view (Best & Kellner, 1991), Foucault in particular argues this point and shows how the social and human sciences produce disciplinary processes of which the outcomes are control of society in general and the individual in particular (Foucault, 2003). As part of the social sciences public relations cannot escape Foucault's critique. A postmodern analysis of public relations' complicity in shaping identities and making people subject to power and control through knowledge creation, the specific uses of language, and selective information dissemination would thus form an integral part of this book.

He refers to the modern individual as *subject*: subject to someone else by control and dependence, and in the postmodern sense as having self-knowledge. Self-knowledge, particularly in the form of moral consciousness, is a strategy one can use to resist power (Foucault, 1982, p. 212).

The Death of Knowledge

Baudrillard (1987, pp. 11–12) was extremely critical of Foucault's interpretation of power because Foucault did not take into account new forms of power such as signs, symbols, or media power. Baudrillard even went so far as to suggest that we should forget Foucault because his theory of power is obsolete. Although Baudrillard's concept of power, briefly touched on in the previous section, will be discussed at greater length in the section on politics and power, he did theorize modernist meaning versus postmodernist meaning, which will be discussed here.

W hereas other postmodernists argue that modernist power permeates postmodern society, Baudrillard (1984b) declares modern power structures and meanings to be dead. He views postmodernism as a "second revolution, that of the twentieth century, of postmodernity, which is the immense process of the destruction of meaning, equal to the earlier destruction of appearances" (pp. 38–39). There is no meaning in postmodernity, and theories float in a void. No new meaning is created; everything is a repetition of things that happened in the past. As such, theory has exhausted itself. In the postmodern world no definitions are possible any longer. "It has all been done … It has deconstructed its entire universe" (Baudrillard, 1984a, p. 24). He also declares history to be dead because it has been deconstructed to a position of senselessness. Because history presented modernism with hope for a better future, the end of history destroys all hope for a better future (Baudrillard, 1987, p. 68).

In a critique of Baudrillard, Best and Kellner (1991) say his arguments degenerate into sloganeering and rhetoric without a systematic theoretical position. They believe Baudrillard postmodernizes theory itself and thus "theory … becomes a hypercommodity, geared to sell and promote the latest fashions in thought and attitude" (p. 140). They accuse him of theoretical burnout.

The Role of Postmodern Theory

The concern with theory and its role in how knowledge is generated and perpetuated is an overarching theme in postmodernism. For postmodernists the purpose of theory is to always break up other theories in a process of continuous renewal, never building on what is past, but rather destroying it with the purpose of creating new knowledge. This implies that the barriers between domains might fade away, as is already happening with interdisciplinary research and studies. Public relations is a good example of this. Although Pasadeos et al. (2010) argue that the field is maturing and that it is developing its own theories, their analysis also shows that theory building is largely self-referential between a group of established scholars. The field still has to rely heavily on theories in other domains to inform public relations theory and practice. This is not at all a bad thing and can only enrich the field and bring it in line with other disciplines, such as organization theory. That is also the approach that will be followed in this book.

As with theory, Western philosophy as a totalizing strategy also comes under attack. Postmodernists propose the end of philosophy and regard theory as transcendental and relative, only applicable to specific situations, and ever changing. Lyotard (1984) in particular is the main proponent of this argument and views modernist philosophy and other forms of modernist sciences as metanarratives of which postmodernism is highly suspicious. He in fact calls for the end of the philosophical tradition because its metanarratives co-opt the subject into suppression. The role of the philosopher/scientist is to continuously cut herself free from metanarratives that have been transmitted through the rules, practices, and norms of modernist institutions (Rorty, 1984). Rorty believes Lyotard's approach "necessarily devalues consensus and communication, for insofar as the intellectual remains able to talk to people outside the avant-garde he 'compromises' himself" (p. 43).

Lyotard (1989) suggests that all knowledge is based on narrative, a position I will explore extensively in Chapter 6. "Theories themselves are concealed narratives (and) we should not be taken in by their claims to be valid for all times" (p. 130). Lyotard also refers to theory as "game rules" and describes the postmodern condition as "the state of our culture following the transformations which, since the end of the nineteenth century, have altered the game rules for science, literature, and the arts" (Lyotard, 1984, p. xxiii).

Lyotard (1988) rejects consensus in favor of dissensus because consensus suggests conformity and co-option by power. Dissensus will promote heterogeneity, and instead of agreeing to agree (consensus) there will be agreement to disagree (dissensus). This will force people to recognize and respect differences and to deal with them in everyday life. The issue of consensus is indeed a serious concern for Lyotard (1992) because he believes that through consensus, the intellectual is co-opted into particular metanarratives. The role of the intellectual should be to always oppose any form of metanarrative, to continuously cut free from theory, even those proposed by the individual himself and to always develop new ways of observation.

Modern knowledge excludes views not supporting metanarratives, and as such homogenizes knowledge through consensus. Consensus violates heterogeneity and imposes a false universality on knowledge. Lyotard (1984) champions dissent over conformity and consensus, and heterogeneity over homogeneity and universality. Lyotard's explication of dissensus is one of the core arguments I make for public relations as a form of activism.

Power and Politics

The concept of metanarratives is as valid in a discussion of postmodern politics as it is in a discussion of postmodern knowledge. In its political context postmodernism focuses on ideology as a metanarrative and totalizing strategy of the state to subject the individual. In the same way modernist knowledge is used to control and normalize the individual, ideology is used to gain political power. Because an analysis of postmodern politics has important implications for public relations in terms of the concepts of *publics* and *activist groups*, as well as the obvious implications at the macro level in terms of *government* and *democracy*, this aspect of postmodernism requires special attention.

The Onslaught on Macropolitics

It should by now be clear that postmodernists have in common an onslaught on macropolitics, i.e. an onslaught on the totalizing strategies of ideology. Micropolitics is embraced by all as the authentic terrain for political struggle, and postmodernists suggest that political struggle should be waged through smaller, more agile, political movements such as feminism, environmental activism, and gay and lesbian rights, to mention only a few, in opposition to the oppressive effects of macropolitics. Macropolitics is constituted by capitalism, socialism, the state, sexism, religion, racism, and even the family. Therefore, postmodernists do not regard the labor movement as a democratic form of political struggle because it does not address the multiple sources of power and oppression that exploit labor beyond the work contract.

Again, it was Foucault who laid the foundation for postmodern thinking about macro- and micropolitics. Foucault took an analytical rather than a theoretical approach to power (Best & Kellner, 1991). He views power as *ascending* rather than *descending*. Power is created from the bottom up by establishing power relationships in the smallest societal units, such as the family where, for instance, the father is the head of the household. From there power circulates through divergent institutional networks that make larger power structures such as class and state possible. This is an important distinction because it will explain his emphasis on micropolitics rather than macropolitics. He refers to class and state as *macroforces* and the institutional networks as *microforces*. As such then, power is diffused throughout the social field.

Foucault (1988d), however, theorizes micropolitics beyond the state and institutions, and moves it into the subjectivities of the individual. He argues that political power permeates the individual's knowledge and pleasures, colonizes the body itself, and utilizes these forces to induce obedience and conformity. There are no "spaces of primal liberty" in society, power is everywhere. "(E)very human relationship is to some degree a power relation. We move in a world of perpetual strategic relations" (p. 168). This is an important extension of power in terms of understanding Foucault, because he took power out of the external sphere of the subject into the internal sphere. This distinction becomes an important part of his resistance strategies to power. He believes that things can be changed (p. 156), and that knowledge, particularly self-knowledge, can transform us. He does not regard power as omnipotent in the sense that people are powerless. Power can be resisted from within the individual self and he says, "as soon as there is a power relation, there is a possibility of resistance. We can never be ensnared by power: we can always modify its grip in determinate conditions and according to a precise strategy" (p. 123). This again is an important argument toward the development of an activist approach to public relations practice.

Engaging in Micropolitics

Postmodernists also have in common the rejection of obedience and conformity to the state. The individual has the power from within to stand up against macro power. One tool for transforming the individual in an effort to gain individual power is through knowledge. Thus, political struggle will not only be waged by small groups, but also by the individual. Because power is spread throughout society in many, often undetectable forms, power has to be contested through many diffused groups and many "nodal points" (Lyotard, 1984) throughout society. Furthermore, the struggle for power is inherently a positive force for change. All relationships exist in terms of power relations. Power is also always dynamic and is always looking for new alliances, thereby always regrouping and reshaping itself.

As a resistance strategy to power, Foucault (1980a) calls for a plurality of autonomous struggles waged throughout the microlevels of society—autonomous because the individual has more than one identity and therefore has many opportunities to join specific struggles against oppression. He distinguishes between modern macropolitics and postmodern micropolitics. In micropolitics, numerous local groups contest the diffused and decentered forms of power spread throughout society. In modern society the *general intellectual* speaks on behalf of oppressed groups. In postmodern society the intellectual is demoted to the *specific intellectual* who assumes a modest advisory role within a particular group and form of struggle. He refers to this as a plurality of resistance (pp. 95–96). Because power is decentered and plural, forms of political struggle should also be decentered and plural.

Foucaultian micropolitics includes two key components, namely *discourse politics* and *bio-politics* (Best & Kellner, 1991, pp. 57–58). Through discourse politics, marginal groups attempt to contest hegemonic discourses that position individuals within normalcy. Although all discourses are produced by power, the individual is not wholly subservient and can use discourse as a point of resistance and the starting point for an opposing strategy. In bio-politics, individuals attempt to break from the grip of disciplinary powers and reinvent the body by creating new modes of desire and pleasure. Discourse and bio-politics are intended to facilitate the development of new forms of subjectivity and values

(Foucault, 1982). He believes Western culture views desire as a powerful force and therefore believes it has to be regulated through morality (Best & Kellner, 1991, p. 60), an issue I will discuss in depth in Chapter 2. Foucault thus extends his concept of genealogy (an analysis of institutional discourses of power) to the discourse of the self, reinventing the self as an autonomous and self-governing being who enjoys new forms of experience, pleasure, and desire, emphasizing individual liberty and the larger social context of freedom of the self (Foucault, 1985a, p. 12).

For Foucault, ethics now depends on free choice and aesthetic criteria, thereby avoiding the ethics of the normalized, universal ethical subject (Foucault, 1988c). Although he continues to hold that power and resistance characterized all social relations, he now distinguishes between power and domination. He sees domination as the solidification of power relations that limit liberty and resistance.

Waging the Struggle

Despite their call for micropolitical struggle, postmodernists are against nihilism and total destruction. They suggest that political struggle should be waged from within the system and not from without. There is a point in the process of resistance where one can self-destruct and become a schizophrenic. There has to be a breakthrough without a breakdown. Deleuze and Guattari (1983, pp. 362–363) warn about "deterritorializing" too quickly, both at the macro level of destroying the state and at the micro level of destroying the individual. They agree with Foucault that a new politics requires micropolitical forms of struggle and embrace the concept of politicizing everyday life.

They warn that revolutionary struggle could fail because "groups and individuals contain micro fascisms just waiting to crystallise" (Deleuze & Guattari, 1987, p. 9). Therefore political groups have to wage permanent struggle within their own ranks. They extended their micropolitics of desire by formulating the term *rhizomes*. A rhizomatic method decenters information into divergent acentered systems, and language into multiple semiotic dimensions.[5] Rhizomatics analyzes the various flows of society and looks for lines of escape that can be further deterritorialized in political struggle. Rhizomatics is a form of nomadic thought, as opposed to state thought, that tries to discipline rhizomatic movement through theory. I return to the concept of rhizomatics in Chapter 4 in a discussion of power in public relations and in Chapter 6 in a discussion of postmodern knowledge and public relations. The above postmodern perspectives are important in that they shape the role of the public relations practitioner as an activist. The public relations activist who is involved in micropolitical struggle and resists domination and the concept of local rather than normative action will become important arguments in the discussion on public relations as activism.

Politics as Language Games

The work of Lyotard has been very influential in shaping my thoughts in the context of this book. Because postmodernists believe society is discursively constituted, hence Ermarth's (2001a) "discursive condition" (p. 34), they view politics as discourse. Political change should be brought about through a politics of discourse. Lyotard (Lyotard & Thébaud, 1985) in particular argues that power struggles are inherent in all discourse and hegemonic discourses can be resisted through multiple discourses dispersed throughout society. Although Best and Kellner (1991) believe Lyotard has little to offer in terms of social, economic, and political economy, and should rather be seen in terms of his contribution to postmodern knowledge, an analysis of postmodern political theorizing will be incomplete without reference to Lyotard and Thébaud's book *Just gaming* (1985).[6] Lyotard is mostly concerned with the nature of political judgment and the question of regulation inherent in justice. In *Just gaming* he argues that because political justice takes place in terms of language games, politics is a struggle through discourse. He makes a distinction between descriptive discourse as relating to that which can be described through direct observation, as in the natural sciences, and prescriptive discourse, which is value-based and therefore only can be subjective. All political discourse is bound to be prescriptive discourse. He suggests that the hegemonic political discourses of modernism should be destabilized through the use of language and rhetoric. There cannot be universal rules in language games, but one must acknowledge the basic principle of disagreement, and the right to pose questions and challenges. If no disagreement is allowed there will be terror and no justice. This is one of the most important tenets of public relations as a form of activism that can promote a just society.

Postmodern Theory and Public Relations

Although I have tried to already give some indication of why I view the above theories relevant to public relations, for the uninitiated the links might not be that clear. Postmodern theory remains complex and conflicting, which is the essence of the postmodern drive for multiplicity and diversity in both theory and practice. To make postmodern theory both accessible and explain its applications and implications for public relations, each chapter in this book deals with a particular theme relevant to public relations that is deconstructed from a postmodern perspective.

Chapter 2 deals with one of the most complex issues from a postmodern perspective, namely, values and ethics. Instead of treating this issue as an afterthought, as so often happens, this book addresses this debate upfront. Instead of viewing postmodern ethics as immoral or amoral, I argue that postmodern ethics proposes the purest form of ethics, which is situated in the care of the Other.

This chapter particularly relies on the work of Bauman (1993), whose arguments I find so persuasive that it completely changed my thinking on this topic.

Chapter 3 explores public relations history from the postmodern perspectives on history mentioned before. As with ethics, postmodern perspectives on history are radical, most probably the most radical position in this book. To show how there are different historical perspectives that might inform us of public relations practice I use the history of Emily Hobhouse, the British activist who fought for the right of Boer women and children during the Second Boer War from 1899–1902. Her life also is an example of postmodern ethics and is an example of how forgotten historical interpretations can inform us of public relations practice.

Moving from history to a discussion of postmodern perspectives on power in Chapter 4 is a natural progression. Postmodern discourse links history with power and argues that history is systematically constructed for purposes of domination. In Chapter 4 I discuss the impact of power on public relations practice. This chapter focuses on the political nature of organizations and how strategic relationships and alliances are determined by conflict, power, and resistance to or desire for change (Hatch, 1997). An understanding of the political nature of public relations is essential to the postmodern public relations practitioner. I use Spicer's (1997) perspective that when an organization is viewed as a political system, power is the most important recourse. This chapter will explore how the pursuit of postmodern power, particularly through the previously mentioned work of Foucault and Deleuze and Guattari, is a positive force for organizational change.

Chapter 5 continues the organizational focus of the previous chapter and explores the postmodern turn in organization theory. Organization theory has increasingly become one of the most important theoretical fields applied to public relations. In contrast to public relations theory, postmodern theory has been well explored in organization theory and the field has a journal, *Tamara*, specifically devoted to critical and postmodern perspectives in the field. The postmodern turn in organization theory has direct application for public relations. For example, Deetz (2001) argues that a modernist approach to organizations privileges a management discourse and emphasizes upper management's goals for the organization as given and legitimate. The role of the public relations practitioner in this approach is to ensure that the power of management remains intact. In this chapter I also explore alternative organization theories, particularly in terms of new organizational structures, that might assist public relations practitioners in dispersing power and communication channels more equitably throughout organizations. I also discuss public relations roles theory in the context of postmodern de-differentiation.

In Chapter 6 I specifically focus on how postmodern perspectives on the legitimization of knowledge influences public relations' ability to build a strong community of scholars. I also apply Lyotard's concept of performativity to public relations theory to show how the commodification of knowledge and the modernist insistence on the usefulness of knowledge for a capitalist society has affected theory building in the field. I argue for the role of the postmodern scholar as an academic activist and review research methodologies that would promote such a stance.

In the final chapter I argue that the postmodern agency of public relations is activism. The agency of public relations practitioners is one of the field's most underdeveloped areas, although it is highly relevant to the role public relations practitioners play because economic agency determines the role of practice in organizations. Chapter 7 reviews the differences between the modern and the postmodern agent and the implications of these two perspectives for public relations practice. The chapter concludes with a review of resistance strategies for postmodern public relations activists and reviews the conditions that make postmodern public relations possible. The book ends with the conclusion that public relations as activism is a necessary condition for a just society.

2

POSTMODERN ETHICS AS A FOUNDATION FOR PUBLIC RELATIONS ACTIVISM

Ethics does not have an essence, its 'essence,' so to speak, is precisely not to have an essence, to unsettle essences. Its 'identity' is precisely not to have an identity, to undo identities. Its 'being' is not to be but to be better than being. Ethics is precisely ethics by disturbing the complacency of being (or of non-being, being's correlate).

(Emmanuel Levinas, 1985, p. 77)

Public relations is arguably the communication discipline that is most obsessed with ethics. One likely reason is the nature of public relations practice. Practitioners as boundary spanners are dual representatives. On the one hand, they have to represent the interests of the communicative entity to stakeholders in a fair and judicious way and, on the other hand, they also have to represent the interests of the stakeholders to the communicative entity. Such a situation is obviously fraught with tensions, contradictions, and aporiae.

Another likely reason is that postmodernity offers new danger zones for ethical decision making. Some of these are genetic engineering, cloning, cyberspace, virtual reality, technopolitics, the environment, globalization, bioengineering, corporate monopolies, overdevelopment, overpopulation, poverty, disease, global warming, rain forest destruction, ecological crises, market failure, challenges to human identity, disinformation, and extreme surveillance in a panoptic society (Best & Kellner, 2001, pp. 10–11). It is unlikely that there is a public relations practitioner anywhere in the world who has not confronted at least one, if not multiple, challenges from these examples.

This obsession with ethics has led to numerous publications on the topic. Kirk Hallahan on his website lists more than 60 articles on ethics published in research journals since 1989 (http://lamar.colostate.edu/~hallahan/j13pr. htm) (n.d.). That number excludes the numerous books and textbook chapters devoted to the topic. In addition, every professional public relations chapter has a code of ethics or a code of conduct. Some argue that ethics has become central to the constitution of the field (Christensen & Langer, 2009; Seib & Fitzpatrick, 1995). There is of course nothing wrong with promoting one's ethical values but this situation often also confuses and frustrates public relations scholars, who frequently call for a universal set of ethical standards for public relations to make sense of this confusion.

The problem with postmodern ethics is that it further muddies the water. The question might well be asked: Why another ethical approach and a postmodern one at that? Also, the argument often is made that in the postmodern age nobody is prepared to take moral responsibility and that anything goes, so to speak. But while the lack of moral responsibility might indeed be a trademark of postmodern society, postmodernists argue it is not as a result of postmodern theories. In actual fact, postmodern theorists and ethicists, who use postmodern theories as the mechanism to explain and critique modernism and its outcomes, have interesting and valid arguments explaining this alleged lack of moral responsibility. For instance, Kierkegaard, described as the "first postmodern ironist" (Evans, 2000, p. 30), already argued in 1847 that the creation of a phantom public through advertising and publicity resulted in a level of social impersonality that "withers individual passion and personal responsibility ... that ... allows oppression to flourish" (p. 30).

A postmodern understanding of ethical and moral decision-making actually touches on much more than the lack of moral responsibility in postmodernity. It speaks to the very core of the moral argument, questioning how ethical decisions are made, who makes them, and who they benefit. A study of postmodern ethics makes visible "the sources of moral power which in modern ethical philosophy and political practice were hidden from sight ... while the reasons for their past invisibility can be better understood" (Bauman, 1993, p. 4). The ethical issues of all time remain topical and valid. Some of these are "human rights, social justice, balance between peaceful co-operation and personal self-assertion, synchronization of individual conduct and collective welfare" (p. 4).

Bauman's (1993) use of the terms morality and ethics raises the question of what the differences are between these two concepts. The concept of *morality* is ambiguous (Foucault, 1985) but is generally accepted as "a set of values and rules of action that are recommended to individuals through the intermediary of various prescriptive agencies" (p. 25). Sometimes these rules are clearly stipulated but sometimes they are vague and diffused. Morality also can refer to the extent to which people conduct themselves in relation to the moral conduct expected of them in a particular group. Foucault describes ethical behavior as the extent to which the individual supports the moral code through conduct.

This makes ethics one of the most complex issues in postmodernism. First, a discussion of this topic might evoke the notion that it is just another framework or set of moral codes or ethical rules that one individual formulated for another or others. The postmodern critique of metanarratives would make this an unacceptable approach for a postmodern scholar. Because postmodern ethics speak to the core of postmodern approaches to public relations theory and practice they are fundamental to subsequent discussions. It is appropriate to briefly introduce some of these topics before proceeding to an in-depth discussion of each.

To counteract modernist and Enlightenment thinking on morality and ethics postmodern ethical scholars hark back to the premodern, or primordial, and argue that there can never be a justification for moral codes or sets of ethical rules because they are all socially constructed and therefore serve some hidden purpose in society. The postmodern rejection of universal ethics thus focuses on the moral responsibility of the individual to the *Other* without an institutionally created ethical framework (Bauman, 1993). This resulted in an increased desire for spirituality, and the growth of religious movements is typical of postmodernity. This chapter therefore focuses on the postmodern rejection of universal ethics, while searching for an ethical position relevant to postmodernity and to postmodern public relations practice.

Most of the ethical discussions in public relations focus on the public relations practitioner as the sole ethical decision-maker in the organization. This is typical of the modernist perspective of the powerful individual who can control and direct his environment. In contrast, the postmodern perspective on ethical decision-making highlights its complexity and multiplicity. It suggests ethical decision-making is a situated process rather than being grounded in a universal ethic, which opens the potential for an emancipatory ethic through dissensus, plurality, and diversity.

The most intense debates on this issue are taking shape in religion. One of these was highlighted with the election of Pope Benedict XVI in 2005. Much was written and said about his relationship with his former colleague and fellow Catholic, Hans Küng, and their falling out in 1967 (Marquand, 2007). The Pope's modernist religious approach of radical reassertion of traditional Catholicism is starkly contrasted with Küng's postmodern perspectives on religious tolerance (Küng, 2003; Mansur, 2007). The notion that postmodern ethics is somehow anti-religion is further rejected when one considers that the works of two religious scholars, Søren Kierkegaard in the Christian Protestant tradition and Emmanual Levinas in the Judaic tradition, often are used to support postmodern ethical arguments. But because postmodernism is also very wide-ranging and nomadic in its theory application these works stand shoulder to shoulder with those of Nietzsche, Foucault, Lyotard, Bauman, and feminist philosophers Ziarek, Benhabib and Gilligan when arguments on postmodern ethics are made.

This chapter will discuss the following aspects of postmodern ethics with particular application to current public relations theory and practice:

- The role of discourse in creating the Other, particularly through the contributions of Kierkegaard, Levinas, Nietzsche, and Lyotard as foundational to postmodern ethical theorizing.
- The dilemmas of postmodernity such as fragmentation and alienation, which contributes to an understanding of postmodern ethical decision-making.
- The link between justice, morality, and ethics.
- Power, knowledge, and universal ethics.
- The moral impulse and moral direction in postmodernity.

Finally, the chapter concludes with thoughts on the implications and applications of postmodern ethics for public relations as a form of activism.

The Postmodern Other

Vignette 2.1 provides a good basis to anchor some of the discussion of postmodern ethics because it exposes in many ways how power and ethical decision-making intersects when dealing with those who are perceived as the Other.

What makes the Don Imus saga so appropriate for a discussion of postmodern ethics in public relations is that it provides the opportunity to deconstruct the power relations in the media world, the ethical dilemmas public relations practitioners have to confront in their work, and the ethical decisions female practitioners face. Above all, it exposes how the Other, in this case Black women, are not deemed worthy of moral and ethical treatment and how the media are used to alienate and dehumanize the Other. It also highlights how binary opposites, in this case educated women vs. "hos", are used to demean those on the negative side of the opposite.

The Other and the Moral Impulse

The Other maintains a special position in postmodern ethics, particularly in terms of the self/Other dichotomy. In typical postmodern fashion, which defies any linear development or metatheoretical foundation, philosophers, authors, and scholars as diverse as Kierkegaard, Dostoyevsky, Nietzsche, and Levinas laid the foundation for the ethical tenets of postmodern theory.

An important focus for these scholars is the processes that alienate individuals from the Other. Particularly relevant for public relations practitioners is Kierkegaard's early 19th century critique of the role mass media play in the formation of public opinion and the subsequent alienation of the individual (Best & Kellner, 1997; V. E. Taylor & Winquist, 2001). The media accomplish this alienation by creating a mass audience and public opinion that is devoid of individual thought and compassion. The radio jockey Smith is an example of

VIGNETTE 2.1

The Don Imus Saga

On April 4, 2007 well-known and controversial radio host Don Imus referred to the members of Rutgers University's female basketball team as "nappy-headed hos" and "rough girls from Rutgers" because "they have tattoos." As Poniewozik (2007, p. 32) wrote, "[H]e packed so many layers of offense into the statement that it was like a perfect little diamond of insult."

Despite the severity of the insult, it only became widely known and contentious when Gary Smith, a morning radio show host in Strouds-burg, was fired when he asked listeners to call in and repeat the Imus slur (Cuprisin, 2007). Many argue that until that moment the Imus comments were not widely discussed because people accepted that he said those kinds of things all the time. Once the incident became part of the public debate on who is allowed to use these kinds of words and who not, it became apparent that this was not the first time Imus was controversial and that he had a history of making racial and ethnic slurs. For instance, when the *New York Times* assigned an African-American woman, Gwen Ifill, to be its White House correspondent covering the Clinton administration, he said, "Isn't the *Times* wonderful? It lets the cleaning lady cover the White House" (Tucker, 2007, p. 38).

Imus got a lot of sympathy, although it is important to note that across the board people condemned his words. Many mentioned his charitable contributions. His program was also "a media hangout" and a place to promote books, as Katie Wainswright, executive director of publicity at a publishing house, explained (Poniewozik, 2007, pp. 36–37). Imus also was a Beltway insider and his show was well-known for providing interview opportunities for many well-known politicians, such as Rudolph Giuliani, Senator John McCain, and once Senator Barack Obama.

However, succumbing to the public outcry, and because so many advertisers (obviously scared of a backlash) withdrew from the show, both MSNBC and CBS fired Imus. Media pundits became introspective and with a lot of hand-wringing wondered how they contributed to this fiasco. And it was not only men. Cox (2007, p. 37) wrote how she was so delighted to be "invited inside the circle" that she "found herself succumbing to the clubhouse mentality that Imus both inspires and cultivates." Cox acknowledged that she made a mistake and was unduly enticed to be a part of the Imus show, despite having to tolerate the occasional personal remark about her appearance. She also said, "It's depressingly easy to find female journalists who will tolerate or ignore bigotry if it means getting into the boys' club someday" (p. 37).

> After the debacle, the attention turned to others who used similar language with various degrees of punishment or the lack thereof. Particular attention fell to rap artists, who are generally blamed for stereotyping African-Americans and promoting disrespect for women, portraying women "as little more than animals.... Songs now talk so casually about drugs and murder that listeners are desensitized to the words' effect" (Ross, 2007, p. G3). White people in particular are blamed for the success of the industry because they buy 70 percent of the rap music in the country.
>
> Rapper Snoop Dogg reacted angrily to this type of accusation, defending his right to free speech:
>
>> "It's a completely different scenario ... [Rappers] are not talking about no collegiate basketball girls who have made it to the next level in education and sports. We're talking about ho's that's in the 'hood that ain't doing sh--, that's trying to get a n---a for his money. These are two separate things. First of all, we ain't no old-ass white men that sit up on MSNBC going hard on Black girls. We are rappers that have these songs coming from our minds and our souls that are relevant to what we feel. I will not let them mutha—as say we in the same league as him."
>>
>> (S. Taylor, 2007)

how thoughtless and compassionless the media can be. If he thought through that the people he referred to were real people, his reaction might have been different. The Imus case provides another example of how this alienation and marginalization take place. Kierkegaard's argument that the media "simulate authority and objectivity" (Best & Kellner, 1997, p. 44) and so produce opinions rings even more familiar in this day and age. The Imus case serves as an example of how media people create an aura of authority, which is substantiated by nothing but their own opinions. If Don Imus did not have perceived authority, why would politicians, activists, authors, and other powerful players seek his favor to appear on his show?

It is not a stretch to extend this media role to that of public relations practitioners. It is the very purpose of public relations media relations to influence public opinion and present communicative entities as authoritative, rational, and objective, as in the case of the publishing house publicist who admittedly saw the show as a "media hangout" (Poniewozik, 2007, p. 37). Public relations practitioners are essential to the ability of the wealthy and powerful to gain influence because of the way in which practitioners serve as so-called "objective" third party experts legitimizing the words, thoughts, and directives of powerful communicative entities through their knowledge of and ability to manipulate the media (Holtzhausen, 2002).

Kierkegaard argues that one of the outcomes of media practice is the normalization and massification of thoughts, ideas, and "socially inculcated roles, norms, ideals, desires, expectations, fears, and hopes" (Ruf, 2005, p. 154). The way in which Black women were portrayed and how that portrayal was picked up by another medium without any consideration of the women themselves is an example of the self-referential nature of media. Although in this case public relations practitioners were not directly involved, practitioners, often when practicing crisis communication, use exactly this method to demonize and objectify victims. The media are more than likely to play along. In an analysis of media coverage of the 2002 sexual assault scandal at the Air Force Academy in Colorado the media least quoted the victims and their advocates, and mostly quoted Air Force officials and politicians (Holtzhausen & Roberts, 2009). In particular, the Air Force itself never spoke up in sympathy of the women involved and addressed the issue only at a policy level.

The effects of normalizing practices on morality and ethical decision-making is a consistent theme in postmodern ethics and will come up frequently in different discussions in this chapter. This is also the case in the discussion of the Other. Kierkegaard argues that to live a moral and ethical life it is important to take personal responsibility for one's life, and resist conformity and normalizing practices (Ruf, 2005). Also, to be a fulfilled human being it is important to live a life not guided by rationality but by beauty, emotionality, and the sublime.

Several scholars posit that Kierkegaard was influential in the works and writings of Nietzsche, generally regarded as the earliest postmodernist and one of the most influential in shaping current postmodern philosophical thought (Best, 1995; Best & Kellner, 1997; Ruf, 2005; G. B. Sim, 1996; S. Sim, 1999; V. E. Taylor & Winquist, 2001). Where Kierkegaard saw in religion and spirituality a way to escape the bondage of rationality, truth, and universal ethics, Nietzsche sought ways to expose how power is a motivating force in the Enlightenment project (V. E. Taylor & Winquist, 2001, p. 264). The relevance of Kierkegaard and Nietzsche to postmodern ethics is their challenge to totalizing discourses on morality, metaphysics, and truth that relieve individuals of personal responsibility in ethical decision-making. Nietzsche argues that morality is not situated in the person but in the act, i.e. "we are what we do" (S. Sim, 1999, p. 326), which for public relations practitioners brings a focus on praxis. The praxis/theory dichotomy in public relations ethics remains one of the field's most challenging conflicts and one a universalistic modernist ethical approach cannot solve. No ethics code can predict the fragmented and situational nature of ethical decision-making in public relations practice. Nietzsche views "the drive to find a rational, universal, apodictic foundation for morality, which culminates in the attempt to transform morality into a deductive, ethical science" as the "moral vice of late modernity" (Smith, 1996, p. 147). Also, living by universal ethical codes curtails the freedom of the individual to make her own moral choices.

Ethics as Aesthetics

The notion of Becoming (Docherty, 1993), of setting oneself free is evident in the work of Foucault, who views ethics as aesthetics; as a project of creating the self (Foucault, 1989b; May, 2006). This is not a project of liberation from morality and ethics but rather "an exercise of the self on the self, by which one attempts to develop and transform oneself, and to attain to a certain mode of being" (Foucault, 1989b, p. 433). Foucault insists that this process is not nihil-istic or hedonistic but exactly the opposite, namely a practice of freedom that will allow individuals and societies "to define admissible and acceptable forms of existence or political society" (p. 433). Thus the purpose of postmodern ethical aesthetics is to take personal responsibility for ethics; to accept that with freedom comes the responsibility to transform oneself into "something perhaps new and different, something that would be worthy of being lived" (May, 2006, p. 177). That will mean that we as public relations academics and prac-titioners cannot become "midwives to the 'ethics' of our institutions" (p. 183). To create a life worth living we need to set ourselves free from the normalizing effects of the ethical norms set for us by others.

The theme of struggle for freedom also is evident in the life and work of Küng (2003); a struggle that permeated every aspect of his life and career. Set-ting ourselves free from the ethical norms that form "us to be the sad small creatures we too often are" (May, 2006, p. 183) will allow public relations practitioners to become *a* conscience of the organization (Holtzhausen & Voto, 2002); being *the* conscience will create a metanarrative of ethical behavior for others that will take away their freedom and opportunity to grow. The idea of Becoming is a hopeful one because instead of focusing on what holds us back it helps us focus on what is possible.

The Moral Impulse

So, if the use of universal ethical codes is actually immoral, what would rep-resent morality and ethics? Does that mean that the "anything goes" label does fit postmodern ethics? Bauman (1993, pp. 10–15) describes seven attributes of postmodern morality that are recurring themes in his discussion of postmodern ethics. He argues that human beings are *morally ambivalent*—neither essentially good nor essentially bad. Society is imperfect and despite all the moral frame-works and rules morality cannot, and has never been, guaranteed. Morality cannot be *rule-guided* because it precedes "the considerations of purpose and the calculation of gains and losses" (p. 11). This means strategic decisions are not taken within the context of morality but within the framework of contracts and laws. Moral issues are invariably *aporetic* in that moral decisions can have immoral consequences. Nobody can be totally sure of the morality of a decision. Morality is *not universalizable* because universality leads to "the silencing of the moral impulse and channeling of moral capacities to socially designed targets that may, and do include immoral purposes" (p. 12). Morality and the moral impulse are *irrational*. Yet, the chaotic and autonomous nature of the moral self supplies the raw materials on which society and concern for others are built. Moral responsibility is also "being *for* the Other before one can be *with* the Other" (p. 13). Being for the Other is a pre-rational, primordial impulse, which is "the first reality of the self" (p. 13) and is an impulse without knowing the Other, evaluating his situation, or considering ethical rules. It is indeed the purest form of morality there is.

Instead of the "everything goes" tag attached to postmodern ethics, Bauman (1993) argues that the postmodern perspective on morality is much more taxing than that of modernism, which relieves you of your morality through its many ethical rules and dogmas. He describes universal ethics as "moral parochialism" (p. 14) and argues that enforced ethical codes, on the one hand, and the complex conditions of the moral self, on the other, are essentially incongruous. "It is the ethical codes which are plagued with relativism, that plague being but a reflection or a sediment of tribal parochialism of institutional powers that usurp ethical authority" (p. 14).

The result of the fact that people rather adhere to the rules or laws as set out by the group or society, rather than their moral impulse, is moral and physical poverty, misery, and misrecognition of the Other. This description of postmodern ethics implies that morality is messy and a process that continuously engages the individual. But to fully understand the moral impulse and how it might manifest within public relations practice, it is first important to understand the role of the Other. In the context of postmodern ethics the Other is the binary opposite of the Self, which in modernity is an "independent, autonomous, and thus essentially non-social moral being" (Dumont, 1986, p. 25). Many philosophers describe the Other in female terms, which poses a big problem for feminists and the field of public relations, which is largely dominated by women. Particularly since the Enlightenment women have been viewed as incapable of ethical decision-making and belonging to the private sphere, which is devoid of social ethics.

The ethics of compassion for the Other is largely attributed to the Jewish philosopher Emmanuel Levinas (1906–1995). Like Nietzsche, Levinas greatly influenced Derrida and Foucault and is credited as a key postmodern thinker who has not only provided postmodern theory with an intellectual, but also an ethical foundation (Atterton, 2002). In contrast to the emphasis on the autonomy and freedom of the modern individual, for Levinas ethics begins with obligation and responsibility to the Other, to be interpreted as the face of the neighbor. This obligation is similar to the moral impulse. "The will is free to assume this responsibility in whatever sense it likes; it is not free to refuse this responsibility itself; it is not free to ignore the meaningful world into which the face of the Other has introduced it" (Levinas, 1969, pp. 218–219, as cited in Atterton, 2002). This relationship is asymmetrical in the sense that the moral impulse always privileges the Other. It is an act of self-transcendence—of stepping outside of the self (Ouaknin, as cited in Bauman, 1993). Thus, contrary to focusing on the autonomous self, the postmodern ethical subject has to submit to intersubjectivity, which is asymmetrical in the sense that the moral impulse is invoked without expectations of reciprocity from the Other. "The I always has one responsibility *more* than all the others" [italics in the original] (Levinas, 1981, p. 84).

Levinas transforms the alienated Other to *Face* through a morality that can never evaluate whether the Other is worthy of the moral impulse. In the same way that the moral impulse is activated without preconceived ethical standards, the Face can never expect morality from another. Other attributes of the Face are that it has power over the moral subject in the sense that it *commands* the moral impulse without demanding morality. The Face can never expect anything and can never be expected to reciprocate in any way for a moral act. Bauman interprets Levinas' concept of the Face as that

> the Other is weak, and it is precisely that weakness that makes my positioning her as the Face a moral act: I am fully and truly for the Other, since it is I who give her the right to command, make the weak strong, make the silence speak, make the non-being into being through offering it the right to command me. 'I am for the other' means I give myself to the Other as hostage. I take responsibility for the Other. But I take the responsibility not in the way one signs a contract and takes upon himself the obligations that the contract stipulates. It is I who take the responsibility, and I may take that responsibility or reject it.
>
> (pp. 73–74)

The moral impulse can therefore never be commanded by society or universal ethical standards but purely by the Face, which in turn can never be expected to reciprocate for the moral act. Thus the moral impulse is a truly prerational, unconditional act that becomes before being—an ethic that precedes all other philosophical disciplines (V. E. Taylor & Winquist, 2001).

For the public relations practitioner the implications are that being moral and ethical is ambivalent. We can never know whether our moral decisions in our practice might not eventually lead to negative outcomes. Nobody else nor a set of rules can make or justify moral decisions for an individual. Individuals take moral responsibility and that responsibility is based on the moral impulse. The moral impulse should also not be confused with financial expediency or strategic intent. In the Don Imus case advertisers did not withdraw because of their moral impulse but because their respective brands were threatened. That is neither a moral nor ethical act but a merely practical decision. If the moral impulse is pre-rational it is also clear that an organization or corporation cannot be moral but only the people who work in those organizations, and then only as individuals, not as a group. In the Imus incident it is clear that Imus felt no moral responsibility toward the Rutgers students, and neither did Snoop Dogg, based on his description of the Black women in die "hood." Both argued that they were entitled to say what they want, falling back on legal issues of free speech. This is typical of what postmodernists argue is wrong with modernist ethics, where the law and universal ethical codes replace morality and compassion.

Morality, Ethics and The Law

Vignette 2.2 is typical of the dilemma of the law when one argument is incommensurable with another in that the one argument does not exist in the language of the other. The American Indians argue within a framework of religion and the developers within a framework of capitalism. The American Indians argue from a basis of their own history and ethnicity. "The paradigm is so different. One elder said, 'Are we now playing God?'" The developers argue from the basis of their rights in a capitalist society. Is this merely a case of justice or is it a case of ethics? That is the question postmodernism poses and that articulates the tension between the two fields.

Because of this tension the relationship between ethics and the law is an important discussion in postmodernism and particularly relevant to public relations, where there often is evidence of tension between legal advisers and public relations practitioners. Postmodernism questions the traditional notion that ethics follow from law and argue law is a contractual agreement between citizens and the state. The same goes for other contractual agreements between employees and employers, clients and service providers. If contracts are broken there are legal ways to solve the problem. But that does not solve the problem of morality. People can be unethical and immoral without breaking the law. That happens every day when corporations lay off people because Wall Street demands more profits, despite the fact that this will result in severe hardship. The corporation is fully within its rights but this step can hardly be viewed as moral. Another daily example is the refusal of health care companies to treat ill or dying people. They are legally within their rights but their behavior is immoral. Their morality (or lack thereof) does not stem from the fact that they are abiding to the stipulations of the contract but rather in the way they ignore their moral impulse toward the Other. Ethics stem from morality, which for postmodernists is a pre-rational impulse of unconditional love. It comes from the moral impulse. These examples show how difficult moral decision-making in the workplace really is and that it goes well beyond the simplistic statement in many public relations ethical codes that practitioners should be open and honest.

VIGNETTE 2.2

Snowmaking plan pits ski area against tribes, environmentalists

March 2005

U.S. Water News Online

FLAGSTAFF, Ariz.—For residents of sun-drenched Phoenix, the quickest route to skiing and snowboarding is a two-hour drive to this northern Arizona community—if there's snow, anyway.

Arizona Snowbowl, which sits in the Coconino National Forest outside Flagstaff, has hosted skiers in search of powder since 1938. But the drought gripping Arizona has meant hardly any skiing in some recent seasons.

Snowbowl's operators hope to change that with the addition of snow-making equipment, pitting them against tribes and environmentalists in a dispute that the U.S. Forest Service must now decide. A decision from a Forest Service supervisor is expected in the next month or two.

Snowbowl wants to operate the snowmaking equipment with reclaimed Flagstaff city wastewater to offset dry years and to lay bases in good years, like this one. It has also asked the Forest Service to allow it to upgrade lifts, build new trails and build an area for sledders.

Coconino National Forest officials have already identified that proposal as its preferred choice, compared to allowing no new development or allowing expansion but not snowmaking equipment. A final decision, which will be made by Forest Supervisor Nora Rasure, is being drafted, said spokesman Ken Frederick.

Whatever decision is made, however, it will likely be appealed administratively and could end up in court, detractors say.

J.R. Murray, Snowbowl's general manager, said Snowbowl needs snowmaking equipment to be competitive, and the current owners have indicated they will try to sell the resort if they can't get permission to make the addition.

"If you're a ski area without snowmaking, you are on financial thin ice," he said.

Snowbowl is enjoying a good season this winter, as El Nino-driven storms have brought consistent snow to the San Francisco Peaks. It opened Thanksgiving weekend.

But during the ongoing western drought, snowfalls have been inconsistent from year to year, and Snowbowl has been open as few as four days in an entire season, Murray said.

"To operate a ski area as a successful business, you have to have some degree of predictability," he said.

Environmentalists and American Indian tribes, however, have objected to the addition of snowmaking equipment, in part because of its use of reclaimed wastewater. Reclaimed water is commonly used in Arizona to water golf courses and parks and to recharge groundwater aquifers.

Ski areas elsewhere have used reclaimed water blended with other fresh water, but Snowbowl would be the first to use reclaimed water alone, Murray said.

The issue is particularly sensitive for Indian tribes that hold the peaks sacred. Various ceremonial sites dot the peaks area, and native healers often gather plants here.

The Hopi believe Kachinas live in the San Francisco Peaks. Kachinas, messengers who take prayers to the Creator, bring rain and snow, said Leigh J. Kuwanwisiwma, director of the Hopi Cultural Preservation Office.

"The paradigm is so different. One elder said, 'Are we now playing God?'" said Kuwanwisiwma. "Will the Kachina spirits feel rejected? If they feel that rejection, does it mean they will no longer give us that blessing?"

Tribes and environmental groups have opposed Snowbowl for decades, contending that it desecrates a sacred site and mars a unique environment.

Andy Bessler of the Sierra Club said he's concerned about what the reclaimed water would do to the soil. The group doesn't oppose the use of reclaimed water but believes it should be used for groundwater recharge rather than snowmaking.

He also said that cutting trees to expand trails and other infrastructure is a concern in a forest that's been hit hard by years of drought.

"Any reduction of habitat is a significant environmental impact," Bessler said.

Murray argues, however, that the ski area affects just 1 percent of the peaks area and the demand for winter recreation is demonstrated by the nearly 200,000 people who visit in good ski years.

"Look at the people out here," he said on a recent weekday when snow was falling and parking lots were filling. "If the snow is here, they will come."

Water officials have already certified the type of wastewater Snowbowl wants to use for snowmaking operations, Murray said.

He acknowledged that tribes consider the mountain sacred, "but it's public land, not a reservation."

Kuwanwisiwma counters that public lands officials shouldn't have to save Snowbowl from poor seasons.

"The Forest Service shouldn't be in the business of bailing out private business," he said.

(Anonymous, 2005)

Incommensurable Language Games

Lyotard (Lyotard, 1988; Lyotard & Thébaud, 1985) in particular highlights the tension between different and incommensurate arguments, as in the case of the American Indians and Arizona Snowbowl. He argues that ethics and justice are two genres of thought with incommensurable language. Each of these discourses takes place in terms of their own "language games" (Lyotard & Thébaud, 1985, p. 50). Lyotard explains the difference by arguing one "absolutely cannot put on the same plane a language game of scientific denotation ... and, let us say, an 'artistic' language game [which is] quite difficult to define" (p. 50). To understand the difference between morality and justice it is also important to understand Lyotard's distinction between *denotative* (descriptive) and *prescriptive* language. Denotative language belongs to the sciences, to the *what is* category. Justice belongs to the *ought* category. "There is a change of language" (p. 17) between the two, representing two different language games. "One [denotative] describes a model of strategy, of society, of economy, and then, when one passes to prescriptions, one has jumped into another language game. One is without criteria, yet one must decide" (p. 17). This brings into clearer focus the pre-rational emphasis on the moral impulse where no language can reach, where no judgment can be made, and only the extreme love of the Other counts. Lyotard argues that prescriptive language games, which he views as theoretical, come from the "will to power" (p. 17) and are politically motivated because they are used to persuade and bring about changes in the current state of affairs (Malpas, 2003).

The moral impulse functions without judgment and without political motivation. But even judgment cannot be universal. It can only take place on a case-by-case basis. People cannot live without making judgments; but judgments cannot be universal—only specific and individual. To ensure justice, each case prescription must be made "one by one and without appealing to ontology or claiming universalizability" (Best & Kellner, 1991, p. 161).

Lyotard follows the fact-value distinction that argues *ought* cannot follow from *is* because ought is based on subjective value judgments. Linking is and ought is dangerous particularly when a collective *we* does not recognize the language games of others, as in the case of the American Indians. For Lyotard the only way to be just is to recognize that there are others who speak in a different genre of discourse. Ultimately the only justice is to allow the other party to speak, using its own genre of discourse. "To be just is to allow others to participate in the 'game of the just', to respect their difference and allow them to speak for themselves" (Malpas, 2003, p. 57).

So, finally we understand the implications for public relations practitioners. Moral and ethical conduct is deeply personal and based on the pre-rational moral impulse. Just practice is based on allowing stakeholders to participate in the *game of the just* and allowing them to speak for themselves. This has nothing to do with symmetrical or asymmetrical practice. Asymmetry exists when people argue within the same genre of discourse but the most powerful determines the outcome of the discussion. Symmetry exists when people using the same genre of discourse have equal power to determine the outcome. Just practice exists when the parties recognize that they are using different genres of discourse and that an equitable outcome is impossible. In such a case no outcome should be enforced and if it is, both parties need to acknowledge that the outcome is unjust.

But there is also a difference between judging and the law. Lyotard (Lyotard & Thébaud, 1985) comments on the role of a judge by arguing that even justices deal with cases on a case-by-case basis, despite the perceived universality of the law. In the postmodern context judgment can be interpreted as ethics in the context of critiquing law's judgments (Loizidou, 2007). Thus, postmodernists would argue that morality and ethics come before the law and that legal decisions can also be submitted to ethical judgment. In fact, as Patterson (1994) mentions, "postmodernist jurisprudence represents a break with the past in so far as it embodies a conception of justification which is at odds with the key assumptions of modernism" (p. xii). In contrast, in "modern ethics these principles [of right and wrong] are typically given a jural conception" (Loizidou, 2007, citing *The Cambridge dictionary of philosophy*, 2001, p. 286). Patterson (1994) follows Lyotard by saying legal arguments, because they are from the genre of prescriptive language, can never be true. "Nothing—not the world, not morality, not economy—makes a proposition of law true. We use forms of legal arguments … to justify our assertion of the truth of legal propositions" (p. xiv).

Murphy (1994) points out that all language games are both descriptive and prescriptive. Elaborating on Lyotard's arguments, Murphy argues that although scientific language is descriptive of phenomena it is also prescriptive in that there are standards and norms for the ways in which the descriptive language is produced. The difference between descriptive language and prescriptive language is that with descriptive language there are "*criteria* to judge the truth of statements, but *no criteria to judge the justness of the prescriptions we make*" [italics in the original] (p. 5). Thus, in all matters of ethics, justice, and politics there are only opinions and no knowledge. Murphy uses the complex systems of knowledge, particularly those around the core values of Western societies, as proof of the inabilities of these societies to make conclusive judgments. This leads to the need for prudent judgment because there are many valid arguments and "*the claims of rival paradigms need to be taken into account whenever we judge and decide*" [italics in original] (p. 8). Contrary to the argument that postmodernism makes people ethical relativists incapable of judgments, this awareness "may end up making our judgments less black and white, more subtle, more rich" (p. 9).

What is important to public relations practice is the postmodern contention that one language game cannot be privileged over another. What follows is that public relations as a language game (consisting of many different language games in the form of different approaches and philosophies) is not *less than* the language game of a communicative entity's legal representative. Privileging one language game over another will be unjust. The aim of the postmodern is respect for a diversity of language games. "Postmodernism judges prescriptions in terms of how they contribute to cognitive diversity" (Murphy, 1994, p. 15). Also, public relations is but one language game competing within some or all of many competing spheres, all making up the *bricolage* of society and human life:

> Community emphasizes norms; the economy, reciprocal ends and roles; bureaucracy, organizational goals and rules; the civic realm, procedures and processes; the cultural sphere, values; the reconstructive sphere, changes; and finally, the public sphere, equilibrium and balance. Each of these spheres makes distinctive claims. Each backs up its claims with its own vision of a good society.
>
> (p. 4)

Public relations is a language game within all of these spheres, which each in turn has its own language games. To perform their public relations roles practitioners have to understand the criteria of each of these spheres and should be able to participate in all of them without giving preference to one over the other. Furthermore, there cannot be a grand narrative, not of "Theology, Science, Philosophy, Hermeneutics, or Art" (p. 10). All of these have to become little narratives, and all of them have to be considered and included in the pastiche that makes up the fabric of society. That is a postmodern approach. It is the justice of multiplicity.

Power and Ethics

One of the main concerns postmodernists address is that of power. Again, power is addressed at two levels: how knowledge shapes power and how knowledge and discipline are used to gain political power. In a discussion of postmodern ethics these two perspectives are again front and center.

In the case of ethics it is more difficult to untangle these two arguments. The question for postmodernists is not what the content of a postmodern ethical stance would be but rather who makes ethical decisions and on whose behalf they are made, or who benefits from them. The aim of the postmodern ethical project is that "the source of moral power which in modern ethical philosophy and political practice were hidden from sight, may be made visible while the reason for their past invisibilities can be better understood" (Bauman, 1993, p. 3). Thus, the postmodern ethics project is to show how power shapes ethical debates and decisions. The postmodern stance that morality, and subsequently ethical behavior, should be guided by the moral impulse to the ultimate Other is now a familiar one. The postmodern argument that will be explored here is that any group decision, or decisions made in the name of a group, relieves the individual of his ethical responsibility. This is also true for public relations professionals. To illustrate the complex environment in which public relations practitioners have to make ethical decisions, particularly as it pertains to the influence of power, Vignette 2.3 shows how this affected a public relations executive.

The fact is that the moral impulse makes people in power very uncomfortable because it awakens those who have to perform their public relations duties to the reality of their practice, as in Vignette 2.3. The moral impulse means taking care of the Other without any legal or social obligation toward the Other. The Other cannot ask for anything, might not even know there is someone who cares, and cannot insist on being cared for. Love for the Other can only be given unconditionally and unquestioningly. No wonder that both Kierkegaard and Levinas use erotic love as an analogy for the moral impulse (Bauman, 1993). Bauman argues that the modern project aimed at freeing people from tribal and religious strangleholds to make it easier to reconstitute them in the framework of a new social dispensation. The modernist human agent is understood as rational, as having a complete understanding of and insight into herself, has a "supposed unity and homogeneity of the ensemble of its positions," and is viewed as "the origin and basis of social relations" (Laclau & Mouffe, 1985, p. 115). Thus, the modern individual had to be free to make his own decisions, but this time in the framework of the nation state, which now has replaced the Church as the supreme societal authority (Bauman, 1993).

But because those in power do not trust ordinary people to make the correct moral decisions, a whole cadre of people such as teachers, philosophers, and other surrogates of modernist ideology, which included medicine and disciplines such as psychology, was tasked to shape ethical mores and norms. Here the postmodern attack on knowledge creation in general and philosophy in particular becomes very clear. The philosopher in particular had access to the knowledge about what to dictate to others, to "those less endowed who cannot find them on their own, and [have to] do it with the authority of 'people in the know'" (Bauman, 1993, p. 28). In Western society these people are mostly teachers and philosophers who, with their high-brow and expansive analysis of philosophical questions raise ethical decision-making to an elitist level where few dare to go.

This creates a paradox. On the one hand, people are now free from the constraints of old orders such as religion and ethnicity and, on the other, new systems of behavior have to be created because people cannot be trusted to make their own judgments. But people, now free to choose, would not again voluntarily subject themselves to new sets of rules. That was when the law became entangled with ethics because what was upheld as law was also presented as moral. The modernist project is to unsettle the moral impulse. It wishes to create distance between the individual and the Other and then fill that distance with laws and sets of rules presented as ethical decisions.

VIGNETTE 2.3

Situated Ethics

"Every social structure or organization has power relations, be it in government, religion, business, family, or social clubs. To function in such an environment behavioral guidelines or requirements are used to reach and satisfy the objectives and expectancies of those in power in a particular environment.

The ethical behavior and moral decisions that come into play while satisfying job expectations may clash with what is acceptable in other environments. For example, acceptable and expected conduct in the workplace might not be acceptable in a social club or religious affiliation.

It is possible for a communication practitioner to adhere to the values of the workplace and adjust his moral approach without questioning whether such values will be acceptable in another environment. It is also likely that the work environment can bring about a change in the moral perspectives of the practitioner over time.

Satisfying the requirements and expectations of a workplace is viewed as a prerequisite to its success. The moral conduct of the practitioner must therefore be such that it will guarantee the required results, or at least not contribute to an organization's failure. Sometimes, however, in this process the practitioner might be expected to behave in a way that she would view as amoral in another environment. This happens not only because the employer requires it but also because non-compliance will threaten the practitioner's career, financial well-being, standard of living, or even her family. To balance the moral and personal incongruity and interests of all concerned, the practitioner has to meet the unattainable demand of switching between or satisfying several sets of moral principles in the course of a day.

This will inevitably result in inner moral conflicts that could devastate or disrupt the behavioral effectiveness of a professional practitioner. If not addressed successfully and in a professionally accountable and coherent manner, both the employer and/or the practitioner may fail or be destroyed. Most likely the victim will be the weaker and less powerful communication practitioner.

Typically such employers would be ones that operate in environments where secrecy and security are prerequisites, such as military institutions, armaments manufacturers, and state functions responsible for high level global interests, such as state departments and departments of defense. I experienced that myself.

The military acquisitions corporation I was working for was responsible for obtaining state-of-the-art military equipment and paraphernalia to maintain my country's military strength. Because my organization could not satisfy all the acquisitioning demands of the country's military due to international constraints, it was forced to develop military manufacturing capabilities.

To conceal the military's vulnerability from adversary interests, the developments and shortcomings needed to be dealt with at the highest level of covertness. For instance, a specific component was unattainable but required to complete the missile firing-system of an attack helicopter, in turn tied to a critical military development program. The acquisition of this component had to be achieved under utmost secrecy and concealment. This meant that people needed to be networked or appointed to obtain knowledge or blue-prints. Against the backdrop of ever-ongoing industrial and sensitive undercover work by adversaries, as well as avoiding the transparency sought by media, such a venture called for an unusual business approach.

These "cloak-and-dagger" circumstances called for behavior that placed extraordinary, perhaps bizarre, demands on the people involved. This included me, the communication practitioner, who needed to be drawn into this network of dangerous confidentiality. As a result, my career, financial reality, and way of life became burdened. To maintain secrecy and keep the project secured, I was required to perform under a set of survivable, "professional" communication values. I was often required to make a prompt diagnosis of a situation and then come to a decision to either appropriate undamaging spin or venture a risky disinformation approach.

This meant I was required to conceal the *bona fide* facts and save the day for my organization irrespective of whether the facts were accurate or true. To be successful, I had to manage my employer's image in a seamless manner, despite the contorted moral basis and despite forfeiting my personal moral values or preferences. However, over time I came to realize that I was actually confronted with a choice. On the one hand, I could accept falsehood and astute deception as a means to ensure an affluent standard of living that would have benefited all and secured my family's future. On the other hand, I could listen to the moral dissonance and act. I slowly started to resist and eventually confronted myself with the dilemma. In the end I was unable to suppress my moral values and walked away but I and my family paid a heavy price in terms of our financial security."

The Importance of Information for Ethical Behavior

It is important to note that this dissemination of knowledge about what is "newly ethical," so to speak, needs to be done through communication. The more complex society becomes the more complex these communication systems will be. Where in the pre-modern era it was enough for a tribal leader to get his people together or for the powerful clergyman to preach from the pulpit, new technologies are now required to disseminate this new knowledge. Two ways are used to disseminate the required ethical knowledge. The first is the creation of social systems that distribute knowledge, which Althusser (1971) calls ideological state apparatuses (ISAs) and include units as small as the family and as big as political government systems, spanning the Church, government departments, schools, universities, and social organizations. The other is the use of people who can objectify this knowledge and hide the powerful interests behind this distribution of knowledge. Here public relations practice becomes important to powerful players. Together with other communication practitioners, including advertising practitioners and journalists, public relations practitioners are systematically used to create this new moral order and justify the actions of the others. Bourdieu (1977) argues powerful people need agents to cover up their real interests because this subversion is what allows them to accumulate wealth. That is how public relations becomes part of the system that alienates people from their own moral responsibility and helps objectify the interests of powerful entities while presenting them as moral and ethical instead of exposing the underlying desire for power and wealth (Holtzhausen, 2002).

Bauman's (1993) argument is reminiscent of Bourdieu's when he says that some people have more moral freedom than others. "Individual autonomy and heteronomy in modern society are unequally distributed" (p. 29). The only people who are trusted to make their own moral judgments are those in power. "You can trust the wise (the code name of the mighty) to do good autonomously, but you cannot trust all people to be wise" (p. 30).

Nowhere is this issue more obvious than in giving tax breaks to the wealthy. Who is not familiar with the *trickle down* concept—the argument that the people who control the resources necessary to create wealth will know what to do with their money, will put the necessary systems in place, and wealth will trickle down to the rest. They will use their wealth for good works, for those less wealthy, and for those who do not know how to help themselves.

> So, in order to enable the resourceful to do more good, one needs to give them yet more resources (they will, one hopes, put them to good use); but in order to prevent the resourceless from doing evil, one needs to further restrict the resources at their disposal (one needs, for instance, to give more money to the rich, but less money to the poor, to make sure that good work will be done in both cases).
>
> (Bauman, 1993, p. 30)

Communication practitioners in general, but public relations practitioners in particular, because of their close relationship with those in the dominant coalition and the very nature of what public relations work entails, form part of this wealth creation system, which needs for its very survival that its codes of conduct be translated into ethical behavior instead of the power grab it really is. Ironically, public relations practitioners do not gain power themselves but are merely used in the process.

As a result of the insertion of agents and laws to present normal social rules as ethics, people do not take responsibility for their own ethical behavior because they have relinquished that privilege to others. That is the only way in which people can be coerced into doing the will of those in power. The modern system needs intermediaries who can teach and guide others to obey those social rules, presented as ethical rules. Perhaps one of the most powerful tools for public relations educators is to make their students aware of this situation and to teach them to not uncritically accept whatever is thrown at them in the workplace with arguments that it benefits the bottom line. It is always important to understand whose bottom line benefits from public relations work.

To further stress the importance of these social rules and make them useful for control in a society where people believe they have freedom of choice, they need not only to be presented as ethical but also as universal. Universality in the context of ethics requires the presentation of these rules as applicable to all people in all circumstances. This ignores the inherent complexity of postmodernity. Bauman (1993) makes a distinction between the unencumbered self and the situated self, who is "always set against a self differently situated—rooted in another polis" (p. 40). The argument that the unencumbered self is always different from the situated self is indeed a valid one. First, people are situated differently in multiple ways at different times, which leads to the concept of fragmented identities. Second, public relations practice, like so many other professional practices, differs depending on the environment in which it is practiced and requires a different situatedness depending on the environment of practice. For these two reasons public relations can have no universal ethical rules. Universal ethics can be nothing more than meaningless, toothless lists of rules that cannot address the complexity of practitioners' lives, as in the case of the practitioner in Vignette 2.3.

Ethics and the Group

But will it then not be postmodern for communities to define their own ethical rules, as in the case of an organization, such as was obviously the case with the practitioner in the armaments industry, or in the case of professional organizations, of which there are many in the field of public relations? Can one not see these as moral communities? Unfortunately, the problems remain the same as for universal ethics in broader society. Sometimes these smaller moral communities can even be more destructive of moral responsibility than those universal social ethics. Now the group takes the place of the powerful individual in society. Adherence to the group is more important than adherence to the rest of society. This need for universal ethics in the group stems from insecurity because the only basis for the group's existence is discourse. It is a postulated group, which is per definition insecure. One cannot help but wonder whether the drive for universal ethics in public relations stems from the field's insecurity, because ultimately public relations practice is only a postulated profession.

A discussion of ethics also cannot take place without some focus on human rights. Far too often human rights, i.e. the rights of the individual, are confused with culture or group rights. Many crimes are perpetuated in the name of culture under the guise of human rights. It is not difficult to think of examples. One close to home is the rights White South Africans claimed for themselves but not for Blacks in the name of cultural differentiation between them and Black South Africans—the so-called right to self-determination. Fortunately, the rest of the world did not accept that argument and eventually forced the country to transform. But how often do we support this claim, particularly when it comes to the status of women? Would the world but demand the same rights for women as they claim for men to live out their cultural values! One reason for this is the subordinate role philosophers assigned to women. The other is that the group in these instances is situated above both the universal and the individual. Bauman (1993) argues that even communitarians, who would argue vehemently against universal rights, will in an instant deny human rights in favor of the interests of the group. Human rights, like in the case of White South Africans, become a way to assert power in the name of group rights. As Kierkegaard (1968, p. 51) said, "The truth is that in a herd we are free from the standards of the individual and the ideal."

The problems for public relations practitioners are that we are far too often confronted with having to deal with group rights while being required to ignore individual rights. South African law, for instance, recognizes tribal law and gives women a choice to live under tribal law or common law. Because tribal law entrenches the rights of tribes and particularly their chiefs, they have been slow to change. A Black female practitioner in South Africa, a thoroughly modern young woman, working for one of the largest public relations agencies in the country, tells how she was responsible for an HIV/AIDS campaign in one of the country's far-flung rural areas. To do her job, she had to have access to the tribal leader. First, she had to make sure that she was conservatively dressed, covered from head to toe. Second, she had to be accompanied by a man, who first had to ask the chieftain permission on her behalf to speak to him personally. Then she had to ask the chieftain permission to communicate with his people. When asked whether she resented that, she said no, because that was what the job demanded and to get the job done that was what she had to do. This is an example of how group rights often trump the law of the land and how practitioners can get caught up in perpetuating discriminatory practices, particularly when they communicate cross-culturally and are afraid to offend. Situations like these further emphasize the extreme complexity of ethical decision making that has very little to do with codes of conduct of professional organizations.

Ethics and the Problem with Women

These perspectives on how powerful interests shape ethical and legal decisions have particular bearing on the issue of women and ethical decision-making. Without fear of contradiction one can argue that women as a group have been and still are subjected to discrimination that is systemic, systematic, deliberate, and often cruel. This discrimination takes on different forms in different settings, but remains nonetheless pervasive and global. For those who argue that women in Western society have been fully liberated one only has to show the statistics in the United States, for instance, that femicide is the major reason for the death of pregnant women, or that despite the fact that public relations tracks at U.S. universities are filled with female students, they not only make less money than their male counterparts but also are less likely to reach the top of their profession. These manifestations of discrimination might not be viewed as severe in the United States as in other parts of the world but are nonetheless a form of violence perpetrated against women. No matter how one argues this, women are still seen predominantly as second class citizens who need to be seen but not heard. Postmodernism, as a Western philosophical tradition, will not comment on how this came about in other societies and cultures but does point to the role modernism has played in segmenting the role of women as *less than*. If one uses this lens to view the media coverage of Senator Hillary Clinton's campaign to become the Democratic Party's presidential candidate for 2008, it not hard to often find a misogynistic subtext in how she was judged and reported on. This is partly due to the fact that women are not supposed to be part of public life, which is a direct outflow of the Enlightenment project.

The argument that women are positioned as the binary opposite of men is now a familiar one. If men are the rational self then women are the irrational other. As Simone de Beauvior (1949, as cited in Thornham, 1999) points out, man has assigned himself the category of self whereas "she is the incidental, the inessential as opposed to the essential. He is the Subject, he is the Absolute— she is the Other" (p. 43). Whereas modern man is upheld as the universal being, this being is "far from being ungendered and 'transcendent', was not only gendered but very specific: a Western, bourgeois, white heterosexual man" (p. 43).

One of the problems with philosophical arguments that reflect on women is that women's philosophical perspectives are relegated to the sphere of the private, while the typical male-oriented philosophical approach that focuses on justice and rules is viewed as part of the public sphere. As a result definitions of the moral domain and moral autonomy "lead to a *privatization* of women's experience and to the exclusion of its consideration from a moral point of view" (Benhabib, 1992). Benhabib argues that the "relevant other" (p. 152) in universalistic moral theories is always brother and never sister.

Moral theories differentiate between justice and the "good life" (Benhabib, 1992, p. 153). The good life is "the spheres of kinship, love, friendship, and sex that elicit considerations of care [and] are usually understood to be spheres of personal decision-making" (Kohlberg, Levine, & Hewer, 1984, pp. 229–230). The good life is considered the informal and personal part of the moral domain, whereas issues of justice are viewed as the formal and public. If politics is played out in the public sphere and primarily concerned with legislation, i.e. justice, it is understandable why so many men do not feel Senator Clinton has a place in public life as the president of the United States. Women are tolerated to be legislators but only as long as they do not aspire to the highest level of service.

Many of Kohlberg et al.'s (1984) assumptions are questionable from a postmodern perspective. First, postmodernists would argue Kohlberg's assertions are value judgments—not descriptive but prescriptive. Lyotard (Lyotard & Thébaud, 1985) argues that the moment something becomes prescriptive it becomes political. Thus, what Kohlberg presents as universal moral assumptions are deeply political statements; statements, one can argue, to keep women out of the public sphere. Second, discourses on the public and private moral spheres are what Lyotard would identify as language games. Thus, the way in which Kohlberg privileges the public over the private would in Lyotard's terms be unjust because one language game is not better than another.

This raises the question of how the marginalization of women from the moral sphere came about. Indeed, Derrida comments that this exclusion might in historical perspective be one of the biggest scandals of the 20th century (Kearney, 2004). Benhabib (1992) argues that the way in which the moral sphere was separated into private and public domains started with Hobbes' defense of the "privacy and autonomy of the self" (p. 154) in the religious, scientific, and philosophical spheres. For Hobbes "free thought" was part of the autonomous self. To preserve this privacy and autonomy of the individual (read men), justice became the center of moral theory. "As long as the social bases of cooperation and the rights claims of individuals are respected, the autonomous bourgeois subject can define the good life as his mind and conscience dictate" (p. 154). At the time when moral and political theories started to be formulated this did not mean that women became equal but rather that gender was removed from the public sphere and issues of justice. Women were relegated to the domain of the conventional. While males remained the independent heads of the household and could negotiate within the realm of justice, the intimate sphere remains removed from the reaches of justice and was restricted to the reproductive and affective needs of the bourgeois pater-familias. An entire domain of human activity, namely, nurture, repro-duction, love and care, which becomes the woman's lot in the course of the development of modern, bourgeois society, is excluded from moral and political considerations, and relegated to the realm of 'nature'.

(p. 155)

By being relegated to nature, women become earth and no longer the bearer of all human beings, thus finally freeing "the male ego from the most natural and basic bond of dependence" (p. 156). In this way the early modern woman is not recognized as having life experience of her own but only exists in terms of what men are not. This distinction was made across racial lines, as is evidenced by the fact that in the United States Black men received voting rights, which is representative of the public sphere, long before any women did. In South Africa women were only granted voting rights when the colored population was given the vote in 1920 because Whites feared they would be outvoted. It was argued (correctly) that women would vote as their men instructed (Giliomee, 2003).

Unfortunately this relegation of women to a different moral sphere did not remain only part of philosophy but was subsequently carried over to other social sciences, most notably psychology. In her hugely influential book, *In a different voice*, Gilligan (1993) uncovers how the assumptions of moral theory discussed above penetrated Freud's thinking on moral development in children. She shows how Freud built his psychosexual theory of child development on the experiences of the male child. Because of the basic theoretical anomalies in applying the theoretical assumptions about male children to female children, Freud came to the conclusion that women made ethical decisions different from men because of the "strength and persistence of women's pre-Oedipal attach-ments to their mothers" which he saw "as women's development failure" (p. 7). But instead of merely observing and describing these differences he made the value judgment that women "show less sense of justice than men, that they are less ready to submit to the great exigencies of life, that they are more often influenced in their judgments by feelings of affection or hostility" (Freud, 1925, pp. 257–258), placing the "problem" of women's early development at the level of emotion and relationships. Gilligan (1993) shows how boys' natural prefer-ence for rules became the standard against which child psychologists such as Piaget, Lever, and Erikson measured girls' moral ability and found it wanting, simply because morality was viewed as synonymous with justice and "playing by the rules." Girls identify themselves through their relationships with others, whereas boys show a level of individuality, a much more desirable attribute and a preferable moral stance in modern philosophy.

The deference to the values and opinions of others and the inclusion of the voices of others in their judgments have thus led to assumptions of women as immature adults, instead of being their biggest moral strength (Gilligan,

1993). Gilligan argues that this conceptualization of adulthood that favors the individual and autonomous self over interdependence of love and care is itself out of balance. Through her research Gilligan concludes that when it comes to morality women speak in a different voice. They see their individual self not as autonomous but "as a standard of relationship, and ethic of nurturance, responsibility, and care" (p. 159) rather than defining themselves through their academic and professional prowess. Contrarily, "[power] and separation secure the man in an identity achieved through work, but they leave him at a distance from others, who seem in some sense out of his sight" (p. 163). While a definition of morality as integrity and care is the same for women and men they come to this debate from two very different truths, which Lyotard would identify as two genres of discourse. Gilligan quite rightly identifies these two opposing viewpoints as two different moral ideologies but she also shows how men and women, despite the different paths they take, get to the same place in later adulthood. In this stage of life justice and caring are equally important and "judgment depends on the way in which the problem is framed" (p. 167). These perspectives on moral development would question any study that would measure moral development of public relations practitioners, e.g. Lieber (2008), because a single standard of moral development is impossible.

An Ethic of Caring, Relationships, and Community

The arguments of Gilligan and Benhabib are important to public relations practitioners in that they legitimate an ethic of caring, relationships, and community. These are the building blocks of public relations practice. It shows how the fact that public relations practitioners are situated in a social context and are in a position to listen to the voice of the Other allows for the practice to be ethical. Allowing the voice directly into the sphere of practice without representation is the truly ethical: "Without engagement, confrontation, dialogue and even a 'struggle for recognition' … we tend to constitute the otherness of the other by projection and fantasy or ignore it in indifference" (Benhabib, 1992, p. 168). This is how we can differentiate between the *generalized* others, who are people like us, or the *concrete* Others, who are people with irreducible differences from our own.

This engagement with the Other is fraught with danger. As Bauman (1993) mentions, sometimes the voice of the Other is absent or so distant that it cannot be engaged directly. In public relations this means we need to represent the voice of the Other and try and articulate that voice, which speaks in such a different genre, to ensure justice. This presents the danger of "pastoral power" (p. 103), which means people submit themselves to the goodness of others and then that goodness is used to suppress those who are under their care. In the case of pastoral power love becomes power. This often happens in the work environment when women are prevented to perform certain tasks, such as traveling alone internationally or meeting with people after-hours. This is done for fear of their safety but preventing them from performing those tasks is eventually also what prevents them from being promoted. Another example is the way in which the sexual liberation of women, which was a philosophical argument about how women were held to different social and ethical standards than men, has been co-opted by powerful entities to make money from rampant pornography and the sexual exploitation of women. It will truly be hard to find morality in this kind of exploitation except to argue that it gives some women a source of income without becoming criminals. As Best and Kellner (2001, p. 36) argue, "sexuality is a domain of power" made possible by forms of "male domination, the connection between militarism and patriarchy, and the extension of male power throughout the interstices of everyday life." The new ruling elite now consists of "military men, capitalists, scientists, bureaucrats, media moguls, shadowy figures who use intelligence and technology as modes of domination" (p. 36).

To fight this kind of oppression, it is important that female public relations practitioners speak in their own voice, and strongly at that. It is inauthentic and untruthful to try and live a man's moral life. If we understand why and how the different voices of women have been marginalized and when we can speak of its injustice we can also move to a "more integrated vision of ourselves and of our fellow humans as generalized as well as 'concrete others'" (Benhabib, 1992, p. 170). Similarly, McKinnon (1987) encouraged two women who ascended to the Minnesota Supreme Court to "use the tools of law as women for all women" to determine

> what our identifications are, what our loyalties are, who our community is, to whom we are accountable. ... we have no idea what women as women would have to say. I am evoking for women a role that we have yet to make, in the name of a voice that, unsilenced, might say something that has never been heard.
>
> (p. 77)

By putting forth the voice and reason of women outside of logocentrism, or *phallologocentrism,* which Derrida argues is what women need to deconstruct, it will be impossible to return to the former "logocentric philosophies of mastery, possession, totalization, or certitude" (Kearney, 2004, p. 152).

Fragmented Discourse and Ethical Decision-Making

One problem with hearing women's voices is their fragmented nature. Postcolonial perspectives on feminism have argued that there is no homogenous identification of womanhood and that women's lives differ hugely from context to context. This of course also is the case with men. Derrida says despite the huge changes in perspectives on the feminine, women are not and will not be any freer than men are (Kearney, 2004). With the disappearance of a single understanding of what the human condition means and with the questioning of the once (perceived) stable categories of power, knowledge, and social roles, every human being's life in Western society has become fragmented.

Modernism's big claim was to determine categories and organize society in ways that helped people to know their place. For instance, men were the bread-winners, the decision-makers, and carried the authority in society. Women's role was determined to be care givers, have families, and take care of the private side of men's lives, while men took care of the public side of life. Children, of course, were subject to both parents. So, in modernism, everybody had a place and it was easy for people to have a single identity by which to live and by which to make decisions, also ethical ones. In today's society, of course, people have multiple identities. Gone are the days when men are the sole decision-makers in society or home. Men now, as much as women, have different roles in public and private lives. In democracies the role and place of people in power are increasingly questioned. Thus the old, stable categories of where people belong and who can be questioned or whose words one has to accept uncondi-tionally are disappearing. This is the case as much for politicians as it is for other institutions such as universities and churches, and also executives and managers in corporations.

In this fragmented society, people are also confronted with complex ethical decisions that are most often quite specific to a particular event or situation. For people to have one stable set of ethical rules is no longer viable because there is no one set of rules that covers all ethical dilemmas, as our practitio-ner in Vignette 2.3 said. One of the reasons for this practitioner's dilemma is the modernist project to create mutually exclusive categories such as work vs. home, church vs. work, mother vs. professional, technician/artisan vs. profes-sional, and so forth, each with its own set of ethical rules. Every public relations practitioner will understand this differentiation and subsequent fragmentation. The ethical rules of the workplace in the case of the practitioner in Vignette 2.3 actually required professional deception and deviance, while these were contrary to the value system of honesty and openness expected from him in his religion and his relationship with his family. In the parlance of the postmodern, each of these situations are socially constructed and produced through political discourse, which means that powerful entities shape the ethics of each of this practitioner's life experiences in different ways and different contexts.

Another issue in ethical decision-making is that the issues presented to peo-ple are unfamiliar. With biotechnology and other technological issues that sim-ply did not present themselves to past generations, ethical decision-making has become a complex area where different voices are vying to shape ethical frame-works to present to others as the most appropriate (Best & Kellner, 2001). This is of course again indicative of the postmodern question of who makes ethical decisions and on whose behalf they are made. It is clear that in postmodernity that question becomes increasingly complex.

This brings the postmodern argument on ethics to the role of evaluation and choice in making ethical decisions. Bauman (1993) argues that we are merely actors who play a role in each position and no one role identifies who we truly are. As a result the postmodern subject is morally ambiguous. This is contrary to the generally accepted view that holds integrity and morality as "an uncorrupted condition" (Austin, Rankel, Kagan, Bergum, & Lemermeyer, 2005, p. 210). Because of the view that humans are supposed to have a single moral condition, when confronted with morally ambiguous situations, it can lead to moral distress, particularly among working practitioners, as Austin et al. found. However, Bauman (1993) believes moral stress is a natural outflow of being ethical. When public relations practitioners can choose to live in the "Zone ... a sphere of openness, of interdeterminancy, in which people have options, can make choices, and may create their own domains, cultural forms and life" (Best & Kellner, 2001, p. 42), moral ambiguity will set in.

The moment we start to evaluate we are faced with the criteria we use to evaluate. For instance, what do we value in our own practice of public relations? Is it the bottom line? Then our ethical stance is clear: We will do whatever it takes to make money. However, practitioners should be mindful when they make a choice such as this because "no moral impulse can survive ... the acid test of usefulness or profit" (Bauman, 1993, p. 36).

Similar to Best and Kellner's (2001) argument, Lyotard (Lyotard & Thébaud, 1985) too argues that the postmodern represents the necessity of judging without criteria, which he calls paganism. Those decisions are always prescriptive, i.e. political, because value judgments are always based on prescriptive meanings. For Lyotard paganism is a metaphor from Greek mythology where "a society of gods [was] constantly forced to redraw its codes" (p. 17). Criteria, or prescriptions, always have to be argued. "[B]etween statements that narrate or describe something and statements that prescribe something, there is always some talking to be done" (p. 17). Thus, the way in which public relations practitioners communicate would become an important part of their ethical framework. Postmodernism argues that ethical discourse is based in conflict and dissensus, rather than consensus.

Postmodern Ethics as Dissensus and Dissymmetry

Introducing activism as ethical behavior in public relations might sound like a universal statement but to understand activism it is important to understand the concept of dissensus. Dissensus does not suggest that practitioners should defend a single perspective but rather focus on the process of communication as one of ethical concern (Holtzhausen 2000; Holtzhausen & Voto, 2002). Postmodern feminist scholar Ziarek (2001) makes a similar argument. She emphasizes antagonism as a way to negotiate the role of power in shaping discourses. Antagonism emerges through dissensus, which is "formative antagonism" (p. 218). Dissensus takes place when focusing on the inability to articulate one's voice in the genre of the Other, as in the case of the American Indian tribes in Vignette 2.2, and when analyzing the relation between power and *embodiment*. Ziarek describes embodiment as the disruption the binary opposites created through a discourse of power. She approaches this from a feminist perspective, namely, to disrupt the man/woman dichotomy, but the two issues of voice and power inherent in embodiment also are the foundation of an ethic of dissensus. This also prepares the way for a postmodern ethic of public relations as activism and describes the way in which public relations practitioners should disrupt the many dichotomies that privilege one group over another.

The concept of symmetry has arguably become the most dominant theoretical approach in public relations and can be described as one of the field's true metanarratives (J. E. Grunig, 1989, 1992a, 1994; J. E. Grunig & Hunt, 1984; Pearson, 1989a). From South Africa, Botswana, and Nigeria to Korea, Taiwan, China, and Singapore, India, the Middle East, Europe, and North and South America scholars have applied, argued, theorized, and compared the concept of symmetry in public relations to different philosophical systems and arguments. Two arguments are predominantly associated with symmetry: collaboration (Spicer, 1997, 2007) and consensus (Pearson, 1989a). There is a distinct difference between the two.

Collaboration and Consensus in Public Relations

Collaboration entails "the development of evolving common purpose" (Spicer, 2007, p. 37), and results in increased mutual understanding and trust. Collaboration implies working together, possibly only for immediate goals. It also has a focus on vulnerable stakeholders, i.e. "dependent or silent stakeholders" (p. 38). Whereas collaboration has as its outcome a specific action, it appears consensus has as its outcome a broader focus on social change, as "a social construction of reality, a form of knowledge" (Fairclough, as cited in R. L. Heath, 2001, p. 44). Consensus is based on dialogue, which consists of "exchange and challenge" (R. L. Heath, 2001, p. 44). Sometimes these two terms are used interchangeably by arguing that collaboration takes place through dialogue (R.G. Heath, 2007). Nonetheless, both these approaches hold forth that symmetrical communication is the way to both collaboration and consensus.

Spicer (2007) and R. L. Heath (2001) conclude that collaboration and consensus, respectively, represent ethical public relations practice. This is consistent with Habermas's (1984) theory of communicative action, which is an effort to re-establish communication as central to the "emancipatory project of modernity" (Venturelli, 1998, p. 22). The work of Habermas has been applied to public relations particularly in terms of his concept of consensus (e.g. Burkart, 2009; Pearson, 1989b). Similar to postmodernists, Habermas stresses the importance of communication and language as central to reaching understanding (Gunaratne, 2006). Habermas articulates rationality as universalistic and a "form of communicative action aimed at achieving agreement with others in an 'ideal speech situation' where people put forward moral and political claims and defend them based on rationality alone" (p. 118). He argues that the life world (consisting of the private and public spheres) and the system world of economic and administrative power exist in complex societies through a self-regulating media-system independent from its social environment (Habermas, 2006). Democracy and deliberative politics take place "if anonymous audiences grant feedback between an informed elite discourse and a responsive civil society" (p. 2) through which consensus is reached. Consensus is central to the ideal communication situation and "is the central experience of the unconstrained, unifying, consensus-building force of argumentative speech" (Habermas, 1984, p. 10). Habermas posits that his theory of communicative action is both normative and universal (Gunaratne, 2006), with the result that his work harks back to the beginnings of the Enlightenment (S. Sim, 1999).

In public relations ethics the Habermasian principles, which (Gunaratne, 2006) calls neo-Kantian, also are reflected in the work of Bowen (2005), who bases her practical model for ethical decision-making in public relations on Kant's deontology. The first step in this model is based on the possibility of reason alone and/or group consensus. This will eventually lead to the ethical outcome of symmetrical communication. The concept of ethical reasoning or ethical decision-making in public relations is also apparent in the work of Seib and Fitzpatrick (1995) who suggest deontology and teleology are the foundations of ethical decision-making. They emphasize the importance of codified standards for ethical decision-making in public relations without which "the practitioner would be forced to wing it, relying on wobbly situational ethics. This is asking for trouble" (p. 113).

By now it is clear postmodernism challenges the underlying concepts of rationality, consensus, and the individual, rational public relations practitioner as the sole ethical decision-maker. Holtzhausen and Voto (2002) and the practitioner in Vignette 2.3 showed how people with organizational power can enforce unethical behavior in the public relations environment. The notion that consensus conceals the hidden power relations in the communicative action is the most consistent critique of both Kant and Habermas. Stauber and Rampton (1995) offer many examples of how corporations co-opt unsuspecting (and sometimes suspecting) activist groups through the creation of a false consensus. Reason and rationality imply that there is some truth out there that we can find through reasoning. The postmodern argument that no such truth exists make the Kantian and Habermasian approaches unpostmodern.

The Differend *as an Alternative Communicative Approach*

Of all the postmodernists Lyotard (1984) is the most critical of Habermas's theory of consensus, "which is nothing more or less than the latest variation of the grand narratives and the cultural imperialism (terrorism) that comes with them" (V. E. Taylor & Winquist, 2001, p. 168). Lyotard (1988) argues consensus is impossible because of the *differend,* which refers to a discussion taking place in the frame of reference of only one party:

> A case of differend takes place when the 'regulation' of the conflict that opposes them is done in the idiom of one of the parties while the wrong suffered by the other is not signified by the other in that idiom.
>
> (p. 9)

He refers to this idiom as a "genre of discourse" (p. 29). All discourse is political, and political debates consist of arguments that aim to silence or persuade the Other (p. 149). As a result, Lyotard champions difference and division against reconciliation, the absence of which is generally also the biggest critique of Habermas, whose work points to an inability to accommodate conflict and difference and ignores social inequality and unequal power relations (Gunaratne, 2006). Consensus is impossible because the *differend* is a barrier to efforts aimed at resolving differences and explaining events. In addition, consensus sacrifices the recognition of differences for superficial treatment. Consensus represents an unjust outcome because a resolution that satisfies both parties is impossible. Lyotard does not believe there is legitimacy in consensus. Consensus does violence to the heterogeneity of language games, and he associates consensus with the end of thinking. Inventions and novel ways of thinking are always born out of dissensus (Lyotard, 1992). The only way to be just is to strive for dissensus, which is based on a postmodern dialectic. The classic understanding of dialectic communication is "discussion and reasoning by dialogue as a method of intellectual investigation: the Socratic techniques of exposing false beliefs and eliciting truth" (*Webster's new collegiate dictionary*, 1975). But Lyotard (Lyotard & Thébaud, 1985, pp. 4–5) describes postmodern dialectics as follows:

> [I]f you take dialogic discourse, as Plato presents it, it is a discourse in which each of the participants is, in principle, trying to produce statements such that the effects of these statements can be sent back to their author so that he may say: This is true, that is not true, and so on. In other words, so that he can control, or contribute to the control of, these effects … the regulating of dialogic discourse, even of dialectical discourse in the Platonic sense, seemed to me to be associated with power, since ultimately it aims at controlling the effects of the statements exchanged by the partners of the dialogue; I was trying, on the contrary, to limit myself to the delivery of a mass of statements barely controlled in themselves, and, insofar as the relation of the addressee is concerned, they were drawn

up more in the spirit of the bottle tossed into the ocean than in that of a return of the effects of the statements to the author.

In this sense postmodern dialectics "aims to produce effects upon the reader, and its author does not ask that these effects be sent back to him in the form of questions" (p. 4). Harland (1987) uses the metaphor of dominoes toppling forward to describe the postmodern dialectic process. Whereas consensus is a means of arresting the flow of events (a philosophy of Being), the search for dissensus extends thinking (a philosophy of Becoming) (Docherty, 1993).

How then should public relations practitioners deal with these deep conflicts? The sides in a conflict must be awakened to the depth of their conflict and must testify to the irresolvability of their *differend*. One has to wonder whether the *differend* in Vignette 2.2 can ever be resolved within the confines of the law, or within any other context. The acceptance of different viewpoints is of extreme importance because terror occurs when subjects cannot make claims to be different or represent something outside the system (Williams, 1998).

An event that has the potential to involve intermingling or opposing and different forces is a "tensor" (Lyotard, 1993a, p. 54). The role of public relations practitioners is not to strive for consensus but to identify the tensors between the organization and its stakeholders. Through the identification of tensors practitioners will promote and create situations where new meaning is produced through difference and opposition. Instead of creating the impression that consensus has been reached, those involved in a dispute would rather admit that the outcome of the event was unjust to a particular side, and that the most powerful won because they were powerful. Symmetry is thus impossible in the same way that consensus is impossible. Symmetry and true consensus will only be possible when there is total equality in the communicative relationship. Creedon's (1993, p. 164) concept of dissymmetry—defined as symmetry in different directions rather than a lack of symmetry—aligns with the postmodern dialectic process. The concepts of difference, dissensus, a postmodern dialectic, tensors, and dissymmetry point to one of the most pervasive underpinnings of postmodernism: respect for differences and an emphasis on differences to create positive change. Once public relations practitioners understand that symmetry is not per definition ethical, it will become easier for them to properly analyze a situation and decide on the best action to take. Sometimes it might be appropriate to be asymmetrical in the favor of stakeholders to ensure the survival of the organization (Holtzhausen, 2005). Even if we call it symmetry, the end game for all of us is still winning.

An understanding of dissensus can serve as an explanation for the fact that practitioners find it difficult to practice the two-way symmetrical model of public relations, which admittedly is a normative model, i.e. "how public relations *should* be practiced" [italic in original] (L. A. Grunig, Grunig, & Dozier,

2002, p. 310). To use the words of Lyotard (Lyotard & Thébaud, 1985) symmetry is prescriptive and not descriptive, which is evident in the use of the word *should*. The authors of the Excellence theory, which has as its foundation the concept of symmetry as normative practice (J. E. Grunig, 1992b), concluded after an exhaustive analysis of empirical data that practitioners use advocacy and symmetrical communication in the form of collaboration (L. A. Grunig, et al., 2002). They suggest a two-way contingency model would better describe public relations practice. They found "no organization and no communication program to be exclusively symmetrical or asymmetrical" (p. 472). Describing this practice as the pursuit of "enlightened self-interest" (p. 472), the authors argue practitioners make decisions contingent on who need to be persuaded in particular situations and use both symmetry and advocacy in practice. The two-way contingency model thus is descriptive in nature.

Postmodern Public Relations Ethics as Activism

In summary, it is apparent that there is no list of ethical rules for postmodern practitioners but rather a series of concepts that will contribute to our understanding of moral and ethical decision-making in postmodernity. Although most of these tenets point to the potential of practicing public relations as activism that will lead to positive change and to the inclusion of previously marginalized voices in our practice, there is no single point when a practitioner can be called an activist. Rather, many different actions, opportunities, and contexts exist in organizations and society where practitioners can exhibit activist behavior. As such activism is part of the whole that makes up practitioner behavior and not the only identifying attribute. Much of what practitioners do is routine and takes place within a shared genre of discourse. Practitioners are not confronted on a daily basis with the very complex choices that trigger postmodern activist behavior. But they should be aware when these opportunities arrive and should live in the Zone, as earlier described by Best and Kellner (2001), which "is a sphere where corporate and state power do not yet dominate, and where freedom and meaning ... still are possible" (p. 42). The chaotic nature of the Zone renders room to maneuver.

The guiding principle in a postmodern ethical approach is dissensus and a postmodern dialectic, which can be described as ethical concern through a process of communication. This means continuously unsettling long-held positions by asking questions—not to protect a particular viewpoint or seek definitive answers but to question the power motives in a particular action. It is the understanding that all prescriptive language is political and aimed at a specific outcome. One outcome of dissensus might well be an asymmetrical relationship with stakeholders in favor of the stakeholders and not the organization. Because postmodernism challenges modernist categorization and ordering mechanisms it also questions the modernist notion of the organization as autonomous. Organizational boundaries are viewed as porous and ever-fluctuating, which places the public relations practitioner as boundary spanner in a position of choosing sides and speaking out when she perceives an injustice, even when that injustice takes place outside of the organization.

In the boundary spanning function, a position of dissensus will force the public relations practitioner to recognize and respect differences on the side of both the organization and its publics. Where an insurmountable dispute arises, the public relations practitioner should encourage the sides to come to grips with the tensor and the depth of the conflict between them because conflict leads to new solutions. This represents an approach outside the perceived rules of public relations and is one of the many challenges in the field opened up by postmodern perspectives. Really the only tool practitioners have in this role is the use of language, in the form of the spoken and written word and the use of symbols and artifacts. Practitioners should give recognition to the equality of discourses and should also ensure that the discourse of the practitioner is not marginalized, as so often happens in organizations.

Perhaps the most important dialectic is that between public relations and legal practitioners. As this analysis shows, matters of law are not to go unchallenged because the law is not the truth and is as subjected to prescriptive arguments as is the discourse of public relations. Both are advocacy-based and the dialectic approach is one of the few tools the practitioner has to challenge the dominance of legal practitioners. Legal discourse should not be privileged over public relations discourse. Public relations and legal practitioners need to co-create ways of dealing with organizational crises. In these situations the public relations practitioner needs to stand up for stakeholders when he perceives an injustice is being done to that stakeholder. Also, solutions are always temporary and do not hold for the rest of the time. Solutions lead to new problems and issues, which can seldom be anticipated. Hiding our moral impulse behind legal solutions is not activist behavior.

Resistance to power is another tenet of the postmodern ethic of activism. Institutional power does not mean change and often leads to resistance to change. However, power does not only exist at the top of the organization. Postmodern ethics are about the individual resisting power. Practitioners need to be conscious of their moral impulse, which often is activated by resistance to power. Because power is diffused throughout the organization there are diffused opportunities to resist power. This is done through the use of language and by recognizing the political nature of all language, which always aims to persuade. Another way to resist power is to include as many different voices as possible or at least present the voice of the Other in the organization. At the same time the practitioner needs to realize that inclusion of all voices is likely impossible. As Lyotard (1993a) says: "We need not leave this place where we are … there is no good place" (p. 123). Postmodernity is indeed an imperfect and fragmented place.

Postmodern ethics represents an ethic of caring for the Other, grounded in the moral impulse. But if the moral impulse can never be given in exchange of anything or even demanded, who would be deserved of such a powerful impulse? The environment comes to mind, as do the poor, sick, and oppressed. But it can also be the co-worker or manager who lost his job under questionable circumstances and who needs someone to speak up on his behalf. In postmodernity there is no limit to the list of issues or people who can trigger the moral impulse. The practitioner has to be particularly aware of the need to represent to the organization the voiceless Other, or the Other who speaks in a genre of discourse that is different from that of the organization. At the same time moral ambivalence is inherent in a response to the moral impulse because of the inability of the individual to always know what the outcome of moral decisions might be.

Also, practitioners have to walk the tightrope of synchronizing individual conduct and collective welfare. In organizations practitioners are also not the sole ethical decision-makers and their moral decisions become part of the bricolage of moral decisions made in the organizational context. Because of this the only way to work ethically is to take personal moral responsibility. Therefore, a postmodern ethic can never be universal and never relativist. Somebody else's set of ethical rules cannot govern the moral impulse, nor can the individual decide under what conditions moral behavior should take place. That is determined by the Other.

But it is not only speaking for the Other that is important. Speaking in one's own voice is equally important. This promotes honesty, openness, and authenticity. While honesty and openness are often times viewed as requirements of ethical public relations, this is always promoted as service to the public sphere. Seldom is honesty to the self viewed as ethical behavior. This does not only hold true for female practitioners who work in a male-dominated world, but also for practitioners from other cultures and races. Instead of buying into the dominant organizational paradigm, speaking in one's own voice can be a powerful tool to stand up for the Other.

3
A POSTMODERN VIEW
OF PUBLIC RELATIONS HISTORY

No universal history leads from savagery to humanitarianism, but there is one that leads from the slingshot to the megaton bomb.

(Adorno, as cited in Steven Best [1995, p. 20])

Humanity does not gradually progress from combat to combat until it arrives at universal reciprocity, where the rule of law finally replaces warfare; humanity installs each of its violences in a system of rules and thus proceeds from domination to domination.

(Foucault, 1980, p. 151)

Historical narrative is not benign and can have significant conse-quences. History in public relations is no exception. For instance, one of, if not *the*, best-known histories of public relations is the pre-sentation of the four historic models of public relations (Grunig & Hunt, 1984). The authors argue that public relations-like activities have taken place through-out history but that the real history of the field started in the 19th century with the appearance of fulltime press agents.

The very first model of public relations practice was thus identified as press agentry/publicity. Well-known historical figures who benefited from this model were "Andrew Jackson, Daniel Boone, Buffalo Bill Cody and Calamity Jane" (J. E. Grunig & L. A. Grunig, 1992, p. 287). The best-known practitio-ner of this model was P. T. Barnum, who skillfully promoted his circus. The underlying value system for this type of practice was one of deception and propaganda, particularly based on Barnum's dictum, "There is a sucker born every minute" (p. 287).

The beginning of the 20th century saw the emergence of the public information model, which large corporations and government used to counter attacks from muckraking journalists (J. E. Grunig & L. A. Grunig, 1992; Grunig & Hunt, 1984). These organizations now employed their own journalists to state their case, generally in a truthful and accurate manner. The poster boy for this practice was Ivy Lee, who started out as a business journalist and was subsequently employed by organizations to explain "complicated and misunderstood facts to a popular audience" (Hiebert, 1966, p. 39). The underlying value system of this model was one of truthful and relatively objective dissemination of information.

The third model in this *progressive* history of the field was the two-way asymmetrical model of public relations, which was essentially developed by Edward Bernays through his use of scientific research, particularly grounded in psychology (Grunig & Hunt, 1984). With the help of newly developed social science techniques organizations could now determine what members of their publics knew and believed and could then persuade them to do the "right" thing. This model also introduced the concept of symmetry to public relations practice. But because the underlying value system of this model was to persuade publics of organizations to do the will of organizations even if it was not in their own interests, the model was viewed as asymmetrical.

The final, and fourth, model, the two-way symmetrical model, was similar to the asymmetrical model and historically succeeded it. It too used social science research but the underlying value system was not one of persuasion but to facilitate "understanding and communication rather than to identify messages most likely to motivate or persuade publics" (J. E. Grunig & L. A. Grunig, 1992, p. 289). Thus, as the years passed from the mid-19th century to the 1980s this history of public relations indicated it did not only improve in terms of practice but also became more ethical.

It is important to note that the four historic models of public relations are not the only historical perspectives in the field. Subsequently public relations historians have examined in more depth the practices of the practitioners mentioned above and many others. Most of these histories are those of practitioners who practiced in the context of organizations, either government or corporation. Some other notable histories are founded in politics. Cutlip (1995) reviews public relations practices mostly in the context of the political and social developments in the United States and calls it an *antecedent* history. He argues that the histories in his book are "the forerunners of modern public relations" and cautions students of the field to "not shrug them off as ancient, or worse, irrelevant history" (p. 279). According to Cutlip's analysis the real practice of public relations started in the 20th century. A notable exception to the historical analysis of public relations as an institutional practice is Hon's (1997) study of the role communication and public relations practices played in reaching the goals of the Civil Rights Movement. Hon's analysis showed that although

African Americans still have a long way to go in gaining equal rights in every aspect of society, public relations practices helped them to make important gains toward their goal. One of the most recent historical analyses (Lamme & Russell, 2010) provides an exhaustive and non-linear analysis of public relations history in the United States to argue that corporate public relations' development did not take place in a progressive manner from naïve to sophisticated but rather that different developments at different moments "created a framework over time through which the understanding and practice of public relations is now filtered" (p. 354).

It is difficult to say whether scholars in other countries have a similar emphasis on the history of the field because of language barriers. In Britain L'Etang (2004) focused on the development of public relations as a profession in Britain during the 20th century. L'Etang's analysis is significant, because while U.S. scholars largely viewed the development of the field as a phenomenon of the military-industrial complex, i.e. grounded in capitalism and its institutions, L'Etang grounded her analysis in the political, social, and economic contexts in Britain in the 20th century. She found that professionalization of the field in that country stalled because public relations practitioners were "an occupational group pursuing its own interests in relation to the state and social elites as the source of cultural and ideological power. Professional status has been sought to establish social legitimacy" (p. 221). For L'Etang the development of public relations was linked to a class struggle, whereas U.S. historians generally viewed the field as a major player in promoting the interests of capitalist and government institutions.

This brief review is not in the least meant to be a definitive analysis of historical representation in public relations. Rather, this review is meant to serve as a point of reference for a discussion of postmodern approaches to history and their application to public relations. It is less concerned with individual histories of practitioners than with the basic assumptions public relations historians bring to their analyses. The postmodern debate on writing history and what that history represents goes well beyond establishing alternative historical perspectives or *mixing in* a few female contributors to the development of the field. In fact, the postmodern challenge to history is so controversial that it offers the most radical critique of public relations in this book. Whereas the postmodern perspective on ethics challenges the individual practitioner to take responsibility for ethical decision-making in daily practice, postmodern history challenges the very foundations of the field and its Anglo-Saxon and Eurocentric practices.

The postmodern challenge to history by, particularly, Derrida, through his method of deconstruction; Foucault, through his genealogy project; and Lyotard, through his concept of the *differend*, has shaken the very foundations on which history as an academic discipline is built. These philosophers, and others such as Rorty and White, challenge History, or upper case history, which refers to histories that have an ideological foundation (Jenkins, 1997). Other perspectives in this category are those from feminist and postcolonial scholars such as Morgan (2006) and Said (Sim, 1999a) respectively.

The other perspective is the postmodern challenge to lower case history. This is particularly an attack on academic historians and is "the attempt to pass off the study of history in the form of the ostensibly disinterested scholarship of academics studying the past objectively and 'for its own sake' as 'proper' history" (Jenkins, 1997, p. 6).

An analysis of postmodern history is no more complex than other forms of postmodern analysis and again there are recurring themes. But the analysis of postmodern historical discourse is more profound and challenges the very principles that hitherto have sustained Western civilization. This chapter will be organized around some of these recurring themes and how they apply to public relations in terms of both historical representation and its ideological content. As such it is not a linear argument, which is one of the most important critiques of modernist history, but rather random and eclectic, with the ultimate purpose of destabilizing the linearity of modern history and its underlying discourse of progress. Thus, this chapter will be organized around themes such as the nature and role of history and the concept of *endism* in historical writing and its relation to the discourse of progress. It also will address the ideological nature of history and the relationship between history, power, and politics, including postcolonial and feminist history. In public relations it will focus on the role of upper case history and how lower case history manifests in the form of public relations case studies. It will conclude with the emancipatory potential of postmodern historical representation in the field.

What is History?

One of the first inklings that a major debate was brewing on what history represents and the role it plays in Western society was a seminal text by British historian Plumb (1969/2004).[1] Although Plumb's work cannot be viewed as postmodern it bears the imprint of the social changes that led to postmodernity: race riots in Memphis, Tennessee; resistance to the Vietnam War; student unrest in the United States and Europe; and the introduction (and acceptance) of new musical styles from artists such as the Beatles and the Rolling Stones. "Rarely have traditional attitudes and structures seemed as ripe for interment as they did in the spring of '68. The past was never more moribund" (Ferguson, in his introduction to Plumb, 2004, p. xxv). Ferguson believes that Plumb's contribution lies in the following question: "whether or not academic history, in dismantling our received notions about the past, is essentially a destructive enterprise, capable of dislodging but incapable of replacing the largely mythical but socially functional 'past'" (p. xxvi).

This question Plumb raises already introduces the major postmodern issues with history: history as myth; history as a function of social cohesion; history in the service of politics and power; and the role of academics in the production of history.

Plumb (2004) draws a distinction between the past and history. Societies and cultures use the past to determine the future and as "a moral, a theological, or even an aesthetic truth and not merely a factual one" (p. 12). The past, although (sometimes) factual and transferred in many different forms from one generation to the next, also has a major social role. History, on the other hand, is an intellectual exercise and is viewed as largely a Western intellectual enterprise. Similarly, Berkhofer (1988) argues that, because historians selectively gain facts from the past and put them into a coherent narrative, the past, in the form of history, becomes more than the sum of the totality of the facts used to tell that history. Thus, the past gains significance because someone has ordered it in a certain way.

Partly because industrial society has no need for the social role of history and partly because of the way in which history has been used to sustain certain ideologies and power, Plumb (2004) argues the role of history is dissolving. The past has been used to sustain governments, ruling classes, and religions from the earliest days through a process he calls the domestication of time and the past. This domestication of the past always excluded the peasantry and laboring class, and here one can include women. The genealogies of societies have been used to show the authority to rule and "outbreaks of genealogical fever occur most frequently when new classes are emerging into status" (p. 31). As a result genealogy, which was traditionally needed for social and political authority, "became the plaything of snobbery or of mere nationalist obsessions" in industrial societies (p. 34). Genealogy has been appropriated and invented to secure a lineage that could support social authority. In a certain sense one can refer to the four historic models of public relations as a genealogy, or lineage, used to secure the social authority of the discipline.

Another way in which history has been used is through the concepts of defeat and victory. This is a very simple concept: the victorious is good and the defeated is evil. Plumb calls this annalistic history, which is used "to explain the past in order to strengthen and to serve the authority of the ruling powers" (2004, p. 38). As societies become more sophisticated annals have to employ literary and narrative techniques to try and solve the problems posed to annalists. In complex societies it becomes more and more difficult to use annals to show where power and authority originate. Periods of conflict also bring with them conflicts of historical representation. "Warring authorities mean warring pasts" (p. 40).

All these factors contribute to Plumb's argument that the past is dead. The past no longer has the purpose to sustain power and authority, particularly for "new scientists and technologists" (2004, p. 42) for whom this past is of no use, except to bring a level of nostalgia. The use of the past for moral and social examples and entertainment further erode the significance of the past. Finally, education has adapted to the needs of the present and as a result history has become redundant in most educational institutions. Similarly, the past has lost its grip on the conditioning of the sexes, on concepts of the family, and on sexual activity itself.

Postmodern historians challenge the social cohesion, social compass, and moral authority functions of history precisely because they argue history is always theory, subjective, and representational (Jenkins, 1995, 1997, 1999, 2003). Jenkins, likely the most prominent and vocal activist for postmodern historical perspectives, argues history is self-referential, reflects self-interest, and is ideologically based. It is a "useful fiction" (1999, p. 14) built only on already accessible historical artifacts and has no access to those historical facts not recorded or lost. The past is always only partially accessible because the evidence is incomplete and limited (McLennan, 1984). Jenkins (2003) eventually rejects the very necessity for history and argues the only reason why history should continue is when it is "articulated through the reflexive foregrounding of a postmodern discourse wedded to the idea of emancipation" (p. 2).

Postmodern historians argue that even though historians view their work as objective and empirical they analyze historical evidence from the basis of a theory. Empiricism itself is a theory and an inadequate method because it cannot provide the necessary reasons why certain facts are selected and others are discarded, or why certain facts are more important than others. The selection of historical facts always is based on a theory (Jenkins, 1997).

Some postmodernists go so far as to view historical writing as a literary genre. First, they argue historians selectively choose facts to support an argument, and second, they present those facts as linear, with a beginning and an end. This is similar to storytelling. Historians present a chaotic past as a complex but nonetheless related series of events that they help to construct through a narrative structure using an omnipresent narrator (Berkhofer, 1988). The reasons for this argument are apparent:

> Our continuities are storytellers' devices to give order and progression to the plot; the periodisation, by which we set such store, is a strategy for narrative closure. Events are singled out for attention not because of their intrinsic interest, but because of the logic of the text; they are not material realities but the organizing units of historical discourse, highly coded tropes that "read" or allegorize the past.
>
> (Samuels, 1992, pp. 220–221)

These arguments bring into focus a number of postmodern debates about what history is and does. It explains perspectives on the role of upper case history as history that is used to establish a universal narrative to sustain power and authority through genealogy, annalism, and ideologies. Lower case history, on the other hand, is the work of academic historians who no longer are trying to write the history of mankind but view history as essentially an empirical and scientific enterprise, where history speaks for itself. These historians assume the rationality and objectivity of their enterprise (Jenkins, 1997). By this time it is clear that postmodernists would have a lot to say about both upper and lower case history and would critique notions of rationality, objectivity, and the use of history in the service of power.

Deconstructing History

Postmodern historians argue that history is nothing but theories of the past and how the past should be appropriated to serve our understanding of the present. White (as cited in Jenkins, 1995) does not believe that this means the past never existed but rather that the past has been and is being used in any way people want. History is narrative discourse because the past does not come in stories. Because past events are interpreted from a current position all history is present-centered.

One of the major pillars supporting the postmodern argument that history is not a definitive science or that historical representation is neither true nor factual is based on deconstruction as proposed through the phenomenon Derrida describes as *différance* (Derrida, 1973). Although Derrida's aim was to destabilize philosophy and Western logocentricity in particular through the process of deconstruction, many theorists have applied this approach to historical analysis. As mentioned before *différance* means both *to differ* and *to defer*. Because all knowledge is mediated through language and, in the Western historical tradition in particular, the written word, Derrida shows that historical interpretation and representation will always be unstable because *différance* makes it impossible to ever create a fixed meaning of what happened in history. Thus, Derrida shows "the impossibility of reducing the infinite possibilities of thinking about what history might be to the finite or to the knowledgeable" (Jenkins, 2003, p. 19). Because humans do not have any transcendental signifiers, i.e. words that mean the same to everybody and hold their meaning stable across space and time, words get their meaning through other words and relative to other words, which in turn refer to others words, and so forth. As a result all meaning is forever unstable and historically speaking it is impossible to know what words meant in a particular context or what other words would signify those words at that time. It logically follows that all historical texts, built on written texts, are unstable. As explained before, the signifier (the one who writes or speaks) becomes unimportant because meaning is now determined by the people receiving the text, who can interpret the text in many different ways. "The act of interpretation of the text thus becomes more important than the writing of the text" (Wilson, 1999, p. 33).

It also implies that all history, at some level, is fiction. Wilson (1999) believes, "The implications for history are staggering: (1) the disappearance of the author and the historical actor as a coherent subject, (2) the disappearance of the text as something with a discernable meaning, and (3) the disappearance of any teleology in history" (p. 33). This last point is important, because history is often used for moral reasoning particularly as it pertains to future human goals. As Sim (1999a) argues, deconstruction implies that "no method of analysis (such as philosophy or criticism) can have any special claim to authority as regards textual interpretation" and "that interpretation is, therefore, a free-ranging activity more akin to game-playing than to analysis" (p. 31). He uses the concept of *erasure* to show how he has different interpretations of terms used by others.

Deconstruction is not only a philosophical approach or a critical method but an obligation. No effort of deconstruction can ever be complete. Every act of deconstruction can and, in turn, should be deconstructed. Full meaning is always illusive and always deferred. Derrida introduces the concept of *trace*, which refers to "something that is no longer present, yet has left its mark" (Sim, 1999b, p. 372). Although traces are invisible they are ever present, which complicates any analysis of phenomena, both present and historical. "It is in the nature of deconstruction not just to see the wider context (those traces or specters, stretching back into the past in an infinite regress) but also the fluidity, the flexibility, the ultimately incontrollable nature of that context" (Sim, 1999a, p. 50). To view any history as a complete interpretation is therefore impossible and totalitarian.

Thus, we return to the four historic models of public relations for a postmodern deconstruction of public relations history as presented in the United States. In defense of the authors, they most likely never thought that these models would become the most prominent theory in public relations internationally. What started out as an interpretation of a U.S. history of public relations became the theoretical foundation for public relations practice in research conducted in many countries and has been the dominant paradigm for theory development in the field in the United States since the early eighties. I am particularly critical of scholars from countries other than the United States who seamlessly adopt theories of symmetry and asymmetry because of their unique American original. But even in the United States, following from Derrida's principles of deconstruction, allowing any interpretation to become hegemonic is a questionable practice. The ways in which the four historic models are presented have several attributes typical of historical representation, which point to the selectiveness of the practice.

First, the history of the four models is presented in the form of a narrative, with distinct characters who are representative of the most excellent practitioners of that particular model. It is a narrative with a beginning and an end, i.e. a linear progression from one model to the next to show improvement as knowledge in the field increases. I discussed before the implications of history as narrative, namely, that narrative represents storytelling, whether it is based on factual or fictional events. The authors of a historical narrative selectively compile facts to support their historical representation. From a deconstructionist point of view one can ask why the authors elected to start their historical narrative of public relations at that particular point. Is it because of the name given to press agents or publicists? Is it because media became role players in commercial interests? Why would a history only begin with giving something a name? This is particularly questionable if one supports Derrida's *différance* as the instability of all meaning. It is impossible to determine in retrospect the traces that led to naming a practice in the mid-19th century. Thus, the first issue raised with a deconstruction of the four models is the validity of the claims made on the historicity of these models as truly representative of public relations practice in the United States.

Second, a typical narrative technique that has been used through the ages is to identify heroes who typify certain practices that people can aspire to (Southgate, 2000). Southgate points out, "these choices are 'political' and far from value-free. They are not made without a 'purpose' for all are inevitably linked with a variety of views about society and the sorts of people we admire" (p. 27). Thus, our heroes in the four historic models are P. T. Barnum, Ivy Lee, Edward Bernays, and Scott Cutlip. Each of these theorists developed these models normatively and "then implemented them in the real world or taught others how to implement them" (J. E. Grunig & L. A. Grunig, 1992, p. 292). Again, when deconstructing the representation of these heroes of the four historic models it is clear that their inclusion in the historical representation was selective and most likely based on the premises of their theoretical possibilities from the perspective of the academics who developed these models. It is problematic that the historicity of these models was neither explicated nor questioned by other scholars. Moreover, these models did not remain historic but silently made the transition to empirically tested models, which blurs the lines between historical narrative and modern-day practice.

A third problematic aspect of the four models is their teleology. A Derridian deconstruction of history does not leave any space for drawing moral conclusions (Wilson, 1999). It is clear that the aim of proposing the four historic models was to present them as having moral content. This is yet another function of history, namely, to teach by examples (Southgate, 2000). "That history can best achieve its moral aim by recording the lives of the great and the good has been an assumption motivating numberless historians and educationists" (pp. 20–21). While some scholars argue that all public relations practice is unethical (e.g. Gandy, 1989), J. E. Grunig and L. A. Grunig (1992) argue that only the two-way symmetrical model is inherently ethical. They argue that the press agentry, public information, and two-way asymmetrical models are unethical because they do not allow for the opinions of others nor do they provide for behavior change on the part of organizations using public relations. This comes from the critique of scholars that all persuasion is similar to propaganda and therefore unethical. However, because it is impossible to determine why certain practices took place at a particular stage in history, it is impossible to look back from a current ethical and moral perspective and make such a determination.

Lastly, the use of binary opposites is a method Derrida (1976) argues is applied to devalue one term over another. Laying bare binary opposites is a procedure Derrida uses to "dismantle the tacit, violent hierarchy found in … binary opposites…. In subverting the binary, the goal is not to reverse the hierarchy but rather to destabilize it in order to leave the opposition in an undecidable condition" (Taylor & Winquist, 2001, p. 36). The binary opposites used in the four historic models are clearly value-laden, based on the values of the authors. Not only is asymmetrical bad and symmetrical good, but symmetrical is in actual fact *excellent*. In a later development the press agentry and public information models were explained as *craft* models, while the two two-way models were described as *professional* (J. E. Grunig & L. A. Grunig, 1992, p. 312). It is clear which of these two are the most desirable. The way in which these models are explained is a catch-22 situation for scholars and practitioners. Who would not want to practice modern, professional, and ethically acceptable public relations? As a result, through exploiting the historicity of these models, the hegemony of the two-way symmetrical model, also called the excellence model, was secured. The conceptualization of these four models goes virtually unchallenged because they are presented as historically accurate and therefore factual. This might account for the spread of these models throughout the United States and into some of the most far-reaching countries, which do not share Western approaches, schema, and worldviews.

History as Progress

As we have now seen, postmodernists challenge the very basis of the modernist historical enterprise, particularly the notion that it is possible to objectively and rationally present the past, or let the past speak for itself. Another area where the postmodern critique of history is very influential is the notion of history as progress. For instance, Plumb (2004) argues that there is an inherent difference between Western and Chinese historiography. He maintains Western historiography is largely influenced by Christian perspectives, which link the past to

> the future in a much more dynamic fashion, for the Christian cosmology stretches over time future as well as time past in an intricate narrative *that predicted particular and precise events* [italics added]. The movement of the past in the West was linear, in the East cyclical, though not without a concept of betterment.
>
> (Plumb, 2004, pp. 11–12)

What is important in Western history is the concept of progress or destiny. History is viewed as linear and should lead somewhere, particularly to a better future. It should have some predictive qualities in the sense that what happened in the past will predict the future. At the same time the future needs to be an improvement on the past. This is particularly true for the Judeo-Christian tradition, which translated the notion of improvement into the personal destiny of the individual, who should learn from the tales of history, particularly in terms of moral conduct. "The past, even a man's [sic] life, still possessed an unfolding drama which the future would complete" (Plumb, 2004, p. 84).

Similarly, Plumb (2004) argues, history was used to project the belief that nationalist histories, particularly those of Britain and the United States, were moral and political examples to mankind. American historians in particular wrote a history of the United States that projected it as a natural progression toward man's ultimate destiny. These histories of progress were further supported by the theories developed by Darwin and Hegel, which in turn were used to justify expansionist and imperialist policies of both countries and became universal histories of the destiny of all mankind. Marxist history has been used in a similar fashion, particularly when exported to China.

Sim (1999a) calls this "endism," which refers to "a wide range of positions and thinkers whose common element is that they are announcing 'the end' of something or other—history, humanism, ideology, modernity, philosophy, Marxism, the author, 'man', and the world being the most popular candidates of late" (p. 12). Historical endism, however, is closely tied to the notion of progress. Progress, in turn, is closely tied to the notion of improvement and development. To repeat what Bauman (1993) said in his discussion of ethics, progress moves from inferior to superior. Modern memory is linear and in this linearity that which has become before is inferior and outdated. Furthermore, what is inferior is that which has been defeated in battle; "superiority is tested and proved in victory" (p. 226). It will be impossible to tell this story of progress without creating a linear narrative logic, particularly through events such as wars, which in turn is only possible if facts are selectively presented as if the past is a total past, i.e. that there is a single past that can be accessed, understood, and investigated (Berkhofer, 1988).

One of the important postmodern critiques of endism is that it projects an ideal end, a level of fulfillment where all human life reaches a point where everything that has ever been strived for, has been concluded. Fukuyama (1989 as cited in Sim, 1999a, p. 16) believes that mankind has reached the "end point of mankind's ideological evolution." Fukuyama particularly believes that humanism has reached its peak in the form of liberal democracy and that man has now reached his full potential. Because human progress is now complete, history has served its teleological purpose—therefore the end of history. Fukuyama's interpretation of endism coincides with the collapse of communism, which ended the ideological struggle between the East and the West (Sim, 1999a). He believes liberal democracy has now settled all possible problems and as a result there cannot be any more development of new ideas.

This postmodern deconstruction of history as progress is also evident in the development of the four historic models of public relations. What started out as a practice of conmen developed through three subsequent models, each one improving on the previous, into the pinnacle of excellent public relations. Indeed, the excellence model of public relations is held forth as subscribing to the very basic principles of a liberal democracy: "inherently consistent with the concept of social responsibility" [Dozier (1989) as cited in J. E. Grunig and L. A. Grunig (1992, p. 310)]; and because "it uses research to facilitate understand and communication ... Symmetrical communication is balanced; it adjusts the relationship between the organization and the public" (p. 289).

Postmodernists clearly have different interpretations of the end of history. For Jenkins (1997) a postmodern interpretation means "the end of the peculiar ways in which modernity conceptualized the past; the way it made sense of it in upper and lower case forms" (p. 9). Thus, instead of viewing history as progress with a utopian end as closure, postmodernists argue that history has a very different function or no function at all. Technology and the drive toward technoscience play no small role in postmodern interpretations of the end of history. L'Etang (2004, p. 7), citing Hall (1969), mentions the move to make public relations a technoscience in an effort "to diffuse a glow of respectability" on the field. What Hall specifically referred to was the effort to make public relations part of the management sciences. Hall, however, viewed public relations as trivial, "a walking case-book of the technicisation of culture" (p. 7).

Technoscience refers to the intersection between science, technology, and engineering, which, through their interaction, "denotes a dynamic relationship between instruments and people within a cultural context that brings about conceptual and practical change" (Taylor & Winquist, 2001, p. 389). Lyotard (1984), in particular, is associated with the later development of the term. He identified certain steps necessary for the development of technoscience. These steps reflect much of Kuhn's explication of scientific revolutions. One such step is the development of a universal language and rules on which a group of experts agree. The four historic models of public relations have contributed a great deal to the development of such a language in the field, even if there is no consensus on the concept of symmetry as such. Lyotard describes this as "a metalanguage that is universal but not consistent" (p. 43). Much research has been conducted in public relations to test the principles of symmetry and asymmetry. Similar to Kuhn's concept of scientific paradigm, Lyotard argues that scientific proof is another requirement of something becoming a technoscience. Because proof has to be proven, technology became part of the development of scientific knowledge. But because technology requires a monetary investment, proof of effectiveness and return on investment is required. I wish to argue that public relations as a form of technology, which requires a specific investment, had to become technoscience. The field, to prove that it is more than a communication system between humans, had to become part of the technoscientific community. The need for theories in this science was fundamentally what drove the development of the four historic models of public relations.

However, postmodernism seriously challenges the link between history and current practices. Baudrillard (1997), for instance, believes that history has been dissolved into a hyperreality created by

> technology, events and media [that] has propelled us to 'escape velocity,' with the result we have flown free of the referential sphere and of history. We are 'liberated' in every sense of the term, so liberated that we have taken leave of a certain space-time.
>
> (p. 39)

This liberation has also removed our ability to see events coherently in terms of cause and effect and linearity—clearly the marks of modernist history. Because there is no point of reference to what has become before or even what is taking place at the moment, everything has become fragmented and torn apart. Baudrillard welcomes this and simply dismissed the necessity for history because he believes, "It is precisely in history that we are alienated, and if we leave history we also leave alienation" (as cited in Sim, 1999a, p. 24).

Although Sim (1999a) holds forth that Lyotard has a very negative view of the end of the world, i.e. the eventual destruction of the earth, I wish to argue that Lyotard's concept of metanarratives provides a much more enlightening perspective on the role of history in postmodernity. Lyotard argues for the end of history because of the destruction of metanarratives, of which the biggest and most dominant is history itself. History is the ultimate metanarrative. Once one understands this and accepts Lyotard's (1984, p. 60) position that all metanarratives should be broken down into little narratives, one can truly decenter history as a method through which we understand our past and predict our future. Through little narratives we can displace our interpretation of history as progress. They provide a rationale for the end of the four historic models of public relations, not only as a public relations metanarrative but also as the end of public relations history. Thus postmodern perspectives can also set public relations scholars and practitioners free from the conjecture of public relations as four models of practice, with symmetrical communication as the only really ethical and effective model. At last public relations scholars and practitioners, if they so wish, can develop new and exciting language to describe the daily practice, set outside of the linearity and endism as articulated in the language of the four historic models.

History as Power

Modern history established a single Western perspective, which Morgan (2006) describes as a Western philosophical gaze, that justified existing forms of knowledge, social organization, and power and its institutions. Its aim was to establish a single truth by presenting this history as rational and objective knowledge, thus making it impossible to challenge its underlying concepts and belief systems. We can see this trend in the history of public relations. It is actually quite amazing that this U.S. history to this day is being applied in different ways in countries that do not have a Western cultural heritage. The blame for this should also be put at the feet of scholars in those countries who willy-nilly apply these concepts to their own practices, thus making themselves and their own cultures invisible.

It is these practices that lead to universal claims of truth and knowledge. Foucault (2003), for instance, argues that rationality itself is a historical construct and that general theories of knowledge must be abandoned in favor of specific and local understandings of theory. Knowledge develops in discontinuous forms with the result that all knowledge is theory-laden in character. Lyotard also applies this to an analysis of history. The Lamme and Russell (2010) analysis of public relations is reminiscent of this argument and their interpretation of historical facts is evidence of the theoretical nature of historical interpretation.

Thus one of the aims of the postmodern project is to establish alternative historical perspectives that challenge the underlying rationale of modern history. Foucault's (2003) argument that the interface between modern forms of power and knowledge has served to create new forms of domination comes alive in public relations history, particularly through the application of the four historic models of public relations as defined by Grunig and Hunt in 1984. Foucault's take on the connection between power and knowledge will be examined closer in the next chapter, but he is particularly interested in the relationship between history and power. He argues that those who have control over historical knowledge can occupy a specific strategic position. The outcome of this is "the constitution of a historic-political field" which came about by telling a history of wars and then turned into "a history that continues the war by deciphering the war and the struggle that are going on within all the institutions of right and peace" (p. 171). This historic-political field is very important because it enables the use of history in the struggle. "History gave us the idea that we are at war; and we wage war through history" (p. 172). He argues that history has never been about what brings about peace and order, but has always been about conflict and "the events in which relations of force are decided" (p. 173). Here Foucault describes the task of the historicist, which fits in with the role of the postmodern historicist, "We must try to be historicists, in other words, try to analyze this perpetual and unavoidable relationship between the war that is recounted by history and the history that is traversed by the war it is recounting" (pp. 173–174). Although Foucault refers to real wars as shaping history, he clearly articulates wars also as struggles, what he calls "the relational character of power" (p. 168). These struggles permeate society and force all of us into one side or the other. Exposing relational power thus becomes the task of the historicist.

In returning to our topic of public relations history in the United States it is important to expose the interrelationship between this history and its relational power with the state. Through teaching public relations in the United States I have come to learn that although public relations is often viewed to be "as old as civilization itself" (which gives us the dubious distinction to be the oldest trade in the world, with some others) the American history of public relations is viewed as emerging through the use of the term *public relations* and *press agent*. Therefore, the founding fathers of public relations are seen as P.T. Barnum, Ivy Lee, and Edward Bernays, and the history of these figures are closely tied to the development of American commerce and industry or the development of the industrial/military complex, i.e. the development of American capitalism. In this history the history of public relations is intimately tied with the history of journalism, which is why public relations are so often located in schools of journalism or mass communications. This history of public relations also is tied closely to the history of the state and its institutions, including the media, which can be interpreted as a history that also gives power to public relations as an institutional practice. Furthermore, the dominance of Western theoretical perspectives in the field can be interpreted as the Anglo-Saxon colonization of the field.

Lower Case History

The above dealt mostly with upper case history, or history as metanarrative in the service of power. This kind of historiography has now been debunked by professional historians as "not history at all but improper, positioned ideology" in favor of *lower case* history (Jenkins, 1997, p. 14). Jenkins describes this kind of history as a history practiced by professional and/or academic historians who claim that they can write a true and objective history through the empirical analysis of data, be that data texts, oral representations, numerical data, or other means.

While Jenkins refers to it as lower case history, several other terms are used to describe this movement in historiography. For instance, Burke (2001b) calls it "new history" after the French term *La nouvelle histoire* (p. 12). This kind of history is identified by the wide range of topics subjected to historical analysis and is also referred to as "history from below" (p. 4). "Everything has a history," J. B. S. Haldane (as quoted in Burke, 2001b, p.3) famously said. This new history is conducted "for its own sake" or "sakism" (Southgate, 2005, p. 11), with historians either merely enjoying the practice, or determining the future through learning from history. The assumption is that this kind of history, because it is empirical, is objective because it removes the historian from the historical facts and artifacts. The empirical method in the representation of history thus becomes paramount.

The role of lower case historians is

> to try and understand what happened, purely in its own terms and not in the service of religion or national destiny, or morality, or the sanctity of institutions ... to see things as they really were, and from this study to attempt to formulate processes of social change which are acceptable on historical grounds and none other.
>
> (Plumb, 2004, p. 13)

From this use (and abuse) of the past, history as we know it today emerged. Plumb (2004) believes,

> The purpose of historical investigation is to produce answers, in the form of concepts and generalizations, to the fundamental problems of historical change in the social activities of men [sic]. These generalizations about societies will, of course, not be immutable but always tentative. They must, however, be accurate, as scientific, as detailed research and a profound sense of human reality can make them. The historian's purpose, therefore, is to deepen understanding about men and society, not merely for its own sake, but in the hope that a profounder knowledge, a profounder awareness will help to mould human attitudes and human actions. Knowledge and understanding should not end in negation but in action.
>
> (p. 106)

Plumb's interpretation of lower case history, which had been the dominant one for a couple of centuries, gave rise to the belief that historical investigation is a scientific, empirical enterprise from which the historian stands aloof. The ideal historian, Plumb argues, is like the historian Bloch, who "possessed the power to abstract himself from any preconceived notions about the past and to investigate an historical problem with detachment" (p. 106) and which Bloch himself referred to as "a rational attempt at analysis" (p. 108). Plumb argues that the foundation for modern history in terms of accumulation of materials and the critical method was laid in the 17th century, which in the 20th century became "a study for professionals by professionals" (p. 133). These professionals saw the purpose of history as limited, as mainly training in criticism and satisfying curiosity, instead of the Enlightenment view of history, which is that history should "interpret the destiny of mankind" (p. 134).

Despite Plumb's outstanding explication of the philosophy of history he and other major historians of his time, such as Elton (1997), still held on to the notion that it is possible to present history objectively, rationally, and empirically through the study and analysis of historical documents, artifacts, and personal histories. Lower case history is always theoretical because historians investigate history from a particular theoretical perspective, even if they do not acknowledge it. The history of events, or annalistic history, is now replaced by the history of structures and everyday phenomena. History from below focuses on "the views of ordinary people and ... their experience of social change" (Burke, 2001b, p. 4) and is determined to take ordinary people's views of their experiences into consideration. Finally, history from below is no longer an isolated subject but interdisciplinary and collaborative.

It is important to note that history from below is not necessarily postmodern. Whenever historians make claims of objectivity because of their empirical methods, history cannot be postmodern. However, as is the case with upper case history, postmodern perspectives on history have also permeated lower case history. We are now familiar with some of these arguments, for instance the rejection of the claims of rationality and objectivity of lower case history, as well as the social and cultural construction of reality, which also pertains to the construction of history, which become relativist (Burke, 2001b).

So where does lower case history fit into historical representation in public relations? I wish to argue that in public relations case studies represent the field's (modernist) lower case history because they have several of the attributes mentioned above. First, there is the empirical nature of case studies. Generally, case studies are conducted by using multiple methods, including quantitative methods (Stacks, 2002). In a discussion of the methods used in history from below, Burke (2001b) mentions that official records are no longer adequate because these are reflections of history from above (or upper case history as per Jenkins). Lower case historians now have to rely on multiple sources to reflect the experiences of ordinary people. In public relations those *ordinary people* will be practitioners. To do this historians now have to read between the lines, for instance by being aware of the omission of women or minority groups, or rely heavily on oral accounts. Other historical materials are photographs and images; pictorial images such as paintings, drawings, or graffiti; physical artifacts, such as media releases, media coverage, print and other media materials in the case of public relations practice; and quantitative methods, such as longitudinal surveys, opinion surveys, or satisfaction surveys. In fact, Sharpe (2001) validates the use of case studies as a form of historiography from below that can become a counterpoint for antiquarianism, particularly through the use of thick descriptions similar to those used in anthropology. This allows for more direct representation of present-day events than the study of antiquated documents and artifacts. As such, case studies become a much better recording of immediate history. But if lower case history/history from below/sakism is not postmodern history, what is? Is history even possible considering the postmodern arguments raised above? And if it is, what would be the role of the postmodern historian?

The Purpose of Postmodern History

Southgate (2005) argues that history always had a purpose. Sometimes it was overt and sometimes it was hidden. I have already discussed the (modernist) purpose of history as one of *learning from*, or helping us on our path of progress to the perfect society. Southgate argues the need for transferable skills has become an important purpose of modern historical practices. Threatened by the requirements of market economies that all skills must have "real world" applications "teachers of humanities often attempted to take refuge in a list of so-called transferable skills ... which could then be duly applied in other contexts to the 'world of work'" (p. 33). She mentions cultivation, myth-busting, and obligations to the dead as other reasons given to justify the practice of historiography. In public relations the purpose of case studies and histories of events and major characters are mostly to promote or determine best practices. However, we also know that all the evidence presented in case studies is subjective with a particular (often self-serving) aim, namely, to emphasize the usefulness of public relations practice or the practitioner, particularly in terms of its contribution to organizational goals. Sometimes the "benefits" derived from practice verge on the fictional, as in the case of the Tylenol crisis. Dezenhall (2007) claims the Tylenol case became so iconic because "a PR firm that didn't handle it wrote a case study declaring it brilliant. They rewrote the facts and went around on road shows for years proselytizing the case."

Instances like this support the notion that history is narrative, often imagined and found (Jenkins, 2003). This is a typical example of the kind of history that drives the postmodern onslaught on history that challenges the very existence of the field by pointing out its service to power, the subjective nature of the practice, and the futility of its quest for the truth. That does not mean that history has no purpose. It is not more flawed than any other discipline in the humanities and social sciences. Foucault (2003) provides a clue to the postmodern purpose of history when he talks about historicism, i.e. "try to analyze this perpetual and unavoidable relationship between the war that is recounted by history and the history that is traversed by the war it is recounting" (p. 174). I interpret this as the continuous analysis and exposure of the underlying power relations that are served in historical representation, even in one's own work.

As mentioned, in the U.S. context there is another voice trying to be heard in terms of creating an alternative historical stream for public relations practice, specifically embedded in major political events (Cutlip, 1995). Although activism is viewed as part of the development of public relations tactics (Wilcox & Cameron, 2006) not many of these histories are explored in depth. One of the few histories that focuses on activism, and women in particular, is that of Margaret Sanger (Center & Jackson, 1995). Sanger's history inspired me to be more interested in the role women played as activists in shaping historical events, which brought me to contemplate the roots of public relations in my country of origin, South Africa.

The history of South African public relations practice as it emerged through the Public Relations Institute of Southern Africa (PRISA) clearly followed the development path in other Western countries (Holtzhausen, Petersen, & Tindall, 2003). However, this history is, as we now know, embedded in a particular view of what public relations is and what its social function represents. Said's perspectives on postcolonial history (Walia, 2001) reminded me of my own colonial heritage and led me to the conclusion that resistance to colonialism could create a joint (not linear) history in countries subjected to colonialism that could lead public relations practitioners to a better understanding of what activist practice might be—a moral tale that we could use to break away from the oppressive history of public relations in the service of power. I could immediately see an analogy in the life of Emily Hobhouse (see Vignette 3.1). The fact that Emily Hobhouse was an activist does not make her history postmodern, however. It is how I interpret this history and interface with these historical facts that have the potential of making this postmodern history.

Before moving to a discussion of the attributes of postmodern history it is important to take note of the typical historical narrative techniques I used to create an understanding of the postmodern critique of history. First, I selected Emily Hobhouse as the historical hero of the story—the woman from whose life we can learn a lesson that, if we use her as an example, public relations practitioners have the ability to improve society. In typical historical fashion I wish to teach by example. I selectively and artificially chose a time period, electing to focus on the period of the war itself, 1899–1902, largely ignoring the events in Hobhouse's life that led her to a life of activism. White calls this a chronicle (Jenkins, 1995, p. 150). In my brief narrative in Vignette 3.1, I selectively chose the facts I presented to make a linear argument. This is typical of the postmodern critique that "histories are fabricated without 'real' foundations beyond the textual" (Jenkins, 1995, p. 179).

This historical interpretation also supports Foucault's (2003) argument that history is told through war and conflict. One can argue that my interpretation of the Hobhouse history is grounded in nationalism—a part of my heritage as an Afrikaner whose own family fought and lost in that war and for whom the treatment of the Boer people will always be a source of humiliation. In fact, when reading Hobhouse's book that humiliation becomes very apparent in the British arguments justifying the war, as Bauman (1993) so succinctly described: they brought progress and civilization to the barbaric Boer people; their invasion of the two republics were done for the sake of progress and development of the Boer people; the Boer women and children were interned for their own benefit because they were ignorant, dirty, and unhygienic. In typical colonial and traditional historical fashion, that which has been defeated in battle proved to be inferior, with the Boer people becoming the binary opposite of

VIGNETTE 3.1

The History of an Activist

Emily Hobhouse, born in Cornwall in 1860, was the daughter of the Anglican Archdeacon Reginald Hobhouse and Caroline Trelawny. She grew up in a Victorian environment where typically as a girl she could not claim much of an education. Her education came from the family's rectory in the small mining town of St. Ives. As a young woman her only recreational activities were related to the church and social work.

Only after the death of her widower father, of whom she took care until he died, could she break away and pursue her own interests. At this time she was 35 and regarded as an old maid. Her first venture was a visit to Minnesota where she did social work. After a broken engagement she returned to London. At this time Britain was at war with the Zuid-Afrikaanse Republiek (South African Republic) and the Republiek van die Oranje Vrijstaat (Republic of the Orange Free State)—two republics established by the descendants of the Dutch who first colonized the Cape at the southernmost tip of Africa. The Dutch (known as Boers) moved away from the Cape because they perceived being oppressed by the British. This did not bother the British until rich deposits of gold, diamonds, and other minerals were discovered in these two territories. When prospectors and miners from all over the world descended on the mining areas and the Boer republics did not want to grant them voting rights, the British decided to invade.

When Emily returned to Britain she found herself in pro-Boer circles, where her uncle Lord Hobhouse, played an important role. Emily, like many other members of the radical wing of the Liberal Party, was opposed to the Boer War, which lasted from 1899–1902. During the first weeks of the war Emily spoke at several public meetings where she denounced the activities of the British government.

In late 1900 Emily was sent details of how women and children were being treated by the British army. This particularly related to the British policy that gave British soldiers the right to burn down the farms and kill the animals of Boer families whose male members were fighting in the war. The women, children, and farmworkers were placed in concentration camps where close to 40,000 people died, indeed this was the first holocaust of the 20th century and most probably Western history.

In October 1900 Emily formed the Relief Fund for South African Women and Children, an organization set up "To feed, clothe, harbour and save women and children—Boer, English and otherwise—who were left destitute and ragged as a result of the destruction of property, the eviction of families or other incidents resulting from military operations" (Biggins, 2004). Except for members of the Society of Friends, very few people were willing to contribute to the fund.

Undaunted, Emily decided to go to South Africa, a country she did not know or had ever visited, and arrived in Cape Town on December 27th, 1900. After meeting with Alfred Milner, who was the governor of the Cape at that time, she gained permission to visit the concentration camps that had been established by the British Army. Because of time constraints, she kept a journal of her experiences and later published a book, *The brunt of the war and where it fell* (1902) with many letters from eye witnesses in the two republics. Her aim was to document the atrocities of the war and bring them to the attention of the British public.

Her book was meticulously researched and essentially consisted of original documents, reports, newspaper articles, legal documents, transcriptions of parliamentary proceedings, and most of all, letters from eye witnesses, both English and Boer, that chronologically reported on the atrocities of the war. This book became a monument of remembrance of what Boer women and children suffered in the war. It excruciatingly reported letters and written reports of British soldiers who were forced to burn down thousands of farmhouses, kill or capture stock, ransack homes, and take women, children, and the frail elderly into custody.

Hobhouse never took her eye off her aim, namely, to create better conditions in the concentration camps. She used every possible tactic at her disposal. She wrote letters to British newspapers, used her network of political influence in Britain and later South Africa, she constantly wrote personal letters to Lord Kitchener, challenging him and turning his own arguments against himself. She used the law and legal arguments; cited eye witness accounts; created a network of women's organizations outside of Britain to exert political pressure on the British government; and exhausted her personal means to reach her goals.

After her first visit she decided to return to England in an effort to persuade the Marquis of Salisbury and his government to bring an end to the British Army's scorched-earth and concentration camp policy. The Minister of War was unwilling to take action and when the issue was raised in the House of Commons few members showed any sympathy. Emily was not daunted. She closed alliances with the Liberal Party and continued her letter writing campaign in the British media. Eventually the government agreed to set up a committee of women to investigate Emily's allegations. She was, of course, not included in the committee. But slowly public opinion turned in her favor and the British public itself started to question their government's actions.

Despite warnings that she would be refused permission to visit the camps, she returned to South Africa in October 1901 but was not allowed to leave her ship. By this time she suffered from poor health, and decided to recuperate in the mountains of Savoy. It was here that she heard that the Boer leaders had signed the Peace of Vereeniging, which ended the war.

Her fight was not only for the Boer women and children but also for the honor of her country. In 1913 she wrote a letter to the people of South Africa saying of her visits: "I came quite naturally—in obedience to the feeling of unity or oneness of womanhood and of those noble traditions, characteristics of the life of the English people, in which I was nurtured and which I inherited from time memorial" (Simkin, n.d.).

After the war she continued her work of upliftment among the Boer people of South Africa. She established many home industry projects to make women more self-sustaining and able to rebuild their lives after the war. But by this time she suffered severe financial hardship herself. In 1921 the people of South Africa, impoverished themselves, raised £2,300 and sent the money to Emily in recognition of her work. The money was sent with the explicit mandate that she had to buy herself a house on the coast of Cornwall, where she lived until her death in 1926.

the intellectual, well-educated, and civilized British. These types of rhetorical strategies have become known as ideographs or ideographic analysis (Delgado, 1995; Hasian, 2003; McGee, 1980) because they allow for the study of "political struggle among competing elements and contestations between dominant and non-dominant groups" (Delgado, 1995, p. 447). Hobhouse (1902) did not need a postmodernist to explain this concept to her. She wrote:

To the plain man and woman, outside the political and military worlds, it seems as though in war an arbitrary line is drawn, one side of which is counted barbarism, the other civilization. May it not be that, in reality, all war is barbarous, varying only in degree? History shows that as nations have advanced in civilizations this line has gradually been raised, and watchful care is needed lest it slips back. None of us can claim to be wholly civilized till we have drawn the line above war itself and established universal arbitration in place of universal armaments.

(p. xvi)

The above example of my appropriation of Hobhouse's involvement in the Boer War gives credence to the postmodern interpretation that all history is rhetoric, "*all* histories are of the aesthetic, postmodern type" [italics in original] (Jenkins, 2004, p. 382). The postmodern interpretation of history then leads one to Steedman's (2001, p. 154) conclusion, as cited in Jenkins (2004, p. 280), that historical representation is

> about something that never did happen in the way it comes to be represented (the happening exists in the telling or the text) and it is made out of materials that aren't there [those inferred structures that act as real referents] in an archive or anywhere else, a nothingness that we take to be, nevertheless, 'a sign of history.'

Despite all these arguments, postmodernists do believe history has a role, but only under very specific conditions. Again, the history of Emily Hobhouse above can serve as an example.

The Emancipatory Potential of Postmodern Public Relations History

Much has been written about a postmodern critique of history but few have actually clearly formulated a path to postmodern historiography. There are some themes, mostly parsed together from the work of Southgate (2000) and Jenkins (1995), which can serve as guidance for public relations historians who wish to do postmodern historiography.

Reflexivity and Openness

One of the most important criteria for appropriating historical events when writing history from a postmodern point of departure, are the concepts of *reflexivity* and *openness*. When telling Hobhouse's story I as the author of this specific representation have to remain conscious that my interpretation of and interest in her contribution is deeply personal from an ethnic, gender, and professional perspective. As I said in the introduction to this book, I was raised at the intersection of race, class, and gender. Similarly, Hasian (2003), citing Krebs, argues that the public debates Hobhouse's work in the concentration camps generated "tell us a great deal about the gender, race and class hierarchies that operated in imperial circles at the turn of the century" (p. 2). Growing up with the history of Emily Hobhouse as the heroine of the Anglo-Boer War while living my own first experiences with race, class, and gender discrimination most likely triggered my continued, and now academic, interest in her life and work.

Let us first look at the issue of gender. In a classic example of gender stereotyping Hobhouse was portrayed as "a 'hysterical' woman, a busybody who was overreacting to wartime conditions" (Hasian, 2003, p. 2). This aspect of Hobhouse's history always fascinated me because as a woman she stood up against a system and culture that did not appreciate outspoken women. In British culture, as in my own, women had to know their place and politics was not one of them. Thus, from my perspective, not knowing one's "place" has to be one attribute of activism.

The second factor, class, also motivated me to be personally involved in the Hobhouse history. Growing up in Grahamstown, in the Eastern Cape province of South Africa, I became acutely aware of the class system that existed within British culture, as I explained in the Preface to this book. In addition to the class system within the South African British culture, I was also acutely aware of the way Afrikaner children were perceived and of the names we were called, thus further strengthening my perceptions of social class systems. Although Hobhouse came from a privileged class and moved in privileged circles, she preferred to stand up to her own class, even though she was rejected and ridiculed. Having some insight in how privileged the upper class was and how difficult it must have been to stand up to that privilege, further inspired me to explore her history from an activist perspective. It also guided my understanding of the activist as outsider, similar to the position of Said who argues for the academic as outsider "who always tries to put his [sic] views outside of the domain of dogmas and rigid party positions" (Walia, 2001, p. 7).

But no history of South Africa can be complete without a focus on race. I also grew up with the knowledge and understanding that while the English viewed the Afrikaner as inferior, Afrikaners projected those feelings on to Blacks. Thus I also have to be aware of the Afrikaner people's collective responsibility for *apartheid*. Instead of learning from our own experiences of humiliation and subsequently treating Black South Africans with compassion, humanity, and respect, Afrikaners preferred to treat Blacks with the same contempt and disrespect with which the British treated them. Hobhouse, however, felt tremendous compassion for Afrikaner women and children, as well as the many Blacks who were interned with them. Her actions show the true meaning of the moral impulse at work as discussed in the context of the work of Bauman (1993). While even talking about *apartheid* is painful and shameful, redemption is possible if one can become an activist striving for equality, fairness, and compassion.

Although the above might appear indulgent, being honest to oneself and others about the personal issues that motivate one to focus on a particular event is very important to a postmodern historic analysis. This level of reflexivity is one of the major criteria for conducting postmodern history. It is important to know from which perspective a scholar enters into her subject matter. What the above also shows is how insidious one's life experiences are in terms of the subject matter one studies, not only in terms of postmodern, critical, or qualitative work but also in what is generally termed empirical research. All researchers have a personal interest in their work, even when using statistical methods in their analyses. The fact that I used Hobhouse as an example of the possibilities of activism in public relations was therefore influenced by my own experiences and not an objective rendition, as is so often claimed in historical research. Being reflexive goes hand-in-hand with openness and honesty about one's intent in conducting the historical analysis.

What flows logically from this kind of reflexivity and honesty is that history is open-ended. Everybody who interprets history from a reflexive perspective has to admit that there are multiple interpretations of the same historical event and that all historical interpretation is incomplete and open to multiple interpretations. For instance, one can also argue that the Afrikaner people were a flawed people from the very beginning and that the British invasion was for their own good, as so many argued at the time. Even today there is an admission among Afrikaner historians that the Afrikaners could not and would not be ruled, that they failed to adopt new technologies and that many preferred to live a nomadic existence (Giliomee, 2003). Thus, painting Hobhouse's support for the Afrikaner women and children as support for Afrikaner nationalism would be a seriously flawed interpretation. There might have been multiple reasons why she chose this path, one of which could be her love for her country:

> I take also this opportunity of publicly denying the accusation, so widely made in the Press and elsewhere, that I have slandered the British troops. No one has yet substantiated this accusation from my words or writing. I have, on the contrary, done my utmost to uphold the honour of the army. It is true that as long as war exists the honour of a country is confided to its soldiers, who will never cease to shield it; but is not the converse also true, and is it not often forgotten? Viz. that the honour of the soldiers is confined to the country? If advantage is taken of the necessary obedience of soldiers to demand of them services outside the recognized rules of warfare, or in performance of which their moral duty must clash with their professional duty, the blame lies on the country and its Government but not upon the army.
>
> (Hobhouse, 1902, pp. xv–xvi)

It is important to see this interpretation of the Hobhouse history as only one particular interpretation. Alternative interpretations of her conduct as activism are clearly also possible. Neither would this interpretation of her activist behavior be definitive for all activist behaviors.

Acknowledging the Influence of Ideology and Power

All historical representation is ideologically positioned. I state that as a given based on the previous arguments on upper and lower case history. Ideology in upper case history is often times quite obvious. In the case of the Anglo-Boer War the ideological battle was between British imperialism vs. the Boer republics' ideology of self-determination. As can be expected, the dominant ideological perspective that emerged from this war was that of the British Empire; namely, that the establishment of the Union of South Africa was for the good of the people and that Britain would lead the people of South Africa to a better future. Hobhouse was very outspoken in her critique of this ideology, as mentioned above.

Determining the impact of lower case history is far more subtle. Two lower case ideological influences are at work in this historical representation. First, there is the ideological influence of Hobhouse the historian. She was clearly motivated by and moved in some of the highest political circles in London, albeit that of the radical left wing of the opposition Liberal party. Her interpretation of the events in South Africa would be influenced by her political perspectives, which were very much against war in any form. She was particularly critical of the British government's betrayal of the Hague Convention, which governed wars at that time, and the British commanders' willingness to ignore their own rules and regulations as set out in the 1899 Manual of Military Law. Her writings and interpretation of historic documents could have been influenced by her moral impulse toward the Boer women and children as much as it was driven by her political associations and ideological perspectives. Ignoring the possibility of Hobhouse's political aspirations would make for a less rich interpretation of her role as an activist.

The second argument regarding lower case history is that of my own interpretation of the events. Jenkins argued that all historians enter their historical analysis and selection of facts and documents with a theory. In this case my theory is that although Hobhouse's activist behavior was not called *public relations* it nonetheless sets a template for current public relations practitioners to follow. The theory further holds that public relations in the hands of activists can bring about social change and social justice. Public relations as a function supporting or being part of institutional power harms the field and undermines its credibility and its ability to bring about positive change. I would argue involvement in positive social change is the highest form of practice in a democratic society. As Martin Luther King Jr. wrote, as cited in Hon (1997, p. 163): "Public relations is a very necessary part of any protest of civil disobedience.... In effect, in the absence of justice in the established courts of the region, nonviolent protesters are asking for a hearing in the court of world opinion."

This is largely what Hobhouse also believed. When she could not get justice for the victims of the war she went to the court of public opinion, not only in Britain but in several European countries and the United States. I have long argued that public relations practice as mostly defined in the West only can exist in a democratic society. In undemocratic countries where so-called public relations is practiced it is either in the form of government propaganda or used in the service of marketing communication to promote products or services. While the markets are free, the people are not. This is likely one of the most distinct ideological differences between public relations and marketing communications.

The many case studies in public relations, which I have now put in the category of public relations history, indicate that most scholars wish to situate practice in the context of modern organizations and the free market. Recently a whole issue of the *International Journal of Strategic Communication* (Zerfass, 2009) was devoted to the institutionalization of communication practice. Participating authors investigated to what extent communication practice is becoming an inherent part of modern institutions throughout the world. These perspectives place the use of public relations in the category of administrative control over organizations and societies. But the practice can as easily be situated in social change, empowerment, democracy, freedom, conservation, and human rights, even when it is part of institutional practice.

Accepting Chaos, Complexity, and Ambiguity in Historical Interpretation

The postmodern historian also has to accept that he is always creating an order that never existed, from the chaos of historical facts. As Best and Kellner (2001) argue, it is important to preserve the inherent complexity of any historical or theoretical interpretation. Scholars have to be aware of contradictions and aporiae when developing theories and interpreting or representing history. For instance, my argument that marketing communications is not necessarily a function of a democratic environment does not mean that it cannot bring about social change. Marketing techniques often are used for this very purpose as is evident from the term *social marketing*. In an effort to make sanitary hygiene freely available to women in a time where the subject was a social taboo, Kimberley-Clark created the word *Kotex* to help women ask for sanitary napkins without embarrassment (Heinrich & Batchelor, 2004). The company promoted the open display of the product so that it would be easier for women to buy it without having to ask for it. The authors claimed this was the start of the self-service concept. Their appropriation of the Kimberley-Clark history can certainly be critiqued from a public relations perspective but in the end it is good to remember that all histories are appropriated, all are written from a theoretical perspective, and all data are applied selectively. Therefore one history cannot be privileged over the other, particularly if the other history has an emancipatory subtext.

Another important outcome of acknowledging chaos and complexity in historical interpretation is resistance to the accumulation of "a coherent body of knowledge, with its modernist agenda of rational ordering and prediction and control" (Smith, as cited in Southgate, 2000, p. 135). Creating normative theories for the field, or even a metatheory, is doggedly pursued in public relations. This not only happens in the United States where so much emphasis is put on the concepts of excellence and two-way symmetry but even internationally, for example through the work of Sriramesh and Verčič (2003), who set out to further the global study of public relations by using the Excellence Project as a building block for their own work (p. 2). European public relations scholars pride themselves on their ability to examine public relations from a social perspective and their application of social theories to the field. What is seriously lacking in most European scholars is a critical look at the field. In fact, most critical work outside of the United States is conducted in the United Kingdom by scholars such as Jacquie L'Etang and Margaret Pieckska, and by New Zealand scholars such as David McKie, Shirley Leitch, and Judy Motion.

Looking at international public relations practice through the lens of an appropriation of historical data from the United States is reductionist to the extent that it is illogical. Looking at the field as essentially chaotic and disorderly will allow for a much richer interpretation of historical possibilities of practice rather than investigating the field through a few narrowly pre-defined concepts.

This state of theoretical and practical ambiguity goes against the grain of most practitioners and scholars, however. The problem is that ignoring the ambiguities inherent in practice and in academic interpretations of practice merely creates an illusion of orderliness. We all do students, clients, bosses, owners, audiences, and publics a huge disservice by presenting our knowledge as truth, while in fact it remains a narrow interpretation from a very limited perspective. It will be much more beneficial to acknowledge our limited understanding, lay bare the chaos and complexity, and invite as many new perspectives and understanding as possible into finding solutions for public relations problems, both academic and professional. It is much better to teach future professionals how to live and deal with ambiguity because never before have established structures and thoughts crumbled so quickly before our eyes as now. Helping students and practitioners to be reflexive and understand their own premises when approaching problems will enable them to be more open to alternative solutions, help them to become life-long scholars, and open their eyes to the validity of others' arguments. That is what will change professionals' attitude from striving for consensus to recognizing the tensors inherent in their practice, which in turn will lead to a better flow of ideas and more open discussion, without the desire to force the viewpoints of their clients or superiors on those who do not agree (Holtzhausen, 2000). The reality is that we live in a permanent state of chaos and ambivalence. The problem is that we choose to ignore it and deal with it by returning to simplistic and naïve places (Southgate, 2005).

The only way of preserving the chaos and ensuring the prominence of aporiae is to bring as many different perspectives to the analysis as possible. And while it will benefit practitioners to consider the emancipatory potential of their practice it will also be important to ask how their practice can be tempered "by reverence for nature, respect for all life, sustainability, and ecological balance" (Best & Kellner, 2001, p. 11). This is also true for historical analysis, which "should engage both negative and positive developments, criticizing forms of oppression, domination, and exploitation, while valorizing positive possibilities for moral and technical evolution" (p. 15).

Paying attention to the structure/event continuum is one way of preserving the complexity of historical narrative (Burke, 2001a). Historical events and the underlying structure that affects events were formerly not seen as the opposing ends of a continuum but rather as two different and opposing approaches to the writing of history. Events refer to the practice of representing history through major events such as wars or social transformations, for example the French Revolution. These events are narrated through the perspectives of those who had the power to leave behind key documents, for example, kings, emperors, and generals, and are regarded as descriptive history. They prefer "to couch their explanations in terms of individual character and intention" (p. 287). Structural historians, on the other hand, are critical of event historians, view event history as shallow and even "vulgar" (p. 283) and point to the narrative nature of event history because it excludes large periods of history between so-called historic events. Structural historians rather focus on the analytical, i.e. on the structural elements in a culture that influenced historical events and were outside the control of leaders, such as "the economic and social framework to the experience and modes of thought of ordinary people" (p. 285).

Burke (2001a), however, argues it is best to see history as an event/structure continuum and suggests historians should tell their stories (again an admission of history as narrative) from different viewpoints, by making themselves visible in their narratives, and making their descriptions thick enough in the Geertzian tradition "to bear a heavy weight of interpretation" (p. 291). Burke thus argues for explaining macrohistory (or upper case history) in terms of microhistory (or lower case history).

To demonstrate, doing a structural analysis of Hobhouse's environment could also lead us to a better understanding of the factors motivating activist behavior and provide for a richer description and a better understanding of how individuals become activists. This is an important contribution to the concept of public relations as activism because it allows for a focus on individual attributes of activists rather than some aggregated traits among a group of activists. In the case of Hobhouse her womanhood brought on great sympathy for the Boer women and children. In her writings she consistently stressed that her only reason for becoming involved in the war was to improve the lot of the aged, women, and children and that she could not be concerned with the Boer warriors. Her sympathies were most likely further encouraged by her religious upbringing and her desire to work as a social worker, as she did in America. Hobhouse's actions are an example of the moral impulse at work: she was not asked to interfere, she expected nothing in return, and she stood up for the Other who had no voice.

Another structural factor that facilitated her ability to become an activist was her skills as author and thinker, as is evident from her book. Having grown up in the house of an Anglican Archdeacon meant that she most likely had access to books and different kinds of writing. She made clear and logical arguments supported with actual documents meticulously collected, similar to the academic empirical method. Her birth also provided her access to political circles and to the upper class. She knew how to use her social networks, the political system, and the media to further her goals. Her letter-writing campaign displayed a media savvy most likely rare among women of her class and status at that time. Her experience as a single woman used to traveling alone likely prepared her for her journeys into Africa. Had she been married with children her personal history would most likely have taken a different path, particularly against the backdrop of the status of women at that time. The political system and players of that time were structural elements that might have enabled her ability to influence public opinion, particularly as Britons started to reflect on the expansionism of their empire and its effects on local populations. The way she pursued her cause also suggests that she had a strong personality and was most likely thick-skinned. She stood her ground when confronting the commander of the British forces in South Africa and the British governor and never gave an indication that the consistent critique and ridiculing of her in the press bothered her. She single-mindedly pursued her cause without considering her own well-being, health, and financial status.

However, in the end it still is important to remember that all forms of history are narrative and even thick historical description cannot escape the postmodern critique of historical representation as theoretical and selective. Thus another role of postmodern history is not to put order on past events but rather to point to the ambiguities in historical analysis. It is important to keep all historical analysis open-ended, as Southgate (2005) said, "a questioning of past closures becomes a central part of what history in postmodernity might be for" (p. 115).

The Power of Language

Deconstruction, frequently discussed in this text, is a powerful tool to ensure the openness of historical texts. The act of deconstruction itself ensures openness to the Other. It does not mean dispensing of the Other but rather opening oneself up for new possibilities of interpretation of the Other (Kearney, 2004, p. 155). Deconstruction thus particularly highlights the role of language in postmodern historical analysis. Deconstruction, *différance,* and *difference* expose the complexities of communication in daily life, which are multiplied infinitely in historical analysis. The meaning of words and the contexts within which they are used in historical documents and artifacts change over time. References to other words in sentences get lost as the meanings of those words change or words simply disappear in the modern idiom (Southgate, 2005). This is also the case with historical documents that are translated from a language foreign to the historian. Meaning literally gets lost in translation.

As thorough as Hobhouse was in collecting letters and other documents that recorded what happened in the concentration camps, she did not include letters from people who could not write in English. As a result the voices of the women, who wrote letters in Afrikaans about their experiences in the concentration camps, were not included in her book. This is referred to as a *trace*, or undocumented history (Jenkins, 1995). Language itself is not only inaccessible in terms of realistic interpretation but inaccessible because there might not be recorded historical evidence available in a language the historian understands. This is problematic for public relations because the American-centered approach to public relations has been widely adopted in countries where the language to explain the practice does not yet exist. Scholars in those countries often create language to describe practice, which might be inherently different from the deeper meanings of the words in their original American interpretation. One example that comes to mind is the translation of *public relations* into German (*Öffentlichkeitsarbeid*), and Dutch (*Openbare Schakelwese*), which is similar to Afrikaans (*Openbare Skakelwese*). In the United States public relations practice is increasingly interpreted as public relationships, whereas a translation of the German, Dutch, and Afrikaans terms implies *work that takes place in the public sphere* or *work in service of the public*. This means that there are deep philosophical differences between what the practice means in these different geographical regions. Therefore, taking the four historic models from the United States and transplanting them onto practices in other countries, even those where the practice is well established, is not logical. It would behoove scholars and practitioners to be aware of how, and for what purpose, language at any time is used. As Jenkins (2004) wrote, postmodern "notions of ... the *aporia*, undecidability, incommensurability, the *differend*, the event, the figure, the trace, difference, the symbolic, anamnesis" mean "without exception ... all historical representation are failed representations" [emphasis in original] (p. 369).

Another function of historical deconstruction is the analysis of texts to expose how language is used to create totalitarian systems and metanarratives, or in the words of Southgate (2005), an awareness "of the ways that language is used by those in power, whether political or economic, in our own time" (p. 144). I will discuss language in the use of power in more depth in the next chapter, but suffice it to say that public relations scholars assign historical importance to certain events, words, and phrases, which sometimes are used to prevent new thoughts. To again refer to the four historic models so frequently discussed in this chapter, the words *press agentry* and *asymmetrical* have been tainted to such an extent that many practitioners would not admit to their use in practice. Since the use of two-way symmetrical communication historically is represented as the only ethical practice, one can argue that the use of these terms has been raised to an ideological level that affects practice and steers academics away from studying these phenomena and their effects in practice. The role of the postmodern historian is to expose the ideological underpinnings of their own work and of the language that is used in their own texts and those of others. It is the role of postmodern public relations academics to ensure that they foster "self-reflexivity, linguistic awareness, ability to live with ambiguity" (p. 147) in their students and promote that practice among their colleagues.

Finally, language in its representational and repetitive functions creates a distance between practitioners and their audiences or publics. In this role language helps to disassociate us from those our practice harms, as Bauman (1993) pointed out. Not only is it the role of public relations historians to show how practitioners in the past used language in a similar way but also how current practices promote the use of language in the service of power. Here the work of Benoit comes to mind. Although Benoit (see Benoit & Pang, 2008, for a thorough review of Benoit's work) does not set out to critically analyze organizational discourse during times of crisis his analyses do show how language is used to euphemize or hide the real impact of organizational behavior and how public relations practitioners are actively involved in this process.

Fragmented History

Fragmentation is a persistent theme in postmodernism and also is applied to historical interpretation. History does not escape the postmodern critique of progress and the very purpose of postmodern history is to break down the linearity of modern history that leads us to imagine a utopian state where humans have reached the ultimate civilization. Postmodern historians aim at breaking down and decenter thoughts such as those of Fukiyama who professed to the end of history. To understand Fukiyama's notion of the end of history it is important to understand the modernist interpretation of history as linear. A linear history has a beginning and an end and Fukiyama argues that we have reached the pinnacle of our history of emancipation, thus the end of history. Postmodernists, on the other hand, view history as non-linear and use a variety of terms or metaphors to portray this non-linearity. As is typical for postmodernists, new images and metaphors such as fragmentation, rupture, collage, and bricolage are used. The idea is that historical events and interpretations are similar to the flowers on a shrub. Although the shrub holds them together, they exist and display their beauty individually.

If there is any linearity in history it is not in the sense linearity is normally understood. One such example of non-linear linearity is from postmodern philosophy. Several scholars have discussed how Kierkegaard, Nietzsche, and Levinas form part of the postmodern philosophical tradition (Best, 1995); however, these scholars did not know each other, nor did they form a postmodern "dynasty" because the development of postmodern philosophy was much more organic than that. Foucault (1984) in particular argued for the unraveling of history to see how power structures create the value systems that are historically established. One such example could be to examine how the colonial values and norms the British generals used in the Anglo-Boer War again emerged in the American invasion of Iraq in 2002. Some of the arguments and justifications the British used to invade the Boer republics were also used during the invasion of Iraq, such as that the invasion was to help the local people become better (more democratic, more civilized, etc.). As in the Iraq War, the British invaded the republics, laid claim to them, and declared that anybody who opposed them would be treated as traitors because they acted against the crown. When it suited the British they ignored the agreements they made at the Hague Convention and proceeded with the "scorched earth" approach. This sounds eerily familiar when one considers the debate in the United States about torture and the Geneva Convention. Thus, rather than seeing events of war as humanity's progress toward an ideal society, Foucault argues that it is the responsibility of the historicist to lay bare the underlying value and power systems that make this kind of abuse possible. Only when these underlying value systems are exposed can they be challenged and prevented.

The Hobhouse history is not part of a progressive history of activists who inherited and built forth on others' legacy. There is no linear progression of activist history in public relations. There are only rare moments and people who allow scholars to study what activism demands of practitioners. The goal of the study of the communication behavior of activists also is to decenter and fragment any efforts to accumulate a hegemonic body of public relations knowledge. By pointing out that public relations practice can and does exist outside of the four historic models of public relations or any other linear historical narrative and outside of society's dominating institutions, public relations history becomes fragmented, ruptured, and discontinued. To understand activism it also is important to lay bare those power structures, institutions, and value systems that activists have to be aware of. For instance, to be an organizational activist it is important for practitioners to always evaluate and analyze the organization's assumptions when communicating with activists. It is important for activist practitioners to understand how power works, where power points are, and what the possibilities for resistance are.

History as Therapy

Postmodernists such as Derrida often refer to the playfulness of deconstruction (Kearney, 2004). The approach to postmodern thought should be like that of a child in the sense that a childhood creates the potential for new possibilities, thinking about possibilities that have not yet taken place, literally living in the future and being "pre-mature" (Jenkins, 2004, p. 369). The postmodern philosopher should be like a child, who has no

> habitual baggage to weigh it down. It just likes to play. It just has to make things up as it goes along—experimentally. Analogously, postmodernism is also future-oriented. Postmodernists are those people who we might grow up into if we can escape being governed by the past or by the beckoning termini of teleology or by pre-programmed schema.
>
> (p. 370)

This playfulness can also take the form of "what if" questions such as, What if public relations scholars sought their historical roots in political activism and not in commerce and industry? How different would our practice have looked? Would we have been part of schools of mass communications, or speech communication, or would we have been part of sociology, political science, or anthropology? Would we perhaps have taught our students the dynamics of social movements, advocacy, civil rights, and social change rather than the importance of the bottom line? Would we now not be the step-children of journalism departments? These questions pose the other possibilities for public relations practice and provide hope for its future because of alternative interpretations of its past.

In this vein, Southgate (2005) argues postmodern history presents therapeutic possibilities because it allows us to decenter previous histories and to question those histories that created categories of ourselves from which we thought we could not escape. We can actually escape the grips of history. At the same time history allows us to choose (perhaps outside of existing categories) historical figures with whom we like to associate ourselves, people who we believe have in the past articulated or lived those values that we ascribe to as individuals. The Hobhouse history provides such a historic figure to public relations practitioners who are abhorred by the way in which their discipline is and has been used to support existing power structures and maintain systems of discrimination; and for those of us who believe that public relations practice is a necessary practice to fight for equality, democracy, and sound environmental practices. It also provides an alternative interpretation to the perception of public relations as just another, and less ethical, form of journalism.

Thus postmodern history provides us with possibilities of hope for the future because we can choose those histories that give us hope for and pathways to the future. As Southgate (2005) says, "To a great extent, we fashion that 'reality' ourselves, looking back with regrets and forward with anxiety, or back with delight and forward with high expectations" (p. 127). Hope for the future is made possible by looking back at those histories that show us that it is possible to affect change, although this kind of hope also comes with responsibility to act in a way that change for the better is possible.

Although this text might appear to be hyper-critical of the four historic models of public relations, their historical trajectory can be revised to be therapeutic. It is quite possible that the therapeutic potential of the four models is exactly what makes it so popular to practitioners and scholars all over the globe. Practitioners choose this history that leads to two-way communication, which they see as more ethical, democratic and fair, rather than the history of lies in press agentry, the do-nothing history of providing information, or the manipulative history of using science to the benefit of organizations in two-way asymmetry. This history has generated a vast body of research and has influenced modern-day practice, which is indeed a hopeful event. However, it is important to note that the history of public relations as presented in the four historical models remains a narrative and selective interpretation or events, just like any other history, and should not be elevated to the level of scientific or normative truth.

The Emancipatory Potential of Postmodern History

Postmodern history has the potential for both personal and social emancipation, although social emancipation is not possible without personal emancipation. The issue of personal emancipation will be discussed thoroughly in the next chapter but needs to be addressed briefly here to highlight the role between personal emancipation and historical analysis. Foucault (1984) argues that historical analysis allows people to become aware of those practices that made humans subjects and subjected and so has the potential to set us free. He argues for "a historical investigation into the events that have led us to constitute ourselves and to recognize ourselves as subjects of what we are doing, thinking, saying" (p. 47). From Foucault's perspective then the goal of historical interpretation is "human freedom.... Subjectivity and sociality are mutually connected insofar as limits of the self point to social constraints" (Best, 1995, p. 126).

But scholars also warn against an interpretation of freedom that could lead to self-destructive behavior (Best, 1995). Southgate (2005) perhaps articulates it best when she says historical interpretation should lead to a "deracinated" selfhood, which will allow us "to know ourselves" (p. 116). That kind of historical analysis will take care of our memories and help us to find our own identity. We can find historical figures or social groups with whom we can identify or perhaps articulate who we wish to become and so help us toward leading a good life. It provides hope for a better future. As shown in Chapter 2, postmodern ethics do not imply an "anything-goes" philosophy but rather a deep responsibility to compassion for the Other and knowledge of what we stand for. Through the process of reflexivity the postmodern philosopher develops a "philosophical consciousness" that is not only caring toward those without a voice but also helps us to gain a voice that resists our and others' submission and subordination (Jenkins, 1995). Reflexivity helps us to monitor the extent to which we harm others.

Being reflexive in the business world can be very difficult because so much knowledge comes to public relations practitioners in the form of "objective" knowledge through survey research, information presented in the form of graphics, or in the form of power from above. This kind of knowledge makes it very difficult to keep the emotional links to the people affected by our practices. It glibly removes the complexity and ambiguity inherent in all situations and desensitizes and dehumanizes us, as Bauman so powerfully argued. So much knowledge comes to us as given that it is easy to forget that "[t]he assumed fixity of knowledge mitigates against life" (Southgate, 2005, p. 178), insisting that we "be" rather than "become." That is the very reason why it is important to resist fixed interpretations of history and why we should always explore alternative interpretations of history that can point us to a more egalitarian and compassionate future. Postmodern historians all have one argument in common, namely, we can never assert to have found the final truth in history because all historical interpretation must be kept open to new and emancipatory interpretations.

It is not necessary to rewrite the whole of history but rather to be cognitive of the *event*; which in postmodern terms refers to life-changing experiences that come to us as everyday occurrences (Jenkins, 2004, p. 374). So we return to Lyotard's *différend*, which argues that the cognitive of the event is incommensurable with what happened and why it happened. In Chapter 4 I will discuss in more depth the concept of the *tensor*, which refers to situations where mutual agreement is impossible because of the incompatibility of genres of thought. But the tensor is also important in historical interpretation because history often conceals tensors and smoothes over those deep differences often inherent in events. As a result those in power who write history present events from their perspectives, and the voices of those whose thoughts are incommensurate with their own get lost in history. Hobhouse's book (1902) is a powerful reminder of how differently the Boer women and children saw the destruction of their homes and property from the soldiers who had to execute the "scorched earth" policies and how these policies became concealed in the British representation of that war. It is the role of the postmodern historian to preserve the *différend*, to expose "that which prohibits that the question of the just and the unjust be, and remain, raised" (p. 377).

The emancipatory role of the postmodern historian lies in resisting dominating and closed interpretations of historical events and pointing to the underlying political motivations of all historical representation. If all historical representation is political, then there is "something to institute. There is no politics if there is not … a questioning of existing institutions, a project to improve them, to make them more just" (Lyotard & Thébaud, 1985, p. 23). This is a clear instruction to the activist public relations practitioner: question your existing institution, improve it, and make it more just. So history becomes strategy. Reinterpreting history from an emancipatory perspective becomes a strategy for transforming society and creating a more hopeful future.

Historical Underpinnings for the Practice of Public Relations as Activism

This chapter thus far has clearly articulated a historical foundation for public relations as activism and for the reinterpretation of history as an activist strategy in public relations. At a 2002 get-together of major players in the public relations industry I was surprised and heartened that Daniel Edelman of Edelman

Public Relations and the CEO of Ketchum Public Relations stressed the concept of activism, namely, that the time is ripe for public relations practitioners to take the high road. At that occasion Edelman used Alexander Hamilton as a role model for today's public relations practitioners.

However, recent events in the United States do not point to an influential role for public relations practitioners in changing the outlooks and actions of powerful role players in a broad range of organizations, from the White House, to financial and industrial institutions such as energy companies. Public relations practitioners largely remain the henchmen and women of power players, an issue that will be discussed in the next chapter. Somewhere we lost our activist fervor, as Dozier and Lauzen (2000) so aptly mentioned. Somewhere we became co-opted by big business to do the bidding of management, loosing not only our role in society but also our reputations. Fortunately, a historical re-examining of the role of public relations provides hope for the future. So, let me conclude with my interpretation of a historical profile of the public relations practitioner as activist based on the involvement of Emily Hobhouse in the Anglo-Boer War of 1899–1902 and my reading of postmodern history.

Hobhouse's reaction to and interaction with the Boer women and children sets a fine example of Bauman's (1993) concept of the moral impulse. Nobody in the two Boer republics knew of her existence and she had no obligation to help these people other than her moral calling. With fierce and unswerving commitment to her cause she exemplifies the meaning of activist fervor. She gave voice to the voiceless. Not only did she speak on their behalf but through the many letters she published in her book she made their actual voices heard. She did not represent them as much as she became a channel for their voices and so tried to bridge the gap between them and her representation of them. What a wonderful example for modern-day public relations activists. Instead of being the messenger, we should rather be the channel through which decision-makers can hear the voices of our stakeholders and publics loudly and clearly in all their raw emotion rather than sanitizing and summarizing their opinions through our surveys and focus groups.

To be the channel for the voices of the Other Hobhouse had to become physically involved in their cause. This was not humanitarianism or charity from afar. She spent her own money and used her own resources to travel to Africa, to the point where she was nearly destitute. Similarly, postmodern activism consistently argues for direct involvement in communities and political issues. Postmodern activism is daily practice. No longer can the practitioner stand apart and merely execute the demands of their seniors. Being involved in changing policies at national level creates a metanarrative for all people. Action at local level directly addresses the needs of local stakeholders, which vary from place to place and situation to situation.

To change the fate of the Boer women and children Hobhouse did not hesitate to take on people in power at the highest level. She fearlessly attacked the British government and did not hesitate to get into altercations with Lord Roberts, the commander of the British forces in Africa, and the British governor of the Cape. She went toe-to-toe with Lord Roberts, pointing out the discrepancies in his policies and unfair and exploitative practices of his forces. She engaged in the politics of the day, was aware of those groups who would benefit politically from her cause, and joined their ranks. She gathered like-minded people around her and used them in a letter-writing campaign to the media. As such she not only influenced the politics of the day but was activated by it. Public relations practitioners have to understand that public relations is political, no matter what the action. The aim of all communication, particularly that which takes place in the public sphere, is to influence, assert, or affect. This is an important issue that the field needs to accept and come to grips with. There is no neutral communication. Even providing information is a political act. To live consciously and reflexively in this political world is part of being an activist. Denying it makes public relations practitioners mere tools of power.

The fact that her ideas went against popular opinion, which supported the war, did not bother Hobhouse. She did not mind being unpopular or in the minority. What drove her was her fight for the powerless, the poor, the underdog. Her actions were motivated by her resistance to political oppression. She was a democrat who believed in equality and fairness and that all people have a right to be heard. She loudly and clearly used her voice to affect change and was ashamed of the behavior of the British government that used the troops for such shameful operations. How often do practitioners stand up for stakeholders and/or employees whose voices are silenced? How often are they ashamed of the behavior of their organizations but do not speak up? How many practitioners subscribe to organizational power hierarchies that would never stand the test of daylight in our democratic societies? To be a public relations activist means that you can no longer stand on the sidelines. You have to become politically involved.

Another aspect of activism Hobhouse highlights is the variety of tactics she used. Even more than 100 years later her tactics are still valid to the public relations activist practitioner. As mentioned, she closed alliances and formed pressure groups with others of similar mindsets. In today's parlance we would call it networking. She understood how society works and how power is formed and knew how to assert political pressure. She was a wordsmith who wrote documents, letters, books, and articles. Her style was clear, persuasive, and succinct. She did not mince words but also knew how to make a logical argument. She would use Lord Roberts's arguments against him to show how wrong he was. She made it her business to understand the treaties of the day, such as the Geneva Convention, and was informed of military and other relevant laws. Her writing was both passionate and logical. Despite the accusations there was no sign of hysteria; only clear indignation that came from her knowledge that she occupied the moral high ground. Practitioners should remember that it is easier to argue for a case when one occupies the moral high ground.

Her impact on history was further facilitated by her excellent use of strategy. She knew which messages she needed to convey to whom and made sure she made the biggest impact possible. She never compromised and consensus building was not in her vocabulary. On the contrary, she worked hard to create dissensus and conflict to reach her goals. She used the social and political upheaval of her time to drive her point home. All times have upheavals which should drive the public relations practitioner to become involved.

Finally, Hobhouse was not in the battle for herself but for others. Although she fought for the immediate relief of the women and children in the concentration camps, she returned after the war to help them back on their feet. She understood that big changes are slow to come but the rewards are huge. She most likely never saw the results of her activism and involvement in the future. Nonetheless, her reward is a place in history and the eternal gratefulness of a people.

So, "What if" our history is written through the lives of activists and not press agents? "What if" our common history emanated from resistance to British colonialism and not from P. T. Barnum, Ivy Lee, and Edward Bernays? "What if" our heroes are Thomas Jefferson, Margaret Sanger, Alexander Hamilton, members of the Civil Rights Movement, Emily Hobhouse, the African National Congress, and Nobel Peace Prize winner Jody Williams? Perhaps practitioners would be less fearful of losing their jobs when they know they are doing the right thing. Perhaps they would be less enamored with management. Perhaps they would play a much more important role in helping their organizations survive by aligning corporate values with the democratic principles of the societies in which they live. Perhaps they would have a better reputation. Perhaps their contribution to society would be recognized and celebrated instead of vilified.

4

POWER AND THE PUBLIC RELATIONS FUNCTION

Make rhizomes, not roots, never plant! Don't sow, grow offshoots! Don't be one or multiple, be multiplicities! Run lines, never plot a point! Be quick, even when standing still! Don't bring out the General in you! Don't just have ideas, just have an idea.

(Deleuze & Guattari, 1987, pp. 24–25)

Public relations practitioners like to think of themselves as *the* or *a* conscience of the organization (Holtzhausen & Voto, 2002) but events during the past decade, and particularly those that resulted in the scandals of indulgence in financial organizations after the U.S. government bailed them out financially, are proof that public relations practitioners are not fulfilling that role. These incidents are indications that public relations practitioners are either marginalized in organizations or are so cozily seated at the table that they have lost touch with what is ethical and how their organizations will be viewed in the public sphere. These incidents also go unchallenged from both professional organizations such as the Public Relations Society of America (PRSA) and some academics, for whom corporate practice is the holy grail of the discipline.

When I raised this issue at an academic conference a scholar defended the practitioners from the company mentioned above. His response was that he personally spoke to the practitioners involved, who said they tried to warn top management. However, top management did not listen to them, which speaks to the lack of influence public relations practitioners have in the organization. He also said the issue was complex and the company was now losing a lot of money because the particular junket was canceled, in effect defending the organization's behavior. As we know, all practice is complex and complexity is not an excuse for doing the wrong thing. Second, as Bauman (1993, p. 84) said, if the only value system is money it negates any ethical arguments.

Another problem that exacerbates the power relationship between public relations and management often is the function's reporting line. It often is a source of great pride when public relations departments and their heads report directly to the CEO or the most senior executive in the organization. However, this has an inherent danger. I can attest from personal experience and direct observation that in that type of reporting structure the CEO becomes one's direct supervisor, which means that the practitioner no longer works for the organization as such but becomes the personal publicist for the executive. This kind of reporting structure is blatantly unethical because the executive is using organizational resources to build his own image, which comes in very handy on the way to the next top position or government appointment. It also endangers the whole public relations function because if things go wrong for the executive it affects the whole department and the image of the organization. Vignette 4.1 highlights the importance of a serious consideration of the role of power in practice. It also will behoove public relations practitioners to remember that they only work for the CEO if the CEO pays their salaries and not the organization.

This vignette shows how CEO and other top executives can abuse the communication function in an organization for their own benefit and testifies to the emotional violence practitioners often are subjected to in the environments in which they work (Spicer, 1997). The vignette also speaks to the issue of power and the public relations function. Postmodern theory provides a unique and alternative lens through which to view power, but it does not only theorize how power permeates society, it also provides resistance strategies to power. In fact, one of the mainstays of postmodern theory is its resistance to and disdain for dominating and unfair forms of power. For a serious discussion of power in public relations it is important to again remember that public relations practice is not a benign, neutral force but is deeply political, which in postmodern parlance translates into a struggle for power.

This chapter will focus on the role of public relations in creating power systems in organizations through mostly Foucaultian perspectives on the relationship between knowledge and power, particularly the knowledge organizations create in the public sphere. I will revisit these perspectives in Chapter 6 in a discussion of the role of academic knowledge creation and public relations research and education. As my point of departure I use Spicer's (1997) work on the political nature of public relations practice and view the organization as a site of political struggle.

Next I use some academic liberty to include the work of Bourdieu in my discussion on the political role of public relations. Bourdieu's interest in language and power (Ihlen, 2009) can be seen as a precursor to the link between knowledge and power theorized by Foucault. Bourdieu is not a postmodernist

---

Vignette 4.1

A very senior communication practitioner related how he was appointed as the communication executive for a very large South African multidivisional organization. Although he was a member of the management committee of the organization the CEO was his direct report. It did not take long before the CEO started making demands to raise his personal profile, arguing that when people think of the organization they think of him. The practitioner was instructed to ensure that every speech the CEO made was publicized and that special efforts were made to get him involved in every possible organization that could enhance his profile. One of these institutions was the local university and the practitioner was instructed to raise the CEO's profile to such an extent that the CEO would be offered an honorary doctorate. The practitioner was uncomfortable with his reporting arrangement and proposed that a special reputation management board should be constituted that would involve every department and division in the organization, as well as the chair of the board of directors. That would ensure a holistic approach to managing the reputation and communication of the organization. This suggestion was ignored.

After a few years things went very wrong for the CEO and he literally disappeared from the organization over a weekend due to serious financial questions raised in the media. Fortunately the practitioner had already resigned and was on his way out. As expected, when the CEO's reputation suffered, so did the reputation of the organization. In addition, the practitioner received a call from the CEO over the weekend asking him to lie to the media on his behalf because "he was in any case on his way out." Needless to say, the practitioner declined.

---

and an avid supporter of the Enlightenment. Thus my postmodern reading of Bourdieu in terms of public relations practitioners' role as agents who create symbolic capital is quite radical. But I believe Bourdieu's work elucidates us on the role of the agent in the process of wealth and power accumulation, which sets the stage for the subsequent discussion of knowledge and power.

The Political Nature of Public Relations Practice

One of the first scholars to recognize the political context of public relations was Spicer (1997), who posits the following proposition: "Organizations are political entities in which power, in its many forms, is used to influence others toward desired individual or organization outcomes" (p. 13). Spicer emphasizes that this does not constitute a negative view of power but rather refers to its ubiquity. He also highlights the importance of recognizing the political function of public relations. All politics is about power relations and in organizations specifically politics focuses on strategic relations and alliances determined by conflict, power, and resistance to or desire for change. The term *politics* thus does not only refer to recognized political processes such as elections but to all actions linked to change or resistance to change (Williams, 1998). Whereas modernist power more often than not is viewed negatively, postmodernists also view power as a positive force, but they do separate the individual pursuit of power from the centralized and hegemonic power so often predominant in organizations.

Thus, power in the organizational context cannot escape postmodern scrutiny, particularly because power is so obviously present through organizational hierarchies and positions such as supervisor, manager, executive, team leader, strategic apex, and other structural and differentiated forms of organizing. This is the overt face of organizational power. But power also has a covert face. Overt and covert power are not dichotomous but in the postmodern perspective work together to create different forms of suppression. Modern interpretations of power differentiate between categories of power in organizations, such as administrative power, managerial power, supervisory power, decision-making power, expert power, and so forth (Hatch & Cunliffe, 2006). There also is a difference between authority, which is a legitimized and institutionalized form of power that mostly works its way from the top of the hierarchy downwards, and for instance expert power, which is much less hierarchical and more multidirectional.

These power perspectives and interpretations have been very influential in public relations theory. The most well-known theoretical perspective is the need for practitioners to be part of the dominant coalition (L. A. Grunig, J. E. Grunig, & Dozier, 2002) and to gain "a seat at the table" (Berger & Reber, 2006, p. 7). These theoretical approaches stem from a focus on the desirability of hierarchical power. For public relations the benefits of hierarchical power in traditional organizations are obvious and cost-effective—and the easy way out. To benefit from informal power or "non-authorized power" (Hatch & Cunliffe, 2006, p. 255) one needs to exert oneself to gain additional knowledge, build relationships, or negotiate support on issues outside of formal authority. Not everybody is prepared to exert herself in this way because it is much easier demanding action than negotiation or explaining those actions.

These categories of power are based on the assumption that public relations takes place in bureaucratic organizations. But, as I argue in Chapter 5, bureaucratic organizing systems are being replaced and/or supplemented with other hybrid forms of organizational structures, which require alternative perspectives on organizational power. A much more useful perspective of organization is that of organization as collective action, which is one of the predominant approaches in organizational communication. Mumby (1996, p. 266) argues "organizations—of whatever form—are based on some notion of collective action; there is presumably a logic that undergirds such collective action, however far it might deviate from bureaucratic models of organizing." This approach to organizations not only provides for including different kinds of organizations in public relations theorizing but also allows for power perspectives other than those from modern organization theory, particularly from postmodern theorists who have extensively theorized power.

Particularly in bureaucratic organizations hierarchical power is known to create a power distance between managers and employees (Hofstede, 1991). Power distance is viewed as a function of societal cultures that are hierarchical and authoritarian in nature. The societal attributes of power are then transferred to organizations in those cultures. Even at universities that have more decentralized structures than most organizations, the idea of communicating up or down the chain of command is firmly entrenched. One can therefore argue that hierarchical power creates a power distance in organizations because of fear of authority and lack of communication between authority figures in the organization and its employees. Thus, purely from a practical viewpoint the importance of hierarchical power for public relations is questionable because it is the function that has to break down fear and barriers to communication. The wisdom for public relations practitioners to be part of the dominant coalition is therefore questionable because it often breaks down trust between them and their internal and external publics (Holtzhausen & Voto, 2002). Berger and Reber (2006) have made a similar point and we all have argued for multiple resistance strategies to overcome negative perceptions of practice.

Control in modernist organizations goes beyond the categories of power mentioned above. Boje and Dennehy (1993) critique modernist organizational control from a number of perspectives which also provide space for a postmodern critique of public relations practice. For instance, the authors argue one of the mainstays of modernist organizations is their desire to predict the future. One sees this on Wall Street, where shares go up or down depending on whether organizations match their predictions for financial performance during a particular quarter. This also emphasizes the short-term results orientation. Boje and Dennehy ask, "What is the quarterly return? The result is that physical plan, human resource, and production systems are gutted to gain short term advantage. The cumulative gutting of the corporation takes it out of effective long term competition" (p. 316). Organizational environments are far more complex than these simple predictions suggest, which is one of the reasons for the sometime extreme fluctuations in share prices. Similarly, the reality is that complexity in organizational environments affects the ability of managers to monitor performance according to pre-set performance standards and makes outcome predictions difficult and unrealistic. Language categories, for instance in strategic plans, and accounting standards (which really also is a form of language) are used for control at every level, which results in a system where rigidity rules and people are evaluated and compensated for their conformity rather than value-added behavior.

The Dangers of Public Relations Power

Although postmodernism does not critique capitalism in the same way Marxism does, not since the Depression has the postmodern suspicion of predatory capitalism been as vindicated as at this stage in world history. Postmodernists focus on how power is *discursively constituted* through political and knowledge processes and view Marxism as merely another form of capitalism (Holtzhausen, 2011). Thus, postmodernism focuses on the use of language and meaning creation in establishing systems of power in society. The postmodern project further focuses on how power is sustained through historical processes of knowledge and political institutions and not capitalism per se; however, capitalism has become part and parcel of institutional processes that aim to dominate and that determine "how science and technology, the military, and reason produce a form of rationalized social organization, driven by the search for power and money" (Best & Kellner, 2001, p. 29). It is important for public relations practitioners to understand how their practices sustain the systems of power run by the new ruling elite, which Best and Kellner, drawing on Pychon, describe as military men, capitalists, scientists, bureaucrats, media moguls, and "shadowy figures who use intelligence and technology as modes of domination and power" (p. 37).

This sounds pretty radical for public relations; however, Mickey (1997) was the first public relations scholar to grasp the significance of Baudrillard's (1983, 1984) concern with the way in which public relations practitioners use signs and sign systems to assist in creating a new world order. Mickey uses a postmodern cultural analysis to understand the role one of the world's largest public relations agencies, Hill and Knowlton, played in the start of the Gulf War. Through an analysis of the signs Hill and Knowlton produced, Mickey proposes the firm created a hyperreality that disenfranchised many voices and privileged a small group of people. This hyperreality creates a hypercivilization or "semiurgic society" (Best & Kellner, 1991, pp. 118–119) where the image and the sign are used to change the course of society. Indeed, Mickey's work reflects the Best and Kellner interpretation of the role of public relations in the new world of "infotainment" (p. 120), which is typical of the collapse of boundaries between information and entertainment. They argue there is a similar implosion between politics and entertainment "where image is more important than substance, and political campaigns become increasingly dependent on media advisors, public relations 'experts', and pollsters who have transformed politics into image contests or sign struggles" (p. 120). Note the single inverted commas used in terms of public relations, which surely must be a mocking use of the term. This is typical of postmodern scholars who do recognize and analyze modern manifestations of techno-sciences, of which public relations is deemed one.

Postmodern theory allows us to focus on three aspects of public relations power: its media relations function, its creation of messages on behalf of power actors, and its relationship building function. It also provides for an alternative approach to the concept of symmetrical communication.

The media relations function of public relations can be critiqued from the perspective of a crisis of representation (Jameson, 1984), which, similar to the Best and Kellner interpretation, can be viewed as the "replacement of the factual by the representational" (Hassard, 1996, p. 50). The Hill and Knowlton incident is an example. Representation involves the presentation of a reality that does not exist—it is "a perfect copy for which there is no original" (p. 50) and which creates a sublime state of detachment where the horrors of society are viewed with cynicism and disinterest. Public relations practitioners so become the "disinterested third party" (Bauman, 1993, p. 114) that creates distance between the individual and the Other, which in turn leads to a removal of passion for and the objectivizing of the Other.

I noted previously (Holtzhausen, 2002) that this replacement of the real with the hyperreal in public relations already starts at college level where students are trained to write, act, and think like journalists. The emphasis on writing skills and journalism training is arguably the most dominant concept in the training of undergraduate public relations practitioners in the United States. This creates a hyperreal image of the practitioner as a legitimate journalist who plays an "objective" role, thus mimicking the role journalists are perceived to play in society and imploding the boundary between simulation and reality. It is no wonder that journalists view the field with skepticism. These perspectives directly relate to my interpretation of Bourdieu's concept of symbolic capital.

Public Relations Practitioners as the Agents of Power

In Chapter 7 I review the concept of agency in terms of economic and human agency and the implications of these theoretical concepts for public relations. I will argue that the concept of economic agency has played an important role in public relations. But here economic agency is particularly relevant in the role of the public relations practitioner as the economic agent of the manager. Vignette 4.1 shows how this agency helps to create and maintain *managerialism* (Deetz, 1992, p. 221). Managerialism implies that management co-opts workers into suppressive workplace practices that benefit managers more than workers and that lead to the formation of a new corporate class system. This creates the appearance that these managers are not ordinary workers but so special that the ordinary rules of organizations do not apply to them.

Ihlen's (2009) application of Bourdieu to public relations focuses on the organization; however, I do not believe it is a helpful reading, particularly not from a postmodern perspective. Ihlen's perspective elevates the organization to a level of struggle, while a postmodern approach focuses on the role of the individual practitioner within a larger network in the particular field in which he operates. Associating public relations practice so closely with institutions and institutionalization undercuts the possibility to critique the institution itself as an oppressive force in society and in public relations practice itself. Ihlen focuses his application of Bourdieu on public relations' need for financial capital, its possession of a specific type of knowledge capital, and social capital through the function's ability to create and operate within social networks; I prefer to focus on Bourdieu's more encompassing perspective of symbolic capital, which he defines as "a reputation for competence and an image of respectability and honourability" (Bourdieu, 1984, p. 291).

Symbolic capital is the socially recognizable form of economic capital and is a necessary form of capital to gain wealth. Symbolic capital is founded on

> symbolic violence ... when domination can only be exercised in its *elementary form*, i.e. directly between one person and another, it cannot take place overtly and must be disguised under the veil of enchanted relationships. [This is] the only way in which relations of domination can be set up, maintained or restored ... through strategies which, being expressly oriented towards the establishment of relations of personal dependence, must be disguised and transfigured lest they destroy themselves by revealing their true nature; in a word, they must be euphamized.
>
> (Bourdieu, 1977, p. 191)

Vignette 4.1 shows clearly how this process works and how important the agent is for wealth creation. This also sets up the link between Bourdieu and Deetz's concept of managerialism, which is discursively constituted, particularly through agents. As economic agency theory in particular states, agents are people acting on the behalf of others called principals. In the case of public relations principals often are powerful organizational managers. Bourdieu (1977) argues agents are interpellated into a system to legitimize the discourse of those in power. The ultimate aim of the managers who utilize the agency of public relations practitioners for their own needs is the accumulation of wealth, "the ultimate basis of power" (Bourdieu, 1977, p. 195). Public relations practitioners in particular are used to create symbolic capital, which is the only way through which economic capital can be accumulated. This application of Bourdieu to public relations practice sets the scene for the introduction of a postmodern interpretation of the relationship between public relations practitioners, power, and knowledge in the context of collective action, specifically in the context of organizations.

Power, Knowledge, and Public Relations

Public relations practitioners are knowledge workers. One might even argue that information, how to deal with information in its many manifestations, and the establishment of powerful connections are the critical resources of public relations practitioners. That places public relations practitioners at the intersection of the debate on how organizations and their powerful actors create knowledge and the appearance of rationality.

Postmodernists also critique management power from perspectives of rationality and control and question managers as rational beings who have the power to make objective decisions (Deetz, 2001). They argue the very notion of management rationality is nothing else but emotional and subjective decisions by political players who use their power not only to exert authority but also shape the organization to their benefit. For instance, women often are accused of bringing their emotions to work. This argument is then used to rationalize why women are incapable of being managers. This leads to the question of what counts as emotions (Mumby & Putnam, 1992). If one thinks this through, the implication is that men have no emotions or do not bring any emotions to work. However, competition, aggression, assertiveness, and anger typically associated with male behavior are all emotionally-based. This is a typical example of how irrational behavior is often framed as rational, appropriate, and logical.

This is an example of what Foucault (1988a, p. 28) means when he says "reason is self-created." By that he does not mean the disappearance or collapse of rationality but rather "multiple transformations" of reason. "Other forms of reason are created endlessly" (p. 35). Rather than being a given truth that exists outside of humans and for humans to find, Foucault argues rationality is based on human and historical practice. Because rationality is man-made it can be unmade through a deconstruction of the history of the specific rational reasoning, particularly when reasoning is used for domination. The example of workplace emotionality above shows how this process takes place but also shows how it can be deconstructed.

Power as Revolving Upward

The concept of discourse further enlightens us on how power is created in organizations. Power at the top of the hierarchy is made possible through institutional practices in the lowest and smallest units of societies. Power revolves upward through institutional practices and not downwards from power at the top of the hierarchy. This is also true for organizations.

Traditionally, the father is designated as the "head of the household," the smallest social unit, and is supposed to serve as a strong role model for his son or sons. The resistance to single mothers or gay households is widely known and partially stems from adherence to this basic organizing principle of Western society. (Not that it does not exist in other societies. The institutionalized power of the man of the family, be it father, brother, or uncle, in Middle-Eastern families is well known.) In this way boys are socialized to be strong, aggressive, and competitive so that they can become leaders in whichever field they choose. They are therefore not supposed to grow up without a strong male role model, which is one of the reasons why single and gay mothers are criticized for raising boys all by themselves. The societal expectations of girls are well known and with women's impulse to lean to community, cooperation, and the use of language to negotiate their way through life they are socialized not to be competitive, strong, and aggressive (Gilligan, 1993).

Once these children go to school and/or attend religious institutions these social roles are further enforced. Although there has been much hand-wringing about school practices that allegedly now empower girls to such an extent that boys have become marginalized, boys are still expected to take on leadership positions in society. They go to business school, become engineers, lawyers, doctors, sport stars, or professionals of one kind or another to fill the leadership positions in the military, law enforcement, commerce, industry, education, and religious institutions—all the institutions that assert power and determine ideology in society. They also earn more than women, who are still only earning 77c to every dollar a man earns.

Financial empowerment is as important to social power as is social structure. Of course not all boys have this privilege because going to college is mostly facilitated by money and even more status is acquired if money and connections allow privileged boys from the upper classes to go to Ivy League colleges where they mix with their own class and further establish the networks that will sustain them through their leadership careers. It only requires an elite few to take on the leadership roles required to maintain a society. In actual fact, too many of these kinds of people might not be good for a society of this nature and might lead to unnecessary competition and conflict. It is fine, and required, if women and other less fortunate men, particularly from minority groups, play the supporting roles. Even in the largest organizations one will find that more than 60 % of employees are women, while very few actually occupy leadership roles in those very same organizations.

Once the basis of power has been created for men in institutions such as the traditional family, the education, sports and entertainment systems, and religious institutions they enter other institutions of power where they expect to be leaders. Their entrance into these institutions often already is facilitated through their powerful connections. They are immediately familiar with the male institutional discourse of power, competition, and assertiveness (or barely hidden aggression) and buy into this because they believe that will take them to the top. They do not question hierarchical structures and know how to use them to gain access to power. Once these men, now even fewer because at this level competition gets tougher, reach the pinnacle of their organizations, they become part of an elite group that is designated for leadership positions in the political field. Empowered by position, power networks, and money they can now become senators, governors, and eventually president. Indeed, few and far between are those women, men from minority groups, or men who do not come from a traditional background who make it to the very top. Although the election of Barack Obama is indeed proof of a major social shift in the United States, he too is a product of an Ivy League education.

This process might explain why, once the most senior positions in public relations become available, the function experiences encroachment, i.e. people with more power (both covert and overt) but little knowledge of communication practice are appointed, often over women who have the academic background and experience. These people, because they do not have the necessary knowledge of the field, perpetuate the myths of practice, namely that it is a reactive practice focusing on crisis communication, publicity, socializing, and event organizing. This is indeed a contributing factor to the image crisis public relations is experiencing.

Disciplining the Subject

Foucault's famous archaeological and genealogical projects form the basis of his analyses of power. These two approaches (Foucault insists they are not methods) offer different but complementary ways to investigate specifically how power comes about. The archaeological project focuses on "rules, discourse, and knowledge" and the genealogical project focuses on "practices, institutions, and power" (Best, 1995, p. 113).

It is particularly the genealogical approach that is important to a postmodern critique of public relations practice, although Foucault's archaeology does explore how knowledge is formed through "a theory of discursive practice" (Foucault, 1973, p. xiv). Although the archaeological project focuses on formal knowledge creation, I believe it clears space for an analysis of how public relations practitioners use discursive practices to shape institutional and individual power on behalf of others through institutional knowledge creation. For Foucault the aim is to overturn forms of domination (Best, 1995). This approach politicizes his work and Foucault now sets out to expose institutional practices that appear to be neutral and benign but in fact are politically violent.

This leads to the postmodern focus on how public relations uses discursive practices to establish perceptions of truth and objectivity and construct binary opposites that devalue certain terms and positions to create and promote organizational ideology. Several recent examples show how spin doctors (I will not call them public relations practitioners) use language to shape public opinion, while also laying bare the underlying ideology of language. In the United States there are efforts on the far right to not refer to President Obama as Barack Obama but rather use his middle name, Hussein. Hussein obviously comes with a lot of symbolic baggage in the United States. As President Obama jokingly said, he was given the name Hussein by someone who never anticipated that he would become the president of the United States. The use of his middle name is an effort to perpetuate the myth that he is actually a Muslim and has close ties with the Muslim world. Another example is the Republican Party's efforts to rename the Democratic Party as the Democratic Socialist Party. Similarly, Bentele and Wehmeier (2009, p. 345) relate how a neoliberal campaign has tried since 2000 to reposition the term *social* in "new social market economy" to be "transformed into a capitalist meaning that is freed from welfare connotations."

Several scholars from organizational communication (e.g. Deetz, 2001, p. 9) argue that a modernist approach to organizations privileges a management discourse and emphasizes upper management's goals for the organization as given and legitimate. Organizations and their functions are evaluated in terms of economic contribution and "rational" economic goals. The goal of the modernist approach is a world that can be controlled through administrative procedures, the elimination of dissension and conflict, and the blind acceptance of organizational goals and roles. The role of communication in this approach is to ensure information transfer from the supervisor to the subordinate to gain compliance and to establish networks to ensure the organization's power in relations with the public. This perspective includes the concepts of strategic message design, management of culture, and total quality management. Theoretical approaches include covering laws, systems approaches, and an emphasis on skills development, particularly in the areas of communication and management (Deetz 2001; Hatch 1997).

Through a process of deconstruction of the language systems used in organizations we come to understand the role public relations practitioners play in creating and maintaining power relations in organizations. Public relations practitioners translate the language of managers into apparently benign and easy-to-understand language. For instance, public relations students are taught in writing classes to use power verbs, short words, and paragraphs, and to adhere to journalistic principles when writing. This contributes to the perception that management language is rational and neutral. Additionally, through their technical skills in web design, content management, blogging, tweeting, videography, graphic design, and other forms of communication, public relations practitioners are used to create perceptions of truth and rationality and create the binary opposites without which modernist systems cannot operate. Practitioners who are not aware of this will not understand how their role is used to "facilitate organizational control and to direct innovation and change" to the benefit of management (Hassard, 1993, p. 117).

One of the main outcomes of this use of language and the social science and human relations approaches so predominant in public relations theory and practice is the concept of administration and control, of which postmodernists are so critical and which they describe as social science engineering (Boje

& Dennehy, 1993). This does not necessarily refer to relationship theory as it has been developed in the field but rather to the belief that there is "an exact science of man" (p. 194). The method that is used is mathematical calculations where human behaviours and human responses become numbers on a spreadsheet. The aim of this form of science is control under the pretension of social goodwill. "Human relationists put on the mantle of the good therapists and appear mild-looking and mild-mannered helpers" (p. 195). This is reminiscent of Foucault's concept of *pastorship*, which he argues is used to rule and control the individual (Foucault, 1988b, p. 60). Pastorship is a deeply paternalistic form of leadership, which Foucault compares to the shepherd responsible for a flock. In societal terms the shepherd is responsible for the behaviour and moral well-being of the flock outside of government structures.

I will return later to a discussion of the relationship building function of public relations but suffice it to say at present that public relations practitioners are very much a part of the pastoral technology system. Their role is to listen to employees who are dissatisfied, have grievances, and even more benignly, have suggestions for process improvement. The role of the public relations practitioner is to ensure that these employees adjust to their work group and that their suggestions align with the aims of upper management, not vice versa. This is done under the pretence of a caring attitude. Through the use of social scientific methods "it became possible to prescribe scientific norms for relating the individual to the group and plan her promotion in the group. Individuals who depart from the norms of the majority are deviates" (Boje & Dennehy, 1993, p. 197). Using social science methods, the objects of research become faceless, mere categories of human beings for whom compassion is impossible (Bauman, 1993). That is one of the reasons, Bauman argues, why rationality leads to the inability to be moral. No wonder that Foucault (1980b, p. 84) argues that our main concern should be with centralized power created through social science discourse, "for it is really against the effects of the power of a discourse that is considered to be scientific that the genealogy must wage its struggle."

The Power of Segmentation

One of the reasons why public relations practitioners use social scientific methods is for the purpose of segmentation. In particular, identifying publics as conceptualized in public relations is a segmentation technique. Let us consider why we use segmentation techniques, which is where the arguments about publics, stakeholders, markets, and so forth come from. All of these terms refer to the segmentation techniques we use and all are aimed at grouping people together so that we can better communicate with them. From a postmodern perspective, the ultimate aim of this segmentation is typical of the social scientific method of creating categories of people for the purposes of administration and control. Thus, the concept of publics most certainly is not a benign term. In this context it directly opposes the aims of participation in the public sphere, which according to Habermas, is where communicative action should take place (Habermas, 1984, 2006). We engage publics to minimize their impact on the organization in particular.

This situation is typical of the aporiae public relations practice as such grapples with. On the one hand, we try to identify those individuals who can harm or advance our cause or organization, and, on the other hand, we also believe that we have a responsibility to promote communication in the public sphere. It is important to remind ourselves that, although this argument is not intended to exclude people from Asia, Africa, and the Middle East from this debate, the philosophers cited here and whose work is used to formulate arguments on the public sphere, such as Lippmann, Dewy, and Habermas (Self, 2009), come from Western philosophical thought. We simply cannot apply these concepts to all countries and all situations.

Traditionally, in Western society the media have played an important part in shaping the public sphere. They have held that they are objective in this process. We know now that that is not true. All information is presented within the framework of the presenter (or signifier) and is not objective knowledge. I believe that part of the demise of traditional news outlets today is partly due to the gatekeeping role and arrogance of the media. For instance, Brian Williams from NBC News advertises his role as "making sense of it all." What arrogance. People are more than capable of making their own sense out of things. We do not need mass media to drive our conversations. Beyond the fact that people themselves are quite fit to do that, we also know that people make sense of things within their own understanding, knowledge, and life experiences. With the new media, it is possible to completely by-pass the traditional media.

Beyond the issue of control, segmentation does not make much sense. Practitioners are imposing their understanding of issues on other people, who might not share their understanding of the issue or agree with the "segment" in which they were placed. It will be better to let go of segmentation. Our environments are far too complex to segment them. Dewey's idea of the public is built on the Enlightenment concept of the individual who is all-powerful in shaping his or her own environment (Self, 2009). The postmodern approach recognizes the complexity inherent in every aspect of our society, both local and global. The individual is not a unified entity but rather fractured with multiple positions and multiple opportunities to resist. This presents a better understanding of the environments in which we have to communicate. That position makes segmentation redundant because individual positions and alliances are never stable but always in flux. I believe the very idea that we can segment our publics is outdated. It might be a theoretical construct but no longer a pragmatic one.

In place of segmentation a return to our belief in and support of a democratic debate in the public sphere presents a better opportunity for us to communicate. We have an obligation to drive debate in the public sphere so that all people have the opportunity to participate in or at least have an opinion about something if they so desire. That is where our social responsibility lies. We now have the means to do that. The many new media formats and outlets allow for much more information seeking behavior and subsequent action. People almost daily go online and check on the issues that are important to them. In some instances they will become involved and in others not, but they never know from day to day.

By opening ourselves, our organizations, or our clients to the discourse of the public through new media platforms, we facilitate the development of postulated communities forming and emerging through discursive practices, i.e. communities formed around ideas and issues through a process of radical dialectics, not through consensus but through *dissensus* (Lyotard, 1988)—a process of *becoming* rather than *being* (Docherty, 1993). In that way our work will be more likely to contribute to the emergence of new ideas and solutions in which anybody who wishes can participate and contribute. This allows for a much more democratic participation in the public sphere. We should rather use the new media to allow anybody who wishes to engage us come to us, rather than us imposing our predetermined categories on others. The prerequisite for this is that practitioners need to create interactive communication channels to assist members of the public to engage them, their organizations, and their causes. Then it is also the duty of those practitioners to engage those people in active discussion, listen to them, and become audience centered rather than organization centered. Lyotard (1984) recognizes the dual purpose of new technologies. While, on the one hand, it has the ability for more control and regulation, it "could aid groups discussing metaprescriptives by supplying them with the information they usually lack for making knowledgeable decisions." This is only possible if "the public [has] free access to the memory and data banks" (p. 67).

In addition to democratizing the public relations process, this also will make the work of practitioners easier. One of the problems with the situational theory (J. E. Grunig, 1983, 1989a, 1997) is its practical application. Although it might be accurate in terms of predicting communication behavior, it is difficult to engage members of publics at an early stage before they become activists. New media environments allow us to identify and engage with individuals within the public sphere at an earlier stage than normal and so secure a democratic social sphere for all.

Bio-power and the Postmodern Subject

Another important contribution Foucault made to the postmodern theorizing of power is the focus on the subject and subjectivity. Diverting from modern interpretations of power as either economic or juridical, Foucault "interprets power as dispersed, indeterminate, heteromorphous, subjectless and productive, constituting individuals' bodies and identities" (Best & Kellner, 1991, pp. 48–49). This postulation of power has significance for public relations practice in that it helps us to understand how organizational practices discipline practitioners and the role practitioners play in disciplining others, while simultaneously creating an understanding of the possibilities of resisting power.

Foucault (1980a) coined the term "bio-power" (p. 140), which is a collective term for the many techniques used to control individuals and whole populations. Bio-power emerged in the 17th century. He described two forms of bio-power that are connected through a complex set of relations but on opposing sides. Thus, the one form makes the other possible. The one he calls "an *anatomo-politics of the human body*" and the other "*regulatory controls: a bio-politics of the population*" [italics in the original] (p. 139). Anatomo-politics focus on procedures of power, the aim of which is the simultaneous usefulness and docility of the body for purposes of economic control, i.e. to utilize the body for economic purposes it also had to be disciplined and controlled. As Bauman (1993) so succinctly put it, the aim was "control of the morally indolent classes" (p. 121). In public relations the use of social scientific methods to understand groups of people with whom institutions need to communicate in an effort to control their behavior for the economic benefit of the organization is typical of anatomo-politics.

Bio-politics, on the other hand, is directed at the regulation of the population (a faceless mass of people with similar traits and specific attributes) through biological processes to ensure its health and propagation; to ensure that there are adequate bodies to accomplish economic production. What differentiate these two forces of bio-power, "this great bipolar technology" (p. 139) from the medieval acceptance of death as the human condition is the "calculated management of life" to ensure the order of life (Foucault, 1980a, pp. 139–140). This led to the direct supervision of the population through newly created scientific methods and the expansion of "fields of knowledge, power and techniques" (Best & Kellner, 1991, p. 50). As Mumby (1996) explained, "subjectivity is an effect of discourse, constructed through the various power/knowledge regimes that constitute the disciplinary mechanisms of our society" (p. 268). Bio-power then describes the process that "takes the modern subject as data to be accounted for, rather than as a source of privileged accounts of the world" (Ferguson, 1993, p. 15).

An understanding of bio-power and its effects in shaping the human as a subject to control through disciplinary procedures of the body (external control through knowledge) and morality (internal control through self-discipline) is essential to the individual's ability to resist systems of power and control. One way to free oneself from this self-imposed discipline is to first understand that these norms and behaviors "are not available to us performed, that they have not been inscribed from the beginning of time in a book of eternal and universal verities" (Racevskis, 2002, p. 140). This understanding develops through subjectivity. Subjectivity refers to "the property of being a subject" (Edgar & Sedgwick, 2002, p. 389) and in the postmodern context represents the process of how one has been constituted as a subject through normalizing and disciplining processes. The only way to resist dominating power is through the deconstruction of the self and reflexivity to create under-standing and self-knowledge.

Postmodernists share a disdain for the uncritical acceptance of power and argue that power is a necessity for each person. Individual power should be a sought-after commodity. Although Foucault's (1980a) concept of bio-power emerged from his analysis of how the discourse about sexuality was actually a discourse on power, he argues that people only tolerate modern power because it is hidden (Foucault, 1975, p. 86). The more hidden power is, the more suc-cessful it is. The only way to expose hidden power is to lay it bare and resist it. Because all relations are concerned with power he argues "as soon as there is a power relation, there is a possibility of resistance. We can never be ensnared by power: we can always modify its grip in determinate conditions and according to precise strategy" (Foucault, 1988c).

Although this does not relate to Foucault's concept of bio-power I have earlier argued that it is possible for individuals to tap into their own bio-power, based on knowledge of those forces of power that govern them and under-standing of the processes they implement that sustain those forces of power. To briefly return to a discussion of ethics, Foucault (1989a) refers to this as "'governmentality' [which] cover the whole range of practices which consti-tute, define, organize and instrumentalize the strategies individuals in their freedom can use in dealing with each other" (p. 448). He argues that the more freedom there is in societies the bigger the desire to control each other. Ethics are the responsible care of freedom for both the self and the Other. To be able to care for the freedom of the other it is important to take care of the self. To take care of the self it is important to know oneself. It is this knowledge (or knowledges) that will allow practitioners to identify forms of power and resist or subvert them.

Public relations practitioners are in a particularly strong position to resist this kind of domination because they are expected to communicate with stakeholders, who have become increasingly important to organizations. For instance, organizations are instructing their employees to put their customers first. This has led to the decentering of management in favor of a stakeholder perspective (Hatch & Cunliffe, 2006). Evidence already exists to support this trend. I reported in an earlier study (Holtzhausen, 2005) that South Afri-can public relations practitioners adopt an asymmetrical stance that favors the interests of external stakeholders over that of the organization because of heavy government pressure on organizations to adapt to political and social changes in their environment. Although this is enforced through government regula-tion, practitioners recognize the political nature of the process and respond accordingly.

The Political Nature of Public Relations Power

One of the attributes of modernist power is the lack of a central point of power that can be resisted. In some sense, this is a blind kind of power because it is "impotent" (Foucault, 1989b, p. 258), which created the necessity to create relationships between forms of knowledge and control. Similarly, Deleuze and Guattari (as cited in Best & Kellner, 1991, pp. 102–103) use the term *rhizomatics* to explain how power permeates society while they use the concept of "nomadic movement" to explain how one can free oneself from "all roots, bonds, and identities, and thereby resist the state and all normalizing power." What these philosophers have in common is the way they describe power as multidirectional. But even though it is multidirectional it still forms part of a system that aims to control and discipline through a process of micropolitics. As explained earlier, it is exactly through micropolitics, i.e. power structures at the lower levels of society, that macropolitics, i.e. more centralized power, is made possible. Three postmodern approaches are relevant to a discussion of public relations practice and political power, namely, the relational nature of power as explained by Foucault and Deleuze and Guattari, the concepts of grand narratives, and the *differend* as postulated by Lyotard.

The Relational Nature of Power

Over the past 20 years or so public relations practice as relationship building has become a dominant approach in public relations research in the United States (e.g. Ledingham & Bruning, 2000). Vignette 4.1 also emphasizes how the practitioner was expected to build relationships or make connections for the powerful CEO to ensure a power structure not only embedded in the organization but also in other power structures in society. This example shows how intuitively people in power understand power and use it to influence and dominate. This relational attribute of power is recognized in other theoretical approaches such as network theory (Barney, 2004) and complexity theory, particularly as it is applied to public relations practice (Gilpin & Murphy, 2009).

Complexity theory, in particular, argues that during times of crisis or chaos the system goes into self-organizing mode that eventually leads to a new and better system. I have argued that postmodernism diverges from complexity theory in that it focuses on the role of power during times of chaos and shows how already powerful people use such situations to realign, maintain, and strengthen their power (Holtzhausen, 2007). It was interesting to watch this process during the South African transition to a democratic society. Organizations, including government departments, were under enormous pressure to appoint more Black South Africans. This necessarily meant that a great many White South Africans lost their jobs. However, those in the most senior positions somehow managed to maintain their own positions while getting rid of White South Africans at lower level. Cynically, these senior managers openly stated their support for transformation, but only as long as they did not have to transform themselves. Thus it is specifically during times of dramatic change that it is important for public relations practitioners to be cognizant of how their power is used and for them to resist the re-emergence of unfair and exploitative power.

So, is it wrong to theorize public relations practice as relationship building? Of course not. But it will be important to ensure that relationships are built with exactly those people who have been marginalized and ignored previously. To merely build relationships that will benefit the organization will not do justice to the practice as activism. This also will require a much wider definition of stakeholders. If one deconstructs the concept of *principal* in economic agency theory, principals should include communities that facilitate businesses through tax breaks and investment incentives and taxpayers whose money is used to facilitate big business in every conceivable way. Depending on the level of economic development of a country, it is important to remember that many people might not have access to modern communication technologies. Relying on technology to build relationships through networking will be very important but it also will be important for practitioners to emerge themselves in stakeholder communities to truly try and understand what their issues are. It is important for practitioners to remember that power is diffused and spread throughout society in many different sites or nodes. One way to resist power is in the same way. By building relationships with disempowered groups practitioners help marginalized communities build their own power resources.

One of the main foci for postmodernists is hidden sources of power. To expose them is also to disempower and resist them. Instead of resisting hierarchical power at the macro level, it is more effective to resist power at the very nodes where it exists. Thus resistance to power should be diffused and should be a form of micropolitical or "nomadic" struggle (Deleuze & Guattari, 1987, p. 159). Instead of accepting the status quo, it is important for public relations practitioners to resist controlling power in organizations through micropolitical struggles. This can be done through the creation of alliances with diverse marginalized groups in the organization and society and by resisting the use of public relations' voice to further assert power. This can be done through creating platforms and opportunities for open and free discussion and by making senior managers aware when they ignore the voices of different organizational constituencies. In this way practitioners can give voice to the silences, i.e. speak up for those whose voices have been ignored or speak up on issues that in the political process are being swept under the rug. Similar to those in society, hegemonic discourses in organizations can be dismantled through the use of language and a postmodern dialectic rather than a dialogic approach (Lyotard & Thébaud, 1985).

It might, however, be difficult for practitioners to resist domination and power exactly because it is so ubiquitous and pervasive. In organizations, for instance, employees' actions are highly regulated through administrative procedures such as job specifications, policies, and procedures. There also are many technologies that, more than ever, can trace what employees are doing, where they are, and what they say by tracing communication through emails, telephone calls, automated entrance and exit procedures, and many more. In agency environments, for instance, every call and every minute of the day has to be accounted for and billed to a client. The result of this immanence of power in a panoptic society (Foucault, 1975) is that people discipline themselves and so internalize their own submission. In this way it becomes easy for people in powerful positions to control the less powerful, without having to adhere to these principles themselves.

A study among members of the Arthur Page Society found that middle managers were more likely to consider the organization's vision, mission, and strategic intent when making decisions about corporate philanthropy than more senior members, who were more likely to make these decisions based on corporate politics (Nunemaker-Bynum, 2000). The results indicated senior practitioners did not view themselves as regular employees but rather as a separate class of people who did not have to consider such "minor" issues as organizational strategy. As a result they were more likely to break the rules than their more junior counterparts. In this way the organizational strategy itself became a disciplinary tool to ensure compliance at lower levels (Bynum, 2000). This is an example of the incidence of managerialism in organizations.

"The impossible consensus"

In Chapter 2 I argued that dissensus provides the best opportunity for ethical public relations practice. Dissensus also has an application in terms of power and it is worth repeating some of my previous arguments and expanding on them in a discussion of power and public relations practice. I do this because I believe the concept of dissensus is crucial to our understanding of postmodern public relations practice and public relations as activist practice will be impossible without understanding this concept.

"The impossible consensus" is what Lyotard and Thébaud (1985, p. 3) called the first day of their conversation. Lyotard's explication of *consensus*, however, goes well beyond that of agreement through dialogue. He links dialogic discourse and consensus within the context of persuasion. The debate about public relations as persuasion or two-way symmetry is well known but Lyotard also views dialogic communication as a form of persuasion. He describes the person using persuasion as "the maker of simulacra, of the sly one, the one who deceives" and "who seeks to produce effects upon the other, effects that the other does not control" (p. 4). This is very similar to the concept of two-way asymmetrical communication as conceptualized in the Excellence Theory, where the ultimate aim of social science research is to persuade publics to do the bidding of the organization (J. E. Grunig, 2001, p. 12).

Two-way symmetry is generally interpreted as dialogue, as a two-way conversation between a communicative entity and its "publics." Lyotard argues that dialogue itself is persuasion of a different kind and is directed at the Other in the conversation in order to "control or contribute to the control of, these effects" (p. 4). In public relations theory two-way symmetry is aimed at this kind of mutual control and mutual change (L. A. Grunig et al., 2002). Lyotard thus associates dialogic discourse with a desire for power because the ultimate aim is "controlling the effects of the statements exchanged by the partners of the dialogue" (Lyotard & Thébaud, 1985, p. 4). Dialogue erases the possibility of politics because dialogue only can take place when everyone in the discussion has agreed on the rules and the "language game" in play under these circumstances. He describes consensus as "the manufacture of a subject that is authorized to say 'we'" (p. 81), which means that in addition to the underlying agreement of the rules of the language game, the one with the most power has the ability to determine the outcome of the discussion.

He further argues that the rules determining language games are not denotative but prescriptive. Even in the sciences the language games used are prescriptive in nature (Lyotard, 1984). He critiques Habermas for suggesting that it is possible for all participants to reach universal consensus by agreeing on the rules of a universal language game, which will make a truly democratic and emancipatory debate possible. Lyotard argues that all language games are highly heterogeneous and pragmatic, determined by the immediate players in the game. Contrarily, consensus is an "outmoded and suspect value" (p. 66) in the search for justice. He proposes recognizing the heterogeneity of the rules of all language games. If the outcome of language games is dissent it will lead to a more just system. The ultimate rule for language games is that the rules of consensus should be determined locally by those who are participating in the game. The inherent persuasive nature of all communication is likely the reason why it is difficult to move symmetrical communication from a normative to a positive theory.

The question then arises: What would replace consensus as public relations practice? Postmodernists argue for dissensus and dissymmetry. First, it will be important for practitioners to understand the concept of the *differend* (Lyotard, 1984). When a member or members of the public complain about the actions of a communicative entity or even when the practitioner is in such a position, as in Vignette 4.1, a *differend* will occur when

> the plaintiff is divested of the means to argue and becomes for that reason a victim. … A case of differend between two parties takes place when the "regulation" of the conflict that opposes them is done in the idiom of one of the parties while the wrong suffered by the other is not signified in that idiom.
>
> (Lyotard, 1988, p. 9)

This is particularly the case in capitalist organizations where the conflict is more often than not cast in economic terms, while the relevant publics most likely have other concerns such as community health, environmental sustainability, or cultural and religious beliefs, as in Vignette 2.2. Lyotard (1988) refers to these different frames of reference as *genres of discourse* that are incommensurable. In these cases it is important for the practitioner to recognize the extent and depth of the differences and make the parties aware of them. Agreement can never be forced because it will result in injustice since the most powerful player in the consensus process will always have the upper hand, as stated before.

Dissensus, on the other hand, is a much more powerful strategy to affect change (Docherty, 1993; Lyotard, 1992, 1993a). While consensus represents a philosophy of Being, dissensus represents a philosophy of Becoming (Docherty, 1993), which means consensus aims at arresting the flow of new ideas and does violence to language games. The sense of *becoming* is an important concept in postmodernism. Lyotard articulates the idea of becoming in a conversation with Thébaud he says his writing is "an attempt to produce a new book ... I have written books that have been sent off like bottles to the sea" (Lyotard & Thébaud, 1985, p. 6). This implies that thoughts and ideas are sent off never to return or never to return in the same form. This is the essence of dissensus, i.e. never going back to try and determine the correct meaning of what was said, which is impossible, but rather going forward finding new meanings and new solutions. This concept is of great importance to public relations practitioners because far too often consensus is determined by those in power (see Holtzhausen, 2000 for examples and a thorough discussion of consensus), which limits free speech and growth of ideas.

Respect for and acceptance of differing viewpoints is of the utmost importance to Lyotard because he believes terror reigns when participants cannot raise issues outside of the accepted system (Williams, 1998). To describe these deep philosophical divisions between participants in a conversation Lyotard (1993a) uses the term "tensors" (p. 54). I have argued previously (Holtzhausen, 2000) that a typical example of a tensor is the debate between public relations and marketing and journalism respectively. Each of these disciplines comes from a different philosophical place and cannot be compared. As a result the debate about which is the best approach or more ethical approach is futile because the underlying philosophical assumptions are incommensurable.

Creedon (1993) introduces the term *dissymmetry* and explains it as symmetry in different directions. I believe dissymmetry also is useful to understand the postmodern approach to power as multidirectional. However, I would rather interpret dissymmetry as multidirectional dissensus, i.e. promoting conflict and difference at every node of the power network. This will inevitably put practitioners in their boundary spanning role at the center of organizational conflict. They now will have to choose sides and speak out in an ethically responsible way on the side of the party to which an injustice is taking place. In the case of tensors, practitioners will need to make the different parties aware of the depth of their conflict but cannot force any resolution. This approach certainly is outside established public relations practice but so is the whole concept of activist practice.

The Political Struggle

Metanarratives vs. little narratives and macropolitics vs. micropolitics are as inherent to a discussion of power and politics as the consensus/dissensus debate and are the essence of the postmodern condition. "Simplifying to the extreme, I define postmodern as incredulity toward metannarratives," Lyotard (1984, p. xxiv) famously said. But what is a metanarrative? Lyotard associates a metanarrative with a "grand narrative" or a "metadiscourse," which is a philosophy "to legitimate knowledge" (p. xxiv). In other words, a metanarrative, as also explained in Chapter 3 in terms of upper case history, is a system of meaning that tries to include all other narratives in an effort to legitimate itself. Metanarratives are typically ideological or at least support forms of dominating ideologies. The purpose of metanarratives is to normalize and standardize thought and suppress alternative voices. Lyotard focuses in particular on the sciences, a topic I will explore again in Chapter 6.

What we can take away from his interpretation of metanarratives is that the ultimate aim of metanarratives, be it in society or in the sciences, is to control, which makes their purpose political. Metanarratives can be resisted through little narratives, which should always be local and temporary. Through a process of reflexivity it is the duty of the narrator to always question the narrative put out for consumption. Thus the creation of little narratives also becomes an important factor in the struggle against domination. Foucault (1980b) too holds this view, namely, that it is important to acknowledge their legitimacy because it is through "local popular knowledges, these qualified knowledges, that criticism performs its work" (p. 82). What his genealogical project does "is to entertain the claims to attention of local, discontinuous, disqualified, illegitimate knowledges against the claims of a unitary body of theory, which would filter, hierarchies and order them in the name of some true knowledge" (p. 83). To create little narratives can be compared to a guerilla tactic, i.e. coming out of the blue and at a place and time nobody expected.

A consistent theme in this book is the way public relations practitioners are used to create metanaratives in organizations and in society on behalf of those in power. Also, public relations theories and practices are used to sustain the ideology of capitalism, often times predatory capitalism, as is evident from those practitioners and the academic who defended the use of taxpayers' bailout money for a trip to Las Vegas. But capitalism is not the only metanarrative that is promoted in this way. Public relations practice is used to defend political ideologies and religious beliefs and to sustain discrimination on issues such as gay rights. One can argue that these are merely issues put out in the marketplace of ideas to be argued and discussed. However, these issues are virtually without exception sustained by existing ideologies and systems of power deeply embedded in ideological discourse and that cannot survive without exerting their power in the public sphere. What little narratives also imply is the legitimation of alternative perspectives and knowledges. Public relations practitioners can no longer depend on aggregates of opinions collected through social science research. Their role as activist practitioners will be to divert from these types of research practices in favor of emergence in marginalized communities and so legitimate their knowledge, experiences, and interpretations, through a process which is anecdotal, "savors detail and reserves a special place for what is unique in each and every life" (Rosenau, 1992, p. 83).

Segmentation is yet another process of control that is linked to metanarratives (Deleuze & Guattari, 1987; Lyotard, 1984). The ultimate aim of control is to ensure the efficiency of the system's performance. Lyotard and Deleuze and Guattari argue segmentation overlooks the complexity of society and is an oversimplification.

> The decision makers … attempt to manage these clouds of sociality according to input/output matrices, following a logic which implies that their elements are commensurable and that the whole is determinable. They allocate our lives for the growth of power. In matters of social justice and of scientific truth alike, the legitimation of that power is based on its optimizing the system's performance—efficiency. The application of this criterion to all of our games necessarily entails a certain level of terror, whether soft or hard: be operational (that is commensurable) or disappear.
>
> (Lyotard, 1984, p. xxiv)

Similarly, Deleuze and Guattari (1987) say, "We are segmented from all around and in every direction. The human being is a segmentary animal" (p. 208). In contrast to segmentation in primitive societies, segmentation in modern states is linked to centrality of control. First, the state and institutions exert control over those segments not allowed to sustain or survive. Second, they create their own segments for their own purposes. These segments are rigid and it is difficult to escape them. This kind of segmentation functions particularly strongly on binary opposites and the main question should not be so much about the status of those on the negative side of the binary opposite but about the type of organization that benefits from the particular segmentation strategy.

In public relations practice one might argue that organizations benefit from paying female practitioners less by merely viewing them as not as efficient as men. To take Deleuze and Guattari's argument to full conclusion in this example, it is not so much that these systems or institutions view women as inferior as that the capitalist system benefits from such segmentation. In actual fact, these systems know that they get top-quality and well-qualified workers at less pay, which makes the segmentation even more important. This is but one example of how segmentation supports the capitalist system. There are many systems of segmentation based on race, culture, ethnicity, social orientation, social development, education, geography, income, age, and so forth that are used in this way. Deleuze and Guattari further argue that these segments are closed and rigid, "The segments, once underscored and overcoded, seem to lose their ability to bud" (p. 212). Geometry and arithmetic are the two techniques used in this process, which allows the different segments to relate to each other; "the wage regime establishes a correspondence between monetary segments, production segments, and consumable-goods segments" (p. 212).

Here again the issue of segmentation in public relations practice comes to the fore. In the same way that segmentation leads to an undemocratic communication environment, the many segmentation techniques (so inherent in the social science research methods public relations theorists and practitioners use) lead to discriminatory practices that further enhance the power of a few. This is done by segmenting people into categories and then treating them according to those categories. For instance, if women between 18 and 35 are the most influential in terms of buying a certain product or voting on a particular issue, the other groups are ignored. If the lack of affluence of a certain group is not beneficial to an organization, they are left out of the communication process. However, those in powerful positions never allow themselves to be segmented and categorized. Those rules of society are not for them, as explained in Chapter 2.

In a next step, segmentation is linked to resistance. Deleuze and Guattari (1987) make a distinction between molar and molecular segmentation. Molar segmentation refers to rigid categories, e.g. typical of those we refer to as demographic segments, while molecular segmentation refers to segments within molar segments. The two segmentation techniques facilitate each other. "If we consider the great binary aggregates, such as sexes or classes, it is evident that they also cross over into molecular assemblages of a different nature, and there is a double dependency between them" (p. 213). This interdependency also links macropolitics and micropolitics. To resist macropolitics it is important to participate in micropolitics because macropolitics would not be able to exist if "molecular escapes ... did not return to the molar organizations to reshuffle their segments, their binary distribution of sexes, classes, and parties" (pp. 216–217). As soon as molecular movements show signs of deviance they are again *reterritorialized* and *overcoded* (similar to coded all over again) (p. 220).

All these philosophers have in common resistance to power through micropolitical struggle, for example, it might be important to resist being segmented or segmenting certain people in a certain way. Both Lyotard and Foucault refer to the local and regional resistance to power through the use and legitimation of regional knowledges, while Deleuze and Guattari propose a micropolitical struggle through "rhizomatics" (Deleuze & Guattari, 1987, p. 15). To understand their concept of rhizomatics it is important to know that a rhizome refers to a rootlike plant a "horizontal subterranean plant stem that is often thickened by reserved food material, produces shoots above and roots below, and is distinguished from a root in possessing buds, nodes, and usu. scalelike leaves" (*Webster's new collegiate dictionary*, 1975, p. 994). They juxtapose the metaphor of the rhizome with the metaphor of the tree and its roots. While a rhizome is capable of independent and uncontrolled growth, the roots of the tree are always attached to the centrality of the tree trunk, as are the branches and leaves. While the metaphor of the tree (the molar system) describes its links to the roots (the molecular system), i.e. the link between macropolitics and micropolitics, rhizomatics describes a different kind of micropolitics based on the metaphor of the rhizome. "The rhizome itself assumes very diverse forms, from ramified surface extension in all directions to concretion into bulbs and tumors" (Deleuze & Guattari, 1987, p. 7). They describe the properties of the rhizome as

> [p]rinciples of connection and heterogeneity: any point of a rhizome can be connected to anything other, and must be. This is very different from the tree or root, which plots a point, fixes an order … A rhizome ceaselessly establishes connections between semiotic chains, organizations of power, and circumstances relative to the arts, sciences, and social struggles.
>
> (p. 7)

Rhizomes also adhere to the principle of multiplicity. "A multiplicity has neither subject nor object, only determinations, magnitudes, and dimensions" (p. 8). A multiplicity is something that does not have a central value or meaning but rather multiple meanings and therefore can always escape categories or segmentation. Rhizomes cannot be destroyed. Where the rhizomatic line is broken, it will again grow somewhere, which is a metaphor for a micropolitical struggle that always creates a line of flight because macrosystems can always exert themselves (through processes such as public relations practice) and because microsystems such as "[g]roups and individuals contain microfascisms just waiting to crystallize" (pp. 9–10). Rhizomes allow one to establish "a line of flight, enabling one to blow apart strata, cut roots, and make new connections" (p. 15).

Again the implications for postmodern public relations practices become clear. Through a process of micropolitical struggle or rhizomatics practitioners can help to break down segments at both the macro and micro levels and so destabilize power systems. They can do this through challenging the very process of segmentation, by broadening their views on stakeholders, destabilizing existing meanings and understandings, and always coming up with new ideas.

Resistance Strategies for Activist Practitioners

As Deleuze and Guattari, Lyotard, and Foucault suggest, activist public relations practitioners will have strategies to resist power. But these are not resistance strategies to everything and anything; these are strategies only aimed at breaking down hegemonic and centralized power, dehumanizing behavior, and unfair practices. Not every situation is unfair or a struggle. Most public relations work takes place in shared genres of discourse where there is equal distribution of information. But when there are tensors, a lack of information, an unequal distribution of power, or any other postmodern moment activist practitioners have to become involved. Since power is something everybody needs the implication is that while there is resistance to dominating power, there should be facilitation of multidirectional power, which in its turn also can resist and decenter hegemonic power structures. The concept of resistance in public relations is not new (Berger & Reber, 2006; Holtzhausen, 2000; Holtzhausen & Voto, 2002) and it will be worthwhile for activist practitioners to have at hand an array of resistance strategies.

The need to pursue change in organizations and society has never been greater. Nearly ten years ago I remarked that people might wonder why it is necessary to pursue change when "capitalism is thriving and public relations is playing an important role in making this possible" (Holtzhausen, 2000, p. 100). However, recent developments in particularly multinational conglomerates and financial institutions laid bare the moral bankruptcy of capitalism in some quarters, undoubtedly facilitated in many ways by public relations practices. It truly is time for public relations activists to stand up and be counted.

There are different postmodern perspectives on forms of resistance and one, in particular, focuses on whether it is best to stay in a system and resist from within or to leave and work from without. I would argue that it depends. Sometimes working from within cannot change the system and one might have to leave, like the case of Wendell Potter who was a corporate public relations executive for CIGNA. Potter left his job when he could not reconcile his conscience with his organization's resistance to health care reform (Potter, 2009). The argument is not about leaving or staying but about legitimation. Legitimation should not come "by inclusion or identification with dominant forms" but rather through opposition to domination, an act of "disidentification" (Connor, 1989, p. 236). Drawing on Pêcheux, Connor argues *identification* means living within the terms of a certain discourse. In public relations this is similar to the Berger and Reber (2006, p. 226) arguments on how practitioners can gain influence as public relations practitioners. *Counteridentification* "is the mode of the trouble-maker who stays within a governing structure of ideas, but reverses its terms" (Connor, 1989, p. 237). *Disidentification* happens when one leaves the agreed upon terms of engagement and engages from the outside.

Postmodernists generally do not promote disidentification and are against destructive opposition that can lead to nihilism; they warn against self-destruction (Deleuze & Guattari, 1983). Foucault (Eribon, 1991) argues for engagement at the local level and several times traveled to other countries in support of some local cause in a particular environment. This struggle also is never-ending because power permeates our world and always shifts its grip. For that reason activist public relations practitioners always need to be on the lookout for instances of autocratic power. "As soon as there is a power relation, there is a possibility of resistance. We can never be ensnared by power: we can always modify its grip in determinate conditions and according to precise strategy" (Foucault, 1988c, p. 123). The ultimate purpose of resistance to power is "showing what is intolerable in a situation that makes it truly intolerable" (Eribon, 1991, p. 234). Postmodernists thus rather promote counteridentification. Lyotard (1993a) said, "We need not leave this place where we are ... there is no good place" (p. 262).

Knowledge and Insight as the Basis for Resistance

Coming to grips with the complexity of life is a prerequisite to gaining the knowledge and understanding that facilitates empowerment. "Resistance and empowerment emerge out of conditions of understanding the complex relationship among knowledge, power, and social structure, and the ability to constitute alternatives to dominant framing of this relationship" (Mumby, 1996, p. 284). Thus, practitioners who have a desire to reduce complex issues to simplistic solutions, such as linear cause-and-effect relationships, will not understand why they even need to resist dominant power structures because dominant power structures often force reductionist solutions. Complexity implies uncertainty; thus, coming to grips with the uncertainty brought on by complexity and embracing the notion that there is no single correct answer to problems but a multitude of possibilities is a first step toward becoming an activist practitioner.

To truly understand the role a public relations activist can play it is important to understand what the critical resources of practitioners are. One can make a strong argument that information is that critical resource, be it in the process of relationship building, promotion of debate in the public sphere, or knowledge building in an organization or society. The question is: Whose information is privileged? As discussed so many times in this book, it is clear that the penchant for most practitioners is to legitimate and privilege the information of managers over that of workers or external stakeholders. One way to resist that reflex action is for practitioners to become "critical worker researchers" (Kincheloe & McLaren, 1994, p. 174). This implies a questioning of existing organizational practices, an analysis of one's own role in the creation and maintenance of the organizational hierarchy, and the legitimation of the knowledge and experience of co-workers (Foucault, 1980b; Garrison, 1989).

Encouraging "alternative discourse communities"

Encouraging reflexivity and initiating discussions about issues of power among co-workers would be one way of addressing this issue. Discursive strategies can raise awareness of and resistance to power, particularly by encouraging "alternative discourse communities" both internally and externally to the organization (Mumby, 1996, pp. 281–282). Discursive communities will help people to become postmodern subjects who are able to resist power and who can clearly articulate their position of resistance (Birch, 1992, p. 293). I have previously noted that there is ample evidence that public relations practitioners do display activist behavior in their organizations and so become organizational activists. Discursive communities also can be facilitated within organizational settings where it is important to ensure that the knowledge of co-workers are legitimated and recognized. Building relationships with informal leaders and employees who are outspoken about organizational practices in general is an example of how a discursive community can begin. Not all employees are fearful of retribution and one strategy is to identify other internal activists in other departments to form a discursive community for the informal discussion of issues. Having an open door and creating a safe space where people know they can come in and talk also encourages the formation of discursive communities. It will be important that these communities in themselves do not become thought police or drown out the voices of others. Ethical responsibility remains the most important aspect of the postmodern practitioner.

Another way to ensure that co-worker practices are recognized is to treat strategic planning as emerging from the knowledge and experience of those who work on the frontlines of the organization every day, such as those working with customers, clients, suppliers, community members, and other stakeholder groups. Rather than communicating the strategic plan devised by top management downward a more appropriate approach would be a reversed strategic planning process that originates from employees at lower levels and revolves upward for top management input and re-alignment. This does not mean that top management should not have any inputs but rather that top management, when making final decisions about strategic intent and direction, should consider the contributions of all employees who, after all, are the people who have to execute the strategic plan. In my own practice departmental strategic planning was always a team effort. Each employee led the strategic planning session on her area of responsibility, with input and open discussion from others in the department. If it can be afforded, it is good to leave the office environment and get an outside facilitator. Whichever technique is used, employees learn a great deal about the process of strategic planning and build important skills in the facilitation of open discussion. Internal activism also means that public relations practitioners should resist the marginalization of certain organizational functions, such as the public relations function itself, against dominant functions, e.g. marketing and accounting, that often drown out concern for stakeholders in favor of short term capital gain and focus all the attention on consumers or the financial community.

To facilitate external discursive communities practitioners will need to become involved in the communities they serve as practitioners. I still find it surprising how infrequently stakeholders use opportunities for interactive communication between organizations and their stakeholders. Few people realize that a good way to engage an organization is through its public relations department and that they can likely find the email address of an organization's communication practitioner if they search an organizational website. Often practitioners do not provide their email addresses but only a mailing address. That is done deliberately because many practitioners have no desire to engage individuals from the public and it becomes a strategy of suppressing open communication, often because practitioners do not have the necessary conflict resolution skills.

Additionally, practitioners will need to actively promote dissensus by being honest when the views of these communities represent the existence of a tensor. They also will need to clearly articulate the existence of the tensor to the communicative entities they are representing. By being entrepreneurial, original, and creative public relations practitioners can become activists and can continuously recreate themselves and their practice. Through promoting diverse ideas and legitimating many different and heterogeneous forms of meaning and understanding through their practice public relations practitioners will contribute to a more meaningful and participative form of democracy that will also benefit those they represent. Discursive communities also can be facilitated by encouraging communicative entities to speak out on humanitarian and environmental issues and encouraging community participation in discussion and activism on these issues, even if it means taking on government actions.

Personal Power

I previously argued that Foucault's term bio-power also can apply to the power of the individual. An individual can gain or tap into his bio-power if he understands the forces of power governing him and how he contributes to sustaining those forces. In this way bio-power can act subversively to resist dominant power. It will be very difficult to resist power if the practitioner herself is part of the organization's power structure. Practitioners often express how being too close to organizational power structures contributes to mistrust of the practitioner and the public relations function in general. But public relations executives do use various subversive tactics such as whistle-blowing or counterculture initiatives to affect organizational decisions and so become organizational activists even when they are part of the dominant coalition (Berger & Reber, 2006). Perhaps the best kept secret in public relations practice is the fact that practitioners do use their media contacts to fight issues they cannot resolve within the organization. But generally practitioners strive to have a seat at the table. This can be problematic as the research of Kanter, as cited in Boje and Dennehy (1993) showed. In Kanter's study middle managers became socialized in organizations by being taught the values of upper management. Admittance to the dominant coalition was based on conformity to its values and action. This led to self-censorship and a loss of self. Not being in the dominant coalition obviously can have an effect on the practitioner's formal power but practitioners do find ways to gain that without being embedded in formal power structures. They argue they can obtain personal influence by building relationships with influential people inside and outside the organization. Mid-level practitioners build personal relationships with top executives, CEOs, or top influencers in the community rather than relying on authoritative power (Holtzhausen & Voto, 2002). In that way they can secure their sense of self and be allowed to speak out without jeopardizing their positions.

What is important in resistance is that practitioners need to use their personal power to resist unfair or untruthful actions. This necessitates an immediacy of action that stems from situational decision-making and micropolitics. As discussed in Chapter 2, practitioners will need to open themselves to the moral impulse, which will be triggered by focusing on issues of injustice or inhumane actions. This implies an ethical responsibility and immediate action triggered in the individual himself rather than ethical responsibilities formulated for him by others. Because power revolves upward macropolitical changes need to start at the micrological level. By becoming involved in immediate action through micropolitics practitioners can start chains of reaction that can eventually create significant change. They can do this by building alliances and identifying possible areas of micropolitical power with which they can align their practice. Through awareness of how power is constituted practitioners can resist at the very moment when a situation with the potential for unfair or harmful treatment emerges. This can happen in apparently insignificant ways, such as through an email from someone outside the organization, reading a news report, or witnessing unfair workplace treatment.

Workplace Practices that Promote Resistance

Several organizational scholars have made suggestions for practical strategies to resist dominating power and promoting power sharing. Employees increasingly would be confronted with dualistic modern and postmodern power modes, e.g. autocratic organizational power vs. relational power. The idea is to "rebel and go underground" (Boje & Dennehy, 1993, p. 317). Informal power networks can be more powerful than formal ones. To break down the extreme differentiation and specialization of modern organizations, practitioners should strive to learn new skills and become involved in different work groups. Boje and Dennehy suggest flat organizational structures, development of circle networks, and network planning as postmodern strategies to resist postmodern power.

In my own practice I always implemented a flat departmental structure, even operating within a bureaucratic system. In such a scenario each employee becomes an expert in his area and the team leader in terms of that specific expertise when planning or implementing projects. All employees work on all projects and so learn the skills of their co-workers through observation and, eventually, execution. This leads to de-differentiation and multiskilling, which makes employees more marketable and empowered when they decide to move on. Accepting that employees will move on as their skills sets develop is a fact of life and should be encouraged and welcomed. I have always viewed it as a compliment when an employee found a more senior job because it implied that I did mine.

Another form of participative and empowering practice is postmodern network planning, which is planning that "bring[s] the ad hoc stakeholders together to shape, bend and untwist the network relations" (Boje & Dennehy, 1993, p. 84). Network planning would include a wide array of stakeholders, including internal and external customers, and would consider the interests of the communities in which organizations are situated as well as the environment. The stakeholder is at the center of the planning process, i.e. in public relations terms it will be audience-centered and members will be "social auditors, employees, managers, customers, vendors, and stockholders" (p. 85). This is similar to the concept of emergent strategy, as discussed above. Other useful resistance strategies are delegation and empowerment, quick modification of plans, decentralization, and rebellion through the promotion of conflict, similar to the promotion of dissensus (pp. 142–143).

Social network theory holds that the way to understand power in organizations is to understand the "network of relationships that exist between social actors" (Bouquet & Birkinshaw, 2008, p. 484). In a radical reading of social network theory, I would argue that it can be related to an extent to Deleuze and Guattari's (1987) description of centralized power. Bouquet and Birkinshaw (2008) argue that the power relations in networks provide critical resources, which they argue "is of paramount importance to the pursuit of power, irrespective of legitimacy objectives" (p. 484). I have previously argued that the critical resource for public relations practitioners is information. To have power public relations practitioners need access to information. However, the aim of the postmodern practitioners is not to control information but to *disperse* it through the many informal networks they have established. Thus, instead of creating a network that circles back to central power, the postmodern practitioner will create rhizomatic networks, which will never lead back to confirm established power networks but rather always find ways to escape management, or even personal, control over information.

Bouquet and Birkinshaw (2008) propose more strategies for gaining power that also are reminiscent of Deleuze and Guattari's (1987) strategies for resistance, i.e. having new ideas, entrepreneurship that involves the pursuit of new opportunities, profile building, creating projects that benefit the environment or marginalized communities, and breaking rules (not the law). Strategies to gain power are the disruption of hierarchies, implementing organizational strategies in ways that benefit marginalized groups, and the "cooptation of elites" to "facilitate the continuous exchange of information and expertise" (p. 496). They also suggest that low-power actors use their communication skills and technology to influence local and international public opinion to "promote the adoption of advanced practices such as labor rights, environmental standards, and economic and social working conditions" (p. 497). These are all practical examples of projects activist practitioners can champion and facilitate in their own work environments.

Practitioners will experience management resistance because of team work and it might feel to them that they also delegate their power. However, based on Foucault's (1989a) concept of governmetality, Ibarra-Colado, Clegg, Rhodes, and Kornberger (2006) argue that by taking care of the freedom of others managers themselves become ethical subjects. This means that ethics cannot be invoked to control the behavior of others. Resistance through different forms of networks, be they informal discursive communities, network planning, work groups, team work, shared responsibilities, and promotion of co-worker skills, also takes care of ethics of the self as much as recognizing the importance of power for others.

5

PUBLIC RELATIONS AND
THE POSTMODERN TURN
IN ORGANIZATION THEORY

Surely one of the great ironies of the modern world is that democracy, imperfect as it is in the political realm, seldom extends to the workplace. In fact, most U.S. citizens do not even question the fact that they are required to "check their voice at the door" of the shop or office.

(Cheney, 1995, pp. 167–168)

Despite the far-reaching changes new technology has wrought in public relations practice, fundamentally the work of communication practitioners has not changed. Practitioners still manage communication, build relationships, and are professional communicators who formally communicate with publics on behalf of "communicative entities" (Hallahan, Holtzhausen, Van Ruler, Verčič, & Sriramesh, 2007). That is what sets the field apart from other areas of communication studies.

But *how* the practice is performed has changed considerably. The reasons for this are manifold. One reason, of course, is technology. Other factors are changes in philosophical approaches brought on by internationalization and globalization and, like virtually every other discipline, organization theory is also being scrutinized from a postmodern perspective.

The application of organization theory to public relations in the early eighties was probably the most pivotal point in the development of public relations theory as we know it today. That was the moment public relations became a management function. Up to that time communication theory served as the major theoretical framework for the development of public relations theory, although the discussion of the management role versus the technician role was mentioned as early as 1978 (Broom & Smith, 1978). Since that time organization theory has become the other pillar on which public relations theory has been built. Broadly speaking one can argue that if public relations theory is a three-legged stool, one leg will be communication theory, one will be philosophy/metatheory, and the third organization theory.

A number of important theoretical approaches have emerged from organization theory:

- roles research,
- the impact of organizational structure on practice,
- the impact of organizational environments,
- decision-making processes,
- the concept of strategy and the role the practitioner should play in this,
- the importance of power for the public relations function,
- the impact of organizational technologies on practice,
- the role of public relations in strategy formulation,
- the role public relations plays or does not play, in shaping organizational culture,
- the impact organizational change has on practice, and
- contingency theory.

Thirty to forty years ago organization theories were largely shaped through modernist thought and what today is called classical organization theory (Hatch & Cunliffe, 2006). Since that time two other important theoretical approaches in organization theory have developed: symbolic-interpretivism and postmodernism. These two approaches have some critical thoughts in common, such as the social construction of reality, the problems of representation, and the necessity for reflexivity. However, the postmodern focus on the role of language clearly sets this approach apart from symbolic-interpretivism.

Every so often claims are made that this or that theory represents a general theory for public relations, i.e. provides a framework for understanding the whole field. Suggesting that a single theory can explain all the phenomena in a field is typical of a modernist approach in many ways:

1. It offers a simplistic and reductionist approach to public relations that ignores the inherent complexity of postmodern society where the interpretation of most issues is contested.
2. It assumes that public relations practitioners all do the same things, much like surgeons use the same procedures all over the world, and that the reasons why they do what they do are the same across different environments.
3. It proposes that there is one single correct way of arguing about public relations practice, and that a few, simple categories or topics can explain every complex situation, like for instance in contingency theory that "take the seductive form of recipes for success," i.e. proposing that if a specific situation exists, there is a single action that will solve the problem (Hatch & Cunliffe, 2006, p. 41).

4. It maintains that knowledge can be rationally and objectively determined and that knowledge accumulated in this way leads to progress.
5. It argues that technological development is desirable and progressive and will lead to the improvement of the human condition.

Many of these approaches often are still fundamental in the application of organization theory to the development of public relations theory. However, both postmodern thought and the postmodernization of society have led to legitimate and serious challenges to the application of modernist organization theory to public relations. Modernist approaches to organizational structure is one area where this is apparent.

New Directions in Organization Theory

The term *organize* conjures up images of things neatly ordered, of everything under control, of things or people being where somebody else expects them to be, doing what someone in control expects them to do.

That was indeed the modernist approach in organization theory with metaphors of organizations running like well-oiled machines or functioning as disciplined armies going to war. The crown jewel of this approach was the bureaucratic structure where people were neatly put into boxes, with the most powerful at the top and the least significant at the bottom. Admittedly, this perspective of organization was more often than not normative—something to strive for rather than something that could exist exactly as conceptualized in real life.

New approaches to organization theory provide concrete explanations why the link between normative theories and positive behavior is unlikely. Both symbolic-interpretive and postmodern approaches argue organizations are not created as rational structures that exist in the form of buildings or other structural formats that are first organized and then equipped with people and technology. Organizations are co-created through the discourse of participants, both internal and external to the organization, and are therefore emerging. Consequently they are part of a continuously evolving process and concomitantly always changing entities. Language plays a vital role in this evolution. Organization is viewed as "a concept of social actors that is produced in contextually embedded social discourse and used to interpret the social world" (Gephart, Boje, & Thatchenkery, 1996, p. 2). Citing Gergen, Hassard (1996, p. 49) argues that the postmodern turn in organization theory came about as a result of a "sense of unease" with the lack of alternative theories modern organization theory offered and the sense that these theories were based on an "ideological mystification." Hassard also cites Clegg's critique of bureaucracy and differentiation as the organizing principle of organization theory and mentions the challenge to "the modernist objective of determining factual relationships through the empirical method" (p. 50) as another reason for the shift to postmodern organization theory.

But this understanding of how organizations evolve is not the only challenge to traditional approaches to organization theory. A critique of capitalism, the questioning of the very notion of theory, and changes in culture and society are some of the issues that brought their own challenges to organization theory (e.g. Gephart et al., 1996; Jameson, 1995). As a result public relations theory, because of the way in which it has been impacted by organization theory, is facing the same theoretical challenges.

One of the biggest challenges facing organization theory in the postmodern context is the legitimation crisis of capitalism whereby the very existence of capitalism is viewed as a "snake chewing at its tail" (Bauman, 1993, p. 209), referring to capitalism's continuous need for new commodities, new markets, and new consumers, which will eventually lead to its demise. Postmodern theorists are not critical of capitalism per se but rather are critical of a new kind of predatory capitalism (Lyotard, 1992), which Jameson (1995, p. 3), citing Ernest Mandel, calls "late capitalism", which is a "third stage … in the evolution of capital" and "a purer stage of capitalism than any of the moments that preceded it."

The commodification of science, education, culture, and even religion is one of the attributes of this stage of capitalism and is further promoted through the use of representational images, such as brands. These representational images bring about "a prodigious exhilaration with the new order of things, a commodity rush, our 'representation' of things tending to arouse an enthusiasm and a mood swing not necessarily inspired by the things themselves" (Jameson, 1995, p. x).

As has been argued consistently throughout this text, postmodernism challenges the universality of theoretical claims. This is of course also the case for organization theory. Hassard (1996, p. 57) proposes a "synthetic prospect" for theory development in organization theory in which it is impossible to separate theory and practice. One can therefore argue that the development of organization theory will always be embedded in the practice of a particular organization, which is inseparable from the culture and society in which it exists. While Clegg (1990) focuses his attention on differentiation as the single biggest problem facing modernism, Hassard (1996, p. 58) cites Gergen's (1992) "relational theory of organizational power" as another focus for postmodern organization theory. Gergen argues against the traditional theoretical notion that individuals are centers or agents of power, but rather that power is gained through "social supplementarity" or "social interdependence" (Hassard, 1996, p. 58).

If all theory is local, regional, and situational and always based in praxis, it also is necessary to be reflexive in postmodern theory building. This is also the case for organization theory. Not only is it important to reflect on the ability of one's theories to enter society and change relations but it also is important to challenge theories that lead to "repulsive forms of behavior" (Hassard, 1993, p. 128).

These postmodern tenets in organization theory also are recurring themes when organization theory is applied in the development of public relations theory. Exploring every possible area where postmodern organization theory can be applied to public relations from a postmodern perspective is far too large a task for a single chapter of a book. As a result only the following theoretical applications to public relations will be scrutinized: organizational structure, strategic planning, crisis communication, change management, and leadership. Two other postmodern emphases, power and roles, were discussed in Chapter 4.

Organizational Structure

Two modernist perspectives on organizational structure have been influential in building public relations theory. The first is the concept of *bureaucracy*, which remains one of the most dominant forms of organizing and often is used in conjunction with other organizational forms. Clegg (1990, p. 73), citing Donaldson, pointed to the "iron cage" of organizational structure. This perspective does not limit organizational structure to bureaucracy but rather points to "the existence of a structurally limited range of organizational types." Bureaucracies are typically hierarchical in nature, have a strict division of labor with fixed roles, and have well-defined rules and regulations that govern the organization. Thus, organizational structure determines task allocation, reporting lines, and formal co-ordination mechanisms and interaction patterns (Donaldson, 1985).

Structure is traditionally measured in terms of three components: *complexity*, *formalization*, and *centralization*. Complexity refers to the degree of specialization of an organization's employees, how labor is divided, the number of levels, and the geographical dispersion. Formalization is concerned with the degree of rules and procedures. Centralization refers to levels of decision-making. The more complex an organization is the more supervisory levels are required. Because managers have bounded rationality, i.e. an inability to exert control beyond a certain level of reach, more and more managers have to be appointed. Managers are typically appointed for their technical abilities and knowledge. In extension, agency theory holds that managers become agents of the owners and act on their behalf. The actions of agents are governed by contracts that determine their exact roles and expectations (Williamson, 1975). Labor is not only divided into individual roles but also is grouped together into departments, divisions, and other operational units.

The second perspective is Mintzberg's (1979) influential work on the structure of organizations where he draws a distinction between an organization's strategic apex, line functions, and support functions. In this perspective public relations is a support function in which practitioners mostly supply professional-type knowledge and counseling. Line managers, on the other hand, move up through the operating core of an organization to become a part of the strategic apex. It appears that public relations roles theory, in particular, has been influenced by these two perspectives, which are both driven from a structural approach. Thus, organizational structure has been influential in the building of public relations theory in terms of the concepts of differentiation, i.e. by shaping perspectives on manager and technician roles, and other derivations such as the expert prescriber, communication facilitator, and problem-solving process facilitator (Dozier & Broom, 2006), the cultural interpreter role identified in international public relations (Grunig, Grunig, Sriramesh, Huang, & Lyra, 1995) and the strategist role (Steyn, 2007). It has also been influential in terms of emphasizing the importance of public relations as being part of the strategic apex (or dominant coalition) of an organization to influence strategic decision-making on organizational communication.

Critique of roles theory abounds but focuses on binary opposites, namely, whether public relations is a craft or profession, why men are more likely to become managers than women, or whether the manager role is preferred over that of the technician, to name but a few of these dichotomies. Indeed, looking at current roles theory in public relations one has to come to the conclusion that organizational structure is an "iron cage."

However, a number of new structural forms have emerged over the past decade or two, largely facilitated by advances in communication technology. Although few of these structures are applied as pure forms and are more likely to emerge as hybrid forms, they have been conceptualized and empirical testing is starting to emerge. For example, Stokes (2005) tested the impact of structure on public relations roles and found that four distinct organizational forms emerged: *multidivisional, matrix, network*, and *virtual*. Although this study used a small sample of 100 randomly selected public relations practitioners, the emergence of the structural forms was significant. Subsequently, the conceptualization of these structures was confirmed in a comprehensive survey of public relations practitioners in the United States (Holtzhausen & Werder, 2008). Two of these structural forms are closely associated with bureaucratic organizing structures: multidivisional and matrix (Hatch & Cunliffe, 2006). Multidivisional structure develops when organizations become too large to be effective and are then reorganized according to specialization or geographic area. The bureaucratic structure is then duplicated in these decentralized structures. Network and virtual structures are typically associated with the use and development of technology, particularly communication technology.

It is difficult to provide a definition of a matrix structure because it shifts according to organizational needs and might incorporate different structural arrangements (Kolodny, 1979). In matrix organizations functional managers assign employees to project teams and oversee them to ensure their expertise in the specific function. Project managers oversee project development. Thus employees who are assigned to projects have dual reporting lines: to their functional manager and to their project manager. Once the project is successfully completed the employee will be assigned to a new team with a new project manager (Galbraith, 1977). While this organizational arrangement might result in conflict because of dual reporting structures, it is flexible and adaptable and employees learn to apply their expertise in different operational environments. Although traditionally associated with bureaucracies, matrix structures are now challenged in terms of design and project execution due to the complexity inherent in the coordination of businesses, functions, countries, and customers, in what Galbraith (2009) calls a four-dimensional matrix.

For postmodernists, however, the two most intriguing organizational structures are *networks* (Raab & Kenis, 2009) and *virtual organizations* (Gibson & Gibbs, 2006) because these two structural types are directly linked to changes in society facilitated by technology while also exemplifying the shift to postmodern values in society. In general terms a network describes the way in which different nodal points in a society (often a global one) are linked together through "ties" (Barney, 2004, p. 2). In organizational terms this means different organizations are linked together sometimes, but not always, through technology. These networks also change our notions of time and space because people can work together on complex problems and projects without being physically close and despite major time differences.

Public relations practice offers an excellent example of how networks operate. Independent practitioners have become such a mainstream phenomenon in public relations that PRSA has recently established the PRSA Independent Practitioners Alliance, which "provides resources and a virtual gathering place for independent practitioners, whether they work alone or in teams, from home, small or shared offices" (PRSA, 2008). These independent practitioners can set themselves up as part of a network organization that can function as well as a large, fully-fledged agency. They can provide all necessary services in-house by creating nodal points with other similar independent firms that provide auxiliary services clients might need. At the same time the independent practitioner becomes part of a network that can call on her services when necessary, thus extending the service network of the independent practitioner. Increasingly these networks form alliances when pitching for large projects and it is not uncommon for nodal points consisting of a business consultant, a small graphic design house, a media placement agency, a media relations practitioner, an event organizer, and other specialty services to put presentations together for multimillion-dollar projects. In turn, each of these nodes has networks consisting of other nodes offering similar services, which reduces each one's dependence on a single other node and exposes it to many other business opportunities. In this way networks form "clusters of firms or specialized units coordinated by market mechanisms or relational norms rather than by a hierarchical chain of command" (Walker, 1997, p. 75). These networks favor independent practitioners because they are more flexible and adaptive than large organizations. They can also decrease their administrative overheads through cost sharing. By their very nature these networks are dependent on the trust, relationships, and high levels of coordination and information sharing between the different nodes. Walker believes network structures raise the levels of information and expertise for those nodes in the network. What makes network organizations particularly postmodern is that they are specifically created for short term, specific goals (Raab & Kenis, 2009).

Network organizations are often used in conjunction with virtual organizations. Typically virtual organizations are associated with organizations such as eBay or Amazon that do not have bricks and mortar offices. However, virtual organizations also are associated with organizations that have virtual employees, i.e. employees who only exist at a remote computer point and who never actually have to enter a physical building. These employees often *telecommute*, and are allowed a lot of autonomy and flexibility (Davidow & Malone, 1992; Verbeke, Schulz, Greidanus, & Hambley, 2008). Virtual organizations also can be geographically distributed and only operate electronically (Rahman & Bhattachryya, 2002). They could be very dependent on a shared vision and goal, and clearly formulated operational protocols. One of the benefits of virtual organizations is their ability to respond in real time to issues. Caplan (2007) reported on the huge financial success of *37signals*, a business software company with eight employees and millions of users. The organization is partly virtual, and its business is designing the software that allows organizations to communicate effectively with virtual employees and partners. *37signals* is typical of the virtual organization that consists of specialized individuals who can participate in the organization from anywhere in the world through communication technology. A strong vision, a learning and developmental environment, an infrastructure that promotes communication, information sharing and job sharing, alternative compensation systems, and quality control are all aspects vital to virtual organizations (Rahman & Bhattachryya, 2002).

From the above it is apparent that organizations often use multiple organizational forms. This is also true for public relations practice in the United States. A recent study (Holtzhausen & Werder, 2008) found statistically significant relationships between the four organizational forms but the relationships between these four structures were weak enough to support the notion that they exist independently as well. Another interesting finding in this study was that, contrary to popular wisdom, men were more likely to work in virtual structures than women. One would expect that virtual structures are ideal for young professional women who have families but in this study it was not the case. It was also found that people who worked in virtual structures were more senior. In deconstructing this situation the question might well be asked whether levels of trust have an impact on this. Can it be that women are not as trusted to work on their own and are deemed to require more supervision? These are questions that cannot be answered in quantitative research studies and is one of the interesting research questions postmodern approaches to organization theory open up for public relations researchers.

Nonetheless, the application of these new organizational structures challenges our notion of organizational structures as fixed and unyielding. Of necessity virtual and network organizations challenge traditional notions of supervisory levels in organizations and require the evaluation of employees' contribution in terms of performance outcomes rather than strict adherence to office hours or executing tasks under supervision. Thus, these organizational forms challenge existing notions of power in organizations and, by extension, our understanding of the roles we perform.

Public Relations Roles

From the above emerging structural forms one can assume that, even at the most functional level, traditional role perspectives in public relations would be challenged. While bureaucracies and divisional structures remain very important organizing systems, particularly in large organizations, aspects of newer structures are busy permeating these structural forms too, challenging traditional approaches to roles. For example, one can argue that matrix organizations are morphing into network structures, with project teams operating increasingly as virtual networks within larger organizations.

The concept of *differentiation* has probably played the most important role in the theorizing of public relations roles. As mentioned before, differentiation has been at the core of roles research in public relations with its focus on the identification and description of exactly what practitioners do and under what circumstances. As a result the manager/technician dichotomy has become one of the most prominent defining mechanisms in roles research. In fact, the foremost scholars driving this research in public relations argue that practitioner roles are central to the development of public relations theory (Dozier & Broom, 2006) and at many levels that is true.

But if one analyzes the concept of differentiation in terms of new organizational structures it becomes much more difficult to clearly differentiate roles. If one analyzes the role of the public relations practitioner in, for instance, organizational network structures at the hand of current roles theory the first obvious question is whether such a practitioner plays a manager or a technician role. The answer will always need to be, "It depends." The roles of public relations practitioners in networks have to be driven by the type of project, the environment in which it operates, the immediate needs of the project, the stakeholders involved, the skills sets of other members of the network, availability of technology, and so forth. Depending on the situation the practitioner will sometimes have to be a strategist by taking the lead in how to handle complex communication issues for the specific project. Other times the practitioner might assume the manager role by managing outside resources required to complete communication assignments for the team. At other times the practitioner might be expert prescriber, communication facilitator, or problem-solving process facilitator when the need arises. While he might still report to a higher level manager, it is clear from this description that the practitioner performs multiple roles and reports to multiple supervisors, which challenges our traditional notion of the manager/technician dichotomy. A colleague and I (Werder & Holtzhausen, 2008) found that out of a total of 784 practitioners participating in their national survey of PRSA members, only 7 identified themselves as technicians. That is less than 1%. These results appear to be consistent with other research that shows practitioners play multiple roles at any time, among which might be some that require technical skills. This, however, does not result in a separate technician role (Holtzhausen, Petersen, & Tindall, 2003; Toth, Serini, Wright, & Emig, 1998). In this organizational form the practitioner performs a role similar to what Toth et al. (1998) call an "agency role," which covers "counseling; research; programming decisions; communicating with clients, peers and subordinates; handling correspondence and phone calls; and making media contacts" (p. 14).

The challenges to traditional roles perspectives in public relations are not new. Leitchy and Springston (1996) argue "meaningful information is lost by categorizing practitioners as either managers or technicians" (p. 475). Another problem with roles theory is that roles are often defined from the outside in, i.e. a researcher uses a theory to define the work and actions of others. Often times, when practitioners themselves are asked to formulate their roles, different and meaningful role interpretations emerge. One example is that of African American female practitioners who identified their roles as educators, mentors, agenda-builders, and females (Pompper, 2004). Similarly, when roles are studied outside of the United States other roles, not necessarily dependent on typical Western bureaucratic structures, are mentioned. Grunig et al. (1995) found cultural interpreter and personal influence roles in India and Greece respectively. In Europe practitioners identified their roles as managerial, operational, and educational (van Ruler & Verčič, 2004).

Another role-related category is that of public relations practice as a craft or profession. The concept of professionalism is, among others, viewed as grounded in a standard education and standard practice (Kruckeberg, 2000). The question remains: "Who would set such a standard and whose standards will dominate?" Such a standard education and practice will of necessity create a metanarrative dominated by single perspectives on economic and political systems, and cultural practices. Also, the very notion of education and standard practice as criteria for professionalism are being questioned. Pieczka and L'Etang (2001, p. 234), for example, argue that practitioners in Britain can be viewed as an occupational group identifying itself "in relation to the state and social elites as the source of cultural/ideological power" rather than a profession.

Another area of differentiation that affects public relations is that associated with the practice itself and that sets it apart from other disciplines such as marketing, human resources, and advertising. Within public relations different aspects of practice are further differentiated, such as community relations, investor relations, media relations, and so forth. Although the notion of describing practice in this way is not per definition wrong, what becomes a challenge is that inevitably one kind of practice, role, or function is privileged over another and assigned a higher status. This is often the function of differentiation, which is associated with creating hierarchical structures in organizations. This then results in a power struggle, which lays at the foundation of the arguments whether public relations is actually integrated marketing, whether it should be separate from marketing, whether it is superior to marketing, and other similar arguments.

One way to break down differentiation is through de-differentiation. Clegg (1990, p. 11) argues that differentiation is one of the cornerstones of modernist organization theory and that the answer is de-differentiation. He believes, "Postmodernity ... may be distinguished from modernity by its earlier tendencies to increase differentiation" (p. 1). One can argue that the concept of differentiation is at its core segmentation with all the implications for power and control as Deleuze and Guattari (1987) suggest. Citing Lash (1988), Clegg (1990) suggests a process of de-differentiation as a resistance strategy to differentiation. He describes de-differentiation as the "blurring of the boundaries between what, under a more modernist impulse, would have been constituted as distinct phenomena" (p. 11). Practitioners who embrace the concept of de-differentiation will be those who resist categorization because they see differentiation and its categories as "the self-imposed limitations of modernism, which in its search for autonomy and purity or for timeless, representational, truth has subjected experience to unacceptable intellectualizations and reductions" (Bertens, 1995, p. 5). Differentiation is equal to self-discipline when you accept the way you are categorized and strictly adhere to that category. Therein lies the danger for practitioners. Strict adherence to certain tasks associated with strict categories lies at the heart of role differentiation, which often leads to lack of development and broader opportunities in organizations. Being able to multi-skill and mastering many different skills and knowledge prevent practitioners from being pigeon-holed, which often happens when practitioners are very good at what they do and become indispensable in a particular role.

One can argue that de-differentiation is the process that leads to fragmentation and that contributes to new structural forms and interpretations of roles. In turn new structural forms and technology have led to both fragmentation and convergence of roles and functions. Network and virtual structures will demand larger skills sets from practitioners and less specialization simply because they are not necessarily part of a predetermined hierarchical structure. This will lead to more convergence of disciplines that have been traditionally separated, incorporating knowledge and skills from marketing, advertising, human resources, and public relations into single practice.

Not working under direct supervision likely requires decision-making in isolation and skills in managing time and outputs. Also, not working under a direct supervisor will shift performance measurement to be based on outcomes rather than on how many hours are spent behind a desk, something academics are very familiar with. New technology also brings changes in work time and space, which in turn challenges the traditional separation between work life and private life. Already many employees go on holiday with communication devices that enable them to check emails and be available if something at the office goes wrong. This blurs the work/private divide. All these trends reaffirm how once stable and isolated categories used to manage society are breaking down.

While technology has largely driven changes in organizational structure, with the subsequent possibilities for re-investigating public relations roles, changes in how we perceive organizational roles also have been brought about by the deconstruction of what those roles mean and represent. The most obvious are the manager/technician, craft/profession, and male/female dichotomies. As discussed in Chapter 1 postmodernism rejects the use of binary opposites in modernist discourse, which implies the superiority of one meaning over another. One area where this is evident in public relations scholarship is the feminist critique of roles research in public relations. One of the most pervasive feminist critiques of roles theory in public relations is that male models of management and practice over the years have become the measure for the performance of women in the field (Creedon, 1990; Hon, 1995). Furthermore, being a manager is viewed as being better than being a technician, and public relations should rather be a profession than a craft.

These are good examples of how language has been used to create binary opposites and illustrate the role of discourse from a postmodern perspective. It also shows how the deconstruction of this kind of discourse helps us to understand the underlying rationale for the creation of categories and to explain that these categories are not as dichotomous and mutually exclusive as they seem at first glance (V. E. Taylor & Winquist, 2001). Deconstruction helps us to articulate the resistance to being categorized in any way through the many little narratives of daily life. Researchers and practitioners who embrace fragmentation are better able to resist artificial categories that empower one group over another. Also, fragmentation provides many more opportunities for resistance and empowerment than merely looking at single categories of the male/female practitioner, the manager vs. the technician, and the educated professional vs. the practitioner practicing a craft. Deconstruction thus can help all practitioners (not only females) to understand the fictional core of patriarchal management practices and language and expose its invisible working (Rabine, 1990). Practitioners themselves are particularly suited to do this because, as also discussed in Chapter 4, Rabine argues that feminist discourse has to operate from within the very structures that need dismantling and restructuring.

Another result of this kind of deconstruction is the concept of *decentering*. Deconstruction shows how all categories are artificially created through the use of language. As Lyotard (1989, pp. 15–16) said: "Men in all their claims to construct meaning, to speak the Truth, are themselves a minority in the patchwork where it becomes impossible to establish and validly determine any major order." This is important for our understanding of roles because it highlights how all roles and role categories are discursively constructed. Not only does the category of *man* become decentered but also the category of *manager*, and all other categories that position one group as superior to another.

Another way to look at public relations roles is through the concept of *agency*. Agency is a "conscious state of activity" that refers to a "postmodern impulse toward self-consciousness with the intention to subvert or undermine social or political oppression" (V. E. Taylor & Winquist, 2001, p. 6). This interpretation of agency supports the activist role in public relations (Holtzhausen, 2002b), which is typified by resistance to suppression of the self and others and by giving voice to silences that represent suppression of any sort. Looking at public relations roles as agency takes the focus away from the technical functions practitioners perform in organizations and society. It is important to note at this point that agency is a highly contested term and that this interpretation of agency differs greatly from the modernist interpretation of the agent who acts on behalf of someone else. Agency is fundamental to our understanding of public relations as activism and will be discussed more elaborately in Chapter 7.

But what the postmodern deconstruction of current public relations roles theory does above all else is to recognize the complexity and multiplicity of practitioner roles, highlight the dismantling of once stable categories, and show how discourse is used to create categories of people that are deemed lesser than others. At the same time it exposes those spaces where resistance to categorization is possible.

Strategic Public Relations

The term *strategic* is undoubtedly the most difficult to reconcile with postmodern public relations. In fact, many communication scholars view strategic as the binary opposite of *dialogic*, arguing that the term cannot be interpreted other than one-way, persuasive in nature.

This often is reflected in the work of Habermas (1979) who poses "strategic" action as directly opposed to communication action, which, he argues, is based on the presupposition of "mutually recognized validity claims" (p. 209). In the strategic "attitude ... only indirect understanding via determinative indicators is possible" (p. 209), implying that strategic means deliberate withholding of information. He does not altogether disregard the use of strategy, as long as it is used to create understanding. He, however, does associate "strategic attitude" with "'deliberate pseudoconsensual' communication" (p. 210) and acknowledges that strategic communication is becoming increasingly important in the public sphere for all players. Despite the inherent discrepancies in power that give groups such as politicians and lobbyists more access to media than the "actors of civil society" the "common construct of 'civil society' certainly invites actors to intervene strategically in the public sphere" (Habermas, 2006, p. 16). The ability to use corporate communication management methods allows "representatives of functional systems and special interest groups" to gain access to media and thus gain political influence. Although the "actors of civil society" have less power, they too have the opportunity and use strategic communication to affect the debate in the public sphere (p. 15).

Although postmodernists are not against being strategic per se we are now familiar with Lyotard's (1992, pp. 138–139) critique of strategic planning as a form of terror because of its relationship with the measurement of outcomes. But postmodernists also argue that Habermas's ideal communication situation is impossible because power imbalances are inherent in and influence all communicative situations. Foucault argues that all relationships are political and therefore strategic. Like Foucault, Lyotard (1988) argues that all discourse is strategic because it is aimed at silencing or persuading, thus leaving strategy open to possibilities of participation in discourse and individual activism.

It is difficult to associate successful activism in any context, be it social or organizational, with a lack of strategy. For example, Burek (2001) showed how a lack of strategic communication knowledge and skills contributed to the campaign failure of a group of community environmental activists. In a world where media and audiences are fragmenting at a lightning rate, it would be professional suicide not to be strategic in one's communication approach. Also, postmodernism argues strongly for living reflexively, or consciously, in the postmodern world. Being strategic would be part of such a reflexive stance because strategy involves high levels of thought, analysis, planning, and review.

But still, strategic remains problematic. Part of the problem with the term is that it has been strongly associated with a modernist approach to management. The term "strategic" was first used in organization theory outside of the military context in the 1950s (Sloan, 2006). It is associated with "objective representationalism" that argues "the purpose of knowledge is to represent, without logical contradiction … the linear, functional causes of actions" (p. 18). The purpose of this approach is to describe how organizations compete in the marketplace, obtain competitive advantage, and gain market share. The above description of a modernist approach to strategic planning is indeed accurate when one considers the original aims of strategic planning as one of controlling the environment and maintaining the organization's autonomy (Pfeffer & Salancik, 1978).

In its most negative context the term "strategic" is understood as having originated in warfare and is in its strictest sense described as "the art of war." The word "strategy" originated from the Greek word for "generalship" (*Web-*

ster's new collegiate dictionary, 1975). As a result the term often has negative associations, particularly in an era where organizations are perceived as using their resources to manipulate their environments to their own benefit without consideration of stakeholders, other constituencies, and the concerns of society in general. Associating strategic as a war metaphor with public relations practice can thus strengthen the existing negative perceptions of the field.

This perception is further strengthened when organizations view the strategy process as rational decision-making (Hatch, 1997). The familiar SWOT analysis is a part of this process, as are goal setting, strategy formulation and implementation, and evaluation (Porter, 1985). In addition to formulating their own communication strategies, public relations practitioners are often tasked to communicate to employees the vision and mission of the organization as set out by management. These perspectives have been strengthened by the fact that strategic planning is being taught in most undergraduate programs in public relations, advertising, and marketing through the rather formulaic and linear process of the Management By Objectives (MBO) approach that emphasizes goal setting, measurable outcomes, and action plans (e.g. Austin & Pinkleton, 2001; Smith & Ferguson, 2001).

Critics of this approach argue that strategy privileges a management discourse and emphasizes upper management's goals for the organization as given, rational, and legitimate. Gagliardi (1986), for instance, argues that cultural assumptions and values determine strategy. He challenges the rational model of strategic decision-making that implies strategic decisions are objective, and culture and gender free.

Others argue the overall aim of strategy in this context is to control organizational outcomes, or as Baumann (1993) describes it, to "colonize the future" (p. 205). This colonization effort takes place through setting up control mechanisms such as administrative procedures, eliminating dissension and conflict, and promoting the blind acceptance of organizational goals and roles. The role of public relations practitioners in this approach is to ensure information transfer from the supervisor to the subordinate to gain compliance and to establish networks to ensure the organization's power in relation with the public. This perspective includes the concepts of strategic message design, management of culture, total quality management, and even change management (Holtzhausen, 2002b). The mere mention of the term "strategic" thus evokes a one-sided approach to organizational management that is based in top-down communication which does not promote alternative applications of strategy. Vignette 5.1 provides a typical example of what can happen when organizational strategies are set in this way.

Another problem is the application of strategy to organizational social responsibility and corporate philanthropy efforts. Using strategy in this context sounds offensive, as does the concept of *social marketing*. It is clear from Chapter 2 that the moral impulse will not, and cannot, be dictated by issues of

---

VIGNETTE 5.1

Emergent Strategy—the Case of the ATM

In the early nineties a workshop was held for communicators in a multidivisional banking organization with the emphasis on how these communicators could assist with helping their divisions reach the goals set for them by head office. Public relations practitioners in the organization were very involved with transferring organizational strategy, which was set at the corporate head office, to "lower levels" in the organization.

By this time the divisional communicators were quite familiar with the demands head office set and had a lot of experience of how these strategies played out every year. They were complaining that nobody ever asked them whether the goals set for them were even feasible. One communicator described their dilemma and said, "Large parts of our region are rural but head office expects us to do a considerable amount of real estate business. That would mean writing a lot of farm mortgages, which is just not going to happen. These farms have been in families for decades, sometimes even hundreds of years. If they had asked us we would have told them that if they put in more ATMs in our rural towns we would smoke the opposition and corner the market but nobody would listen."

If top management had allowed feedback from those people who work on the ground before setting out on strategic planning, they could have set much more realistic goals and get buy-in from those who actually had to implement the strategy.

---

strategy, which by their very nature demand something in return, and demands being measured for effectiveness and outcomes. Thus, at face value, it appears that strategic public relations is irreconcilable with postmodern philosophy.

Viewing strategy in such a very basic manner, however, does not do justice to its usefulness and complexity. Upon closer scrutiny there are indeed several alternative approaches to perceiving the term "strategic" and a thorough deconstruction of the term opens up new ways of viewing and researching communication practice in modern-day organizations. Sloan (2006) in fact describes 10 different approaches to organizational strategy and says that despite these differences there is agreement on the following basic elements:

a will to win;
an element of competition;
a process or framework to win;
an extended time horizon;

determination of a broad and major aim;
unifying intent;
decisions about resource allocation. (p. 4)

Broadly defined, there are two competing approaches to organizational strategy. One approach focuses on *strategic planning* and the other on *strategic thinking*. In one application strategic is associated with power and decision-making.
When used in conjunction with communication strategic implies that communication practice is a management function. Mintzberg (1979) was the first to
describe the "strategic apex" of the organization as consisting of "those people
charged with overall responsibility of the organization—the chief executive
officer ... and any of the top-level managers whose concerns are global" (p.
237). Although he placed the public relations function in the category of support staff, his description of the functions of the strategic apex is similar to
our understanding of the role of communication managers: stakeholder liaison,
boundary spanning, acting as spokesperson, environmental scanning and issues
management, and integration of communication functions.

Alternative, and more positive, notions of strategy have also emerged since
the 1950s. These approaches reject the use of strategic only in a negative context. Quinn, Mintzberg, and James' (1991) perspective on *emergent strategy*
holds that strategy is based on prior experience and action (also see Mintzberg,
1990). Emergent strategy thus legitimates and values the actions and decisions
of employees at all levels of the organization. The concept of emergence is
typical of a postmodern approach to organizational theory, as discussed before,
and its main focus is to, at some level, confirm the democratization of organizational processes. King (2010) argues that communication strategies in
particular emerge through the "interaction between reader/hearer response,
situated context, and discursive patterns" (p. 34). Analyzing communication
from an emergent perspective allows for reflexivity in communication because
the intent of the message and the way it was interpreted can be deconstructed.
Emergent strategy also implies every member of an organization can and should
contribute to future organizational directions and processes in formal and more
organic ways.

Instead of viewing the functional and emerging approaches as binary opposites, several scholars propose a combination of the two, namely, that successful
organizational strategy depends on both visionary leadership and on participation of organizational stakeholders in the strategy formulation process (Canales
& Vilà, 2005; Heracleous, 2003; Rughase, 2006; Sloan, 2006). This approach
requires rigorous communication by both leadership and other stakeholders.
After a comprehensive review of literature on the subject, Hafsi and Howard
(2005) conclude that strategy research takes place at two levels: intellectual and
practical. The five areas informing the intellectual domain of strategy are:

(i)   Strategy as a leader's statement
(ii) Strategy as a community's statement
(iii) Strategy as a guiding track
(iv) Strategy as the building of competitive advantage
(v)   Strategy as a relationship with the environment. (p. 243)

From this it is clear that the strategy process is complex and non-linear.

While organizational leaders have an obligation to include stakeholders in the strategic thinking process, every employee has a responsibility to participate. In the postmodern organization communication can never be the responsibility of leadership only. Employees can no longer abdicate their responsibility to participate and communicate but should rather become strategy activists, speaking out on what they think their contribution could be and how their insights could make the organization better.

The implication of strategic thinking (rather than strategic planning) to communication in organizations is profound. The emergent approach challenges top-down communication and the role of public relations practitioners in "translating" the idea of corporate managers for employees. From a postmodern perspective this is a futile action at best. As discussed in Chapter 1, meaning is not transferred in such a linear fashion. People interpret meaning in the context of their own framework and meaning is always toppling forward, to recall Harland's (1987) dominoes metaphor. It also focuses the attention on the impact of communication on strategy formulation, i.e. how communication about daily practices, in both formal and informal organizational settings, eventually impacts the strategic decisions of organizations. This challenges the long-held notion that public relations managers are the only strategic decision-makers in the public relations function. It confirms that the daily decisions of all public relations practitioners, even if they are web masters, news letter editors, or event planners, have the potential of affecting the future strategies of an organization. They are after all the employees who are most likely to interface with organizational stakeholders on a daily basis and therefore have the most to offer in terms of understanding changes in the stakeholder environment and thus future strategy (Holtzhausen & Voto, 2002).

Another focus of emergent strategy or strategic thinking is that of practice and implementation. Several authors emphasize the importance of execution of strategy and the term "strategic" is often associated with practice and the tactics used to implement strategy (Bigler, 2004; Mintzberg, 1990; Rughase, 2006). Although mostly referring to strategy execution as a task of organizational leaders, Bigler (2004, pp. 6–7) proposes three stages of strategy execution: creativity must emerge as innovation; innovation must emerge as "a priority initiative;" and the priority initiative must go through a process of critical input.

Traditionally, public relations literature argues strategic used in the context of practice rather than management has the potential to reinforce the perception that the practice of public relations and communication is merely tactical and not considerate of larger social, political, and economic factors. Dozier and Broom (2006), for example, strongly link public relations managers with strategic decision-making and argue that practitioners who cannot share their knowledge with members of the dominant coalition cannot add value to organizations. That might indeed be true, but not for reasons of incompetence. The question is: Did anybody ask them? Were they ever invited to participate in strategic planning sessions and was the right environment ever created in the organization to encourage participation? Vignette 5.1 shows how having asked for input from the people who practice at the local level could have contributed to organizational excellence, at least in their own environment. Furthermore, the concept of emergent strategy, as discussed above, does not mean that only managers have strategic insight and implies that it is actually the successful practices of technicians (if such a word is even suitable any longer) that lead to successful strategic decision-making. The term strategic therefore also has the potential to investigate the importance and contribution of the tactical level of public relations practice and so legitimate the work of practitioners at all levels.

In addition to ensuring strategic inputs from public relations practitioners themselves, practitioners also have to ensure that all employees are offered this opportunity. They, in simple terms, need to act as organizational activists. Proposals for such participative processes often are met with strong opposition at many different levels of the organization. Top management might not want to apply the required resources or not think employees' viewpoints are valid in terms of strategic planning. Middle managers often are threatened by processes such as these, fearing direct or such open communication with their subordinates. Oftentimes practitioners do not have the expertise and know-how to go about setting this process in place or the ability to advocate for employees. Emergent strategy invokes images of the *d*-word, which is anathema to many corporate owners, managers, and other organizational leaders. Emergence implies participation, which implies democracy—the *d*-word. It is amazing that the Western world, which claims to have the most democratic systems in the world, has been unable to implement the same principles of democracy and respect for each individual's worth, voice, and contribution in the organizational environment. At some level it is understandable. Individuals, not groups, are held accountable for specific organizational outcomes and are remunerated accordingly. Particularly in decision-making, where immediate decisions are often required, group participation, and particularly group decision-making, will be problematic. Participative communication has long been associated with a more democratic work environment but implementation of such participative processes in large organizational systems are very complex (Holtzhausen, 2002a, 2002b). Making participative processes work also requires perseverance and time and is not for the faint of heart (Holtzhausen, 2005a). It requires a strong, activist stance from practitioners because resistance from supervisory levels is pervasive and consistent.

Because of its many-faceted meanings, the term strategic might offer one of the most inclusive, although conflicting and contradictory, descriptions of the field of communication practice. Although it emphasizes the role of communication as a management practice it does not necessarily imply power and control of management over other stakeholders. It also allows for the study of participatory communication practices which include stakeholder communication, change management, and complex analyses of organizational environments and their contribution to emergent strategy.

Public Relations and Organizational Change

Although change is often used in the context of change management the idea that change can be managed is of course anathema to postmodernists. Few scholars have addressed the role of public relations practitioners in organizational change. In cases where public relations practice has been linked to change agency the theoretical approaches were from postmodernism (Holtzhausen, 2000) and complexity and chaos theory (Ströh, 2005, 2007) respectively. These two approaches are often in conflict with each other.

Chaos and complexity and the resulting uncertainty in organizations and public relations practice now generally go uncontested (Gephart, Thatchenkery, & Boje, 1996; Gilpin & Murphy, 2009; Murphy, 2000). The recognition that postmodern organization is complex often is associated with being complicated and does not implicitly mean that scholars recognize complexity theory as the theoretical foundation for studying complexity. Many scholars still support the modernist paradigm that aims to find contingencies between complexity and other organizational attributes and still try to find generalizable results that can lead to universal theories, as Gephart et al. (1996) suggest. Trying to tame complexity in this context leads to reductionist theories that, even though they might bring a sense of safety and stability, are not based in reality because the world we live in is, and has always been, complex and chaotic.

It is not so much that complexity has been ignored in public relations. Particularly in terms of organizational environments the Excellence Theory has always held that volatile and complex organizational environments would require more strategic public relations, which in turn would force organizations toward symmetrical communication and collaboration. This, for example, is what happened in South Africa during the political transition in the early 1990s (Holtzhausen, 2005b). Essentially based on systems theory perspectives, this line of research was extended with the application of chaos and complexity theories to public relations (see Murphy, 2007 for a comprehensive analysis). Postmodernists, however, argue that complexity theory continues to hold forth the concept of contingency by believing that predictable patterns of behavior emerge from chaos.

Despite the differences there are indeed commonalities between postmodernism and complexity theory that should not be ignored. One of the most obvious is the recognition of complexity, not in the sense of being complicated but in the sense of being unpredictable, random, and spontaneous, as previously argued. While complicated implies difficulty to determine the many links between the components of a system, complexity implies the impossibility of ever identifying all the components of a system or identifying the totality of its networks (Cilliers, 1998). People who try to tame this unpredictability are trying to colonize the future, as Bauman (1993) so succinctly puts it, by setting processes in place that will give them the best control over future outcomes. Postmodern and complexity theories embrace complexity and view it not only as a permanent state of society and organizations but also as a desirable state that offers an opportunity for change. Postmodernists in particular believe chaos is the only way in which hegemonic power can be broken and fragmented, which allows for marginalized voices to assert themselves.

But why would people want change? Are we not at the "end of history," that desirable place where everything has been accomplished? Have we not reached the perfect state of capitalism and free market economies over the globe and will these organizing systems not take care of the poor, the sick, the uneducated, the old, and the young? Are these not the organizing systems that guarantee individual freedom, wellness, and democracy for all? Apparently not; even in the United States, where the end of history is supposedly most evident, some people do not even have the most basic of life's necessities. In 2007, 36.2 million people in the United States lived in food-insecure households and 11.9 million lived with hunger. The fate of marginalized people is even more evident when research shows that of those with the highest level of food-insecurity 22.3% were Black, 22.3% were Latino, 30.4% were from single-mother households, and 17.7% were households with children younger than six (Cook & Jeng, 2009). The divide between the rich and poor within countries and also between countries across the globe has become deeper, with a global class that finds it easy to commute between world cities where they find people who think, act, shop, eat, and live like them. We can even hypothesize that these global citizens form a nation state of their own that spans any geographic, time, and space barriers. Because of their influence and buying power they arguably can do more or less what they want, such as buying alcohol in Muslim countries, or French cuisine in the Far East, and live lifestyles that are outside the norm of many of the societies they inhabit. In addition, these global citizens also are the owners and employees of global organizations, which are increasingly becoming more powerful than governments because of the immense financial power they wield (Roper, 2005).

But this is not the class of people that brings about the need for organizational change. There are three obvious reasons why change is necessary for organizations. The most obvious is that change is so ubiquitous in postmodern society we need to embrace change and uncertainty, learn to live with it, and help our organizations negotiate these complexities in an effort to help them secure their survival. The second is the postmodern stance that change is good and that difference and chaos provide the ideal breeding ground for thinking differently and coming up with innovative solutions to existing problems. The third is the moral call to activist practitioners who still care about the poor, hungry, underprivileged, and marginalized to activate our moral impulse. To respond to these challenges requires changes in the core thinking and approaches in entrenched systems, which will allow them to change into vibrant and alternative systems that will view their role in society differently. In this context then complexity theory and postmodernism are still on the same page. Some of the problems between the two theoretical approaches arise in the context of self-organizing—likely the single most dominant principle in complexity theory.

Complexity theory argues that one of the most defining attributes of complex systems is its self-organizing ability. Cilliers (1998) provides the following definition of self-organizing: "The capacity for self-organising [sic] is a property of complex systems which enable them to develop or change internal structure spontaneously and adaptively in order to cope with, or manipulate, their environment" (p. 90). The attributes of self-organizing systems he describes are often found in postmodern theory, i.e. the emergent nature of organizations, the non-linearity of processes, the local nature of information and organizing, and the local nature of action.

However, what is problematic from a postmodern, activist point of view is the acceptance in complexity theory that the historicity of systems are of the utmost importance during times of chaos. History assists self-organizing systems in remembering what worked and did not work in the past. But this process is not only internal. "Clusters of information from the external world flow into the system. This information will influence the interaction of some of the components in the system" (Cilliers, 1998, p. 92). If one accepts that systems are embedded in other systems, which in turn are embedded in more systems, and so forth, one has to accept that all organizations are situated in social systems. As articulated many times in this text, the critique of power and how it perpetuates itself is one of the most persistent focus areas of postmodern theory. Thus, it would be naïve to think that societal power and those power relations that persisted in the history of the organization will not once again assert themselves during times of change. Several postmodern perspectives in particular motivate organizational activism in these circumstances, namely, the insidiousness of power, the discursive nature of organizations, the benefits of fragmentation, and reflexivity. An obvious example is what happened during the political transition in South Africa in the early 1990s. When it became clear that the transition to a democratic government was a *fait accompli* the South African environment moved to a case book example of a system in chaos. With extreme uncertainty reigning in the country about the future, and particularly about the future of White supervisors and managers, rumors in organizations were rife about who was going to stay and who would be replaced by Black South Africans. Fears of job-loss were indeed well-founded. One of the first steps the newly democratically-elected government did was to start putting pressure on businesses to have employee quotas that reflected the South African population. The biggest immediate changes happened in government departments where new ministers quickly transformed their departments and many senior, White personnel were retrenched. The private sector was another matter altogether. While the power elite held on to their jobs they used the so-called soft jobs, such as communication and human resources, and lower level employees to gain the expected quotas while keeping their own positions intact. It quickly became clear that those in power had no plans to transform themselves but rather to maintain their own powers as long as possible. This is still the case to this day, nearly two decades after the end of apartheid. This is a typical example of how societal power can and will permeate organizations during times of change and, if there is no resistance or challenge to this power, old power structures will merely be maintained. The role of the public relations activist will be to take a stance against this kind of manipulated power and she will use her voice to speak out. For example, Holtzhausen (2000) mentions how the public relations employees of an organization started a trade union to protect the rights of all employees during the transition. This step, which originally was taken to secure rights for women and Blacks in the organization, eventually protected even the positions of managers.

The second postmodern perspective that provides a clue to activism in these circumstances is the notion that organizations are discursively constituted and that the discursive behavior of the system's participants will be what shapes the future of the organization. In South Africa, while many feared the transition, which was indeed uncomfortable for most South Africans, it also became an opportunity for change. In fact, many public relations practitioners saw this as an opportunity to actively speak out and highlight the tensors in organizations (Holtzhausen et al., 2003). Although dissensus contributes to uncertainty in organizations, which is essential for change, it also is liberating in that it allows that which was unsaid in the past to be spoken, as Vignette 5.2 shows. Furthermore, this discourse is essential to the emergence of the new organization that should and would belong to all who participate in it and not only to those in powerful positions.

But dissensus is not only possible in terms of standing up to those with obvious power. The postmodern understanding of the fragmented agent with multiple identities suggests that resistance to power is possible at many different intersections, or nodal points. Although we all have fragmented identities, each of these identities is embedded in a social network. Contrary to the all-powerful, autonomous, modern agent the postmodern agent is part of a complex, inter-connected state of relationships, as complexity theory posits

VIGNETTE 5.2

Chaos Creates Unique Opportunities for Change

To help the employees of the organization I worked for in South Africa with the political transition in the country I asked a consultant to develop a workshop for work groups to help them discuss their fears and concerns and to create trust and open communication in the workplace. This was 1996, two years after the transition to a democracy, and everything was up for discussion, particularly racial and gender attitudes. We trained communicators in the 22 divisional and nine regional offices to in turn train the more than 600 communication champions in organizational units to present these workshops, which meant that I traveled to every region to work with communicators. Sometimes I would present workshops for management teams as well.

In one fascinating case where I had a particularly diverse management group, I decided to veer off from the standard workshop procedure and incorporated an exercise where I broke the participants up into groups that consisted of, for instance, two Blacks and two Whites; two men and two women; and so forth. The two members of the group who were similarly grouped, e.g. the two Black men and the two White men, were instructed to write down all the stereotypes they held of the other group. Subsequently, they had to present their stereotypes to each other and the responsibility of the group on the receiving end was to be reflexive, evaluate what was said, explain the behavior, and to be honest if that was a correct stereotype. This was obviously a sensitive exercise but it was a couple of days into the workshop and I felt a lot of trust was built among the participants.

Amidst much jesting and laughter the different groups would admit to some of the stereotypical behavior but would then explain why it happened. During the discussion it became clear that most of what was originally viewed by both groups as offensive behavior was deeply cultural and as the cultural contexts of the behavior was explained and discussed, so understanding and appreciation grew for the other. It also created an understanding of how cultural behavior could offend and resulted in discussions of how behavior could be modified to create a pleasant workplace.

If South Africa had not gone through such a chaotic and stressful time the opportunity for this kind of open communication would not have presented itself. It was the need for survival that provided me with such a unique experience and opportunity.

(Cilliers, 1998). For the organizational activist it is therefore possible to create dissensus not only at the intersection with the most powerful people in the organization but also at every other nodal point in the organization in which he is involved. Thus, multiple opportunities for resistance to power are possible in the postmodern approach. The use of dissensus is another area where post-modern theory intersects with complexity theory, which argues for breaking the symmetry of systems. Cilliers holds that if a system is too homogenous "the evolving structure can be too symmetrical" (p. 95). One way of breaking sym-metry is through dissensus.

There are many examples of the effects of the homogeneity of systems on public relations practice. First, public relations practice as it is recognized in the West is only possible in democratic systems where every entity has a voice that needs to be heard or where there is free communication in the public sphere. In undemocratic systems the activism that democratic countries take for granted is simply not allowed and, as a result, so-called public relations is either relationship-building between influential entities or, in the case of so-called "developing countries," practiced as development communication where the wishes of governments, in a very paternalistic way, are conveyed to the popula-tion through the supply of information. Second, in very homogenous societies where dissent is viewed as improper social behavior, such as Japan, public rela-tions practice is not developing in a similar fashion as in those countries that are typified by extreme social change through democratization and/or very diverse populations, such as South Africa, Eastern and Western Europe (which is becoming increasingly diverse), and the United States. In both undemocratic and very homogenous countries public relations is developing as a marketing and publicity function because the lack of activism in these societies prevents the development of public relations as activism.

Postmodern theory emphasizes action and practice, particularly because theories have the tendency to create metanarratives and universal principles. If all theories are local and regional, so is all action. In fact, complexity theory too stresses locality as an attribute of a self-organizing system. This supports the postmodern approach to theory as local and regional. The historicity of systems in complexity theory can be equated with the postmodern principle of reflexiv-ity. In the same way that the history of complex and chaotic systems reminds participants in those systems of both the good and the bad that has happened in the system, in the same way reflexivity serves as a mechanism practitioners can use to be cognizant of their own biases, stereotypes, and hegemonic practices. Particularly with an activist approach it is easy to become so enthused that prac-titioners can forget that there are others in the system who interpret situations differently and who have different realities. Postmodernism reminds us contin-uously that we do not create meaning but that meaning is created through the lens of the receiver of messages; a postmodern reality that practitioners should always keep in mind.

A discussion of organizational change, postmodernism, and complexity theory would not be complete without a discussion of organizational crises. Traditionally crises in public relations have been viewed through the lens of linearity, contingency, and rationality with the basic assumption that crises can be managed. Indeed, it would be hard to argue that management of crises is not a reality in public relations practice and often successful—or so we wish to convince ourselves. Also, a very strong tradition of crises as discursive phenomena exists in public relations particularly through the work of Benoit (see Benoit & Pang, 2008 for a comprehensive review of this research). The fact is that crisis communication is a much more complex phenomenon than we believe and much more difficult to "manage" than we would like to admit.

In crisis communication two perspectives dominate, namely, contingency theory in the modernist tradition and complexity theory in the dialogic/dialectic tradition. Contingency theory holds forth a linear approach and "seeks to understand the dynamics, within and without the organization, that affect an accommodative stance [and] ... elaborates on the conditions, factors, and forces that undergird such a stance, along a continuum" from advocacy through accommodation (Cameron, Pang, & Jin, 2008, pp. 136–137). After a content analysis of media coverage of the 2002 sex scandal at the Air Force Academy, a student and I (Holtzhausen & Roberts, 2009) found that so many factors could have affected the outcome of media coverage that a contingency theory approach would not suffice to explain why the Air Force was able to contain the damage within a short period of four months and managed to change media coverage from negative to positive. We concluded that so many internal and external factors could have influenced the outcome of the crisis that

> it will indeed be very difficult, if not impossible, to predict at any time which image repair strategies will be the most effective or which specific situational or predispositional circumstances will successfully predict the appropriate strategies to use during a crisis.

(p. 181)

Although statistical analysis did find empirical support for contingencies, the support was not strong enough to account for the outcome of the crisis. As a result of these findings we support a complexity approach to crisis management as Gilpin and Murphy (2006) propose. These researchers suggest a complexity approach would better prepare practitioners to deal with crises. A complexity approach requires that organizational actors embrace change and complexity and are prepared to learn through the process, rather than being trapped in a fixed crisis plan that does not address the unique issues raised during every crisis.

The postmodern perspective on competing and privileged discourses is also helpful to understand how a crisis proceeds. Somehow public relations as a practice has come to the conclusion that a journalist's discourse is superior to and more valid than that of the public relations practitioner. As a result, the immediate assumption is to accept responsibility and move on. A postmodern approach will argue that no discourse should be privileged over another and that journalists are not more or less objective than public relations practitioners. As the Holtzhausen and Roberts (2009) research showed, the process is dialectic and emergent, which means that the media and the organization changed their perspective during the crisis period based on how the other reacts at different stages of the crisis. Also, when the Air Force used apologia as a message strategy, the media coverage was mostly negative. Dezenhall (2007) argues that apologetics is not necessarily the most appropriate approach and deconstructs how the famous Tylenol case in crisis communication was constructed as a myth to promote the services of a public relations agency. He argues that the media should be taken on aggressively because "modern crises aren't always organic and simple. Instead they're agenda-driven conflicts catalyzed by motivated adversaries. … modern crises aren't communications problems. They're conflicts." In postmodern parlance these conflicts would be tensors between the media and the organization in which the organization is not per definition wrong. Dezenhall says crisis communication is "more guerilla warfare than conventional warfare" and he does not believe public relations practitioners, who have as their aim building relationships, are the best people to deal with a crisis. The best PR person to be in the room is the activist, someone who knows how to deal with adversity and has been through the crisis mill, who "[has] dealt with savage litigation and blanket negative media coverage." It is also someone who has decision-making power. He also believes fighting back assertively is important. Postmodern media approaches will be discussed at length later but suffice it to say that the media, with their short attention span, ratings races, and fragmentation no longer pose the same threat as when they were organized into relatively homogenous and powerful social entities. Organizations now also have many of their own platforms to argue their case, i.e. in the public sphere or through direct communication with their stakeholders.

This does not suggest that organizations should not take responsibility for wrong actions. Personal responsibility is the foundation of postmodern ethics. It merely means that immediately assuming guilt just because a journalist made the claim is not the definitive answer. It is important that the people who did the wrong, if any wrong was committed, should immediately take responsibility. That also means that a CEO who committed wrong-doing does not have the right to use the public relations practitioner to defend those actions. If that happens it is the responsibility of the practitioner to stand up for the function and the other people in the organization affected by but not responsible for the wrongdoing. Schultz (1996) argues that organizational rhetoric diffuses organizational responsibility to *we* and organizations can therefore be viewed as moral actors. I have previously argued that people make up an organization and it should therefore be the people in the organization who take moral responsibility. The use of *we* thus becomes a strategy to hide the individual's moral responsibility. Organizations use three rhetorical strategies to obscure individual causation and control: *decentering* of personal accountability through the submergence of individual voice into that of the organization; *deindividuation*, which is the process whereby individuals are assimilated into an organization's symbolic reality; and *distanciation*, which is used to create diffused responsibility in organizations. It is not hard to conclude that the public relations function stands central to these rhetorical strategies. Although Schultz argues that the postmodern corporation, which is thus constructed, can and should be held morally accountable, it is also hard to accept this as a condition that denies the personal responsibility of the individuals in that corporation, which is the foundation of postmodern ethics. Once again, situations such as crises underscore the complexity of moral decision-making in organizations and raise questions about whether individual members and organizations exist as independent phenomena. Crises themselves often place moral agency and responsibility at the intersection of the individual and the organization (Seabright & Kurke, 1997).

The Democratizing of Organizations

The term *democratic organization* has been an oxymoron for many years. This is partly due to issues of sovereignty (Ibarra-Colado, Clegg, Rhodes, & Kornberger, 2006) but also because traditional interpretations of management did not support power sharing. For many years participative management practice was seen as a weakness and an improbable way to manage, resulting in the term *autocratic management style* as coined by White and Lippitt (1960). However, a discussion of postmodern perspectives in organization theory would not be complete without a discussion of democracy in organizations. Democratic processes are one of the most pertinent concerns for postmodernists because many postmodern scholars are deeply critical and suspicious of management's will and ability to share power. To reassert, postmodernism is not against management per se but rather against *managerialism* (Deetz, 1992, p. 221). It is the focus on management that is one of the main points of a postmodern critique of public relations, which rejects managers as rational beings who make objective decisions for the good of the organization. The modernist approach to management is critiqued for its systematic construction of knowledge and discourse, which makes all human experiences accessible for administration and control. This constitutes a political act on the part of management because it is based in a desire for power.

Some even argue that management itself might be a practice that is on the way out. This is not surprising because in new organizational structures the traditional manager would lose some of that supervisory power so inherent in bureaucracies. Although the following refers specifically to employees affecting their company's stock value, it nonetheless describes how flat organizations have become, which decreases the need for managers:

> The end of management just might look something like this. You show up to work, boot up your computer and log onto your company's Intranet to make a few trades before getting down to work. You see how your stocks did the day before and then execute a few new orders. You think your company should step up production next month, and you trade on that thought. ... All around you, as co-workers arrive at their cubicles, they too flick on their computers and trade. Together, you are buyers and sellers of your company's future. Through your trades, you determine what is going to happen and then decide how your company should respond. With employees in the trading pits betting on the future, who needs the manager in the corner office?
>
> (Kiviat, 2004, p. 4)

Another reason why the manager as an organizational function is disappearing might be societal changes in the first decade of the 21st century. Leadership theory, particularly theories of leadership styles, reflects the political and cultural climate of the time (Eisenberg, Goodall, & Tretheway, 2007). The many changes in organizations, among others organizational structures, brought on by increased use of technology, might be some of the reasons why managers might feel they have become redundant. In recent years the two most studied leadership styles have been transactional and transformational. Transactional leaders gain their influence from organizational variables such as bureaucracy, organizational culture, organizational standards, policy, power, and authority to maintain control and are most effective in stable and predictable environments that do not require change (Aldoory & Toth, 2004; Davidhizer & Shearer, 1997; Kellerman, 1984; S. King, 1994; Northouse, 2007; Tracey & Hinkin, 1998). With the breakdown of traditional hierarchies and power structures in organizations it is questionable whether transactional leadership has a place in organizations of the future. For instance, in a survey of members of the PRSA Werder and I (Werder & Holtzhausen, 2009) found no empirical evidence of transactional leadership attributes in public relations environments. Transactional leadership, also called authoritative leadership, is goal oriented. Subordinates are offered something valued such as recognition, pay raises, and advancement for good performance, or the avoidance of disciplinary action in exchange for reaching their set goals (Bryant, 2003). Many argue that this type of leadership inhibits creativity and risk-taking because, as a result of the impersonal leader-follower relationship, workers only do what is expected of them (Bryant, 2003; Mink, 1992; Yammarino, Spangler, & Dubinsky, 1998).

Contrarily, Werder and I (Werder & Holtzhausen, 2009) found support for the use of transformational leadership in public relations practice. As the name indicates, transformational leadership is associated with organizational change and transformational leaders are viewed as change agents (Eisenberg et al., 2007). Based on social exchange, transformational leaders are viewed as innovative, self-confident, and charismatic and appeal to followers' ideals and moral values. They define a vision for the future, are credible, and accomplish goals by motivating people to work for the greater good of the group or organization. These leadership attributes add to the quality of life of the people and the organization. Transformational leaders will also stand up for what they believe in (Bass, 2000; Northouse, 2007). They not only change others but also are changed in the process. Their deeply held beliefs of integrity and justice play an important role in uniting followers and changing their goals and beliefs because their approach is based on a "relationship of mutual stimulation and elevation" (Burns, 1978, p. 4). New perspectives on leadership argue that the single most important attribute of a leader, cutting across all other factors, is "communication [which is] the essential component of inspiration and change" (Eisenberg et al., 2007, p. 280). Transactional and transformational leadership styles are not mutually exclusive or dichotomous but are practiced on a situational basis. A recent development in leadership studies is the study of leadership traits, which argues that effective, and particularly transformational, leaders share a list of personal qualities that allow them to be successful. These leadership qualities are somewhat reminiscent of the discussions in Chapter 2 on postmodern ethics, which focus on personal responsibility, authenticity, and compassion. These qualities also go beyond the ability to think and argue rationally but rather are more intuitive, creative, motivational, and communicative. Humility and modesty are other traits valued in postmodern leadership (Eisenberg et al., 2007, pp. 281–289).

Werder and I (2009) also identified a participative leadership style in public relations practice, which was conceptualized as a situational approach to public relations practice. There is a strong stream of research on situational leadership, arguing that leaders use different leadership styles depending on the demands of the situation (Eisenberg et al., 2007). This suggests that the environment in which public relations is practiced will influence the field's leadership styles. For instance, if practice is built on collaboration, information sharing, and participative practices (see, for instance, Spicer, 1997) one might assume that the characteristics of collaboration, information sharing, and participative practices will be part of public relations leadership styles. This does not mean that participative leadership is not practiced in other environments. Our study (Werder & Holtzhausen, 2009) found the participative leadership style consisted of more communicative attributes than the transformational style, which was more action-oriented. This interpretation was further supported by the strong correlation between the participative and transformational styles, suggesting participative communication facilitates transformational leadership. A recent

European study (Zerfass, Tench, Verhoeven, Verčič, & Moreno, 2010), which replicated the leadership scales of the Werder and Holtzhausen (2009) study, found overwhelming support for the participative leadership style.

Democracy in organizations has long been associated with participation and decentralization, which are also mechanisms to resist managerialism. Because managerialism is discursively constituted it can be challenged discursively through reflexivity, participation, and, primarily, dissensus. For instance, the activist practitioner can play a role in promoting democratic practices in organizations through the communication process by making others aware of the tensions and contradictions in the workplace. The marginalization of workers in decision-making about their own future and the undemocratic organizational environment has increasingly become a concern over the past decade (Cheney, 1995; S. Deetz, 1992; Monge & Miller, 1988; Strauss, 1982).

An inherent irony is also that organizations, which are along the standards of society inherently undemocratic, manipulate the democratic systems that allow their very existence to further advance themselves through lobbying and donations to political parties, without themselves becoming democratized. Although Miller (1999) argues workplace democracy is more than participation, "for it involves the realization in the workplace of our standards for a democratic society" (p. 188), many scholars link the practice of worker participation with workplace democracy (Cheney, 1995; Deetz, 1992; Locke & Schweiger, 1979; Monge & Miller, 1988). Negative side-effects of non-participation are among others ill health and loss of production (Sashkin, 1984), lack of loyalty (Bennett, 1990), and employee dissatisfaction (Moravec, 1994). Nonetheless, workers have increased responsibility, are working longer hours (Cheney, 1995), and have to bear more intrusion on their private life through the extension of communication technologies (Deetz, 1992).

Although participation is a necessary condition of democracy, it is not sufficient (Cheney, 1995). Cheney views workplace democracy as a process involving "the celebration of self-reflection, collective development and individual opportunity" (p. 171) and offers this rather lengthy definition of workplace democracy:

> A system of governance which truly values individual goals and feelings (e.g., equitable remuneration, the pursuit of enriching work and the right to express oneself) as well as typically organization objectives (e.g., effectiveness and efficiency, reflectively conceived), which actively fosters the connection between those two sets of concerns by encouraging individual contributions to important organizational choices, and which allows for the ongoing modification of the organization's activities and policies by the group.
>
> (pp. 170–171)

Cheney thus argues for the co-creation of personal and company goals through a process of participation and mutual modification. Small group and face-to-face communication is essential for this purpose. He also argues that the core values of an organization should be available for debate by both internal and external interest groups, and "sacred notions of democracy and participation must themselves be open to criticism" (p. 178).

In addition to participative communication Monge and Miller (1988) also identify *representation* which are a dimension of participative systems. They refer to representative participation, which is voting procedures that are more formal. Citing Strauss and Rosenstein (1970) they argue that formal participation has been less successful than direct participation. Nonetheless, several studies show that participation can increase through representative participation, even though management might be less appreciative of such efforts than workers (e.g. D. Taylor & Snell, 1986). Suitable training in representational procedures is required to advance organizational democracy without sacrificing administrative structure and practice. But legitimate concerns remain that representative participation could merely serve as "an institutional façade with no real impact on the lives of either representatives or constituents" (Poole, 1986, p. 235).

There are only a few studies in the domain of public relations that study the effects of democratic practices on an organization's communication climate. I have discussed in several studies (Holtzhausen, 2002a, 2002c, 2005a) how both representative democracy and structural changes to the internal communication in a large organization improved information flow and levels of trust in an organization. However, making these changes is complex and needs years of sustaining before it will become part of an organization's culture. One of the mechanisms used in these studies was the decentralization of the communication function to individual business units. The role of the head office communication function was to be an advocate for the process, create the organizational will and top-level support to implement the process nationwide, and serve as a consultant to other divisions, regions, and other small business units. This provided for possibilities for emergent strategy because even the smallest business units could formulate strategies that would consider how their specific strengths and environmental conditions could support organizational goals. Anderson (2004) argues that a decentralized process for strategic planning and strategy making in post-bureaucratic organizations holds distinct advantages because "decentralized emergent strategy and strategic planning are complementary strategy modes that can coexist and enhance organizational performance, particularly in dynamic environments" (p. 1290). Three factors are necessary to accomplish this: authority for middle managers "to take initiatives, participation in strategic decisions, and strategic planning processes" and the incorporation of these initiatives "into an integrative strategy formation perspective" (p. 1290).

Organization Theory and Public Relations Practice as Activism

Again, like in all other domains, the application of postmodern theory in orga-nization studies is widespread and divergent. The above analysis is typical of postmodern thought as nomadic, wide-ranging, and wandering. Nonetheless, some general postmodern tenets are once again evident and add to our under-standing of how the philosophies and practices of postmodern organization add to our understanding of public relations as an activist practice.

Postmodernism is ultimately concerned about change and continuously emphasizes how changes in philosophical thought, society, and technology shape each other, which in turn lead to a postmodern society that is unique and different from any epoch before. It wishes to undo much of the entrenched thinking that postmodernists believe have led to a society that is inherently unjust and unbalanced in terms of power, voice, and participation toward those who are not in power. Because postmodernists view organizations as porous, they challenge their autonomy and consider them extensions of society.

Not surprisingly organizations do not escape the postmodern concern with language and how it is used to shape power and privilege in institutions. It focuses the attention of how owners and managers present their goals and financial benefits as rational choices founded on objective analysis. Postmod-ernists argue that all discourse is socially constructed and that statements of rationality and objectivity are not valid because they are merely arguments used to hide the underlying desire for power and control over organizational recourses. This in turn highlights the role of public relations in shaping organi-zational discourse and how the public relations function is used to gain power and control in organizations. It also focuses on the use of binary opposites in organizational discourse, which goes beyond the male/female and includes, for instance, the manager/technician and craft/professional dichotomies in public relations literature. It shows how these binary opposites are used to privilege one meaning over another and in this process marginalize certain groups of people. This also explains why public relations practice itself is marginalized because the discourse of marketing and legal practitioners is privileged over that of public relations practitioners. Similarly, the consumer and the organi-zation are privileged over the interests of other stakeholders who are not per-ceived as having a direct benefit to the organization. Increasingly, if something cannot be commodified, for instance public relations practice as symmetry, it will not have any value to the organization. Thus values themselves need to be commodified or are deemed valueless.

In postmodernity the breakdown of traditional hierarchies, such as fixed organizational structure and superficially established categories of work, chal-lenges organizations' autonomy. Subsequently, this questions the assumed power of managers and supervisors in postmodern organizations, described as managerialism. Increasingly questions are raised about the criteria used to privilege certain types of employees over others and why certain work is viewed as more valuable than others. While this legitimizes all work as valued and valid, it places a heavier burden of personal responsibility on the shoulders of all employees. If managers are no longer the sole sources of power in organizations, they also cannot carry the sole responsibility for organizational outcomes. Thus the issue of personal responsibility so prevalent in postmodern ethics is a recurring theme in a postmodern approach to organization theory.

The fragmentation of organizational power does not stop with internal role players but extends to the organization's environment as well. The issue of stakeholder relations, with which public relations practitioners are so familiar, also comes to the fore in postmodernity. But where stakeholders are traditionally identified based on their direct involvement with organizations postmodernism argues that, because of the porous nature of organizations, stakeholders are more fragmented and dispersed than in the past. Thus stakeholders can be people who are affected by an organization's activities without knowing it or even knowing about the organization, and would include the environment and marginalized populations. Again it is the responsibility of the organization, and in particular the public relations practitioner, to identify and take responsibility for these stakeholders without expectations of reaping benefits from those actions.

Because postmodernism embraces change it also embraces organizational crises as ways to make change happen. Organizational crises per definition challenge existing organizational thought patterns and behaviors and are therefore opportunities for the emergence of new thoughts and organizational directions. However, postmodernists are skeptical of the assumption of complexity theorists that crises lead to better systems through self-organization. They argue that those in power and with powerful networks will assert their power during times of crisis. Therefore the public relations practitioner who strives for change will need to identify the power nodes in organizations and society and disrupt these interstices to ensure that old power systems do not perpetuate themselves, thus reverting to old ways of doing.

The postmodern focus on the fragmentation of meaning and identity also challenges the way in which organizations are studied. Instead of looking at organizations as universal entities with similar attributes across nations and cultures postmodernism returns the focus to the local and regional nature of all organizations. Even subsidiaries of international companies would therefore have attributes that are reflective of the local political, social, economic, and cultural environment, which in turn will lead to very specific organizational practices. This also will affect the way in which meaning is created. Postmodernists argue meaning is situated in the receiver of messages and that receivers of messages interpret them in the framework of existing belief systems, cultural frameworks, economic status, class, and personal experiences, to mention but a few. Thus meaning chaotically and randomly bounces off the participants in conversations, toppling forward instead of bouncing back and forth. This approach would make contingency theory approaches, so prominent in modernist approaches to organization theory and so dependent on the linearity of meaning creation, all but redundant.

Finally, the postmodern turn in organization theory challenges command-and-control management and replaces it with the visionary leader who is transformative, charismatic, nonconformist, and a strong communicator. Thus the manager as a rational being who has all the knowledge at hand to make the best decisions is replaced with the leader with strong personal attributes who promotes democratic practices in organizations through participation and inspiration and setting a strong personal example, showing activism in leadership.

6
PUBLIC RELATIONS KNOWLEDGE AND RESEARCH IN POSTMODERNITY

As for what motivated me, it is quite simple; I would hope that in the eyes of some people it might be sufficient in itself. It was curiosity—the only kind of curiosity, in any case, that is worth acting upon with a degree of obstinacy: not the curiosity that seeks to assimilate what it is proper for one to know, but that which enables one to get free of oneself. After all, what would be the value of the passion for knowledge if it resulted only in a certain amount of knowledgeableness and not, in one way or another and to the extent possible, in the knower's straying afield of himself? There are times in life when the question of knowing if one can think differently than one thinks, and perceive differently than one sees, is absolutely necessary if one is to go on looking and reflecting at all.

(Foucault, 1985, p. 8)

Generally, the postmodern concern with knowledge relates to how knowledge shapes and is shaped by power, which subsequently leads to questions of the legitimization of knowledge, i.e. what counts as knowledge and who is accountable for knowledge. This naturally leads to questions of the role of scholarship in public relations and the methods we use to create a knowledge base for the field. This question goes beyond a discussion of whether qualitative and quantitative research methods are the most appropriate. It leads to pedagogical issues, such as the legitimacy of teachers, the relationship between teacher and student, and curriculum development.

In this chapter I will review the postmodern perspectives on the links between power and knowledge, particularly at the hand of the work of Foucault (1972, 1980b), and the legitimation of knowledge (Lyotard, 1984). I will explore the role of the scholar/teacher in theory building in the field and review postmodern perspectives on data and data collection and how these methods can be applied to provide alternative and/or additional insights into public relations theory and practice. I will conclude with a discussion of postmodern perspectives on pedagogical issues as mentioned above.

Knowledge and Power

Is knowledge about the past or the future? Postmodernists would argue that knowledge is about renewal, new ideas, and new understandings, thus more about the future than the past. Again, Harland's (1987) metaphor of how postmodern meaning resembles dominoes falling forward comes to mind. Similarly, past knowledge is only relevant when informing us about the present or serving as the basis for the future. For instance, as I said in Chapter 3, historical narrative serves as a way of understanding the present and guiding us to the future, how fraught those assumptions might be. Also important is to understand that all knowledge is socially created. Societies determine what kinds of knowledge are relevant and create systems that legitimate that knowledge, for instance through school systems and institutions of higher learning. There is no knowledge that exists outside of society. There is no innate knowledge that humankind is born with and there also is no finite knowledge. Humans make up the rules for knowledge as they go along. Sometimes these rules are constructed over millennia, as in the case of philosophy; centuries, as in the sciences; or mere decades, as in computer-based knowledge. This recalls the debate brought about by Kuhn's notion of scientific paradigms (Kuhn, 1970a, 1970b), which essentially argues that scientific knowledge is created within sets of rules and because the rules of paradigms differ, they cannot be compared in terms of which paradigm is better. This is quite similar to Lyotard's (1988) notion of "genres of discourse" or "language games" and the incommensurability of genres of discourse.

With this in mind it is not hard to understand that power is an issue in knowledge creation. Those who have power will have the ability to make the rules and so influence knowledge creation and its legitimation. Public relations itself is subject to this issue. When public relations academics and scholars do not have power in schools of mass communication, their knowledge might be denigrated in favor of the knowledge created in journalism or marketing. With that comes the allocation of resources, which further entrenches the lack of power of public relations scholars. Another example is the preferred use of quantitative methods over qualitative methods, with quantitative research and its data and results viewed as more legitimate than those in qualitative research.

Rupture and Discontinuity in Knowledge

The importance in the development of knowledge is not continuity but discontinuity; "it is no longer one of lasting foundations, but one of transformations that serve as new foundations, the rebuilding of foundations" (Foucault, 1972, p. 5). At the *macroscopic* level knowledge is legitimated not through its inherent rationality but through the continuous use of its methods and theoretical concepts. Therefore, it is important to reveal the ideological nature of the past of a specific genre of knowledge and the "anthropological justification" (p. 7) of its development. As a result postmodern knowledge is not peaceful, certain, and restful but rather quite violent, volatile, and unsettling. Foucault's mission is to expose assumptions of objectivity, rationality, and transcendence in knowledge domains by asking "where they came from, to what historical destination they are moving without being aware of it, what naïvety [sic] blinds them to the conditions that make them possible, and what metaphysical enclosure encloses their rudimentary positivism" (p. 202). Thus for Foucault the archeological project (he stresses that it is not a methodology) is to expose "such concepts as rules of formation, archeological derivation and historical a priori" (p. 206) within knowledge domains with the aim of showing how they were postulated through language and action.

This approach challenges public relations scholars to question the basic knowledge assumptions on which the field is based and to acknowledge that those who participate in the field also are involved in the process of constituting it. Because all knowledge is socially constructed scholars and practitioners should challenge all assumptions about what the field is, whether one approach is more relevant than another, or one methodology superior to another, an issue to which I will return. These challenges should consider who constructed the knowledge in the field, who it is benefitting from those constructions, and what the underlying ideologies are. This is an issue I also discussed in Chapter 3. By challenging these assumptions scholars can disrupt dominating discourses in the field, resist any notions of establishing dominant paradigms, and ensure that all discourse is continuously decentered. These discontinuities would dare scholars to let go of their certainties and arrogances and acknowledge that there are many kinds of knowledge. There is indeed a strong tradition of critical approaches to public relations theory and practice, such as Gandy's (1989) Marxist analysis; the many feminist critiques that started with Creedon (1991) and continued with the works of Toth, L. A. Grunig, Hon, and Aldoory—too many to mention and too significant to only single out a few; and symbolic interpretative and postmodern approaches that are critical of the institutional bias of practice (see for instance Cheney and Christensen (2001); *Journal of Public Relations Research*, 17(1); and *Public Relations Review*, 31(4) for more examples of critical approaches). This critical stance in public relations, whether it is through a postmodern lens or not, is partly the reason why the field is theoretically so vibrant and growing so strongly. At some level, all these critical approaches investigate the relationship between power and practice. The postmodern analysis of the link between power and knowledge adds a further understanding.

Power Creates Knowledge

One of the main arguments Foucault (1980b) uses to explain the relationship between knowledge and power is to show how the desire to control the body through normalizing and disciplinary practices has led to the development of knowledge domains, particularly those of medicine, psychiatry, and other human and behavioral sciences. It is now not the role of the intellectual to serve as advisor but rather to "provide instruments of analysis" to show "where the instances of power have secured and implanted themselves by a system of organization dating back over 150 years ago" (p. 62), referring to the increased use of technology and science in establishing systems of power since the start of the 19th century. The human sciences were created at the moment when the surveillance and record-taking of individuals were formalized and the data gathered organized as domains of knowledge. Obtaining demographic, and now also psychographic, information of publics, stakeholders, and consumers remains one of the mainstays of public relations research. If one were to think it through, Foucault's argument is still very much alive in public relations research where these kinds of data often are used to gain knowledge of specific types of people for the purposes of manipulation or, if that is too harsh a word, at least for selective information sharing, i.e. who are the most powerful stakeholders that need to be communicated with.

The role then of the intellectual also is to focus her analyses on those domains of knowledge where she has experience and should focus on how systems of truth are established in the field under study (in this case public relations), what the effects are of those systems of truth, and how these relate to power. For instance, historical analyses of the development of public relations practice in the United States and the United Kingdom, as discussed in Chapter 3, show how political and industrial power holders used communication practice to further entrench that power. Thus the development of public relations as a social or technoscience can be viewed as parallel to the development of organizations and bureaucratic structures in these countries. This is an example of how the desire to further entrench established power systems facilitates the development of the field. It also shows how the surveying and categorization of the behavior of practitioners and their publics is an effort to control that behavior.

It is important to understand that knowledge created through power becomes entrenched in society through the very systems of power that created the knowledge in the first place. For instance, public relations is legitimated when taught at universities as social or human science. This in turn legitimates the students who go forth to practice as professionals. It is therefore not only the fact that public relations is taught at the university that legitimates the field but also the fact that the university system legitimates the people who practice it, thus further establishing its basis of power in society. As Foucault (1980b) argues, power in its exercise goes much further [than merely institutional power], passes through much finer channels, and is much more ambiguous, since each individual has at his disposal a certain power, and for that very reason can also act as the vehicle for transmitting a wider power.

(p. 72)

Power and knowledge are not separate entities but intertwined. They need each other for their existence. "The exercise of power perpetually creates knowledge and conversely, knowledge constantly induces effects of power" (Foucault, 1980b, p. 52). Although university systems are the most obvious example of this interrelationship they are the least dangerous. The kinds of power Foucault refers to are "[d]iffused, entrenched and dangerous, they operate in other places that in the person of the old professor" (p. 52). The link between power and knowledge also can be positive. As Bauman (cf. Chapter 2) said about the Other, knowledge is an essential component of being with the Other. To know about the Other is to understand and act. Similarly, knowledge is an important component of resisting power. By understanding the processes and discourses through which power is created, it is possible to resist power by using those very same discourses (Abel, 2005) through what Foucault (1985) calls "open strategies" (p. 6).

Examining and understanding those assumptions we take as given, i.e. creating a knowledge base of an issue or event, is therefore the first step to resisting power. Particularly valuable for activist public relations practitioners is the understanding that power is not a given but is continuously shaped through social practice. Organizations in themselves do not have power; it is the people in them that shape their power and practitioners can participate in that process without losing their jobs. This also allows them to change the negative aspects of organizational life, which aim to control society for its own profit and survival, into a positive force that focuses on sustainability, which implies the co-evolution of organization and society rather than a winner-takes-all approach.

Power Subjugates Knowledge

Power subjugates knowledge in two ways: through creating historical narratives that exclude facts and events and by declaring certain kinds of knowledge as inadequate or naïve (Foucault, 1980b). The first type has been discussed at length in Chapter 3 and I have shown how historical narrative excluded vast areas of practice that would show alternative approaches and knowledge fields for public relations, such as anthropology, political studies, international relations, and so forth.

The second type is perhaps more allusive but nonetheless one with which public relations knowledge is intimately familiar. That is the type of knowledge that has been disqualified to count as knowledge because it is viewed as naïve, low-ranking, unqualified, and "below the required level of cognition or scientificity" (Foucault, 1980b, p. 82). Vignette 6.1 serves as an example of how power is used for this purpose.

This vignette shows how the "production-based" courses in that school are viewed as inferior to the other department's focus on media "studies," which focuses on "history, theory, and/or analysis." These words were used to show mass communication knowledge as naïve, low in importance, even lower in the hierarchy of knowledge, and "beneath the required level of cognition or scientificity" (Foucault, 1980b, p. 82) that warrants the use of a title that includes both media and communication. The existing name of that school puts it exactly in its place, namely at the lowest level of the knowledge hierarchy. The statement is wrong in many ways. The school has a graduate program and does offer theoretical, historical, legal, and socio-political perspectives, as anybody familiar with accreditation standards would know. However, this event clearly shows how power is asserted through marginalizing others' knowledge. Foucault stresses the necessity of exposing these instances through a process (not a methodology) of genealogy. He describes genealogical research as "the union of erudite knowledge and the local memories which allow us to establish a historical knowledge of struggles and to make use of this knowledge tactically today" (p. 83). A genealogy focuses not on research methods, issues of positivism, or science but rather on the claims of those disqualified knowledges, in this case the knowledge generated in the school. It is the very act of marginalizing knowledge that must be exposed to show how privilege and power is created.

But it is not only other departments or disciplines that marginalize and suppress the growth of knowledge in the field—it is often disciplines within the field that promote marginalization and suppression through arrogance. One reason why this particular department felt justified acting in this way toward the school is because of the school's history of a stubborn emphasis on journalism and its professional status. Many years ago the school had the opportunity to incorporate the Department of Speech Communication into its structure, but thought it was beneath the status of a school of journalism.

The journalistic hegemony in the school was perpetuated further in the name of the moral and ethical superiority of journalism over disciplines such as public relations and advertising. For many years nearly all the faculty members with Ph.D.s were in the news editorial sequence, which also has been the smallest sequence for a long time. This is one example of how public relations and advertising had been marginalized academically while heavily relying on the student numbers to maintain the hegemony of journalism. It is no wonder that other disciplines think we only teach production-based courses.

This focus on professionalism exposes a certain anti-intellectualism in professional journalists that has harmed schools and colleges of mass communication. There are numerous examples where the focus on professionalism has

VIGNETTE 6.1

"The school of which I was the director recently decided to change its name to include the word 'media' to better reflect what it is we study and teach. The previous name was more than 40 years old and the professional and academic landscape of the field has changed a great deal over that time. I presented the new name to the dean of the college, who distributed the proposed name for comment and feedback to the other departments in the college, the biggest on campus. In reaction I received an e-mail from one department head, who had strong feelings about our name change.

> We have concerns that the name change may also prefigure curriculum expansion which would lead to undesirable duplication of courses in film studies, television studies, or media studies. To be clear, the word "studies" here indicates a course focused on history, theory, and/or analysis, as opposed to the production-based courses [your school] currently offers. In the area of communication the concerns would be about courses in language, discourse analysis, genre analysis, and rhetoric as applied to written and spoken discourse. In general, there is a feeling that a more specifically delimited name would be less problematic.

I responded that other schools and colleges of our nature typically offer courses in these areas and that there are mechanisms in place at both the college and university level to ensure that there is no duplication of courses. Also, we are not interested in treading on their terrain or duplicating their courses. I received the following response:

> We are very well aware that some of your peer schools encompass media and film studies; that is exactly what prompted the concern of our faculty in this area. They wanted to be certain that your school did not have the intention of creating a parallel and competing program in this area. ... It may also be true that you have faculty who work in areas related to media studies ... but an examination of the course catalog suggests that at present you have few courses with this focus at the undergraduate level and none at the graduate level.

In response I pointed out that we have a well-established graduate program and that we are in the process of applying for a Ph.D. program. Finally, there was agreement that we could include the term *media* in our new name but it was clearly articulated that our level of knowledge of this field was seriously lacking and below accepted standards of what would construe a serious theoretical focus on media."

marginalized whole schools and colleges of journalism and mass communication because they do not value critical and alternative approaches to the study of media. The fact is academics with professional backgrounds are the best people to be critical of the fields they study, rather than those who have never worked in a professional environment. It is up to those who are directly involved in a field who are "faced with all the conflicts of power which traverse it, to confront them and construct the instruments which will enable you to fight on that terrain" (Foucault, 1980b, p. 65). That also is the only way to legitimate the local knowledge and experiences of professionals in the field, rather than creating totalizing theories and critiques, as the department did in Vignette 6.1.

The role of the postmodern academic is to be an academic activist, to rebel against the suppression of knowledge. This is done by exposing the relationship between knowledge suppression and the desire for power, mostly to sustain existing institutional arrangements that often stand in the way of new thinking and new approaches. It is this very relationship that gives scientific discourse its power. The reality is that academic knowledge in our field is seriously under attack from within and outside the academy. This needs serious activism of the kind discussed above. Vignette 6.2 shows why.

From Vignette 6.2 it is clear that the real argument was no longer about the name change but about the legitimation of knowledge. In the eye of these two alumni the academic approach to the field was viewed as no longer legitimate. Clearly the experience on the ground by people without graduate degrees was much preferred over people taught by professors with Ph.D.s. Even more prominent were the arguments relating to technology. This journalist argues that technology training in the workplace and using technology on a daily basis is adequate for the future journalism workplace. This leads to arguments about public relations as technoscience.

Public Relations as Technoscience

For both Foucault and Lyotard the Enlightenment aim of scientific discourse is suppression. That is the link they establish between power and knowledge. The aim of their analyses in this regard is not to critique specific research methods or theories, although Lyotard (1984) does provide some specific examples of scientific and theoretical metanarratives. The aim of their work, albeit from two different vantage points, is to challenge the way in which power suppresses certain types of knowledge.

From their perspective the role of science, particularly human and social sciences, is to control the individual. Foucault (1980b) shows how theories of individual rights in democracy have led to processes that aim to control the people who now have the right to act on their own. Bauman (1993) makes a similar argument when he says that the replacement of feudal and monarchic government systems with nation states now requires control of citizens through various, mostly hidden, means. In a democratic society there is a big need for hidden

Vignette 6.2

"The faculty voted and accepted a new name for the school. The faculty vote was overwhelming in favor of the new name but one faculty member would not accept the decision and immediately contacted an alumnus who graduated not too long ago and was working at a major regional paper. Within half an hour of the decision, the dean received an e-mail about the name change, particularly about the fact that journalism will no longer be in the name, and asked me to respond.

I explained to the alumnus that the existing name did not reflect what the students studied because all students graduate from the school with a degree in journalism, while two-thirds of the students actually studied public relations and advertising. I continued to explain that the school would in future offer three degree programs, one of which would be multimedia journalism. Students would in future graduate with a degree that reflects their area of study and their degrees would be more specific and less misleading. I also pointed out that an academic approach and a professional approach in the school are not mutually exclusive and that there is a place for both.

The alumnus responded as follows:

First, the argument about [the university] being a research university and not a vocational school is somewhat insulting. What's needed in journalism education are people who've worked under editors, who've had public records fights, who've learned how to negotiate the bureaucracy—not someone who writes research articles for publications no one reads.

In my newsroom, I work with people who have won Pulitzer Prizes. At my last job at XXX, I worked under a guy who had been a part of three Pulitzers. Before I arrived, he had just guided the newspaper to another Pulitzer finalist spot with their ground-breaking investigation of FEMA before it became a national punching bag following Katrina.

None of those people have graduate degrees. They've been too busy raising hell and protecting the public. Am I seeking to diminish the honors of achieving advanced degrees? Heck no. But if you told me the university was refusing to hire a Pulitzer Prize winner because they didn't have an advanced degree, I'd steer any youngster who listened against attending that school.

In fact, I'll tell you right now that I could walk into a classroom and teach journalism students about how to use GIS software, how to use social science methods in journalism, how to use SPSS and SAS, how to use scripting languages like Perl or Ruby—all in the pursuit of a good investigation—and I was a lousy immature student!

Placing a premium on professional experience over academic honors doesn't make [the university] a vocational school. It means it recognizes what's important in a field. In fact, the argument doesn't really hold water because vocational schools don't have their students getting well-rounded critical [sic] thinking-based educations.

With the rapidly changing media landscape, there's no shortage of journalism academics pontificating on what's needed to "save journalism." Most of the time, the majority are mocked by practicing journalists because their time in the ivory tower has rendered them unrealistic. I look around the country and see journalism schools snatching up mid-career professionals to bring realism to their programs for the 21st century—it seems [the university] is going in the opposite direction.

… we build a department full of Ph.Ds to make ourselves feel important and brag to Newsweek, but has no practical impact on the students. As much as universities seem to disregard students these days while chasing the research dollar, the very history of my alma mater is to educate students. But, thanks to my great journalism education, I was taught it's always about the money.

I again responded that we indeed use professionals with bachelor's degrees to teach students and that we had a Pulitzer Prize winning journalist the previous semester. I again reiterated that "we do not value professionalism over academic accomplishments. I do not believe they are mutually exclusive." But the author would have none of that and wrote back saying, among other things:

I am hammered every single day by nonsense press releases sent by someone who clearly didn't know how to write. You know where it goes? In the trashcan. Seems to me that a journalism background is what set our graduates apart from others. You know the others: They are the ones who send press releases with exclamation points and clichés that make me want to puke.

Media means a lot of things: film studies, English, technical writing, fiction writing, whatever. The university is removing from the school's name a huge part of its heritage, which is producing working journalists.

> ... As for the professional history vs. academic qualifications: I would be willing to guess that under your new policies, several of the professors who taught me wouldn't be hired today. Those professors are who enabled me to get where I'm at today at merely 32.
>
> I'm sorry not everyone wants to be a journalist. This country could use more watchdogs and fewer people producing propaganda. But I understand everyone has a calling in life and understand your desire to include them in the school's name. My distress is that you're doing it at the expense of the rest of us.
>
> At this time I decided not to respond any longer but then received an e-mail from an alumnus related to the one above who wrote in similar terms and indicated that we as academics do not know what is going on in the real world. By this time I no longer responded because what was disconcerting about these e-mails was not the fact that they did not agree with what we were doing but the fact that they were so disrespectful and arrogant. Both these alumni clearly did not respect academic knowledge."

controls. For Foucault the analysis of the relationship between knowledge and power should focus on "an analysis of the mechanisms of repression" (1980b, p. 90). This turns the attention to science, or more specifically *technoscience*.

Lyotard (Lyotard & Thébaud, 1985) makes a distinction between descriptive and prescriptive speech. Although Lyotard speaks largely in the context of justice in this case, the argument can be extended to scientific discourse as well, particularly in the realms of natural and social sciences. Where natural sciences are descriptive (or denotative) in nature, social sciences are values-based. Although social sciences aim to be descriptive in the same way as natural sciences, the way in which social science knowledge is accumulated really is based on the value systems of its theorists and scientists. The results of the social and human sciences are then used to direct society, make policy, and determine specific outcomes. Jameson (Lyotard, 1984) describes this as the crisis of the sciences, namely, that of "representation as the reproduction, for subjectivity, of an objectivity that lies outside of itself" (p. viii). What Lyotard is essentially arguing is that scientific discourse, while presenting itself as denotative, is nothing but narrative. Furthermore, Lyotard argues, the aim of this illogical jump between denotative and prescriptive scientific outcomes is to have control over society.

Foucault (1980b) makes a similar point about the relationship between power and knowledge and argues that these "apparatuses of control" (in the case of public relations—social science as knowledge) cannot evolve without becoming "ideological constructs" (p. 102). Like Lyotard he does not perceive a logical link between the descriptive and prescriptive and argues the object of study should be how knowledge and scientific discourse are used for domination and how they become "the material operators of power" (p. 102). He too makes a distinction between scientific domains, such as physics and chemistry, and argues it is much more difficult to link these kinds of sciences to structures of domination in society than in the case of other forms of knowledge, such as the social sciences. He specifically uses the example of psychiatry, where "the epistemological profile is … a low one" and where its practice "is linked with a whole range of institutions, economic requirements and political issues of social regulation" (p. 109). Thus, for both Lyotard and Foucault the burning issue is how certain types of knowledge, typical of that which includes public relations as a social science, is used to control, discipline, and manipulate. These kinds of power mechanisms are much more indirect in that they do not have overt economic benefit. As a result they were not deemed important in previous analyses of power, where power was overtly linked to economics. However, these knowledge domains are important in that their normalizing and disciplinary practices "are essential to the general functioning of the wheels of power" (p. 116).

This kind of science has become known as a technoscience, of which public relations is a part (L'Etang, 2004). Technoscience's predominant characteristic is its use in creating social control mechanisms for the purpose of improving and measuring output and yield. In public relations the purpose of its social scientific foundation is to understand the communication behavior of its publics in such a way that the messages created and the information disseminated can have an optimal and measurable outcome in terms of controlling those publics to the benefit of the organizations they work for. This kind of capitalism is called *technocapitalism*, which refers to "the synthesis of capital and technology in the present organization of society" (Best & Kellner, 2001, p. 213). This leads to the commodification of knowledge, i.e. knowledge that cannot be measured in terms of its contribution to capitalism will become redundant. Knowledge that public relations scholars build in the name of social science and information processes, measured in terms of their effectiveness and outcomes, contribute to technocapitalism and become *technoknowledge*. Thus, instead of promoting the free flow of knowledge and information through temporary networks that will facilitate the emancipatory potential of information (Lyotard, 1984), public relations as technoscience ensures the domination of those powerful communicative entities in societies that have the necessary resources to ensure their domination. In this way, public relations practice and theory contribute to the repression of new and alternative theories and practices through what Lyotard (1984) calls metanarratives.

Metanarratives in Public Relations Theory

In this discussion I will focus on two perspectives relevant to metanarratives: the link between power, truth, and knowledge; and the suppression of knowledge. Since Lyotard owns the concept of metanarratives, his work will be the focus of this section. Lyotard focuses on two main attributes of metanarratives. One focus is the concept of *narrative*, i.e. storytelling. The other is the concept of a narrative that has become so *meta* that it is no longer questioned and displaces all other narratives or stories.

Metanarratives as Unchallenged Assumptions

The quote from the *Voice Literary Supplement* on the back cover of Lyotard's (1984) text describes metanarratives as "the supreme (and supremely unified and unifying) fictions we tell ourselves about ourselves."

This stance on metanarratives is most likely the defining moment for postmodernism in that it also defines and names postmodernism. Lyotard (1984, p. xxiv) says, "Simplifying to the extreme, I define *postmodern* as incredulity toward metanarratives." Metanarratives become so accepted that they are no longer challenged and go "underground" because we unconsciously use these metanarratives to negotiate our reality (Lyotard, 1984, p. xii). This means that we have become so used to thinking in certain ways that we do not even understand how these metanarratives or "master narratives" influence our thinking. We take for granted that things just are a certain way and no longer question the underlying assumptions. A metanarrative "is a narrative form which seeks to provide a definitive account of reality" (Edgar & Sedgwick, 2002, p. 163). Examples of metanarratives in Western society are concepts of progress, effectiveness, production, and institutionalization through bureaucracy. These basic assumptions are clear in public relations theory building and development, e.g. in the measurement of public relations outcomes.

In postmodernity metanarratives are impossible because there is no longer an overarching language or discourse that can include or describe all the different language games or genres of knowledge. This overarching "language" is impossible because there are no longer single entities that can create and enforce those metanarratives, such as the Church and monarchies during the Middle Ages, or the state and its institutions in modern times. Because people use different language games to justify their arguments, language games cannot be compared and are therefore incommensurable (Williams, 1998). Society itself has now become fragmented because of the fragmentation of language games in what is generally known as an attribute of postmodern society, i.e. different language games competing for recognition.

Similar to language games in society, science also consists of language games. Williams (1998) provides the following explanation of how language games work: a city is divided into four quarters, each with its own basis for the law governing that section. One sector might use property as the basis for its laws, while others could use class, gender, or financial wealth. When laws are broken at the intersection between quarters, there is no common set of laws (something like a metalaw) to address the transgression and the people of at least one of the quarters will be offended by the laws applied. This is also true for scientific research. For instance, different research paradigms are incommensurable because their laws for conducting that research are different. Critical analysis and quantitative analysis cannot be compared in terms of results because their language games make no sense to each other. Also, one language game cannot be viewed as superior to the other because how well a language game is played depends on how well the participants understand and adhere to the rules of that particular game. A language game is therefore only legitimated through the consensus of its players. A researcher really can only play one game at a time.

Metanarratives also can have a strong ideological foundation. In public relations theory itself there are metanarratives, such as public relations as a management function, the institutionalization of practice, two-way symmetry as communication model, relationship building, and so forth. If one deconstructs these approaches it is clear that public relations practice is deeply embedded in the ideology of capitalism and its institutions, as stated in Chapter 3. Not understanding the ideological foundations of these narratives can then lead to a superficial treatment of public relations theory, with students often not exploring what these theories really entail and where they originated. One example is the situational theory of publics, which J. Grunig and Hunt (1984) built on the democratic theories of John Dewey and Herbert Blumer. The concept of *public* is not merely a group of people who act together but is a group of people who in a democratic society has the right to organize and become activists. It is needless to say that these theories belong to Western democracies. However, the reality is that the very principle of the public sphere in Western society is highly contested.[1] Despite the fact that the situational theory is based on an American approach to democracy it is widely applied to other countries, even those that do not have similar histories of democratic development. This is an example of how theories become metanarratives because they are taken for granted, are applied without understanding the original thinking that led to their formulation, and without thinking through what the implications would be of applying theories in contexts other than those in which they were developed. Thus metanarratives in public relations set the parameters of what is studied and how it is studied without questioning the underlying assumptions.

Lyotard (1984) describes two other kinds of metanarratives, which I believe have been influential in the realm of mass communication, particularly in the relationship between public relations and journalism, namely, "narratives of legitimation" (p. 31) of knowledge. He argues that with modernism and through its project of humanism science had to be legitimated for sociopolitical purposes. However, two divergent forms of sociopolitical influence developed simultaneously. Under Napoleon the aim of state institutions in the legitimation of knowledge was to train and educate people to fulfill roles in state institutions and so ensure the stability of the state. Although the ultimate aim of this process was to ensure state control of society, it was portrayed as training people in the name of freedom. Lyotard argues the subject of this narrative is practical—the "hero of liberty" (p. 31). In this narrative the subject of knowledge is the people.

At the same time the German educational system under Humboldt at the University of Berlin developed its own narrative of legitimation and argued that knowledge for the sake of knowledge is an empty act (Lyotard, 1984). The role of knowledge should be to build character and the role of knowledge therefore is philosophical, aimed at creating ethical social and political actors. In this approach knowledge is legitimated if it engenders spiritual and ethical beings whose characters are shaped through complete knowledge. One might imagine that this laid the foundation for what is known as a liberal arts education. Lyotard argues the subject of this narrative is cognitive—the "hero of knowledge" (p. 31). This notion of metaknowledge, that there is a single understanding of society through knowledge that should ultimately define the spirit, is still somewhat apparent in the work of the German scholar Habermas. At the same time the concept of emancipation through liberty is also even now what drives much of modern French philosophy.

I wish to argue that much of what has happened in journalism in Western nations is that it supported the narrative of liberty, i.e. journalists became the heroes of liberty and the subject of their knowledge is the people they report on. On the other hand, public relations has aligned itself with the narrative of cognition, particularly through its information function, i.e. practitioners act as the heroes of knowledge. Both disciplines use these different narratives to legitimate themselves. In the case of the hero of liberty, Lyotard argues the language of legitimation is political. Contrarily, public relations, as the hero of knowledge, distances itself from the people and their fight for liberty and legitimates itself through a narrative of spiritual and moral upliftment through its act of generating information and knowledge. This is another example of how incommensurable the language games of public relations and journalism are.

In postmodern culture, however, the grand narrative is no longer credible because there are no longer forces that hold these metanarratives together. Largely due to the fragmentation of society these grand narratives are challenged and shown not as scientific knowledge but only as language games, and on top of that highly politicized language games. This brings fear because the familiar stories we told ourselves about ourselves are challenged. Some argue that the breaking up of metanarratives is leading to "the dissolution of the social bond" (Lyotard, 1984, p. 15). However, Lyotard argues very affirmatively that the social bond is established through communication and not through metanarratives of individuality. "The social bond is linguistic, but it is not woven with a single thread" (p. 40). The metanarrative of the powerful individual is now replaced with the discourse of the fragmented individual which is constituted through its situated relationship. "Young or old, man or woman, rich or poor, a person is always located at 'nodal points' of specific communication circuits, however tiny these might be" (p. 15). Reminiscent of Foucault, Lyotard argues that language is action and power. "No one, not even the least privileged among us, is ever entirely powerless over the messages that traverse and position him at the post of sender, addressee, or referent" (p. 15). These communication nodal points are opportunities for the use of power through language. Public relations practitioners, too, are situated at many such communication nodal points, which provide them with opportunities to influence the little narratives in which they are involved or to resist unfair communication practices in their environments.

Also, this approach has heuristic value for public relations research. If the social bond is formed through language games, including research (the language game of inquiry), as public relations researchers we need to study individual practitioners to see how they shape and are shaped by their institutions through their discourse and narrative, and how they shape and are shaped by society. Existing stakeholder definitions inhibit us from really understanding and studying our influence on society. I wish to argue that, although we view community as a stakeholder, that definition is not broad enough. For example, an organization (for- or non-profit) that receives tax benefits or in some way profits from government incentives to that particular industry has a responsibility to tax payers because in the end it is their money that is being utilized to generate profits or income. Tax payers cannot be represented through a narrow definition of stakeholders but rather require much more transparency from these companies. This places a much bigger burden of responsible and open communication on the shoulders of public relations practitioners than most companies are prepared to share. Much of this kind of research cannot be conducted through aggregated data collected among any number of practitioners.

Metanarratives thus are fictions and, more so, dangerous fictions because they legitimate other fictions that play by their rules and repeat their stories while labeling those narratives that do not conform to their rules as untruthful. This explains why the *Voice Literary Supplement* refers to metanarratives as "the supreme (and supremely unified and unifying) fictions we tell ourselves about ourselves."

Efficiency/Technology as Metanarrative

Another metanarrative to which Lyotard (1984) pays special attention is the grand narrative of performativity and efficiency. He argues technology has transformed knowledge and theorizes the link between technology, knowledge, and power. The link between these three factors is that only knowledge that can be distributed electronically, i.e. translated into computer language, will be transferred and disseminated. This would further marginalize the knowledge of those communities, or stakeholders in general, that do not have similar access to or knowledge of technology. In public relations this already is happening in that public relations practice is only studied in those countries where knowledge systems have access to technology or where public relations is practiced according to specific rules and practices. Those who do not play the language game of mainstream public relations practice will be excluded.

This also excludes the study of people who practice communication outside of the acknowledged borders of public relations practice. South Africa is a case in point. A recent study showed that the majority of government communicators in that country have never studied public relations but practice a strategic form of communication practice (Holtzhausen & Tindall, 2009). They were mostly selected for these positions because of their ability to communicate with strategic stakeholders, particularly those at grassroots level. The study also found that advertising practitioners performed at higher levels of strategic communication practice than public relations practitioners in that country, despite the fact that South Africa has been educating public relations practitioners since the 1970s and that the Public Relations Institute of South Africa has been active in that country since the 1950s.

It is important to recognize that technology is not about morality or science but about efficiency, which now has become the metanarrative, replacing the metanarratives of emancipation and knowledge. Technology increases performativity (effectiveness), which in turn increases one's ability to produce truth through the creation of knowledge.

> By reinforcing technology, one "reinforces" reality, and one's chances of being just and right increase accordingly. Reciprocally, technology reinforces all the more effectively if one has access to scientific knowledge and decision-making authority. This is how legitimation of power takes shape. Power is not only good performativity, but also effective verification and good verdicts. It legitimates science and the law on the basis of their efficiency, and legitimates this efficiency on the basis of science and law.
>
> (Lyotard, 1984, p. 47)

Because access to information drives effectiveness and performance it increases access to power. If a science cannot prove that its knowledge contributes to effectiveness, "even indirectly," that system will be rejected. Again, this relates directly to public relations. One of the main goals of the field as a social science is to show how effective it is and whole bodies of knowledge are devoted to measuring the effectiveness and outcomes of public relations programs. Practitioners and academics know intuitively that if this cannot be done it will diminish the position of public relations in institutions. This has changed the role of knowledge. Where in the past the question was: "Is it true?" the question now is: "What use is it?" or "Is it efficient?" (p. 51).

This has led to new metanarratives of functionalism and professionalism (Lyotard, 1984), factors that we are all too familiar with in public relations.[2] But Lyotard also provides strategies to resist these metanarratives and allow participants to change the rules of the game. Practitioners now require a new skills set to be functional and professional within the metanarratives of efficiency. He suggests six strategies for survival:

1. immediate problem solving skills;
2. the ability to "organize data into an efficient strategy" (p. 51);
3. imaginative use of data by "connecting information in new and innovative ways" (p. 52);
4. the ability to traverse different disciplinary fields rather than jealously guarding one's territory;
5. an emphasis on team work;
6. changing the rules of the game and creating new language games through little narratives.

This interpretation of performativity and effectiveness, Lyotard argues, is based on the positivist notion that systems are stable, subject to the input/throughput/output model, and that certain outputs can be projected and has very little to do with the pragmatics of postmodern knowledge. This leads us to the differences between modern and postmodern theory building and scientific activity.

Science as Narrative

Enlightenment science is the process of searching for knowledge that exists outside of language and culture, i.e. it is an external reality that can be found (Klein, 2001). Scientific research itself is a narrative, a way of telling a story, and the rules for telling the story are made up or are fabricated by a group of scientists who participate in the particular type of research (Lyotard, 1984). The story a scientist tells is viewed as truthful when that story sticks to the rules of storytelling created within that science. But even in the case of denotative statements emanating for scientific pursuit scientists have to make use of ordinary narrative techniques to explain the results of the experiments, thus eroding the border between scientific knowledge and narrative knowledge. Narrative also has another function, namely to bring communities together through communication, as indicated earlier. Thus it is narrative knowledge that allows public relations to exist as a practice and a community of practitioners and scholars. As I said earlier, it is a postulated community, and it is this group of practitioners and scholars who set the parameters of what can be studied, what practice is, what definitions are used, and what the rules of participation are. We play a language game, or rather several different language games, depending on the community we participate in. This is how we legitimate what we practice and study.

It is in terms of this narrative function that Lyotard takes issue with science, particularly the social sciences. Knowledge is not only formed through science but also through narrative. As I stated above, narrative is what allows a community to set its standards of competence and criteria for performance. But because the narrative form lends itself to many different language games, public relations can never be a stable function. This book, for instance, plays its own language game and its aim is to convince others to join this game. It is, however, incommensurable with the language game of efficiency or social science.

Scientific knowledge is generated through processes of verification or refutation. This is how truth is established in science, because the sender (the scientist) can provide proof of what is known. The addressee (receiver) of the scientific knowledge is equally important because he needs to accept or deny the statement. Science is thus generated through consensus, i.e. the sender and the addressee need to agree on the outcome of the research for it to be accepted as science. The referent, that which is being studied, needs to remain a stable entity in terms of the outcomes of the research before a consensus is reached, which is where replication comes from.

In social science, Lyotard argues, the sender and addressee also are the referents, i.e. human beings, who are never stable entities. This too is typical in public relations research where the researcher also is the referent, i.e. part of the community that is being studied, which means the researcher also is the object of study. Often these researchers are former or current practitioners. This creates a very unscientific environment and is the reason why social scientific knowledge always will be narrative knowledge. From this perspective claiming objectivity and truth of research processes and results appears irrational. Because narrative knowledge is not viewed by the scientific community as legitimate knowledge and is "only suitable for women and children" (p. 27), disciplines in the social sciences feel the need to continue to play the scientific language game to legitimate their own knowledge. Public relations is part of this process because it endeavors to legitimate its practice by pretending its knowledge is scientific and not narrative. This also is how some people are excluded from public relations knowledge and practice, because the community views its knowledge as superior. This is a futile move because even scientific knowledge requires narrative knowledge to convey its knowledge as superior. It has to convince others, through storytelling, that its knowledge is superior and more truthful than narrative knowledge. It can only legitimate itself through narrative knowledge, which puts scientific knowledge on par with other language games.

It follows that no language game can claim effectiveness and performance, which can only be determined if others who participate in the language game agree to that statement of effectiveness. For example, measurements of effectiveness in public relations can only be verified with those who agree with the measures used to determine effectiveness. There is no objective measure of effectiveness and "legitimation can only spring from [scientists'] own linguistic practice and communicational interaction" (Lyotard, 1984, p. 41). This means that other linguistic communities can be created if there is no agreement on the language game. For instance, this text participates in the language game of the postmodern, which is far removed from any discussion about the effectiveness of public relations. There is a pragmatic condition to playing in a language game, namely, it needs to create its own rules and have others join that game.

Postmodern Theory as Narrative

It naturally follows that for postmodernists all theory is narrative. The main aim for postmodern theorizing is to reject any totality in theorizing in favor of plurality and multiplicity as seen in the works of Deleuze (Sellars, 2006), Foucault (Eribon, 1991), Lyotard (1984), and Deleuze and Guattari (1983). To prevent theories from becoming metanarratives it is important to acknowledge the temporary nature of theory, to keep theory development local and situational, and to be reflective of the hegemonic possibilities of one's own theories (Deleuze & Guattari, 1987; Lyotard, 1984; Seidman, 1997).

The role of social theory is well known, namely, to describe and make sense of what we see and do as humans, stepping "beyond the circumscribed boundaries of individuality to assess ways in which the social world shapes subjectivity" and "is necessary to the extent that the world is not completely and immediately transparent to consciousness" (Best & Kellner, n.d., p. 11). Because theories are socially constructed and spatially and temporally situated, postmodernists argue they cannot and should not become metanarratives and hold true for all time. Although they support certain tenets of postmodern theory, Best and Kellner are critical of the notion that postmodern theory only is a language game and does not entail action. In a critique of postmodern theorizing and an approach to theory itself, they argue that particularly Rorty's approach that the theorist cannot "properly criticize, argue, evaluate or even 'deconstruct,' since there is no fulcrum from which to push one claim as 'right,' 'correct,' or 'better' than another" (p. 9) is incorrect. Although they agree with postmodern theorists that our reality is socially constructed and also reject foundationalism, they do argue that the value claims of theories can be compared with one another on the basis of "the criteria of logic and argumentation which are reasonable to hold, and in shared social values that are the assumptions of a liberal democracy" (p. 10). This position remains problematic because as Best and Kellner argue here it means everybody agrees on what *liberal democracy* is. But, while we know that some feminist theories use liberal democracy as their point of departure, the notion of feminist theory implies that women have been excluded from a normative approach to liberal democracy and therefore wish to change its parameters.

This argument truly is the crux of postmodern theory. If everything is arbitrary and anti-foundationalist, can any form of theorizing take place? Here I believe Lyotard, and to some extent Foucault, provide guidance. Lyotard contends that theories are language games and that all language games are negotiated. But he also argues that all language games should be temporary to ensure that they do not become metanarratives. Postmodern scholars need to continuously revisit their own theories with the intent of dislodging previously held positions through a process of reflexivity. Most critical theorists believe that social change should take place at the macro level (Seidman, 1997). However, Lyotard (1984) believes all theory should be local and regional, i.e. all theory should be negotiated at the local level. Instead of being paralyzed by a fear of metanarratives both Foucault and Lyotard were political activists. Foucault in particular physically became involved in protests for causes he believed in all over Europe (Eribon, 1991). For Foucault and Deleuze the relationship between theory and practice is not linear. They argue theory itself is a form of practice, e.g. if one theorizes activism it is an activist act in itself (Sellars, 2006). Also, if the theorist does not apply her own theory it becomes useless. A theory is either practical or worthless.

But that still begs the question of who sets standards, even at the local level. Here again, as throughout this book, I rely on Bauman's (1993) interpretation of the moral impulse toward the Other. Anything that can harm the Other cannot be a part of local and regional theories. Values such as respect, empathy, compassion, dignity, responsibility, and equality of the Other, by virtue of being Human, really do not require any negotiation. And this Other is not only other humans but also other living things such as animals and the environment. *Localness* is not a value because what is called "culture" in local environments often is discriminating and dehumanizing.

Yet another question is what the role of these theories should be. What would they theorize at the local level? Seidman (1997) suggests a postmodern approach would encourage theorists to get involved in local struggles for justice and to analyze how social change can be brought about at the level of everyday life and social interaction. How is this relevant to public relations? A postmodern approach to theory building will analyze how practice contributes to injustice through the ananlysis of the language games brought to bear on any given situation, rather than formulating grand theories that try to describe how public relations works best or how it contributes to global pratices. Postmodernism focuses on how power is discursively constituted through political processes at the local or immediate level. That does not mean that only events in the immediate geographical environment should be submitted to analysis but rather that events currently taking place and currently affecting stakeholders and practitioners should be analyzed for how people are spoken to and about. It can, for instance, also focus on the discursive strategies stakeholders and practitioners use to resist power and how they affect change through the use of narrative strategies.

A metatheory postmodernists use in particular to describe the negative effects of grand narratives is systems theory—a mainstay of public relations theorizing. Systems theory and its modern spin-offs, complexity and chaos theory, view society as "an organic whole" (Lyotard, 1984, p. 11). Critical theory or critique offers a more general approach to theorizing, which is "based on a principle of dualism and wary of synthesis and reconciliations" (p. 12). The purpose of metatheories, particularly systems theory, is to improve the functioning of the system, i.e. it focuses on performance. This indeed is a purpose that is very familiar in public relations theory. The function of public relations as boundary spanner is specifically focused on improving the organizational system. In this function public relations practitioners are intimately involved in each of the three (oversimplified to the extreme) steps of systems theory: input by advising the organization of what is happening in its environment to ensure that it knows how to adjust; throughput by advising organizational subsystems on required changes, helping them to coordinate their communication efforts, and ensuring all employees are on board; and output by actually communicating to entities in the environment with the aim of making them adjust to the organization and vice versa.

This might indeed be a valid approach to public relations *if* the organization is viewed as part of a language game. As long as practitioners play that language game they might very well be successful with this approach. The problem, however, is that the language game organizations play are highly privileged and exclusionary. The link between technology, knowledge, and power has been discussed before but it cannot be stressed enough that this link has created a new ruling class "of a composite layer of corporate leaders, high-level administrators, and the heads of the major professional, labor, political and religious organizations" who have access to data and information systems (Lyotard, 1984, p. 14). By participating in this particular language game public relations assists this new ruling class to gain more power than it ever had.

Similarly, Best (n.d.) is critical of complexity theory, arguing that the social system is not the result of "'self-organization,' 'critical thresholds,' or 'evolutionary peaks,' but rather are determined by socio-economic crisis, profound discontent, class struggle, and political upheaval" (p. 9). I have made a similar argument before (Holtzhausen, 2007) that during periods of deep and chaotic change the system does not organize itself naturally into a new and more just system. The example I used was what happened in South Africa with the transition to a new political system, where the White minority in power, particularly private institutions, made sure that they did not lose their own power but took away the jobs of those Whites who did not have any power. Similarly, ordinary Black South Africans did not receive the benefits they were promised while their new party bosses ensured that they had the best of the old and new South Africa. Thus, during periods of chaos and complexity it is more important than in any other period for public relations practitioners to ensure grassroots democracy and activism in their organizations and society, to speak out about the unjust use of power, and to use strategies to resist power. As Best (n.d.) says, the so-called natural laws supposed to govern self-organizing systems (such as capitalism) are "determined by political struggle and not a self-organizing system" (p. 9).

Following Best and Kellner I propose postmodern public relations scholars should theorize how public relations practice is inhibiting social justice through its theory and practice and how practitioners sustain the new ruling class through the use of their knowledge of technology, instead of focusing on how systems can make more money through public relations practice while ignoring the potentially harmful ethical, democratic, and environmental consequences of practice. As a counter point I also urge theorists to study how practitioners use their practice to create a more just society, sustainable organizations, and an ecologically viable human system through a well-informed and participative public sphere. One way of doing this is to study the concept of activism as proposed in this text in specific situated contexts instead of vague, normative theories that never can have universal value. It would be more useful to create a data bank of case studies of specific events, strategies, and tactics practitioners can use and adapt for their own activist needs. In this role the aim of postmodern public relations theory is undeniably political.

One final point about theories such as the systems theory is the use of metaphors. Metaphors are powerful because they are so simplistic. Metaphors are one of the conditions of speech and are deeply political because they involve relationships and often convey deeper associations with our worldview (Sarup, 1993). For instance, Lyotard (1984) argues that the metaphor of society as a machine is powerful in that it implies that society is a unified whole that can be studied as such. But the argument on metaphors goes beyond the mere use of certain words. Modernists use theories themselves as metaphors, as in the case of systems, chaos, and complexity theories, which were theories from the natural sciences adopted as social scientific theories. This is a very problematic practice and one that is common in the social sciences. The seamless integration of theories from the natural sciences into social science is not logical. The highly regular phenomena in the natural world are vastly different from humans and their actions in social settings. Adopting theories from the natural sciences as metaphors for the social sciences ignores the complexity of social systems and the humans who populate them. It also produces a protective sheen to the particular social theory because it projects the respectability of the natural sciences onto the social sciences, which is misleading to say the least. It also leads to disciplinary practices as Foucault theorized. The assumption on which disciplinary practices is based is that there is some kind of universal human nature as stable as nature itself and that deviation from that stable system can be identified and punished. Analyzing or approaching public relations theory and practice within the framework of these theoretical metaphors is to ignore the complexity of the environment in which public relations is practiced.

The Role of the Postmodern Scholar

Postmodern scholars are unanimous in viewing the role of the scholar as one of being critical. They offer various suggestions about what it means to be a postmodern scholar. Some broad themes emerge: the role of the scholar as activist; the importance of preserving complexity; the nomadic nature of postmodern scholarship; the need to produce new understanding; the necessity of being critical; the need for being an outsider; and the importance of acknowledging other forms of knowledge.

In the past intellectuals who also were critical scholars, such as those in the Frankfurt School, used their knowledge to speak truth to power on behalf of those who did not have knowledge (Foucault, 1977). With more access to information than ever before, that has changed and people no longer need intellectuals to speak on their behalf. However, the system of power has entrenched the role of the intellectual in society, particularly by privileging scientific knowledge over narrative knowledge, as discussed earlier. It is the responsibility of the scholar to be cognizant of how his intellectual capacity is used to entrench power. The role of the scholar also is to become involved in local struggles aimed at revealing and undermining power where it is most invisible and insidious. For instance, in my previous work I have shown how the use of two-way symmetrical communication led employees in a South African organization to be more exposed to power than before (Holtzhausen, 2000).

I believe public relations scholars are uniquely positioned to investigate and make known how communication and public relations practice is used in local contexts to entrench power systems. Already all over the world public relations professors involve their students in the struggles of local non-profit and activist organizations. All they have to do is to refocus their research on an investigation into the relationship between theory, knowledge, and power. To take power away from those who abuse it, it is necessary for the intellectual to work "alongside those who struggle for power, and not their illumination from a safe distance" (Foucault, 1977, p. 208). Also, instead of focusing on how wonderful and successful public relations campaigns are, as is typical in public relations case studies, it will be important to investigate how these campaigns helped entrenched power structures to hold on to power without changing the status quo.

Theory in this context is particularly important. Deleuze (as cited in Foucault, 1977) argues theory is a useful box of tools, not to make practice more efficient, but to provide practitioners and stakeholders with practical ways to gain power. By exposing the power systems at work in a particular environment or situation, practitioners and stakeholders will develop the skills to resist power. The role of theory is to question "the totality of power and the hierarchy that maintains it" (p. 209) and the only way to do that is to work alongside those who are directly involved. That is why the analysis of a specific event is so important. The postmodern scholar is necessarily critical, an activist, and a public intellectual (Best & Kellner, n.d.). Being public intellectuals is indeed one area where public relations scholars are lacking. Whenever a public relations practitioner or scholar is interviewed it usually is about how this or that person can rescue her image or how a company can survive a scandal, but it is seldom to critique the way in which practice is used to entrench power. Where are our public intellectuals who provide public critique of the abuse of the field and provide guidance on how public relations practice can be used to promote positive social change and emancipation?

Another pursuit of the postmodern scholar is to be an intellectual nomad (Walia, 2001) and to easily navigate the borders between intellectual disciplines. Postmodern intellectuals often use the term *aesthetics* to describe how the individual can create himself; much like a painter does with painting. Being aesthetic in the pursuit of knowledge means to create new knowledge, not merely building on what one has previously done and trying to confirm those previous findings. This does not mean conducting yet another relationship study in a different context but coming up with new paradigms for the field. This is similar to the postmodern idea of Becoming rather than being (Docherty, 1993), creating rather than recreating, being reflexive rather than affirming. It also means using a new gaze or lens to view existing knowledge. Being aesthetic means to recover one's own identity and history by becoming aware how that identity has been infiltrated by dominant social paradigms and norms. It is a "historical investigation into the events that have led us to constitute ourselves as subjects of what we are doing, thinking, saying" (Best, 1995, p. 126) and is not about generalization but rather about individual growth through critique.

The postmodern intellectual can only be liberated by and through herself. Nobody but you can take away the liberty of your mind. To be able to do this the intellectual has to view herself as an intellectual outcast, someone living on the border of society (Walia, 2001). The moment an intellectual becomes part of the power system she will lose her ability to provide an alternative perspective. That also will give her the courage to speak. Recent events showed just how important it is to be an outsider to speak truth to power. Three powerful women recently interviewed for *Time* Magazine believed it was their outsider status that made it possible for them to challenge the existing power structures that facilitated the Wall Street meltdown in 2009–10 because they viewed the world differently than men (Scherer, 2010, p. 24). I believe it often is easier for women to do this because they did not come through the entrenched power system and therefore owe fewer people favors in their climb to the top. As with all activist behavior, these women faced a lot of hostility but they remained strong and persevered. That inner strength and clear vision of what is the right thing to do is a core competency of the activist.

Another core competency of the activist postmodern scholar is to have passion. This remains a problem in public relations research and practice (see Dozier & Lauzen, 2000). What are we as public relations intellectuals passionate about? As I see it, it is more about showing how we contribute to the bottom line and how we can better measure our performance and effectiveness, than about social justice and positive change. With the exception of some work on environmental issues and health communication, which often is about powerful corporate interests in any case, there is a glaring absence of how public relations practice can contribute to more democratic practices in the societies in which practice takes place. The role of postmodern public relations scholars is to use our knowledge and research practices to shape our current society.

But we always have to be careful not to become imperialist in our knowledge creation and should always insist that it provides only one lens to view an issue. We also need to be careful that our theories are not socialized and co-opted by those who do not support total equality for all (West, 1997). The work of the postmodern scholar always will have political overtones; at the same time we need to recognize and admit to the aporiae I believe are inherent to our field, and not smooth them over when there are obvious contradictions in our theories.

A consistent theme in postmodern theory is that postmodernists are passionate about acknowledging complexity. They resist categorization, generalization, and segmentation of knowledge and of those who participate in their research. One such aporia is the fact that intellectuals as "critical worker researchers" (Kincheloe & McLaren, 1994, p. 147) or "cultural workers" (West, 1997, p. 74) also are dependent on the institutions they criticize for their livelihood, which makes their criticism "simultaneously progressive *and* co-opted" (West, 1997, p. 66) [italics in the original]. The simplistic either/or reaction is that this makes criticism impossible, which leads to the notion of postmodernism as utopian (Lyotard, 1984). But no change can happen without pressure on the system and therefore even co-opted pressure is better than no pressure at all. The desire for change cannot be reconciled with the need to survive; yet both must be realized.

Postmodern scholars also aim for specific outcomes, e.g. aligning "themselves with demoralized, demobilized, depoliticized and disorganized people in order to empower and enable social action and, if possible, to enlist collective insurgency for the expansion of freedom, democracy and individuality" (West, 1997, p. 66). For the postmodern public relations intellectual the outcome of his work must be empowerment of stakeholders; the enabling of social action for positive and inclusive change; expansion of freedom, democracy, and individuality for all citizens; and resistance to the promotion of senseless consumption.

Other aims are the promotion of organizational sustainability; the preservation of the environment; a just society free from inhibiting cultural practices; and wariness toward the impact of new technologies on society (Best & Kellner, n.d.). This should be accomplished by producing new understandings and interpretations through a critical stance that goes beyond "merely rearranging furniture in the house of modern science … to produce new revolutions in thought and method" (Best & Kellner, 2001, p. 108).

Over the years public relations scholarship has become increasingly empirical and model building is one of the foundations of the field—an activity in which I too have participated (Holtzhausen, Petersen, & Tindall, 2003). However, postmodernists question the degree of accuracy of quantitative research results and reject the notion that only that which the scientist can think of or observe is valid. The use of quantitative data might be useful to identify arguments and define problems, but they merely are tools to facilitate communication and discussion and are neither rational nor true (Rosenau, 1992). All classification of people is socially constructed. Terms such as Black, woman, man, Black woman, White woman, White man, poor, rich, and so forth all are socially and culturally constructed. There is no objective classification system out there to be found; there is no reason for classification except if one wishes there to be so (West, 1997).

Instead of simplistic and reductionist classification systems, postmodernists rather focus on "change, process, indeterminacy (probability as opposed to absolute certainty), complexity, and nonlinearity as fundamental aspects of the world rather than as defects in idealized models, limitations in measurement technologies, or flaws in subjective thought" (Best & Kellner, 2001, p. 111). For public relations scholars this means acknowledging that all our work is value-laden and also acknowledging that our practice is used to sustain injustice through patriarchy, racism, capitalism, violence, and international politics, as Mickey's (1997) analysis of the First Gulf War showed. The role of the public relations scholar is to "provide a permanent critique of our historical era" (Foucault, 1984, p. 43) and show how public relations practice has helped to constitute it, which requires a "permanent critique of ourselves" (p. 43). The aim is not to overthrow the organizations we work for but make them better through working for more democratic practices; questioning the authority of the hierarchy; exposing the hidden power grids; and resisting at every possible opportunity. The problem is that there simply are not enough of these analyses around to show how money has become the basis of the ethical debates in our field (Toth, 2002). Do not be deterred by those who ask what the cost is, or suggest that this approach is idealistic and utopian. As Lyotard (1984) said, these are the strategies used to prevent change and to urge you to give up your work.

The above clearly lays out the postmodern agenda for critique but still begs the question of how we study these phenomena and who is worth studying.

Research Methodology and The Postmodern Scholar

The first instinct is to argue that postmodernists reject quantitative research in favor of critical and qualitative research but there is significant evidence that this is not the case. They might be critical of some aspects of quantitative research, such as the categorization of subjects for the purpose of administration, surveillance, and above all performance measurement and financial gain, but that would be to misunderstand the postmodern stance on all forms of research.

Lyotard (1984) warns against the inclination to distinguish between two kinds of knowledge: positivist vs. "critical, reflexive, or hermeneutic" (p. 14). Foucault (1984) similarly rejects the binary opposites of being for or against the Enlightenment, which he calls the "'blackmail' of the Enlightenment" (p. 42) and suggests that "one has to refuse everything that might present itself in the form of a simplistic and authoritarian alternative" (p. 43). Both offer perspectives on how we might use research in public relations. One perspective focuses on recognizing that research approaches really are "genres of discourse" (Lyotard, 1988, p. 29). Each genre is a language game with its own rules, something all researchers are familiar with. When we do research we even have to write down the rules by which we played, typically in the methods section of our work. The results of our work are judged on how well we played the game. These genres of discourse are incommensurable because they play by different rules and therefore cannot be compared.

While this offers one form of interpretation of research, and indeed a valuable one, yet another perspective would argue that the underlying worldview leading to the research and the purpose of the research also are genres of discourse. For instance, Lyotard (1984) suggests that viewing the world as an organized whole would lead to research of its subsystems as wholly interdependent and their behavior, even in extreme circumstances, as predictable. This approach would privilege research methods that quantify, categorize, and generalize their results and that can lead to prediction and linear relationships. The aim of this kind of research will be to improve the performance of the system through four processes: "selection, normalization, hierarchicalization, and centralization" (Foucault, 2003, p. 181). The critical worldview that rejects the notion of the world viewed as a machine would view the purpose of research to be renewal, reinvention, and the reconstitution of the individual as liberated and emancipated. Research of this nature is underscored by "a philosophical ethos consisting in a critique of what we are saying, thinking, and doing, through a historical ontology of ourselves" (Foucault, 1984, p. 45). The aim of this kind of research is to question "what is given to us as universal, necessary, obligatory" and to look for transgression of that given, i.e. "a practical critique that takes the form of a possible transgression" (p. 45).

Thus the postmodern critique of research methods has little to do with the *type* of research simply because all types of research are language games, but rather focuses on the underlying principles guiding the research and the intent and outcome of that research. Furthermore, postmodernists favor research methods that enable the researcher to conduct "a historical investigation into the events that have led us to constitute ourselves and to recognize ourselves as subjects of what we are doing, thinking and saying" rather than "the search for formal structures with universal values" (Foucault, 1984, p. 46). Even a cursory analysis of public relations research in journals and text books appears to take place with the goal of looking for those universal answers in terms of theory and practice, with culture as the only reason why practices might differ across countries or situations. One of the few texts in public relations that focuses on this type of analysis is the work of L'Etang (2004) even though it uses a linearity of events as the basis for its analysis. However, the text does reveal "an occupational group pursuing its own interests in relations to the state and social elites as the source of cultural and ideological power" (p. 221), which is typical of discourse analysis. Typically discourse analysis takes place in the tradition of critical research, with an emphasis on "structures and those who control them" (Morgan-Fleming, Riegle, & Fryer, 2007, p. 85).

A methodology that focuses on the local or microlevel experience, so often stressed in the postmodern, is narrative analysis, which is a bottom-up process that focuses on how "ordinary people interpret and enact the imposed representations placed on them by those in power" (Morgan-Fleming et al., 2007, p. 85). An example from L'Etang's (2004) history illustrates how narrative analysis and discourse analysis might differ. L'Etang cites an example of how public relations practice introduced modern appliances to Africans in Uganda. In the tradition of discourse analysis she focuses on macrolevel structure and shows how public relations practice "played a role maintaining economic links of benefit to the colonial powers" (p. 97). Narrative analysis would have focused on the narratives of the Africans present at the exhibition to understand how public relations in this instance promoted Western concepts of technology, progress, capitalism, and market expansion in relation to the traditional African lifestyle, while shaping the way in which Africans view themselves in relation to this display of colonial power. Such a narrative analysis would have been conducted with Foucault's (1984) archeological process in mind, namely, "a historical investigation into the events that have led [Africans] to constitute [themselves] and to recognize [themselves] as subjects of what [they] are doing, thinking, saying" (p. 46). As a genealogical method the narrative analysis would have helped Africans understand what public relations really was, how colonial powers used it to shape the identity of Africans, and how the practice was used to expand the market for colonial powers. The next step of the genealogic project would be to make the narrative analysis relevant to "contemporary reality, both to grasp the points where change is possible and desirable, and to determine the precise form this change should take" (p. 46). Thus a narrative analysis would focus on a non-linear linkage between that event and how Africans view themselves today and would make suggestions on how Africans could use this knowledge to liberate themselves from feelings of inferiority and submission. This then would become a subversive history of the role of public relations in expanding and maintaining colonialism at a very particular event in Uganda.

Although narrative inquiry is not identical to qualitative research and they generally are viewed as "two research paradigms" (Pinnegar & Daynes, 2007, p. 4) there are intersections, such as the use of words and stories as the data for analysis. But largely narrative analysis uses all kinds of narrative as both "method and phenomena of study" (p. 5) with an experience as a starting point, much like the vignettes in this volume. This experience is then intertwined with the particular theoretical underpinnings applied in the analysis. In the case of this book the theoretical foundation is postmodernism, intertwined with some of the narratives from the vignettes. Narrative researchers insist that there is not a specific interpretation of what narrative is, but it is used differently in research than in popular culture (Riessman & Speedy, 2007). For instance, in this book different types of narratives are used, sometimes pieced together from different sources. Not only individuals construct narratives but also groups, communities, and even nation states. The United States promotes much of its present-day history within the narrative of the "leader of the free world." From a public relations perspective a narrative analysis would focus on the stories of public relations practitioners and how they promote this narrative. It also would focus on how others perceive and are affected by the public relations efforts of the United States to promote this narrative, particularly how it shapes people's identity and beliefs about themselves and how it empowers or disempowers them.

It also is important to note the differences between narrative inquiry and qualitative research. The way qualitative research is traditionally used in public relations is postpositivist and post-structural rather than postmodern. In this sense qualitative research looks for "taxonomies and conceptual systems ... which look for commonalities across interviews and other things," whereas narrative inquiry focuses on "a philosophical perspective in terms of ... the way we understand human existence" (Clandinin & Murphy, 2001, p. 633).

The underlying assumption of narrative analysis is the notion that narrative knowledge is valid knowledge, as Lyotard (1984) asserted, and that we can use it beyond scientific narrative, which we now know needs narrative knowledge to legitimate itself. Many public relations scholars and practitioners have learnt the power of narrative knowledge while working with publics and stakeholders. The narratives of community members often lead practitioners and their clients or organizations to a better understanding of how policies, procedures, and organizational behavior affect their stakeholders.

Vignette 6.3 also brings into focus action research as a methodology conducive to the aim of the postmodern, namely, working alongside people at the local level to help them get their narrative out, particularly using the legitimacy of the intellectual to validate that knowledge. It also establishes the link between narrative inquiry and action research (McNiff, 2007). Action research is postmodern in the sense that it closes the distance between the researcher and the Other (Bauman, 1993) and removes the necessity for the researcher to speak on behalf of the subject. One example of how fluid the understandings are of narrative inquiry and action research is is Arvay's (2003) definition of a collaborative narrative approach to research. She defines collaborative narrative research as the inquiry into how knowledge is created through the conversations between researchers and those with whom they are working. I would argue that action research combined with narrative inquiry is a fusion of Foucault's (1984) archaeological and genealogical projects because the aim of action research "is to produce practical knowledge that is useful to people in the everyday conduct of their lives" in order to improve the lives of people and communities (Reason & Bradbury, 2001, p. 3). This is done through "a participatory, democratic process...that seeks to bring together action and reflection, theory and practice, in participation with others" (p. 1). Thus, action research brings together the analysis of "the events that have led us to constitute ourselves" with the practical project of defining freedom (Foucault, 1984, p. 46). Vignette 6.3 shows two benefits of action research for public relations research and practice, namely, how the co-creation of meaning and the narratives of study participants can shape public relations practice and how action research also can shape the practitioner in the process.

Action research is not per definition a postmodern research methodology, proven by the fact that some lament the postmodern turn in action research because of the assumption so often made that it precludes any form of emancipatory action, which is the ultimate aim of action research (Dick, 2006). What is interesting about action research is that there is a dearth of examples in the context of communication practice. One would assume that this would be a perfect environment to use action research in the context of activist public relations practice. The areas where most action research takes place are education, community development, participatory development in developing countries, and organizational settings (see Reason & Bardbury, 2001, for a comprehensive review of action research philosophy, practice, and skills). These are all areas where public relations is practiced and where they offer valuable setting for activist research practices in public relations. An example of action research in public relations is the work of Burek (2001) who joined an environmental activist group to conduct her thesis research and became part of the organization to help them in their struggle to oppose a desalination plant in Tampa Bay. One shortcoming of this research was that the people who originally established the activist group did not allow her to co-construct messages with them but rather treated her as an outsider. This research showed how important it is for action

Vignette 6.3

A police officer who was a student in one of my advanced public relations courses made remarks in class that indicated he had a very stereotypical and racist view of Blacks and their experiences. He assumed that his views were mainstream to the extent that he did not even realize his remarks were interpreted as racist. This was problematic, because the class project was to work with a national medical association to study the health gap between Black and White and to see how the organization could reach out to both Black and White underprivileged communities to narrow that gap. As part of the data collection phase of the project this student had to visit one of the housing projects in the area to find out how the residents felt about visits to doctors' offices, accessibility of medical services, transport issues, and much more. This research phase was conducted against the background of secondary research that showed Blacks, for many historical reasons, distrusted the medical profession and would rather take over-the-counter or traditional medicine rather than visit a doctor. The visit to the housing project was an epiphany for this student. After hearing residents' stories of fear and discrimination he realized that there are people whose views differ from his own and that his reality did not reflect theirs. He said, "Even though I do not understand it they have a perception of how they are treated and that is their reality." I am convinced this experience made him a better police officer.

Another powerful narrative that brought home the disparities in treatment for Blacks and Whites during this project was that of a White woman who lived in the housing projects and adopted a White child and a Black child. She related how differently her White child was treated from her Black child during doctor's visits. Were these stories quantifiable or generalizable? No, they were not but they were more powerful in bringing home the aims of the project for the students than any quantitative research could have done.

researchers to explain the process, get buy-in, and gain the trust of the particular community (Pyrch & Castillo, 2001).

As suggested in Vignette 6.3, action research also changes the student researchers through a process of reflexivity. The classroom setting in this case was invaluable because it provided a space for reflexivity, feedback, and exchange—a safe place where students could share their experiences. Action research is "lived like a personal experience…[that] requires us to have energy, patience, vision, sensibility and discipline in order to learn the process" (Pyrch & Castillo, 2001, p. 384). It also requires time to really understand the implications of what we have learned, how we can act on our knowledge, and how it has changed us as researchers. Unfortunately, time is a luxury that we as professors and students do not have in the tight constraints of semester classes. In some cases action research projects can take as long as 10 years (Langan & Morton, 2009).

A research methodology that is an outflow of the concept of reflexivity is the personal memoir or autobiography (Freeman, 2001). The assumption underlying the autobiography is that personal stories are valuable tools to understand the human condition and also are used to explore how narrative inquiry "might lessen the distance between *science* and *art* and thereby open the way toward a more integrated, adequate, and humane vision for studying the human realm" (p. 120) [italics in original]. This suggests that autobiographical data is as valid as social science data collected through quantitative or qualitative means, as per Lyotard (1984). Having said that, I believe researchers should watch against coming across as narcissistic in their strong focus on themselves. While reflexivity in research has now become mainstream, as in the preface to this book, there also is the possibility that "reflexively locating oneself may result in the use of subjectivity in static, deductive, and self-justifying ways" (Bloom, 2002, p. 290). Subjectivity is a much more complex phenomenon than merely some childhood experiences. Subjectivity is shaped through our everyday experiences, writings, and interactions and should not be overly focused on the style of reflexivity (Gough, 2003). A reflexive stance should be "a balance between flat, unreflexive analyses and excessive, hyper-reflexive analyses" (p. 21).

Autobiographical collaboration might be a positive alternative. An example is the work of Frank (2000), which she terms "cultural biography, which combines the genres of ethnography and life history" (p. 2). Frank tracked her interaction with Dian DeVries, "a woman born with all the physical and mental equipment she would need to live in our society—except arms and legs" (p. 1), over two decades. Her writing provides support for the concept of complex subjectivity. Over the two decades the ethnographic project between Frank and DeVries set in motion a "still unfinished, quite irreversible co-construction of lives" (p. 102). At the time of reading the biography I became fascinated by the possibilities of tracking the life of a female public relations practitioner over an extended period of time to determine how practice constructs her identity and how her identity as a female practitioner constructs her practice and her personal life world. Autobiography and cultural biography often are used for feminist research into power relations, identity creation, and female agency. While public relations practice has a very strong tradition of feminist scholars and feminist research, such a study, from a postmodern perspective, might lead to new perspectives, more narratives, and more understandings. Along these lines, L. A. Grunig (2006) proposed a phased analysis of identity construction of both female and male practitioners in public relations, which "recognizes and supports the whole person, the entire range of their responsibilities and life roles" (p. 137). A cultural biography such as the one by Frank might be just such a methodology.

In conclusion it needs to be reiterated that postmodernists do not reject any form of research or any form of knowledge. What is important to understand is that postmodern research relates more to an "attitude, an ethos, a philosophical life in which the *critique* [emphasis added] of what we are is at one and the same time the historical analysis of the limits that are imposed on us and an experiment with the possibility of going beyond them" (Foucault, 1984, p. 50). From this perspective we can use any form of research as often as we want, as long as we address the following questions: "How are we constituted as subjects of our own knowledge? How are we constituted as subjects who exercise or submit to power relations? How are we constituted as moral subjects of our own actions?" (p. 49). This does not exclude quantitative research, although quantitative research is limited in its possibilities for critique. Quantitative data can at best provide broad trends in perceptions of how employees feel about the organization or resource allocation (Miller, 1999) but it is reductionist and over-simplifying of complex problems (Rosenau, 1992). I too have used quantitative research to investigate if democratic communication processes and a decentralized communication function improved communication in an organization (Holtzhausen, 2002a, 2002b) and to determine attributes of activist public relations behavior (Holtzhausen et al., 2003). I still believe that using practitioners' stories and examples of practice provides a better understanding of the potential for emancipatory practices for public relations (Holtzhausen & Voto, 2002).

One of the biggest dangers of any kind of activist oriented research aimed at helping people to empower themselves remains co-optation for purposes of power and control. I have reported previously how processes to implement two-way symmetrical communication in an organization made employees more vulnerable to control (Holtzhausen, 2000) in what Langan and Morton (2009) refer to as a "distressing dilemma" (p. 181) of conflicting agendas, power issues, and divergent interests in research partnerships between academics, community organizations, and institutions. Langan and Morton particularly reflect on the political nature of action research, which is typical of any research conducted within the framework of a postmodern perspective. That is the reason why a common understanding of the particular research methods and the political intent of the researcher should be clearly articulated and supported by all parties in the research process. I had a similar experience in the implementation of internal organizational communication processes in a South African organization, as mentioned above. Only when management started to see and understand the implications of the two-way communication process did they understand to what extent their power was being challenged, an outcome I did not explain to them and for which they were not prepared.

The fact was they expected the new process to provide them with better control over their employees.

The Public Relations Scholar as Activist

Academic and intellectual activism is by no means new. There are many historic and current examples of academics who were and are persecuted, incarcerated, and censored because of their activism and their ideas. Even in the United States there are virulent public floggings of academic ideas in certain media and, as I showed in Vignette 6.2, anti-intellectualism is the order of the day. However, this also does not mean that academics always get it right and there are many historic and current examples where intellectuals align themselves so closely with power that their ideas and ideologies result in grave injustice. One obvious example is the impact of intellectuals on the Nazis in Germany. Similarly, Dr. Hendrik Verwoerd, the first prime minister of South Africa under the Nationalist Party, used his education and theoretical perspectives to formalize and institutionalize apartheid as never before (Giliomee, 2003).

This is exactly what postmodernists do not want to happen and they are opposed to intellectuals as an elite class of people who are used by those in power to translate their ideas into policies. A consistent theme in this book is that people cannot be disciplined without the infrastructure provided by schools, universities, churches, and other institutions. At the same time postmodernism does provide a perspective on academic activism, but not as an action that speaks on behalf of people from an aloof distance but from a perspective of working shoulder-to-shoulder with those in our communities who fight against injustice and for dignity, respect, and freedom.

I believe public relations intellectuals and academics are ideally positioned to play this role because of our unique role in organizations and institutions. A recent text (Heath & Toth, 2009) explores many opportunities for public relations academics to become involved in the development of a fully functioning society through their theories.

But there are prerequisites that will facilitate the academic activist role from a postmodern perspective. For one, we not only should act as activist academics but also as activist practitioners when we get involved in community organizations. We need to recognize that our work is always political; there cannot be neutrality or objectivity. When we align ourselves with the Other we need to understand that this is always about power and power is always political. We need to live our research as a personal experience and need to be passionate about the cause of our research. To do that we also need to acknowledge that knowledge exists in places outside of academia. The experiences and narratives of those outside of academe are as valid and legitimate as that of the academic.

We already do that in our public relations case studies and research but it is the way that we collect and report on that knowledge that makes a difference.

An excellent and early example of this in public relations is the work of Chay-Nemeth (2001) who used an approach based on Foucault's (1972) archaeological process to show how underlying mechanisms of power shaped "a public as a political space" (p. 157). This is an example of how we need to expand our data collection to areas outside of practice and focus on the effects of our practice on social issues in our communities instead of conducting our case studies to tell ourselves how wonderful we are and how we contribute to the bottom line of our organizations.

We need much more self-critique and reflexivity in our research. To do that we need to acknowledge our own interests in our research and admit that it is not an objective process (see Aldoory, 2009 for a similar approach). We need to expose the underlying ideology in our work and be reflexive how our practices sustain existing power structures to the detriment of others. We need to be reflexive on how our work and knowledge is used and acknowledge that our social science approach to practice is prescriptive and thus value-based.

Furthermore, we need to be reflexive of our own theories and make sure that they do not become metanarratives. As postmodern activist academics we need to have an outsider status, as described by post-colonial scholar Edward Said, who saw the role of intellectuals as "responsible and 'oppositional'" citizens who always need to place our views outside of ideology and dogma (Walia, 2001, p. 7). Said lived his life at the intersections of cultures, religions, and philosophies and as a result always viewed himself as an exile. He "sees this position as one of advantage from where he can speak and write subversively because for him the intellectual is always an 'exile or marginal'" (p. 5). Whereas Said used "intervensionist academics politics" (p. 8) to expose instance of colonialism, public relations academics can similarly use our intellectual capacity to lay bare the abuse of power in our own field. Therefore we cannot align ourselves closely and comfortably with power and we need to do more research on how our practice can perform its public role without becoming a part of dominant power structures.

We also need to be public intellectuals and be much more critical of our own practice. Ironically, it is never our foremost intellectuals who are asked to comment on issues of public relations practice but practitioners themselves and often they are practitioners from advertising who have no idea how public relations practice works. We are not even activists on our own behalf. Part of the problem is that we have moved away from our role to promote communication in the public sphere to one of building relationships in the private sphere. That contributes to the image of the field as one that subversively and covertly builds alliances that cannot stand public scrutiny. Transparency is essential to this role (Christensen & Langer, 2009). Even though not everything we do is of interest to the public at least we should be prepared to make it public. We simply cannot play tricks with the public and the media. A recent case in point is BP, which allegedly hired people to clean up the Gulf coast beaches on the day President Obama visited to inspect the area, only to let them go the minute he departed. This is a typical example of what contributes to the cynicism about our practice.

What the field needs is continuous renewal. As Deleuze and Guattari (1987) say, just have an idea and follow through on that. We are far too scared to be critiqued and far too willing to just test existing theories over and over again. Be adventurous and build new foundations for knowledge, as Foucault (1972) suggests. Throw ideas out like bottles on the ocean, as Lyotard (Lyotard & Thébaud, 1985) suggests and see what comes back and in what form. Let us be creative. Be academic nomads who fight against the narrow categories in which we are cast. A consistent voice for this approach to public relations is McKie (2001; McKie & Munshi, 2009) who argues that different theoretical approaches might lead us to a totally different constitution of the field. Let us cast our net far and wide and experiment with how these new foundations can inform us anew of our role and see how our role can contribute to the liberation and emancipation of those who are marginalized and dehumanized. Renewal includes the search and application of new methodologies to inform us differently of our field. I believe tenure-track faculty will be surprised how welcome these ideas will be among the community of scholars. The public relations academic field is generous, encouraging, and welcoming of new ideas.

7

ACTIVISM AS THE POSTMODERN AGENCY OF PUBLIC RELATIONS

The modern era has been dominated by the culminating belief, expressed in different forms, that the world—and Being as such—is a wholly knowable system governed by a finite number of universal laws that man can grasp and rationally direct for his own benefit. This era, beginning with the Renaissance...gave rise to the proud belief that man, as the pinnacle of everything that exists, was capable of objectively describing, explaining and controlling everything that exists, and of possessing the one and only truth about the world.

(Havel, 1992, as cited in Ermarth, 2001b, p. 56)

I have now reviewed the application of postmodern theories and perspectives to some very divergent topics, ranging from ethics, history, and organizations to power, knowledge, and research. As I have repeatedly reiterated in this text, postmodernism is by its very nature nomadic and fragmented and it will be impossible to summarize what public relations as activism means within the confines of a single construct. As such, public relations as activism should and must resist any attempt to quantify or empirically test the practice in order to reduce it to a single, measurable construct.

The practice of public relations as activism will be tied closely to the environment in which the practice takes place and will therefore always resist any normalizing or universal theories that make the practice global or universal. This focus on the local practice of public relations is an important aspect of postmodern public relations praxis, theory, and research because it is one way of resisting universalizing and totalizing practices.

For me, one last question remains, and that is: To what extent does our human condition allow us to be activist practitioners? This relates to the ontological question of the nature of being. What is possible as humans? What is the human condition? This ontological question is closely tied to the concept of the subject and its agency. However, the implications of human agency in organizations cannot be viewed independently from agency perspectives in economics and management, which is an important component of materiality in organizations. This is particularly relevant when it comes to professional communication practice.

Despite the intense focus on agency in scholarly research in recent years, in disciplines as widespread as organizational studies (Hassard & Parker, 1994), organizational communication (Deetz, 1992), history (Ermarth, 2000), economics (Ghoshal & Moran, 1996; Wright, Mukherjib, & Kroll, 2001), political science (Miller, 2005), and sociology (Tucker, 1998), this focus has been neglected in public relations.

This neglect in public relations is possibly a reflection of the same trend in organizational analyses where "the open, reflexive and purposive quality of human agency is either taken for granted or disregarded" (Wilmot, 1994, p. 85). The concept of *agency* is often informally used in public relations when practitioners are referred to as public relations agents, or when counseling firms are called public relations agencies. This use of agency probably stems from "a belief in its self-evidence." As a result the "idea of agency is deployed unreflexively" (p. 130).

Examining the concept of agency more reflexively brings to light very divergent ideas on its interpretation. A dictionary definition of *agent* exposes the reasons for these conflicting interpretations. The *Reader's Digest Oxford complete wordfinder* (1993, p. 30) describes an agent as (1) "a person who acts for another in business, politics, etc." and also as (2) "a person or thing that exerts power or produces an effect." In any discipline the concepts of "acting on behalf of," "exerts power," and "produces an effect" have the potential to be loaded with divergent meanings; perhaps more so in public relations because of its public information and media relations functions.

This raises the question of what public relations agency constitutes. What acts do public relations practitioners execute on behalf of others? Over what do they exert power? What effects are they expected to produce? To an extent one would assume that some of these questions should be answered by the many definitions of public relations. The most dominant understandings of this agency would include the management of communication on behalf of an organization (J. E. Grunig, 1992c; J. E. Grunig & Hunt, 1984) and the building of relationships between an organization and its stakeholders (Ledingham & Bruning, 2000). In the European context the definition is more multidimensional, i.e. public relations is reflective, managerial, operational, and educational in the context of communication practice (van Ruler & Verčič, 2004).

The concept of agency in public relations also brings into focus questions such as whether public relations practitioners only act on behalf of those people who employ them as their agents and who those agents actually are. It raises also the question whether the agency role affects practitioners' ability to speak on behalf of the stakeholders they deal with. It raises the issue of power, namely, whether agents have their own power or whether their power only originates from those who employ them. Also, if practitioners serve at the courtesy of an employer, how does that relationship affect their ability to "produce effects" against which their performance is measured?

This chapter will focus on the different interpretations of *agency* and *agent*,[1] and their implications for public relations practice. It will start out by reviewing the conflicting interpretations of agency in economics and management theory. Subsequently, it will focus on the divergent interpretations of agency in modernism and postmodernism and how agency relates to notions of the subject and subjectivity. Lastly, it will propose a postmodern perspective on the agency of public relations and will suggest that postmodern perspectives on power, knowledge, and language might provide some answers as to how public relations agents can negotiate their role and fulfill their contractual obligations while remaining subject and not object.

Agency Theories

The major debates about agency stem from a number of conflicting assumptions on the subject. One of the assumptions under debate is the individual's ability/inability to control or respond to the environment, which is relevant to the debate between the modern vs. the postmodern agent. This debate is urgent and necessary because it has huge practical implications and agency is the focal point of this debate (Ermarth, 2001a).

The Modern Agent

One of the main reasons why agency has been taken for granted is that the "'individual agent' of modernity exists for and makes possible the 'objectivity' that we have learned to take for granted" (Ermarth, 2001a, p. 37). This belief has emboldened the modern agent (cf. the quote from Havel at the beginning of this chapter). As a result the modernist agent is understood as rational, as having a complete understanding of and insight into himself, has a "supposed unity and homogeneity of the ensemble of its positions," and is viewed as "the origin and basis of social relations" (Laclau & Mouffe, 1985, p. 115).

The agent is therefore viewed as all-powerful in controlling and manipulating his environment. The consequences of this type of agency are expectations of self-assertion; the execution of concrete achievements that can serve as the basis for evaluation and judgment; efforts to change the environment to serve preconceived ideas; acting independently; and being directed by outer rather than inner development (Weick, 2001). These attributes of the agent also serve as the basic assumptions of agency theory in the area of economics. Modernist perspectives of *human agency* assume individuals have much more power and freedom of decision-making than economic agents, who are bound by contracts, but in both approaches the rationality of the agent is uncontested.

The agent and action also are always inextricably linked (Bourdieu, 1977; Giddens, 1979). This is of the utmost importance to the field of public relations practice, which sets itself apart from other competing fields, such as organizational communication, on the very basis of the communication actions practitioners performed in organizational settings on behalf of the organization, i.e. acting as communication agents (Holtzhausen, 2002).

Sociological and critical approaches to agency examine the role of power in agency. Agency is produced through discipline and the struggle to exert power and control is inherent in all agency. "The agency of a person is no less an achievement of discipline than is that of an organization. Agency is achieved" (Clegg, 1994, p. 47). When stereotypical assumptions are made about agents regarding issues such as ethnicity, race, or gender, agents will struggle to break free from that identity. Thus, conflict is often inherent in agency, as is power.

> To be an agent is to be able to deploy (chronically in the flow of daily life) a range of causal powers. An agent ceases to be such if he or she loses the capability to "make a difference," that is to exercise some sort of power.
>
> (Giddens, 1984, p. 14)

It is the ability of the agent to resist power and control that is at the core of the critical debate about agency. Two conflicting perspectives dominate the argument. The one argument holds that agents are interpellated into a system to legitimize the power and position of those already in power (Bourdieu, 1977). From this argument it leads that powerful organizational players will use the agency of public relations practitioners to create norms of discipline and submission of both internal and external publics. Thus, practitioners will actively be involved in creating the rules, practices, and norms of organizations through which they and others are regulated through self-control and self-discipline (Foucault, 1982). Public relations practitioners are the agents used to establish corporate ideologies, a process that is nothing but the creation of meaning in the service of power (Holtzhausen, 2002; Thompson, 1990).

Bourdieu (1977) argues that agency is used to accumulate wealth, "the ultimate basis of power" (p. 195). Economic capital can only be accumulated through symbolic capital. Symbolic capital has as its base symbolic violence. For relations of domination to be maintained, they must be "euphemized" (p. 191). From this description of agency one has to ask whether public relations' agency is used to "euphemize" relationships of domination, and to formulate and propagate corporate ideology, which in turn is used to establish hegemony (Gramsci, 1971).

Several scholars point to ways in which this domination of agency is euphemized. Willmot (1994) describes agency as playing a game. The more successful players, i.e. employees, are at playing the game and following the rules, the more successful, competent, and important they feel. The prestige, accomplishment, and pride that accompany the successful game playing hide the underlying manipulation of employees. Because of the many hidden mechanisms that shape the agency of employees, an analysis of agency will necessarily have to focus on the "myriad of practices" that inhibit employees from becoming powerful through the internalization of discipline by "restricting actions to what is 'obedient'" (Clegg, 1989, p. 200).

Giddens (1984) has a much more positive interpretation of agency. He argues that agents have the potential to deliberately and effectively choose and carry out actions in defiance of established rules. Human agency is therefore possible through reflexivity and knowledge (Wittington, 1994). Reflexivity is the "monitored character of the ongoing flow of social life" (Tucker, 1998, p. 2). Agents can reflexively build their own sense of identity, oppose and change the definitions of society, and so help shape the societies in which they live. Instead of the two opposing views that pit the deterministic role of social structure on agent behavior against the free, decision-making individual unencumbered by social structure, on the other hand, Giddens (1984) places the agent as an active person who can navigate the impact of social structure on his life. From his perspective then, the public relations agent will be able to reflexively resist domination and play an active role in shaping the public relations agency in the organization.

Critics of Giddens' work argue that he ignores the impact of power by paying inadequate attention to "who can structure social relations and who is being structured by them" (Tucker, 1998, p. 6). He also underestimates the impact of culture and how "different cultural orientations ... can promote or deny capacities of creative social action" (p. 7). Several scholars argue that the individual is best understood as a social relation, thus supporting the idea that culture is important in determining agency (Elias, 1991; Shapiro, 2005). Similarly, power, which is based on the individual's scope of action within hierarchically arranged social positions, often arises from factors such as class and gender and is influential in determining agency (Miller, 2005). From the perspective of these theorists the agency of communication will be influenced by organizational power based on the hierarchical importance of the position itself and the class and gender of the agent.

In social theory, perhaps the most applicable to public relations, the main problem is "the tension between agency and social structure" (Edgar & Sedgwick, 2002, p. 17). On a continuum the one extreme argues that agents have no power at all but are merely the products of the structure that dominate them. At the other extreme structure has no power over the individual, while the midposition argues that structure and agency are co-determinate, as per Giddens.

Despite these divergent opinions about the role of agency, the theorists discussed here emphasize a number of issues to be considered. The first is that the power of the agent will influence the agency itself. Second, societal norms, values, and culture will also play a role in how agency is executed. Third, the agent can, and will, be used by people with more power to cement that power and individual wealth. Lastly, the ability of the individual agent to resist domination is in question. All these perspectives challenge the notion of the powerful agent as a rational being. Although the above is a very cursory review of the main arguments about modern perspectives on agency, it clearly has implications for public relations practitioners. The question that arises is whether public relations practitioners have the ability to shape the public relations function or whether they will merely execute what structural imperatives such as power and organizational attributes demand of them. This brings into focus agency perspectives in the area of economics and management.

Economic Agency

Agency theory in economics has been criticized for being too narrow because it focuses on the contract between the owner (called a principal) and the agent and on the way the principal can make the contract more efficient for herself (Wright et al., 2001). The basic premise is that agents and principals have divergent interests, and this divergence translates into differences in risk-taking (Garud & Shapira, 1997). As a result agency theory in economics focuses on ways in which principals can control the self-serving behavior of agents to better serve their own interests. This relationship between principal and agent can also "be generalized to the relationship between lower levels of management and their subordinates" (Hatch, 1997, p. 335).

Principle-agency theory (PAT) is based on a situation familiar to public relations practitioners, namely, the authority of the principal on the one hand and the informational advantage of the expert on the other. Weber was the first to identify this asymmetrical relationship and argued power always lies with the expert (Miller, 2005). However, the principal manages the risk inherent in the principal-agent relationship with the authority to impose incentives. To prevent the agent from withholding important information, the principal provides an incentive to the agent for sharing information. Information asymmetry and asymmetry in the execution of actions are two attributes that might lead to the shirking of duties in the more risk-averse agent. All the relationships in the PAT are executed by people who are stable and objectified speakers or rational economic people.

The problem of divergent interests between agent and principal is handled through a contract in which the principal contracts work with the agent at an agreed price. In fact, supporters of this theory argue that "organizations are aggregates of individual preferences and actions and at times [serve] as a nexus of contracts and agreements" (Jensen & Meckling, 1975 as cited in Pfeffer, 1997, p. 45) and that "power cannot account for organizational outcomes" (p. 45). They also hold that organizations always are in equilibrium.

The theory also holds a negative view of agents. Agents are viewed as opportunistic and always seeking their own self-interest at the cost of the principal (Ghoshal & Moran, 1996; Hatch, 1997; Pfeffer, 1997; Wright et al., 2001). The language used about the negative attributes of agents is cynical and unflattering and supports Bauman's (1993) argument that in modernism people are not trusted to make ethical decisions. Agents' behavior is described as self-interest pursued with guile and deceit (Ghoshal & Moran, 1996), and "making false or empty, that is, self-disbelieving threats and promises in the expectation that individual advantage will thereby be realized" (Williamson, 1975, p. 26). Other attributes of agents' behavior are the misrepresentation of information, diverting resources for personal use, and efforts plagued with "malfeasant behavior" (Nilakant & Rao, 1994, p. 650). Pfeffer (1997) argues that economic theories differ from other social sciences in that human behavior is seen as "strictly instrumental and unconstrained by morals and values, except when behavior may be discovered and have consequent adverse effects on reputational resources" (p. 46).

If this negative approach is also applied to public relations practitioners one might wonder whether the assumption exists that practitioners will abuse their agency and use it to promote themselves rather than their principals, particularly through their very powerful media contacts. In the same vein, agency theory suggests that certain properties of agency might be desirable to others, which begs the question whether the agency of public relations is desirable to other agents (such as managers in the organization), who would like to have control over these self-promoting powers.

At the same time, if Hatch's contention is correct that the theory can be generalized to the relationship between lower levels of management and their subordinates, the managers (principals) of public relations practitioners are agents themselves, who might want to use the agency of public relations to legitimate their own agency. This can indeed lead to at least some conflict in the work environment. Clegg (1994) argues that when people in the organization do not share the same definition of the organizational situation, "contradictory agencies rapidly multiply" (p. 29).

Principals need agents to act on their behalf in their absence, and at the same time need to ensure that the agent will act in the principal's best interest. The contract stipulates the measures and promises rewards in order for agents to act in self-interest while acting on behalf of their principals. Other forms of control over agents are "vigilant monitoring, together with incentive schemes based around money, promotion, negative sanctions, and the like" (Donaldson, 1990, pp. 371–372). To ensure that the agent fulfills the contract, the principal needs information on the agent's behavior. In smaller organizations direct observation is possible, but it is much more difficult in larger organizations. The principal can purchase information about the agent through budgeting and accounting systems, or adding layers of observation to the organization. The agent's performance also can be measured by outcomes but it might become difficult to measure behavioral outcomes, which shifts some of the risk from the principal to the agent, which is undesirable for both agent and principal (Hatch, 1997).

It now becomes clear to what extent public relations practice has been influenced by the underlying assumptions of agency theory. The overriding concern with proving the effectiveness of public relations practice and its contribution to the bottom line stems from the expectation that agents have to prove their contribution and values. The Institute for Public Relations (IPR) (2010), for example, devotes much of its time to this kind of research and hosts an annual conference on the topic. The central question of what it is that public relations practitioners do (e.g. Cropp & Pincus, 2001; Hutton, 2001) can be directly linked to the demands principals make on agents. This might also explain why the big question about the division between public relations and marketing is of such importance to both fields. If public relations practitioners cannot set themselves apart from marketing, and cannot be measured on an exclusive set of performance criteria, principals will simply no longer enter into contracts with them. Also, if principals themselves are vague or unsure about what they can expect from the public relations agency this might lead to conflict between principal and agent. The question might well be asked how often principals have a clear understanding of what they expect from public relations agents, and whether there is not sometimes at least some level of unspoken expectations on the part of principals that practitioners might not be prepared to meet if these expectations were expressed, such as smoothing over problems, or telling half-truths to the media to make principals look better.

At the same time, if Hatch's (1997) contention that outcome measurement is problematic is true, then the evaluation of public relations performance remains a problem for principals. With outcome measurement some of the risk shifts to the agent, because agents might not have control over all the factors that might influence the outcome of their actions. This introduces the concept of *risk* to agency theory. Principals are viewed as risk neutral because they can diversify their shareholding across multiple investment options (Wiseman & Gomez-Mejia, 1998). Agents, on the other hand, are assumed to be risk averse because agents cannot necessarily diversify their income because their employment links security and income to a single firm (Williamson, 1963). Public relations practice, however, is a risky business at best. Practitioners have to deal with crises as a matter of course and often have little influence over factors that affect the occurrence or outcome of these crises. Again, the question might well be raised whether successful practitioners can be risk averse and whether practitioners are adequately compensated for having to deal with risks on behalf of the principal.

In summary, the major concepts in economic agency theory that can be applied to public relations practice focus on the following:

- the nature of the contract between principal and agent (in this case the public relations practitioner),
- the way in which public relations is measured,
- the level of influence public relations practitioners have over the outcome of their efforts,
- the level of risk public relations practitioners display.

Agency in Management Theory

Critiques of economic agency theory abound even though the critique had little effect on the ubiquity of these models in organization theory and social sciences (Pfeffer, 1997). The critique centers around the following: the concept of rational choice, the lack of empirical evidence that these approaches actually work, tautological reasoning that argues organizations are manifestations of the free market, the fact that economic agency theory ignores the impact of cooperation, uncertainty, and authority, and "its difficulty in making unique predictions about empirical results" (p. 51).

Wright et al. (2001) argue that approaches to agents in management theory are much more positive than those displayed in economic theory and that certain tenets of economic agency theory should be relaxed. These theories provide "compelling theoretical and empirical support for incorporating a positive behavioral perspective" in the principal/agent relationship (pp. 413–430). They argue that although some agents might shirk their responsibility because of goal conflict between principal and agent, other agents might enjoy performing responsibly because of their personal need for achievement and the need for love and respect from the principal for good performance. In this search for love and respect the agent is building relationships with others in the workplace, which not only advances the interests of the agent, but also those of other colleagues, and thus indirectly of the principal. They therefore argue that to merely view all agents' behavior as shirking is wrong and the argument of goal conflict should be relaxed.

They also argue that not all agents are risk averse, such as younger agents, or those who display entrepreneurial behavior. Entrepreneurial agents are opportunistic, pragmatic, and performance-oriented (Law, 1994). Agents who work in unsatisfactory situations might also display more risk-taking behavior than those who operate in satisfactory situations. Other factors that might influence risk behavior on the part of agents are governance structures (although the nature of the relationship is unclear) and previously successful risky behavior

(Wiseman & Gomez-Mejia, 1998). When the organization's external environment is turbulent, principals might prefer risk-taking agents because risk-averse agents might not be capable of dealing with new opportunities or threats associated with more dynamic settings (Tushman & O'Reilly, 1997). This focus on relationship building, which has been prevalent in public relations literature in recent years, might be particularly attractive behavior for principals.

The focus on relationship building is expanded when individuals are perceived as agents of their own development. When agents are in control of their own development and are allowed to act independently, they will "continually mix agency and communion" (Weick, 2001, p. 212). This will allow them to build relationships, which in turn will allow the agent to experience personal change, role development, and job evolvement.

In summary then, agents will be successful when they are able to build relationships, take risks, are entrepreneurial, and have a history of successful risk-taking, particularly when the organizations they work for are operating in turbulent environments. A modernist approach to agency theory in economics focuses on the contract between the owner (the principal) and the agent and on the way the principal can make the contract more efficient for himself (Wright et al., 2001). The basic premise is that *economic agents* and principals have divergent interests, and this divergence translates into differences in risk-taking (Garud & Shapira, 1997). The theory focuses on ways in which principals can control the self-serving behavior of agents to better serve their own interests. The problem of divergent interests between agent and principal is handled through a contract in which the principal contracts work with the agent at an agreed price (Hatch, 1997; Pfeffer, 1997; Wright et al., 2001).

Although the basic work contract remains firmly in place in organizations, one of the biggest challenges to this simplistic view of the principal-agent relationship is the fragmentation of worker identities. A strict interpretation of the position of the principal would mean ownership, while agents would be appointed to work on behalf of the principal. In most large organizations, both for- and non-profit, that would mean every person, including the CEO and managers at all levels, are agents. But these roles become fragmented when managers become principals who in turn appoint agents. Also, with shareholding and employee share schemes, agents can also be principals. If the role of the agent is stewardship, one can argue people who are not normally associated with organizations are principals in their role as tax payers or through participation in the stock market.

Finally, the fence between agent and principal is hardly iron-clad. The argument centers mainly on the competitive advantage of manipulating information. Boje, Adler, and Black (2005) argue that Enron's communication actions were highly structured and intentional spectacles of theater intended to lower production and transaction costs in an effort to maximize agent wealth. Their analysis shows how public relations actions were used to mislead the public, which ultimately led to the demise of the organization. This supports my argument that public relations practitioners should not be part of the dominant coalition to prevent co-option of public relations tactics and strategies in order to create wealth for management agents in particular. Boje et al. (2005) describe the implications and outcomes of such collusion:

> Associate delusion describes the principal-agent relationship from an audience-performer perspective when the performer intentionally misleads the audience through metatheatre to gain favorable outcomes and market approval. ... The relationship between principals and agents as an associative group produced convincing metatheatre, and this collective group functioned as a unique form of governance that was moderated by the winning script of unabashed competitive arrogance.
>
> (p. 52)

This kind of dramaturgical analysis of public relations practice, as also suggested by Mickey (1995), employs some postmodern perspectives, particularly from Foucault (1979), to show how organizations create "metascripts" (Boje et al., 2005) to control and punish employees who do not stick to their scripts. Metascripts are "networks of 'little scripts' that suspend employees in 'panoptic surveillance'" (p. 42). It would be a huge oversimplification to suggest that public relations practitioners, through their communication function, are solely responsible for the organization's metascripts. However, the function does contribute to this self-discipline and surveillance, particularly by objectifying management's scripts as rational and reasonable.

Public relations is not practiced in isolation but is "a collective process not adequately explained by public relations theory" with its focus on relationship building (Boje, Rosile, Durant, & Luhman, 2004, p. 767). This critique of particularly the situational theory with its focus on the management of relationships with activist groups points out how in the Enron case public relations was used to minimize the company's interdependence with its publics through creating theatrical spectacles aimed to mislead those publics. This contributed to the demise of the organization. The focus Boje and his colleagues bring to public relations is a very positive development and shows what happens when others take the field and its theories seriously. It not only brings a fresh eye to the field but also shows how invaluable interdisciplinary work is in understanding public relations as a field creating and being created by others in organizations.

Postmodern Perspectives on Human Agency

A postmodern approach would argue that agency theories formulated from a modernist stance are seriously flawed. Postmodern critique of modernist perspectives on rationality, the subject in control of his environment and fully aware of all his positions, and the dismissal of arguments about the impact of emotions and power in the workplace are all now familiar. Furthermore, modernism and positivism are critiqued because of "a practice of closure by which to construct discourses that pretend truth, fixity, and finality" that excludes all other forms of knowledge, which can only be accomplished if one has enough power to enforce such a state of affairs (Westwood & Clegg, 2003, p. 9). As a result "positivism is shorthand for a certain, often unexplicated, set of assumptions guiding the scientific [PR] enterprise" (p. 13). This is why Lyotard (1984) refers to this strategy of exclusion of knowledge as a "terrorist" action (p. 63).

In a similar, but more powerful, argument Ermarth (2001b) proposes that a One World Hypothesis (p. 202) has made the idea of the modern possible—a modern world that presented itself as an "objectified and unified" world and that "posits a world of agreement, not about this or that idea but about the formal possibility of agreement itself: about the possibility of a world held in common, a common 'candid' world" (p. 202). I wish to argue that the world of positivist (and postpositivist) science is what Lyotard describes as a genre of discourse, the rules of which are agreed upon by all the members who participate in the genre and which under modernism was the only genre promoted, legitimated, and acknowledged as real knowledge. Under those conditions it would be hypothetically possible to view the subject as one who totally understands, and accepts, her position in this One World. However, as the power and influence of colonial powers dwindled and eventually were broken they also lost their ability to enforce the One World Hypothesis. People started to contest this one subject as proposed and imposed in modernism, and the modern, unified world consisting of modern, unified subjects came tumbling down.

In contrast to modernist assumptions about agency articulated by theorists such as Giddens, postmodern approaches question this interpretation of agency. Instead of viewing the agent as a rational being that can reflexively resist domination and make rational choices about shaping his agency, postmodern agency is identified as a *state of awareness* or a *stance*.

> The term is used to describe the state of being present, active, or self-actualized in the performance of political, ideological, philosophical selfhood, or community, despite any system which infringes upon or otherwise precludes this ability. As a conscious state of activity, "agency" suggests a distinct, yet culturally variable, postmodern impulse toward self-consciousness with *the intention to subvert or undermine social or political oppression* [italics in the original].
>
> (Taylor & Winquist, 2001, p. 6)

The postmodern perspective on agency posits that all subjects are discursively constituted and everybody exists in a "discursive condition" (Ermarth, 2001b, p. 206). The discursive condition does not tolerate the One World Hypothesis because postmodernity is fragmented and consists of many "worlds." Because of the fragmented nature and varying and contradictory positions of the postmodern subject, it "may or may not be an agent in a given situation" (Taylor & Winquist, 2001, p. 6). Postmodern agency and power are dependent on situational variables. The discursive quality of agency is a positive attribute because it allows agents to actively participate in the construction of their own agency and identity.

Agency and identity are linked concepts. The modern agent had a fixed identity. The postmodern agent can, and does, have multiple identities. This concept of fractured identities was successfully applied to public relations to show that publics do not have fixed identities and that identities are located at different discursive moments (Curtin & Gaither, 2006). It also confirms that despite the sender's intents the message is interpreted through the lens of the receiver and the receiver's identity at that specific moment. Rather than viewing communication as a linear process, activist practitioners "[embrace] the flux and dynamism of communicative processes" (p. 86).

Postmodern practitioners are able to reject your own categorization and fixed identity. Ermarth (2001b) argues postmodernity allows us to have diverse identities because the fixed categories of modernity can be modified to suit ourselves. This makes the fixed categories of social science research even more suspect because the researcher imposes her classification system on those who participate in her research. A case in point is the concept of Whiteness. Everybody who is White will know that they cannot identify themselves in any other way, no matter which part of the world you come from. I, for instance, would like to classify myself as African-American but African-Americans argue I cannot because I do not share their history of slavery. Although I understand and have sympathy for their argument I wish to argue that because I identify so much with their struggle and so wish to participate in their cause, I should have the opportunity to identify myself as African-American, particularly because my own personal history is so shaped by my own African roots. So, even though others do not see me as African-American there are times when I clearly identify with African-Americans, which allow at least part of me to identify myself as African-American. This is an example of postmodern identities that "consist of multilevel and sequential inflections that produce patterns without consensus" [others do not agree with my identification as African-American] and liberate me "from the fatal forward motion of historical causality" [I can claim a certain part of African-American history even though in the most negative connection to apartheid](p. 209) because I have freed myself from the linearity of history.

The subject or subjectivity is often used in conjunction with agency and it is sometimes difficult to determine the relationship between these two concepts. For Foucault (1982), the subject is "subject to someone else by control and dependence" but also has the ability to create an "own identity by a conscience or self-knowledge" (p. 212). Because subjects have been historically consti-tuted through power relations, they now have to resist power and resistance to power is therefore inherent in postmodern agency. Because the subject is discursively constituted we hold "a simultaneous plurality of subject positions" at any single moment (Ermarth, 2001b, p. 210). The postmodern agent does not produce meaning. Meaning is created "in-between potential and practice" (p. 211). Personal identity can only be created in this in-between space. Thus the postmodern public relations agent is co-created through her different positions and relationships. In each of these she will be differently situated and have a different identity.

This concept of *multiple identity* and agency is even more relevant for public relations practitioners than for other organizational agents because its agency is communication. There can never be a single understanding of what the public relations function does because that function will configure differently in any given situation. No matter how we define our function it is defined differ-ently by those who experience our work. That then might explain why public relations practitioners are portrayed as spin doctors and flacks because that is the only role we provide for others who communicate about us. Furthermore, what surprises me most about our field is the general neglect by scholars from other domains and their lack of knowledge. If our identity is co-created with others then we should reach out to others to make them more comfortable with our field so that they too can help with different, although fragmented, identities. We need to understand that a single identity of the public relations practitioner and scholar will never be possible.

In a similar argument, Lecoure and Mills (2008) draw on the work of Bakhtin and Foucault to argue that the postmodern agent is responsible for her own action through dialogue with others. Like Foucault, Bakhtin argues that subjects are responsible for their actions and subjugation. However, Bakhtin argues dialogue depends on a shared culture, which is different from Lyotard's concept of different genres of discourse. According to Bakhtin's argument then identity only can be created in conditions of shared culture. What is valuable from Lecoure and Mills' application is that identity is a discursive condition and that the "self does not exist independently" (p. 8). Similar to Ermarth's (2001b) in-between position, Bakhtin argues that the subject is situated in a boundary position between the self and dialogic Other. Because the postmod-ern agent can never know how the Other sees him and can never convey his own identity to the Other that identity always will be fractured. LeCoure and Mills (2008) maintain that because Bakhtin's concept of the inner self that has multiple identities and therefore multiple inner voices provide tools to realize Foucault's concept of resistance to authority and power at the local level, par-ticular through speech as action.

Thus postmodern agency is simultaneously fragmented and multiple and refuses to be fixed. Tsekeris and Katrivesis (2009) refer to this as a "weak" approach (p. 30) because the postmodern agent recognizes that he has limited knowledge, which allows him to "self-confidently (stand) against all purist, macho aspirations to (Platonic) perfectionism" (p. 30). They argue the acceptance of fragile and limited knowledge is the best way to stand up against Western arrogance of certainty and "self-sufficient/self-immunizing knowledge" (p. 30). The modernist rational agent is replaced with communal agency which, instead of using language as representation of a neutral and objective world, uses language as action to bring about change (Gergen & Thatchenkery, 2004).

Postmodernists agree that all subjects need power to play the strategic game. What is important to remember here, once again, is that postmodern power is diffused. Power is not located in a central point but diffused through society and ever changing (Deleuze & Guattari, 1987; Foucault, 1980a) Similar to Althusser's (1971) position, Foucault (1980a) argues power is ascending. The diffused systems of power make central power at the top possible. "Power is everywhere; not because it embraces everything, but because it comes from everywhere" (p. 93). Deleuze and Guattari (1987) have a similar perspective and coin the term *rhizomatics*, which is both a method for analysis and a strategy for resistance to power. Because postmodern power is diffused and fragmented, it creates multiple opportunities for agents to resist power and postmodernists suggest various strategies to do that.

Resistance Strategies for the Postmodern Agent

Agency as resistance is a consistent theme in postmodern interpretations of agency. Feminist scholars have done some of the most important work in this regard, among others Ziarek (2001), who, like Taylor and Winquist (2001), views postmodern agency as "an attitude, an ethos, a philosophical life in which the critique of what we are is at one and the same time the historical analysis of the limits that are imposed on us and an experiment with the possibility of going beyond them" (Ziarek, 2001, p. 41, citing West, 1993, p. 32).

I have argued repeatedly in this volume that a postmodern approach to public relations proposes a practice of activism for both practitioners and academics. This is particularly facilitated by perspectives on the postmodern agent as fragmented and having multiple identities. Because of fragmented identities it is possible to resist at multiple points. The term rhizomatics also reminds us that it is possible to escape if we are closed in. Activism is possible through the use of language at multiple stages or nodal points in the networks where multiple identities are formed.

The postmodern agent also should know what to look out for and what to resist. I have repeatedly stated that postmodern agency in practice and in the academic environment should resist metanarratives, a concept that now has been thoroughly covered in this volume. This can be done by resisting any attempt to establish normative discourse and should always challenge historically established limits on the agent. I also have repeatedly been challenged that my concept of postmodern activism does not have application in real life practice and that it is impossible. There typically are people who view agency in the modern context, who see their position as fixed in the hierarchy of organizations, and who accept their own lack of power. They most likely see my interpretation of activism and resistance as a grand gesture, as a single moment of truth that defines their whole lives. This is why postmodern agency is so liberating. It is not one big struggle but multiple and continuous struggles—a sort of guerilla warfare that strikes at different and unexpected places and wears down the dominant power that tries to hold on to the One World Hypothesis. Lyotard (1986–1987) says "the idea is no longer physical strength as it was for the man of antiquity; it is suppleness, speed, the ability to metamorphose (go to a ball in the evening and fight a war at dawn)" (p. 219).

This is why it is important that the postmodern agent should resist attempts to fix her identity and in turn should resist fixing the identities of others. The postmodern agent should strive for a philosophy of Becoming, rather than a philosophy of being (Docherty, 1993; Ziarek, 2001). The resistance to metanarratives (Lyotard, 1992) is a consistent theme in postmodern theory. The aim of metanarratives is to dominate through single ideologies and theories, which are presented as truth. It is important to remind ourselves continuously that metanarratives and the truth they pretend to present are merely the viewpoints of some dominant groups in society who wish to maintain their power. This guerilla warfare does not take place overnight but is "a long process by which [public relations activists] resist a variety of pre-existing knowledges and norms" (Loizidou, 2007, p. 12) through "the reactive undoing of the norm" (p. 151).

Disciplinary power, or bio-power, operates on the level of bodies and the life world of the population through disciplinary and normative practices and I have repeatedly shown how public relations practice participates in this process. Eventually people internalize these disciplinary powers and it becomes unnecessary to control people through surveillance. Part of being a public relations activist is to make people aware of the points of self-surveillance and that they can also apply their bio-power to resist these forms of discipline (Foucault, 1988c, 1988d). Instead of fixing the norm, public relations practitioners and academics should strive to break the norm.

While normative power is a threat to postmodern agency, so is the "agentic state" within organizations (Bauman, 1993, p. 125, citing Milgram, 1974, p. 133). Bauman is particularly concerned with the ethics of organizations and although he believes organizations themselves are neither good nor immoral, they render "social action morally adiaphoric" (p. 125). The agentic state removes the agent of authority from the action chain so that organizational agents are never directly faced with the consequences of their actions. Because actions in the agentic state are mediated and mediating there is no real understanding of the contribution agents make to immoral decisions or outcomes of those decisions. Bauman calls this "floated responsibility" (p. 126). Citing Arendt's description of "rule by Nobody," (p. 126) Bauman argues that organizational agents now turn their moral attention inward and their moral responsibility is diverted to others in the same agentic state:

> It renders "loyalty to the mates", to the 'comrades in arms' the main measure of moral propriety, and thus strengthens dedication of all to the task at hand, reinforces discipline and willingness to cooperate, quashing on the way whatever moral scruples about the far-away effects of co-operation might have arisen.
>
> (pp. 126–127)

Bauman consistently argues that postmodern agency only has one moral focus and that is the moral impulse toward the Other. As argued before, the moral impulse cannot be commanded and exists before any rational state. The moral impulse is pre-rational. It is an impulse which calls to act for the Other by judging without rules or criteria and without knowing the Other (Lyotard & Thébaud, 1985). Bauman's moral impulse is similar to Ziarek's (2001) articulation of "anarchic responsibility," which is the "infinite responsibility for justice without the assurance of normative criteria" (p. 6). Thus, being aware of and resisting the agentic state would allow for postmodern agency.

This concern with the Other is yet another attribute of postmodern agency. The modern agent is replaced by a decentered subject who is constituted through fragmented and fractured sets of relationships with others. The image of bricolage comes to mind, or as Linstead and Grafton-Small (1991, p. 39), as cited in Hassard (1996, p. 53), call it, "a weave, a texture, fractured but intertwined rather than hierarchical and integrated, a process and a paradox having neither beginning nor end." The notion that meaning cannot be fixed is a very important one for the postmodern agent. Indeed, as Hassard says, the subject is now "a convenient location for the throughput of discourse" (p. 53). As we have now established, metanarratives are to be resisted. One of the reasons is to challenge the modernist notion of logocentrism, or fixed meanings. Because of the instability of meaning as articulated in Derrida's concept of *différance*, meaning topples forward and can never be retrieved in its original meaning. The role of postmodern discourse is to create new meaning, as Lyotard so aptly describes in a conversation with Thébaud (cf. the quoted at the beginging of Chapter 1).

To ensure that meanings are not fixed and become metanarratives, Lyotard proposes a postmodern dialectic, which is the effort to create new meaning through a process of dissensus, which also has been thoroughly discussed in this text.

I believe dissensus, like metanarratives, is a defining concept of postmodernism and it remains the most dominant strategy to resist metanarratives, particularly for the activist public relations practitioner. Lyotard (1992) forcefully resists a consensual approach to dissolving differences because in consensus the most powerful dominates the discussion and determines the direction of the consensus. I have argued before that in public relations the concepts of asymmetry, symmetry, and collaboration all rest on the principle of consensus because these arguments are all presented in a single genre of discourse. Whoever supports the concepts of symmetry in public relations perceives a single genre of discourse with rules on which everybody in the discussion has agreed. Consensus co-opts people with less power or the powerless to do the bidding of those in power and so not only maintains the status quo but also forces people to make decisions against their own interest. Lyotard (1988) argues that dissensus creates new ways of thinking and problem solving. For public relations dissensus allows for changes to the rules of the game or for the acknowledgment of a totally different game. To ensure one's agency it will be important to make others aware of the tensors in the discourse and to resist consensus. Ziarek (2001) believes dissensus is also the postmodern ethical approach because it "does not transcend power relations but intervenes and enables transformations" (p. 15).

Postmodern agency is always situated in praxis and is always associated with local action. Because agency relates to the practice of the self, i.e. a continuous and perpetual transformation, it is always transformative action. Through everyday practices of resistance, transformation, reflexivity, responsibility, and enabling a postmodern dialectic the subject shapes her agency moment to moment and day to day. There is never a fixed agency. Postmodern agency is not a stable state but continuously transformative.

The above arguments stress the fragmentation inherent in every aspect of the postmodern work environment. It is in this environment that communication practitioners, i.e. people contractually bound to perform communication tasks on behalf of the organization, have to negotiate their roles, power, and morality. First and foremost, they are viewed as economic agents, as in the terms *public relations agent* and *advertising agent*. Of all organizational agents, communicators might face the most daunting task because they are not only supposed to care for the interests of the organization but also of its stakeholders. As argued before, stakeholders can be people in larger society and not only those who are actively involved in the daily activities of organizations. How communication agents address this responsibility; whether they should only communicate on behalf of those people who employ them as their agents; and how power relationships that try to exert influence in their daily work environments might affect their ability to produce measurable results, are all important questions to ask about their economic agency.

But it is equally important to remember that in all these instances there is no single solution because power and agency are fragmented. As a result multiple opportunities for resistance exist. It is the ability of the agent to resist power and control that is at the core of the postmodern debate about agency. Public relations agency is undoubtedly used to create norms of discipline and submission of both internal and external publics for the benefit of more powerful agents and principals. Communication actions of practitioners create and shape the rules, practices, and norms of organizations through which they and others are regulated through self-control and self-discipline.

At the same time postmodern power can be a positive force for change. Postmodern communication practitioners have a duty to use their bio-power (Foucault, 1980b)—their power from within—to assert themselves when they deal reflexively with power issues in the workplace. Foucault (1988c) said, "As soon as there is a power relation, there is a possibility of resistance. We can never be ensnared by power: we can always modify its grip in determinate conditions and according to precise strategy" (p. 123).

I wish to argue that a dialectic of dissensus, dissymmetry, and situational decision-making can negotiate material agency in organizations. This establishes language as the most powerful tool for resistance; not language as written language only but language in its full discursive state. Language is "a site of liberation from the restrictions that modernity imposed upon subjectivity" (Ermarth, 2000, p. 408). It is impossible to not make a difference in the discursive condition. Instead of the grand gesture of opposition "our opportunities [for activism] are ready-at-hand in the daily iterations or revisions of discursive potentials that constitute the real basis for radical change" (p. 413).

To sidestep the dangers of once again becoming the powerful agent of modernity it is important to acknowledge that our identities always are socially constructed and situated differently according to the specific moment in which the self is located. The specific social and institutional climate constrains self-identity at the moment of operation (Broad, 2002). It also is important to acknowledge the others who are co-constructing your identity at any moment. This is particularly relevant to public relations practitioners whose role it is to facilitate the power of the narratives of their publics. Organization and organizational life consists of many competing stories that do not form a coherent whole (Vickers, 2005, citing Boje, 1995, 2001). These stories include "antenarratives [that] are stories that are non-linear, incoherent and unplotted" and that are "never final, never complete, but give[s] attention to what is going on, the sense of the lived experience" (p. 76).

Public relations practitioners, who are supposed to maintain relationships with their publics, should pay special attention to the *antenarratives* and not only to those narratives that confirm and affirm organizational master narratives. The fact that public relations practitioners seldom relate antenarratives is largely due to the fact that personal stories of members of an organization's publics are not supposed to be told because they do not contribute to the aggregate of knowledge and do not count as knowledge. Personal stories, so to speak, throw off the averages and means we are so comfortable working with. The very notion of *a* public points to a group, a mean, an aggregate. Vickers (2005) urges us to become witnesses to suffering and "assume a responsibility for telling what happened" and reinstate "the voice of wounded storytellers." This requires listening, a recognition of "diversity, openness to multiple voices, inclusion, flexibility [and] respect" and "accepting and reinstating the voices of those with less than perfect organizational experiences" (p. 85). That will move us toward justice in organizations. In the past I have argued, based on an analysis of postmodern literature that public relations as activism is possible, and Voto and I have argued that

> the practitioner as organizational activist will serve as *a* [italics in the original] conscience in the organization by resisting dominant power structures, particularly when these structures are not inclusive; will preference employees' and external publics' discourse over that of management; will make the most humane decision in a particular situation; and will promote new ways of thinking and problem solving through dissensus and conflict. These actions will contribute to a culture of emancipation and liberation in the organization.
>
> (Holtzhausen & Voto, 2002, p. 64)

On reflection a fixed definition of public relations as activism is a very modernist stance, which I believe needs to be replaced with a more general evaluation of the conditions that allow for public relations as activism, based on the realities of postmodernity and postmodern assumptions.

Activist Strategies for the Postmodern Public Relations Academic and Practitioner

The world public relations scholars and practitioners in particular occupy is filled with aporiae. To argue otherwise is to live in a world where simplistic and reductivist arguments lead to simplistic and reductivist solutions, the outcomes of which lead to injustice because they do not recognize the impact of power, discipline, and language on our everyday practices. Some of the aporetic situations practitioners have to balance are the interest of the public vs. the interests of specific publics; the economic interests of the organization vs. the broader interest of society; the tensions between economic agency and human agency; the push and pull of a democratic society vs. the often undemocratic environment of organizations; and the pressure to reach consensus on issues that are so irreconcilable that they provoke dissensus.

The aporetic nature of practice is evident in Vignette 7.1 and sometimes the decisions are as big as having to leave your job and becoming a whistle-blower. But postmodern theory shows that it is not about whether emancipatory practices are no longer possible; it is rather about how emancipatory practices come to fruition. Postmodern theories provide us with different strategies to live in this aporetic and confusing world. In fact, postmodernism "can be best defined

VIGNETTE 7.1

Whistle Blowing as an Activist Strategy

Whistle blowing has received a considerable amount of attention of late because of the profound impact it has on organizational outcomes. Whistle blowing often is associated with rogue activities and consequences for whistle blowing can be grave. More often than not whistle blowers lose their jobs and have to bear public scrutiny—the victims become the accused.

I have argued in the past that whistle blowing is easier for women than for men because they often are excluded from the dominant coalition and therefore do not have the emotional baggage that comes with in-group acceptance and loyalties that are formed in social relationships beyond the job. Examples are Sherron Watkins (Enron), Coleen Rowley (FBI), and Cynthia Cooper (Worldcom) who were highlighted in *Time* as "Persons of the Year" because of the effects of their whistle blowing activities (Lacayo & Ripley, 2002).

However, a recent example of whistle blowing challenges that hypothesis and shows that whistle blowing is not gender related. Men can be as good at whistle blowing as women if their moral impulse guides them in that direction. Furthermore, this example is from public relations practice itself, whereas the example of women whistle blowers did not include anybody with a public relations background or responsibility.

The case in point is that of Wendell Potter, a former vice president for corporate communications at CIGNA, the health insurance giant, who became a whistle-blower on the company's public relations tactics to defeat President Obama's health care reform. The turning point for him came when CIGNA declined several petitions for a liver transplant for 17-year-old Nataline Sarkysian. Nataline died hours after they reversed their decision (Hornick & Quijano, 2009). Potter was the CIGNA spokesperson during the incident and was overwhelmed with angry phone calls and e-mails. A free health care event where "volunteer doctors were seeing patients in barns, people in animal stalls" at a fair ground also "changed it for [him]" (Acosta & Knapp, 2009).

Potter resigned in 2007 after a 20-year career in corporate public relations and became a senior fellow at the Center for Media and Democracy with the aim of exposing how the public relations tactics of the health care industry shaped the health care debate (Potter, 2009). He particularly focuses on how the industry uses language and the channels the industry uses to resist health care reform. "Words matter," he said, "and the insurance industry is a master at linguistics and using the hot words, buzzwords, buzz expressions that they know will get people upset" (Hornick & Quijano, 2009). He cites the use of "death panels" and "the government takeover of the system" as examples of linguistic strategies that came directly from the industry. When accused of "purging" small businesses from their company by driving them out by huge increases in premiums, a CIGNA spokesperson responded: "We do not practice that. We will offer rates that are reflective of the competitive group health insurance market. We always encourage our clients to compare our proposed rates to those available from other carriers," which is code for purging without using the actual word.

Potter (2009) says the health care industry uses "its army of PR people" to influence public opinion without the public knowing it. They do this by funneling

> millions of its policyholders' premiums to big public relations firms that provide talking points to conservative talk show hosts, business groups and politicians ... the PR firms set up front groups, again using your premium dollars and mine, to scare people away from reform.

Potter writes that the PR firms the health care industry uses have close ties with media outlets and people who support the conservative movement. He also served on "numerous trade group committees and industry-funded front groups [in which] industry leaders are always full partners in developing strategies to derail any reform that might interfere with insurers' ability to increase profits." The industry goes to great lengths to keep these activities secret from the public. The main reason why the health care companies do this is because they are beholden to Wall Street, Potter said, and it is all about making money.

Being a whistle-blower was not easy. "This is hard to do. It's scary to do something like this. I don't think I'm any more courageous than anybody but I feel I had to do this" (Potter, 2009).

as a method or strategy" (Eagan, 2009, p. 141) to deal with a confusing world that no longer has a single understanding and has thoroughly rejected the One World Hypothesis (Ermarth, 2001b, p. 202). There still are many who support a single understanding of their world but the truth is that they are superimposing their hypothesis on a world that no longer exists. The desire for absolutes is still pervasive, particularly in theory building.

A phenomenon that I find disconcerting is the desire for foundations despite the desire to work with postmodern theory. That is perhaps another example of an aporia. Although there are ample opportunities for using postmodern theory with critical modernist theories, it is important to at least stay within the philosophical realm of postmodern philosophy if one applies a postmodern analysis to public relations. Perhaps the most consistent approach in postmodern theory is the rejection of metanarratives or secure foundations. Two recent examples come to mind where I feel postmodern theory was co-opted to strengthen the theorizing while the theories themselves remain fundamentally modernist.

While espousing a postmodern approach to analyzing activist rhetoric Boyd and Vanslette (2009) provide a caveat to their analysis and say

> a purely postmodern approach to almost anything is inconceivable. The need for closure, certainty, and control ... is a modernist imperative that allows daily life to continue. Without modernist assessments, accountability, and answers it is hard to imagine what the world might look like.
>
> (locations 9213–9220)

If there is one aspect of postmodern theory I set out to show in this book it is that postmodernism challenges notions of closure, certainty, and control. To be a postmodern activist is exactly to reject these approaches to public relations theory building and practice. To experience closure, certainty, and control one needs to willfully impose them on one's life and the lives of others. These are typically the stories we tell ourselves about ourselves to give us a sense of security. Although I am totally supportive of applying Foucaultian approaches to theory building in the context of critical modernism, as Boyd and Vanslette argue, even critical modernism would argue against the type of modernist closure and control they advocate.

Also, although I do not view postmodernism as a rupture with modernism I also do not view it as the one extreme end of a continuum with modernism on the other extreme. It is exactly this kind of linearity that postmodernism critiques and exposes in favor of fragmentation and rupture. For instance, I would indeed be very wary of any work that applies Lyotard's postmodern theories to anything that argues for closure and certainty, as is the case with Degooyer (2010), who applies Lyotard's concept of language games to build a metatheory for problem solving through the use of language. That is an argument I find incommensurable and paralogical, to use Lyotard's terms. Except for the use of metatheory and "metadiscursive commonplaces," citing Craig (1999), Degooyer makes a very interesting and useful argument. But instead of seeking to create a metatheory he would have been better served to propose supple praxis as a strategy, which is more in line with the use of Lyotard's work.

The Postmodern Condition of the Public Relations Activist

I wish to conclude this book with a discussion of the postmodern condition and how it might affect public relations practitioners and academics. I do not wish to repeat the arguments I made in this text. They are many. They are diverse as postmodernism typically is and do not converge into a single coherent argument. That is intentional because postmodernity is not about single understandings and solid foundations. It is a condition, a strategy, a stance, and not a fixed state. Let us first look at the postmodern condition, i.e. what is the nature of this state of our Western society that urges some of us to become public relations activists.

Life is Chaotic and Fragmented

Postmodern public relations activists will recognize and experience life as chaotic and fragmented and will relish living and practicing in this environment. Like Wendell Potter in Vignette 7.1 activist practitioners will overcome their fear and do the right thing. "This is hard to do. It's scary to do something like this," he said. They will reach out to the Other, as he did by reaching out to the family of Nataline Sarkysian after her untimely death and to the many uninsured people who get their health care in animal stalls at a state fair ground. They will display activist fervor (Dozier & Lauzen, 2000) and answer the call of the Other without expecting anything back.

Public Relations Practice is Always Political

Postmodern activists will recognize the political nature of their practice and acknowledge that in politics there is no neutrality. As Lyotard (Lyotard & Thébaud, 1985) said.

> When one says politics, one always means that there is something to institute. There is no politics if there is not at the very center of society, at least at a center that is not a center but everywhere in the society, a questioning of existing institutions, a project to improve them, to make them more just.

(p. 23)

To be just one has to choose, take sides, but one has to do so without criteria, without the absolute moral certainties that are so typical of modernity. It is in this context that the only criterion is the moral impulse to the Other. We have to take sides because we need to resist the objectification of our publics that comes with neutrality, particularly through social science methods and the field's segmentation techniques.

No Nostalgia for the Past

To improve any institution of society one cannot be nostalgic for the past because the past we are nostalgic for has never existed in the way we imagine it today.

Postmodern historical critique shows that history is a narrative of something that we imposed on the past, much like the Disney-like nostalgia for a world of fairy tales and other idealized theatrical presentations as if they really existed. The past can be used for therapeutic purposes (Southgate, 2005) but the self-interest in the historic analysis should always be recognized and acknowledged.

Future-Oriented

Knowledge is not about the past but about the future (Lyotard, 1984). It is not about reinforcing past knowledge because we cannot return to the past or even to meaning created in the immediate past. Knowledge and meaning are always toppling forward and cannot be retrieved in their original form. This challenges concepts of truth because there is no truth that can be verified even within the context of denotative statements because denotative statements also are value-based (Lyotard & Thébaud, 1985). This perspective challenges rationality because there is no social world out there that can be discovered and described because all knowledge and meaning is socially constructed. The role of the public relations activist is to challenge statements of absolute truth and resist becoming the tools through which truth is fixed, as in the case of managerial discourse.

Fluid, Evolving, and New

Because there are no fixed meanings (Derrida, 1976) all meaning is fluid and always evolving. Knowledge also is fluid because it is socially constructed within a specifically situated context. It also is fluid because the postmodern mind does not adhere to the categories modernism created to govern and control the social world and prefers de-differentiation (Clegg, 1990). Ermarth (2001b) aptly and humorously describes the modernist practice of differentiation and categorization:

> Take, for example, the generalization that classifies whales as mammals despite the obvious similarities to fish. Because the culture of representation does not allow for diversity in identification ... the creature must be either a mammal or a fish, and so the poor fish becomes one of us.

(p. 209)

This challenges public relations scholars and practitioners to resist strict role definitions and to look at practice holistically within the context of situated practice, i.e. practice is determined by the situation the practitioner experiences at a particular moment. This also questions the firewalls we have put up between public relations, marketing, and human resources in studying the role of corporate public relations practice. This raises the question of who practices public relations and whether it is only the people who have a specific designation to do so or whether there are others in the organization who perform some public relations duties or who affect the reputation of the organization.

Pragmatic and Situated in Practice

There are no rules outside of practice that determine how a public relations event should be handled. The rules of the game are determined by who is involved in the event, the nature of the event, and the language games that the participants in the event use to articulate their differences. Because the aim of postmodern academics and practitioners is to upset existing metanarratives or resist the formation of new metanarratives, public relations practice is always local and regional (Lyotard, 1984).

Lived, Witnessing, and Involved

For practice to be local and regional it has to be experienced in the local context. In both practice and research postmodern practitioners become activists with those "wounded story-tellers" (Vickers, 2005, p. 85) who do not have our experience of organizations to make their voices heard. Academics can become "critical workers" (West, 1997, p. 74) or "critical worker researchers" (Kincheloe & McLaren, 1994, p. 147) to reflect respect for the diversity and multiple voices of our publics. This will acknowledge the experiences and knowledge of our multiple stakeholders as valid and worth acting upon.

Responsible and Moral

Contradictory to the general belief that in postmodernism "everything goes" postmodernists believe in personal responsibility because we have set ourselves free from the norms and values of others who aim to determine our responsibility for us, invariably to their own benefit. We can no longer blame others for an unjust situation in which we are involved because we hold ourselves responsible for justice in every circumstance. As Ermarth (2001b, p. 212) says, "postmodernists are not loonies unable to kick a stone ... postmodernity is much more respectful of detail than was modernity, in something like the same way quantum theory is more precise just as it becomes less secure in the familiar empiricist terms." Responsibility and morality in postmodernity do not hide behind the norm or the aggregate but face up to what is immoral in every specific event encountered in practice, theory, and research.

The Discursive Condition

It is all about language. Language already is action. No social phenomenon is possible without language, including personal identity. Like all meaning, personal identity is constructed in a complex path of opposing meanings and postulations; it exists in the "linguistic in-between" (Ermarth, 2001b, p. 211) or on the borderline. "The self is half somebody's else's" (Hermans, 2003, as cited in LeCoure & Mills, 2008, p. 7). Because discourse is always situated in a specific context the discursive condition always is temporary. As Potter said in Vignette 7.1, "Words matter" and their meanings can be changed and manipulated. Public relations activists will always live in the discursive moment and can resist situations such as these with their own discursive strategies. The discursive condition is a contested one and rich with diversity. It represents a world that cannot be described in any single way.

A Struggle for Freedom

In his autobiography the postmodern religious scholar Küng (2003) defined his life as a struggle for the freedom to make his own choices. For the postmodern public relations activist this struggle for freedom is one to set us free of norms and expectations others have of us and our behavior and also from our own internalized submission to those norms and different forms of discipline. This will enable us to recognize when powerful interests wish to control us to their own benefit, as in Vignette 7.1. To set ourselves free requires self-knowledge and the need to live reflexively in every moment. It also requires knowledge of how power shapes our world. Only if we understand that can we set ourselves free from its tentacles and assert ourselves powerfully.

The Combative Nature of Postmodern Practice

Postmodern activist practice is combative in the sense that it strives to reclaim organizations and society for those who do not have the resources to accomplish their goals or resist institutions that harm them. It is not combative in the sense of being disrespectful but rather in the sense of resistance and standing up for what is just in a given situation. Postmodern practice is radical in the sense of revolutionary, or what Williams (1998, p. 9) refers to as a "radical philosophy of action." This challenges the public relations activist to bring about fundamental changes in society by addressing societal problems at their very core and not at a macro level:

> The difference between the philosopher of action or commitment and other activists is in the effort of the former to seek out and answer the fundamental questions. What is sought, therefore, is the greatest degree of certainty as opposed to conviction.

(p. 9)

Striving for Participative Democracy

Postmodern public relations practice is egalitarian, democratic, and participative, not representative. Activist practice invites everybody to the discussion table and does not privilege management's views over those of stakeholders. They are as comfortable in the boardroom as in the township or housing project. Activist practitioners and academics are not know-it-alls who pretend that they can articulate the views of others accurately. In case stakeholders cannot be present it is the duty of the researcher or practitioner to first verify the information that will be transferred with the group involved. As I wrote in Chapter 2, allowing the voice directly into the sphere of practice is the truly ethical. "Without engagement, confrontation, dialogue and even a 'struggle for recognition' … we tend to constitute the otherness of the other by projection and fantasy or ignore it in indifference" (Benhabib, 1992, p. 168).

It is Non-Conformist

Because the postmodern activist resists metanarratives and disciplining systems such as social norms or accepted dogma in research and knowledge creation he often will be a lonely voice. This comes with the desire for thinking differently, as Foucault (1985, p. 8) said, "There are times in life when the question of knowing if one can think differently than one thinks, and perceive differently than one sees, is absolutely necessary if one is to go on looking and reflecting at all." As Potter said in Vignette 7.1, it is scary to be a non-conformist but it is important for practitioners to draw on their own bio-power to resist powerful forces of domination and injustice.

Acknowledge and Celebrate Limited Knowledge

Instead of pretending that there is a single world out there that can be known and represented, the postmodern public relations activist will relish the nature of knowledge as fragmented and coming in different forms, such as in the stories of stakeholders or in the disjointed narratives of those affected by our practices. This approach will legitimate the antenarratives of wounded storytellers (Vickers, 2005) or the carnival-like narrative of those who strive to break free from the corporate strangle-hold on society through laughter and humor (Boje et al., 2004), much like Jon Stewart and Stephen Colbert do nightly on Comedy Central. Sometimes it is exactly through pointing to the ridiculous and preposterous that the true nature of institutional discourse comes to life.

Practice is Transparency

Transparency in the organizational environment is a highly contested concept (Christensen & Langer, 2009) and is an example of the aporetic nature of organizational life. From a public relations standpoint transparency is a requirement for building trust but at the same time organizations do have some proprietary information that might harm them in the marketplace and take away their competitive advantage. Public relations practitioners have to negotiate their way through their obligation to transparency with the public, which benefits a democratic society, and their obligation to the organization to be sustainable.

The problem comes when there is a purposeful public relations strategy to keep important information from the public and when public relations tactics are used to deliberately drive a hidden agenda. In the case of Enron public relations was used to create theatrical spectacles to hide the real state of the organization (Boje et al., 2005) and mislead the public, investors, and its own employees, who invested heavily in the organization. Similarly, Vignette 7.1 shows how CIGNA used front groups and public relations agencies to drive its agenda of defeating the health care bill.

One can argue that total transparency is impossible in postmodernity. In the same way that the modern agent who has total self-knowledge is a postmodern impossibility, the postmodern organization also is not totally known and is as fragmented and has as many identities as the people who work there. Transparency is as important as democracy to the postmodern public relations activist. Indeed, as Lyotard (1984) says, it is important that information should be made freely available, which is more possible than ever because of technology. But rather than having a "policy" of transparency for the organization, which might well be an empty promise, as Christensen and Langer (2009) say, it is important for the activist that each and every public relations event should be scrutinized for its transparency or lack thereof. It is as important to understand who benefits from withholding information.

Conclusion

One last point needs to be made and that is that the postmodern project is about fighting for justice. That also is the aim of the postmodern public relations activist as scholar, teacher, and practitioner. This immediately raises the specter of what is justice, whose justice, justice for whom, and so forth. Because postmodernists so consistently argue against any form of essentialism or foundationalism, these are valid questions. However, I wish to argue in the vein of Bauman (1993), that the one thing we have in common is our humanity; that part of humanity that is primordial and was never subject to social construction, namely, that people are born equal, that we care for each other, that we live through and with other people.

To realize this in postmodern society requires a radical, participative democracy that ensures equality for all, respects cultural plurality, and requires confrontational intolerance of injustice. Public relations academics and practitioners are in a unique position to join the fight for justice because so much injustice is institutionalized through laws, corporations, and financial interests—the interests we often represent. We are all aware of the injustices financial institutions perpetrated on a trusting public during the first decade of the 21st century in the United States and Europe and the way in which developing countries often are exploited by world powers, much like the big oil companies are doing in Africa today.

West says it beautifully. We as public relations activists need to align ourselves "with demoralized, demobilized, depoliticized and disorganized people in order to empower and enable social action and, if possible, to enlist collective insurgency for the expansion of freedom, democracy and individuality" (West, 1997, p. 66). All of these goals need "to be tempered by reverence for nature, respect for life, sustainability, and ecological balance" (Best & Kellner, 2001, p. 11). We are shamefully still living in a world where humanity, empathy, compassion, dignity, responsibility, and equality still need to be negotiated and fought for. As long as that is the case, there will be a place for the public relations activist scholar and practitioner.

It is not easy; not for the faint of heart. In his inaugural lecture as professor at the Collège de France on December 2, 1970 Foucault opened with a quote from Beckett (Eribon, 1991, p. 213), which sums up the postmodern condition and the activist position I believe it holds:

> *Behind me I should have liked to hear, behind me, a voice speaking thus: "I must go on, I can't go on; I must go on; I must say words as long as there are words; I must say them until they find me, until they say me—heavy burden, heavy sin; I must go on; maybe it's been done already, maybe they've already said me; maybe they've already borne me to the threshold of my story, right to the door opening onto my story; I'd be surprised if it opened."*

NOTES

Chapter 1

1 Lyon (1999, pp. 6–24) for instance argued that Augustine's concept of providence led to history's forward movement that in turn led to the notion of progress during the early days of the Enlightenment, which resulted in the rejection of tradition in Medievalism. This gave rise to the celebration of reason, which in turn already had the seed of relativism, which led to the notion of nihilism.

2 The work of Gane (1993) and Poster and Aronowitz (2001) provide excellent reviews of Baudrillard's approach.

3 Althusser's essay was written in 1970 but appeared in 1971 in *Lenin and philosophy and other essays*. It was translated by Ben Brewster and published by New Left Books in London.

4 O'Sullivan, Hartley, Saunders, and Fiske (1989, pp. 214, 218) mention three characteristics of a sign, namely, its physical form, its reference to something other than itself, and that it must be recognized by people as a sign. The signifier represents the physical form as perceived by our senses, such as a word, sound, or picture. The signified is the user's mental concept of what the sign refers to.

5 *Rhizomes* refer to underground, rootlike stems bearing both roots and shoots that will re-emerge even when cut off. This serves as a metaphor for the way in which one can escape from power that is centralized. A tree with roots and branches linked to a trunk is their metaphor for centralized power.

6 *Just gaming* was first published in 1979 as *Au juste* and takes the form of a conversation with Thébaud. Best and Kellner (1991) suggested that *Au juste* should be read as *Towards justice*. They said, "it is important to read the English title as just gaming, in the sense of playing the game of the just, rather than as merely gaming in a frivolous way. Justice involves playing by the rules and preserving the autonomy of rules in different language games" (p. 161).

Chapter 3

1 Plumb's text was first published in 1969 and reprinted in 2004 with a foreword by Simon Schama and an introduction by Niall Ferguson. The 2004 edition is referenced in this text.

Chapter 6

1 For an interesting discussion of communication in the public sphere, see the *International Journal of Strategic Communication, 4*(2).
2 The Institute of Public Relations devotes much of its efforts to public relations measurement (http://www.instituteforpr.org/research/measurement_and_evaluation)

Chapter 7

1 The concepts of "agency" and "agent" will be used interchangeably in this chapter because the one concept is impossible without the other, e.g. the *Reader's Digest Oxford complete word-finder* describes "agency" as "the function of an agent" (1993, p. 30).

BIBLIOGRAPHY

Abel, C. F. (2005). Beyond the mainstream: Foucault, power and organization theory. *International Journal of Organization Theory and Behavior, 8*(4), 495–519.

Acosta, J., & Knapp, B. (2009, July 3). Ex-executive accuses insurance giant of 'purging' customers. Retrieved July 27, 2010, from http://www.cnn.com/2009/US/07/02/insurance.purging/index.html

Aldoory, L. (2009). Feminist criticism in public relations: How gender can impact public relations texts and contexts. In R. L. Heath & E. Toth (Eds.), *Rhetorical and critical approaches to public relations II* (pp. 110–124). New York: Routledge.

Aldoory, L., & Toth, E. (2004). Leadership and gender in public relations: Perceived effectiveness of transformational and transactional leadership styles. *Journal of Public Relations Research, 16*(2), 157–183.

Althusser, L. (1971). *Lenin and philosophy and other essays* (B. Brewster, Trans.). London: New Left Books.

Anderson, T. J. (2004). Integrating decentralized strategy making and strategic planning processes in dynamic environments. *Journal of Management Studies, 41*(8), 1271–1299.

Anonymous (2005). Snowmaking plan pits ski area against tribes, environmentalists. *U. S. Water News Online.* Retrieved July 2, 2010 from http://www.uswaternews.com/archives/arcsupply/5snowplan3.html

Arvay, M. J. (2003). "Doing" reflexivity: A collaborative approach. In L. Finlay & B. Gough (Eds.), *Reflexivity. A practical guide for researchers in health and social sciences* (pp. 163–186). Oxford, U.K.: Blackwell Science Ltd.

Atterton, P. (2002). Emmanuel Levinas. In H. Bertens & J. Natoli (Eds.), *Postmodernism. The key figures* (pp. 231–238). Malden, MA: Blackwell Publishers.

Austin, E. W., & Pinkleton, B. E. (2001). *Strategic public relations management: Planning and managing effective communication programs.* Mahwah, NJ: Lawrence Erlbaum.

Austin, W., Rankel, M., Kagan, L., Bergum, V., & Lemermeyer, G. (2005). To stay or to go, to speak or stay silent, to act or not to act: Moral distress as experienced by psychologists. *Ethics and Behavior, 15*(3), 197–212.

Barney, D. (2004). *The network society.* Malden, MA: Polity Press.

Bass, B. M. (2000). The future of leadership in learning organizations. *Journal of Leadership & Organizational Studies, 7*(3), 18–40.

Baudrillard, J. (1975). *The mirror of production.* St. Louis: Telos Press.

Baudrillard, J. (1981). *For a critique of the political economy of the sign.* St. Louis: Telos Press.

Baudrillard, J. (1983a). *In the shadow of the silent majorities.* New York: Semiotext.

Baudrillard, J. (1983b). *Simulations.* New York: Semiotext.

Baudrillard, J. (1984a). Games with vestiges. *On the Beach, 5*(Winter), 19–25.

Baudrillard, J. (1984b). On nihilism. *On the Beach, 6*(Spring), 38–39.

Baudrillard, J. (1987). *Forget Foucault.* New York: Semiotext.

Baudrillard, J. (1997). The illusion of the end. In K. Jenkins (Ed.), *The postmodern history reader* (pp. 39–46). New York: Routledge.

Bauman, Z. (1993). *Postmodern ethics.* Cambridge, MA: Blackwell.

Benhabib, S. (1992). *Situating the self. Gender, community and postmodernism in contemporary ethics.* New York: Routledge.

Bennett, A. (1990). *The death of the organization man.* New York: Morrow.

Benoit, W. L., & Pang, A. (2008). Crisis communication and image repair discourse. In T. L. Hansen-Horn & B. Dostal Neff (Eds.), *Public relations: From theory to practice* (pp. 244–261). Boston, MA: Pearson Education, Inc.

Bentele, G., & Wehmeier, S. (2009). Commentary. Linking sociology with public relations— Some critical reflections for reflexive times. In O. Ihlen, B. Van Ruler, & M. Fredriksson (Eds.), *Public relations and social theory. Key figures and concepts* (pp. 341–361). New York: Routledge.

Berger, B. K., & Reber, B. H. (2006). *Gaining influence in public relations. The role of resistance in practice.* Mahwah, NJ: Lawrence Erlbaum.

Berkhofer, R. (1988). The challenge of poetics to (normal) historical practice. *Poetics Today, 9*(2), 435–452.

Bertens, H. (1995). *The idea of the postmodern. A history.* New York: Routledge.

Best, S. (n.d.). The postmodern turn in philosophy: Theoretical provocations and normative deficits. Retrieved May 5, 2010, from http://www.drstevebest.org/Essays/ThePostmodern-TurninPhilosophy.html

Best, S. (1995). *The politics of historical vision. Marx, Foucault, Habermas.* New York: Guilford Press.

Best, S., & Kellner, D. (1991). *Postmodern theory. Critical interrogations.* New York: Guilford Press.

Best, S., & Kellner, D. (1997). *The postmodern turn.* New York: Guilford Press.

Best, S., & Kellner, D. (2001). *The postmodern adventure. Science, technology, and cultural studies at the third millennium.* New York: Guilford.

Best, S., & Kellner, D. (n.d.). Richard Rorty and postmodern theory. Retrieved May 6, 2010, from http://www.drstevebest.org/Essays/RichardRorty.htm

Biggins, D. (2004). Emily Hobhouse. Retrieved January 6, 2009, from http://www.angloboer-war.com/Other/emily_hobhouse.htm

Bigler, W. R. (2004). *The new science of strategy execution. How established firms become fast, sleek wealth creators.* Westport, CT: Praeger.

Birch, C. (1992). The postmodern challenge to biology. In C. Jencks (Ed.), *The postmodern reader* (pp. 392–398). London: Academy Editions.

Bloom, L. R. (2002). Stories of one's own. Nonunitary subjectivity in narrative representation. In S. B. Merriam (Ed.), *Qualitative research in practice* (pp. 289–309). San Francisco: Jossey-Bass.

Boje, D. M., Adler, T. R., & Black, J. A. (2005). Theatrical facades and agents in a synthesized analysis from Enron Theatre: Implications to transaction cost and agency theories. *Tamara. Journal of Critical Postmodern Organization Science, 3*(2), 39–56.

Boje, D. M., & Dennehy, R. F. (1993). *Managing in the postmodern world. America's revolution against exploitation.* Dubuque, Iowa: Kendall/Hunt Publishing Company.

Boje, D. M., Fitzgibbons, D. E., & Steingard, D. S. (1996). Storytelling at administrative science quarterly. Warding off the postmodern barbarians. In D. M. Boje, R. P. Gephart, & T. J. Thatchenkery (Eds.), *Postmodern management and organization theory* (pp. 63–64). Thousand Oaks, CA: Sage.

Boje, D. M., Rosile, G. A., Durant, R. A., & Luhman, J. T. (2004). Enron spectacles: A critical dramaturgical analysis. *Organization Studies, 25*(5), 751–774.

Bouquet, C., & Birkinshaw, J. (2008). Managing power in the multinational corporation: How low-power actors gain influence. *Journal of Management, 34*, 477–508.

Bourdieu, P. (1977). *Outline of a theory of practice* (R. Nice, Trans.). Cambridge, U.K.: Cambridge University Press.

Bourdieu, P. (1984). *Distinction: A social critique of the judgement of taste* (R. Nice, Trans.). London: Routledge.

Bowen, S. (2005). A practical model for ethical decision making in issues management and public relations. *Journal of Public Relations Research, 17*(3), 191–216.

Boyd, J., & Vanslette, S. G. (2009). Outlaw discourse as postmodern public relations. In R. L. Heath & E. Toth (Eds.), *Rhetorical and critical approaches to public relations* (pp. 328–342). New York: Routledge.

Boyne, R., & Rattansi, A. (1990). The theory and politics of postmodernism: By way of an introduction. In R. Boyne & A. Rattansi (Eds.), *Postmodernism and society*. London: Macmillan.

Broad, K. L. (2002). Social movement selves. *Sociological Perspectives, 45*(3), 317–336.

Broom, G. M. (2006). An open-systems approach to building theory in public relations. *Journal of Public Relations Research, 18*, 141–150.

Broom, G. M., & Smith, G. D. (1978). *Toward an understanding of public relations roles: An empirical test of five role models' impact on clients*. Paper presented at the Association for Education in Journalism.

Bryant, S. E. (2003). The role of transformational and transactional leadership in creating, sharing and exploiting organizational knowledge. *Journal of Leadership & Organizational Studies, 9*(4), 32–44.

Burek, K. (2001). Environmental activism and public relations. Unpublished master's thesis. University of South Florida, Tampa.

Burkart, R. (2009). On Habermas: Understanding and public relations. In O. Ihlen, B. Van Ruler, & M. Fredriksson (Eds.), *Public relations and social theory. Key figures and concepts* (pp. 141–165). New York: Routledge.

Burke, P. (2001a). History of events and the revival of narrative. In P. Burke (Ed.), *New perspectives on historical writing* (2nd ed., pp. 283–300). University Park: Pennsylvania State University Press.

Burke, P. (2001b). Overture, the new history: Its past and its future. In P. Burke (Ed.), *New perspectives on historical writing* (pp. 1–24). University Park: Pennsylvania State University Press.

Burns, J. (1978). *Leadership*. New York: Harper & Row.

Cahoone, L. (Ed.). (2003). *From modernism to postmodernism. An anthology*. Malden, MA: Blackwell Publishing.

Cameron, G. T., Pang, A., & Jin, Y. (2008). Contingency theory: Strategic management of conflict. In T. L. Hansen-Horn & B. D. Neff (Eds.), *Public relations: From theory to practice* (pp. 134–157). Boston, MA: Pearson.

Canales, J. I., & Vilà, J. (2005). Strategy effects on managerial action. In S. W. Floyd, J. Roos, C. D. Jacobs & F. W. Kellermanns (Eds.), *Innovating strategy process* (pp. 33–46). Malden, MA: Blackwell Publishing.

Caplan, J. (2007, May 28). Small is essential. *Time, 170,* Global Section, 8–10.

Center, A. H., & Jackson, P. (1995). *Public relations practices. Managerial case studies and problems* (5th ed.). Upper Saddle River, NJ: Prentice Hall.

Chay-Nemeth, C. (2001). Revisiting publics: A critical archaeology of publics in the Thai HIV/AIDS issue. *Journal of Public Relations Research, 13*(2), 127–161.

Cheney, G. (1995). Democracy in the workplace: Theory and practice from the perspective of communication. *Journal of Applied Communication Research, 23*(3), 167–200.

Cheney, G., & Christensen, L. T. (2001). Public relations as contested terrain. A critical response. In R. L. Heath (Ed.), *Handbook of public relations* (pp. 167–182). Thousand Oaks, CA: Sage.

Christensen, L. T., & Langer, R. (2009). Public relations and the strategic use of transparency: Consistency, hypocrisy, and corporate change. In R. L. Heath & E. L. Toth (Eds.), *Rhetorical and critical approaches to public relations II* (pp. 129–153). New York: Routledge.

Cilliers, P. (1998). *Complexity and postmodernism: Understanding complex systems.* London: Routledge.

Clandinin, D. J., & Murphy, M. S. (2001). Looking ahead. In D. J. Clandinin (Ed.), *Handbook of narrative inquiry. Mapping a methodology* (pp. 632–650). Thousand Oaks, CA: Sage.

Clegg, S. (1989). Radical revisions: Power, discipline and organization. *Organization Studies, 10*(1), 97–115.

Clegg, S. (1990). *Modern organisations. Organization studies in the postmodern world.* Newbury Park, CA: Sage.

Clegg, S. (1994). Power and institutions in the theory of organizations. In J. Hassard & M. Parker (Eds.), *Towards a new theory of organization* (pp. 24–49). London & New York: Routledge.

Connor, S. (1989). *Postmodernist culture. An introduction to theories of the contemporary.* Cambridge, MA: Basil Blackwell.

Cook, G. (1989). *Discourse.* Oxford: Oxford University Press.

Cook, J., & Jeng, K. (2009). *Child food insecurity: The economic impact on our nation.* Chicago: Feeding America.

Cooper, R., & Burrell, G. (1988). Modernism, postmodernism, and organizational analysis: An introduction. *Organization Studies, 9*(1), 91–112.

Cornell, D. (1992). *The philosophy of the limit.* New York: Routledge.

Cox, A. M. (2007, April 23). An Imus guest says no more. *Time, 169,* 32–38.

Creedon, P. J. (1991). Public relations and 'women's' work: Towards a feminist analysis of public relations roles. *Public Relations Research Annual, 3,* 67–84.

Creedon, P. J. (1993). Acknowledging the infrasystem: A critical feminist analysis of systems theory. *Public Relations Review, 19*(2), 157–166.

Crook, S., Pakulski, J., & Waters, M. (1992). *Postmodernization. Changes in advanced society.* Newbury Park, CA: Sage Publications.

Cropp, F., & Pincus, J. D. (2001). The mystery of public relations: Unraveling its past, unmasking its future. In R. L. Heath (Ed.), *Handbook of public relations* (pp. 189–204). Thousand Oaks, CA: Sage Publications.

Cuprisin, T. (2007, April 14). Broadcasters say it's time to talk: Many in radio industry find a lesson in vigilance during fallout from remarks. *Milwaukee Journal Sentinel* p. B6.

Curtin, P. A., & Gaither, T. K. (2006). Contested notions of issue identity in international public relations: A case study. *Journal of Public Relations Research, 18*(1), 67–89.

Cutlip, S. M. (1995). *Public relations history: From the 17th to the 20th century. The antecedents.* Hillsdale, NJ: Lawrence Erlbaum Associates.

Davidhizer, R., & Shearer, R. (1997). Giving encouragement as a transformational leadership technique. *Health Care Supervisor, 15,* 16–21.

Davidow, W. H., & Malone, M. S. (1992). *The virtual corporation.* New York: Harper Collins.

Deetz, S. A. (1992). *Democracy in an age of corporate colonization. Developments in communication and the politics of everyday life.* Albany, NY: State University of New York.

Deetz, S. A. (2001). Conceptual foundations. In F. M. Jablin & L. L. Putnam (Eds.), *The new handbook of organizational communication. Advances in theory, research, and methods* (pp. 3–46). Thousand Oaks, CA: Sage.

DeGooyer, D. H. (2010). Supple praxis: A paralogical strategy for problems. *Communication Theory, 20,* 296–322.

Deleuze, G., & Guattari, F. (1983). *Anti-Oedipus.* Minneapolis: University of Minnesota Press.

Deleuze, G., & Guattari, F. (1987). *A thousand plateaus: Capitalism and schizophrenia.* Minneapolis: University of Minnesota Press.

Delgado, F. P. (1995). Chicano Movement rhetoric: An ideographic interpretation. *Communication Quarterly, 43,* 446–454.

Derrida, J. (1973). *Speech and phenomena, and other essays on Husserl's theory of signs.* Evanston, IL: Northwestern University Press.

Derrida, J. (1976). *Of grammatology* (G. C. Spivak, Trans.). Baltimore, MD: Johns Hopkins University Press.

Derrida, J. (1981). *Positions.* Chicago: University of Chicago Press.

Dezenhall, E. (2007). Damage control: Author Dezenhall challenges Tylenol cyanide scare response, conventional PR wisdom. Retrieved January 7, 2009, from http://www.firmvoice. com/me2/Audiences/dirmod.asp

Dick, B. (2006). Action research literature 2004–2006. *Action Research, 4*(4), 439–458.

Docherty, T. (1993). Postmodernism: An introduction. In T. Docherty (Ed.), *Postmodernism: A reader* (pp. 1–31). New York: Columbia University Press.

Docherty, T. (Ed.). (1993). *Postmodernism: A reader.* New York: Columbia University Press.

Donaldson, L. (1985). *In defence of organisation theory: A response to the critics.* Cambridge, U.K.: Cambridge University Press.

Donaldson, L. (1990). The ethereal hand: Organizational economics and management theory. *Academy of Management Review, 15,* 369–381.

Dozier, D. M., & Lauzen, M. M. (2000). Liberating the intellectual domain from the practice: Public relations, activism, and the role of the scholar. *Journal of Public Relations Research, 12*(1), 3–22.

Dozier, D., & Broom, G. (2006). The centrality of practitioner roles to public relations theory. In C. H. Botan & V. Hazleton (Eds.), *Public relations theory II* (pp. 137–170). Mahwah, NJ: Lawrence Erlbaum Associates.

Dumont, L. (1986). *Essays in individualism: Modern theory in anthropological perspective.* Chicago: University of Chicago Press.

Eagan, J. L. (2009). The deformation of decentered subjects: Foucault and postmodern public administration. *International Journal of Organization Theory and Behavior, 12*(1), 141–162.

Edgar, A., & Sedgwick, P. (Eds.). (2002). *Cultural theory. The key concepts.* New York: Routledge.

Eisenberg, E., Goodall, H. L. J., & Tretheway, A. (2007). *Organizational communication. Balancing creativity and constraint* (5th ed.). Boston, MA: Bedford/St. Martin's.

Elias, N. (1991). *The society of individuals.* Cambridge, MA: Basil Blackwell.

Elton, G. (1997). Return to essentials. In K. Jenkins (Ed.), *The postmodern history reader* (pp. 175–179). New York: Routledge.

Eribon, D. (1991). *Michel Foucault.* Cambridge, MA: Harvard University Press.

Ermarth, E. D. (2000). Beyond "The subject." Individuality in the discursive condition. *New Literary History, 31,* 405–419.

Ermarth, E. D. (2001a). Agency in the discursive condition. *History and Theory, 40,* 34–58.

Ermarth, E. D. (2001b). Beyond history. *Rethinking History, 5*(2), 195–215.

Evans, J. (2000, October 30). The first postmodern ironist. *New Statesman,* 30–31.

Fairclough, N. (1992). *Discourse and social change.* Cambridge, UK: Polity Press.

Featherstone, M. (1991). *Consumer culture and postmodernism.* Newbury Park, CA: Sage.

Ferguson, K. (1993). *The man question: Visions of subjectivity in feminist theory.* Berkeley: University of California Press.

Foucault, M. (1972). *The archaeology of knowledge.* New York: Pantheon Books.

Foucault, M. (1973a). *Madness and civilization.* New York: Vintage Books.

Foucault, M. (1973b). *The order of things. An archaeology of the human sciences.* New York: Vintage Books.

Foucault, M. (1975). *The birth of the clinic.* New York: Vintage Books.

Foucault, M. (1977). Intellectuals and power (D. F. Bouchard & S. Simon, Trans.). In D. F. Bouchard (Ed.), *Language, counter-memory, practice. Selected essays and interviews* (pp. 205–217). Ithaca, NY: Cornell University Press.

Foucault, M. (1977a). *Language, counter-memory, practice.* Ithaca, NY: Cornell University Press.

Foucault, M. (1979). *Discipline and punish.* New York: Vintage Books.

Foucault, M. (1980a). *The history of sexuality. An introduction.* New York: Vintage Books.

Foucault, M. (1980b). *Power/Knowledge: Selected interviews and other writings. 1972–77.* Brighton: Harvester Press.

Foucault, M. (1982). The subject and power. In H. L. Dreyfus & P. Rainbow (Eds.), *Michel Foucault: Beyond structuralism and hermeneutics* (pp. 208–226). Chicago: University of Chicago Press.

Foucault, M. (1984). What is Enlightenment? In P. Rabinow (Ed.), *The Foucault reader* (pp. 32–50). New York: Pantheon.

Foucault, M. (1985). *The use of pleasure* (R. Hurley, Trans. Vol. 2). New York: Random House.

Foucault, M. (1985a). Final interview. *Raritan, 5*, 1–13.

Foucault, M. (1988a). *Michel Foucault: Politics, philosophy, culture*. New York: Routledge.

Foucault, M. (1988b). Politics and reason. In L. D. Kritzman (Ed.), *Michel Foucault. Politics, philosophy, culture* (pp. 57–85). New York: Routledge.

Foucault, M. (1988c). Power and sex. In L. D. Kritzman (Ed.), *Michael Foucault: Politics, philosophy, culture* (pp. 110–124). New York: Routledge.

Foucault, M. (1988d). Social security. In L. D. Kritzman (Ed.), *Michel Foucault: Politics, philosophy, culture*. New York: Routledge.

Foucault, M. (1989a). The ethics of the concern for self as a practice of freedom (L. Hochroth & J. Johnson, Trans.). In S. Lotringer (Ed.), *Foucault live. Michel Foucault. Collected interviews, 1961–1984*. New York: Semiotext(e).

Foucault, M. (1989b). *Foucault live. Collected interviews 1961–1968* (L. Hochrod & J. Johnston, Trans.). New York: Semiotext(e).

Foucault, M. (2003). 25 February 1976 (D. Macey, Trans.). In M. Bertani & A. Fontana (Eds.), *Michel Foucault. "Society must be defended." Lectures at the Collège de France 1975–1976* (pp. 167–187). New York: Picador.

Frank, G. (2000). *Venus on wheels. Two decades of dialogue on disability, biography, and being female in America*. Berkeley, CA: University of California Press.

Freeman, M. (2001). Autobiographical understanding and narrative inquiry. In D. J. Clandinen (Ed.), *Handbook of narrative inquiry. Mapping a methodology* (pp. 120–145). Thousand Oaks, CA: Sage.

Freud, S. (1925). *Some psychological consequences of the anatomical distinction between the sexes* (J. Strachey, Trans., Vol. XIX). London: Hogarth Press.

Friedberg, A. (1990). Mutual indifference: Feminism and postmodernism. In J. F. MacCannell (Ed.), *The other perspective in gender and culture*. New York: Columbia University Press.

Fukuyama, F. (1989). 'The end of history?' *The National Interest, 16*, 3–18.

Gagliardi, P. (1986). The creation and change of organizational cultures: A conceptual framework. *Organization Studies, 7*, 117–134.

Galbraith, J. R. (1977). *Organization design*. Reading, MA: Addison-Wesley.

Galbraith, J. R. (2009). *Designing matrix organizations that actually work: How IBM, Procter & Gamble, and others design for success*. San Francisco: Jossey-Bass.

Gandy, O. H., Jr. (1989). Public relations and public policy: The structuration of dominance in the information age. In E. L. Toth & R. L. Heath (Eds.), *Rhetorical and critical approaches to public relations* (pp. 131–163). Hillsdale, NJ: Lawrence Erlbaum Associates.

Gane, M. (1993). *Baudrillard live. Selected interviews*. New York: Routledge.

Garrison, J. (1989). The role of postpositivistic philosophy of science in the renewal of vocational education research. *Journal of Vocational Education Research, 14*(3), 39–51.

Garud, R., & Shapira, Z. (1997). Aligning the residuals: Risk, return, responsibility and authority. In Z. Shapira (Ed.), *Organizational decision making*. Cambridge, U.K.: Cambridge University Press.

Gephart, R. P., Boje, D. M., & Thatchenkery, T. J. (1996). Postmodern management and the coming crisis of organizational analysis. In D. M. Boje, R. P. Gephart, & T. J. Thatchenkery (Eds.), *Postmodern management and organization theory* (pp. 1–18). Thousand Oaks, CA: Sage.

Gergen, K. J., & Thatchenkery, T. J. (2004). Organization science as social construction. Postmodern potentials. *The Journal of Applied Behavioral Science., 40*(2), 228–249.

Gergen, M. (1992). Metaphors for chaos, stories of continuity: Building a new organizational theory. In S. Srivasta & R. E. Fry (Eds.), *Executive and organizational continuity* (pp. 207–266). San Francisco: Jossey-Bass.

Ghoshal, S., & Moran, P. (1996). Bad for practice: A critique of the transaction cost theory. *Academy of Management Review, 21*, 13–47.

Gibson, C. B., & Gibbs, J. L. (2006). Unpacking the concept of virtuality: The effects of geographic dispersion, electronic dependence, dynamic structure, and national diversity on team innovation. *Administrative Science Quarterly, 51*, 451–495.

Giddens, A. (1979). *Central problems in sociology. Action, structure and contradiction in social analysis.* Berkeley: University of California Press.

Giddens, A. (1984). *The constitution of society: Outline of the theory of strcturation.* Cambridge, MA: Polity Press.

Giliomee, H. (2003). *The Afrikaners. Biography of a people.* Charlottesville, VA: University of Virginia Press.

Gilligan, C. (1993). *In a different voice* (2nd ed.). Cambridge, MA: Harvard University Press.

Gilpin, D. R., & Murphy, P. (2006). Reframing crisis management through complexity. In C. H. Botan & V. Hazleton (Eds.), *Public relations theory II* (pp. 375–392). Mahwah, NJ: Lawrence Erlbaum.

Gilpin, D. R., & Murphy, P. (2009). *Crisis management in a complex world.* New York: Oxford University Press.

Good, G. (2001). *Humanism betrayed. Theory, ideology, and culture in the contemporary university.* Montreal, Canada: McGill-Queen's University Press.

Gordon, C. (1979). Other inquisitions. *I&C, 6*, 23–46.

Gough, B. (2003). Deconstructing reflexivity. In L. Finlay & B. Gough (Eds.), *Relexivity. A practical guide for researchers in social and health sciences* (pp. 21–35). Oxford, U.K.: Blackwell Science Ltd.

Gramsci, A. (1971). *Selections from the prison notebooks.* (A. Hoare & G. N. Smith, Trans.). New York: International.

Grunig, J. E. (1983). Communication behavior and attitudes of environmental publics: Two studies. *Journalism Monographs, 81*, 9–16.

Grunig, J. E. (1989). Symmetrical presuppositions as a framework for public relations theory. In C. H. Botan & J. Vincent Hazleton (Eds.), *Public Relations Theory* (pp. 17–44). Hillsdale, NJ: Lawrence Erlbaum Associates.

Grunig, J. E. (1989a). Sierra Club study shows who become activists. *Public Relations Review, 15*(3), 3–24.

Grunig, J. E. (1992a). Symmetrical systems of internal communication. In J. E. Grunig (Ed.), *Excellence in public relations and communication management* (pp. 531–575). Hillsdale, NJ: Lawrence Erlbaum Associates.

Grunig, J. E. (Ed.). (1992b). *Excellence in public relations and communication management.* Hillsdale, NJ: Lawrence Erlbaum Associates.

Grunig, J. E. (1992c). Communication, public relations, and effective organizations: An overview of the book. In J. E. Grunig (Ed.), *Excellence in public relations and communciation management* (pp. 1–28). Killsdale, NJ: Lawrence Erlbaum Associates.

Grunig, J. E. (1994). World view, ethics, and the two-way symmetrical model of public relations. In W. Armbrecht & U. Zabel (Eds.), *Normative Aspekte der Public Relations* (pp. 69–89). Opalden: Westdeutscher Verlag.

Grunig, J. E. (1997). A situational theory of publics: Conceptual history, recent challenges, and new research. In D. Moss, T. MacManus, & D. Verčič (Eds.), *Public relations research: An international perspective* (pp. 3–48). London: International Thomson Business Press.

Grunig, J. E. (2001). Two-way symmetrical public relations. Past, present and future. In R. L. Heath (Ed.), *Handbook of public relations.* Thousand Oaks, CA: Sage.

Grunig, J. E., & Grunig, L. A. (1992). Models of public relations and communication. In J. E. Grunig (Ed.), *Excellence in public relations and communication management* (pp. 285–325). Hillsdale, NJ: Lawrence Erlbaum Associates.

Grunig, J. E., Grunig, L. A., Sriramesh, K., Huang, Y.-H., & Lyra, A. (1995). Models of public relations in an international setting. *Journal of Public Relations Research, 7*, 163–186.

Grunig, J. E., & Hunt, T. (1984). *Managing public relations.* Fort Worth, TX: Holt, Rinehart & Winston, Inc.

Grunig, J. E., & White, J. (1992). The effect of worldviews on public relations theory and practice. In J. E. Grunig (Ed.), *Excellence in public relations and communication management* (pp. 31–64). Mahwah, NJ: Lawrence Erlbaum Associates.

Grunig, L. A. (2006). Feminist phase analysis in public relations; Where have we been? Where do we need to be? *Journal of Public Relations Research, 18*(2), 115–140.

Grunig, L. A., Grunig, J. E., & Dozier, D. M. (2002). *Excellent public relations and effective organizations. A study of communication management in three countries.* Mahwah, NJ: Lawrence Erlbaum Associates.

Gunaratne, S. A. (2006). Public sphere and communicative rationality: Interrogating Habermas's eurocentrism. *Journalism & Communication Monographs, 8*(2), 95–156.

Habermas, J. (1979). *Communication and the evolution of society.* Boston: Beacon Press.

Habermas, J. (1984). *The theory of communicative action* (Vol. 1). Boston: Beacon.

Habermas, J. (2006). *Political communication in media society — Does society still enjoy an epistemic dimension? The impact of normative theory on empirical research.* Paper presented at the Annual Convention of the International Communication Association.

Hafsi, T., & Howard, T. (2005). Reflections on the field of strategy. In S. W. Floyd, J. Roos, C. D. Jacobs, & F. W. Kellermanns (Eds.), *Innovating strategy process* (pp. 239–246). Malden, MA: Blackwell Publishing.

Hallahan, K., Holtzhausen, D. R., Van Ruler, B., Verčič, D., & Sriramesh, K. (2007). Defining strategic communication. *International Journal of Strategic Communication, 1*(1), 3–35.

Harland, R. (1987). *Superstructuralism: The philosophy of structuralism and post-structuralism.* London & New York: Methuen.

Hasian, J. M. (2003). The "hysterical" Emily Hobhouse and Boer war concentration camp controversy. *Wester Journal of Communication, 67*(2), 138–163.

Hassard, J. (1993). Postmodernism and organizational analysis: An overview. In J. Hassard & M. Parker (Eds.), *Postmodernism and organizations* (pp.1–23). Newbury Park, CA: Sage.

Hassard, J. (1996). Exploring the terrain of modernism and postmodernism in organization theory. In D. M. Boje, R. P. Gephart, & T. J. Thatchenkery (Eds.), *Postmodern management and organization theory* (pp. 45–59). Thousand Oaks, CA: Sage.

Hassard, J., & Parker, M. (1994). *Toward a new theory of organization.* London & New York: Routledge.

Hatch, M. J. (1997). *Organization theory. Modern, symbolic, and postmodern perspectives.* Oxford, U.K.: Oxford University Press.

Hatch, M. J., & Cunliffe, A. L. (2006). *Organization theory. Modern, symbolic, and postmodern perspectives.* New York: Oxford University Press.

Heath, R. G. (2007). Rethinking community collaboration through a dialogic lens: Creativity, democracy, and diversity in community organizing. *Management Communication Quarterly, 21*(2), 145–171.

Heath, R. L. (2001). A rhetorical enactment rationale for public relations. The good organization communicating well. In R. L. Heath (Ed.), *Handbook of public relations* (pp. 31–50). Thousand Oaks, CA: Sage.

Heath, R. L. (2009). The rhetorical tradition: Wrangle in the marketplace. In R. L. Heath, E. Toth,, & D. Waymer (Eds.), *Rhetorical and critical approaches to public relations II* (pp. 17–47). New York: Routledge.

Heath, R. L., & Toth, E. (Eds.). (2009). *Rhetorical and critical perspectives in public relations II.* New York: Routledge.

Heinrich, T., & Batchelor, B. (2004). *Kotex, Kleenex, Huggies. Kimberley-Clark and the consumer revolution in American business.* Columbus: Ohio State University Press.

Heracleous, L. (2003). *Strategy and organization. Realizing strategic management.* Cambridge, U.K.: Cambridge University Press.

Hiebert, R. E. (1966). *Courtier to the crowd.* Ames: Iowa State University Press.

Hobhouse, E. (1902). *The brunt of the war and where it fell.* London: Methuen & Co.

Hofstede, G. (1991). *Cultures and organizations: Software of the mind.* London: McGraw-Hill.

Holtzhausen, D. R. (1995). *The role of public relations theory and research in a postmodern approach to communication management in the organization*. Unpublished doctoral dissertation, Rand Afrikaans University, Johannesburg. South Africa.

Holtzhausen, D. R. (2000). Postmodern values in public relations. *Journal of Public Relations Research, 12*(1), 93–114.

Holtzhausen, D. R. (2002). A postmodern critique of public relations theory and research. *Communicatio, 28*(1), 29–38.

Holtzhausen, D. R. (2002a). The effects of a divisionalized and decentralized organizational structure on a formal internal communication function in a South African organization. *Journal of Communication Management, 6*(4), 323–339.

Holtzhausen, D. R. (2002b). Towards a postmodern research agenda for public relations. *Public Relations Review, 28*(3), 251–264.

Holtzhausen, D. R. (2002c). The effects of workplace democracy on employee communication: Implications for competitive advantage. *Competitiveness Review, 12*(2), 30–48.

Holtzhausen, D. R. (2005a). Improved internal communication in a large South African organization. In M. G. Parkinson & D. Ekachai (Eds.), *International and intercultural public relations: A case campaign approach* (pp. 254–267). Boston, MA: Alan & Bacon.

Holtzhausen, D. R. (2005b). Public relations practice and political change in South Africa. *Public Relations Review, 31*(3), 407–416.

Holtzhausen, D. R. (2007). Activism. In E. Toth (Ed.), *The handbook of excellence in public relations and communication management: Challenges for the next generation* (pp. 357–379). Mahwah, NJ: Lawrence Erlbaum.

Holtzhausen, D. R. (2011). The need for a postmodern turn in global public relations. In N. Bardhan & C. K. Weaver (Eds.), *Public relations in global cultural contexts. Multiparadigmatic perspectives* (pp.140–166). New York: Routledge.

Holtzhausen, D. R., Petersen, B. K., & Tindall, N. T. J. (2003). Exploding the myth of the symmetrical/asymmetrical dichotomy: Public relations models in the new South Africa. *Journal of Public Relations Research, 15*(4), 305–341.

Holtzhausen, D. R., & Roberts, G. (2009). An investigation into the role of image repair theory in strategic conflict management. *Journal of Public Relations Research, 21*, 165–186.

Holtzhausen, D. R., & Tindall, N. T. J. (2009). *Toward a roles theory for strategic communication: The case of South Africa*. Paper presented at the 92nd AEJMC Annual Convention.

Holtzhausen, D. R., & Voto, R. (2002). Resistance from the margins: The postmodern public relations practitioner as organizational activist. *Journal of Public Relations Research, 14*(1), 57–84.

Holtzhausen, D. R., & Werder, K. G. P. (2008). *The emergence of new organizational structures and their relationship with public relations practice*. Paper presented at EUPRERA, Milan.

Hon, L. C. (1995). Toward a feminist theory of public relations. *Journal of Public Relations Research, 7*(1), 27–88.

Hon, L. C. (1997). "To redeem the soul of America": Public relations and the Civil Rights Movement. *Journal of Public Relations Research, 9*(3), 163–212.

Hornick, E., & Quijano, E. (2009, August 12). Whistle-blower: Health care industry engaging in PR tactics. Retrieved July 27, 2010, from http://www.cnn.com/2009/POLITICS/08/12/health.industry.whistleblower/index.html

Hutton, J. G. (2001). Defining the relationship between public relations and marketing: Public relations most important challenge. In R. L. Heath (Ed.), *Handbook of public relations* (pp. 205–214). Thousand Oaks, CA: Sage Publications.

Huyssen, A. (1986). *After the great divide. Modernism, mass culture, postmodernism*. London: Macmillan.

Ibarra-Colado, E., Clegg, S., Rhodes, C., & Kornberger, M. (2006). The ethics of managerial subjectivity. *Journal of Business Ethics, 64*, 45–55.

Ihlen, O. (2009). On Bourdieu. Public relations in field struggles. In O. Ihlen, B. Van Ruler, & M. Fredriksson (Eds.), *Public relations and social theory. Key figures and concepts* (pp. 62–82). New York: Routledge.

Institute of Public Relations. (2010). 8th Annual North American Summit on Measurement. Retrieved July 24, 2010, from http://instituteforpr.com/education/summit_measure

Jameson, F. (1984). Postmodernism, or the cultural logic of late capitalism. *New Left Review, 146*, 53–93.

Jameson, F. (1995). *Postmodernism, or the cultural logic of late capitalism* (6th ed.). Durham, NC:

Jenkins, K. (1995). *On 'What is history'? From Carr and Elton to Rorty and White.* London: Routledge.

Jenkins, K. (Ed.). (1997). *The postmodern history reader.* New York: Routledge.

Jenkins, K. (1999). *Why history? Ethics and postmodernity.* New York: Routledge.

Jenkins, K. (2003). *Refiguring history. New thoughts on an old discipline.* New York: Routledge.

Jenkins, K. (2004). Modernist disavowels and postmodern reminders of the condition of history today: On Jean François Lyotard. *Rethinking History, 8*(3), 365–385.

Kearney, R. (2004). *Debates in continental philosophy. Conversations with contemporary thinkers.* New York: Fordham University Press.

Kellerman, B. (1984). *Leadership: A multidisciplinary perspective.* Englewood Cliffs, NJ: Prentice Hall.

Kierkegaard, S. (1968). *The last years: Journals, 1853–55* (R. G. Smith, Trans.). London: Collins.

Kincheloe, J. L., & McLaren, P. L. (1994). Rethinking critical theory and qualitative research. In N. K. Denzin & Y. S. Lincoln (Eds.), *Handbook of qualitative research* (pp. 138–157). Thousand Oaks, CA: Sage.

King, C. (2010). Emergent communication strategies. *International Journal of Strategic Communication, 4*, 19–38.

King, S. (1994). What is the latest on leadership? *Management Development Review, 7*(6), 7–9.

Kiviat, B. (2004, July 12). The end of management? *Time,* 4–8.

Klein, L. E. (2001). Enlightenment as conversation. In K. M. Baker & P. H. Reill (Eds.), *What's left of Enlightenment? A postmodern question.* Stanford, CA: Stanford University Press.

Kohlberg, L., Levine, C., & Hewer, A. (1984). Synopses and detailed replies to critics. In L. Kohlberg (Ed.), *Essays on moral development* (Vol. 2). San Francisco: Harper & Row.

Kolodny, H. F. (1979). Evolution to a matrix organization. *The Academy of Management Review, 4*(4), 543–553.

Kruckeberg, D. (2000). Public relations: Toward a global professionalism. In J. A. Ledingham & S. D. Bruning (Eds.), *Public relations as relationship management: A relational approach to the study and practice of public relations* (pp. 145–157). Mahwah, NJ: Lawrence Erlbaum.

Kuhn, T. S. (1970a). Logic of discovery or psychology of research. In I. Lakatos & A. Musgrave (Eds.), *Criticism and the growth of knowledge.* Cambridge, U.K.: Cambridge University Press.

Kuhn, T. S. (1970b). *The structure of scientific revolutions* (2nd ed.). Chicago: University of Chicago Press.

Küng, H. (2003). *My struggle for freedom.* (J. Bowden, Trans.). Grand Rapids, MI: Wm. B. Eerdmans Publishing Company.

Lacayo, R., & Ripley, A. (2002, December 22). Persons of the year 2002. *Time, 160.*

Laclau, E., & Mouffe, C. (1985). *Hegemony and socialist strategy: Towards a radical democratic politics.* London: Verso Books.

Laclau, E., & Mouffe, C. (1987). Post-Marxism without apologies. *New Left Review, 166* (November/December), 79–106.

Lamme, M. O., & Russell, K. M. (2010). Removing the spin: Toward a new theory of public relations history. *Journalism & Communication Monographs, 11*(4), 281–362.

Langan, D., & Morton, M. (2009). Reflecting on community/academic 'collaboration.' The challenge of 'doing' feminist participatory action research. *Action Research, 7*(2), 165–184

Lash, S. (1988). Postmodernism as a regime of signification. *Theory, Culture and Society, 5*(2–3), 311–336.

Law, J. (1994). Organization, narrative and strategy. In J. Hassard & M. Parker (Eds.), *Towards a new theory of organization* (pp. 248–268). London & New York: Routledge.

LeCoure, J. S., & Mills, A. J. (2008). Dialogical aspects of the technologies of the self in organizational analysis. *Tamara. Journal of Critical Postmodern Organization Science, 7*(1), 7–20.

Ledingham, J. A., & Bruning, S. D. (Eds.). (2000). *Relationship management: A relational approach to public relations.* Mahwah, NJ: Lawrence Erlbaum.

Leitchy, G., & Springston, J. (1996). Elaborating public relations roles. *Journalism & Mass Communication Quarterly, 73,* 467–477.

L'Etang, J. (2004). *Public relations in Britain. A history of professional practice in the 20th century.* Mahwah, NJ: Lawrence Erlbaum.

Levinas, E. (1969). *Totality and infinity* (A. Lingis, Trans.). Pittsburgh, PA: Duquesne University Press.

Levinas, E. (1981). *Otherwise than Being, or beyond Essence* (A. Lingis, Trans.). The Hague: Martinus Nijhoff.

Levinas, E. (1985). *Ethics and infinity: Conversations with Philippe Nemo* (R. A. Cohen, Trans.). Pittsburgh, PA: Duquesne University Press.

Lieber, P. S. (2008). Moral development in public relations: Measuring duty to society in strategic communication. *Public Relations Review, 34,* 244–251.

Locke, E. A., & Schweiger, D. M. (1979). Participation in decision-making: One more look. In B. M. Staw & L. L. Cummings (Eds.), *Research in organizational behavior* (Vol. 1, pp. 265–339). Greenwich, CT: JAI Press.

Loizidou, E. (2007). *Judith Butler: Ethics, law, politics.* New York: Routledge-Cavendish.

Lyon, D. (1999). *Postmodernity* (2nd ed.). Minneapolis: University of Minnesota Press.

Lyotard, J.-F. (1971). *Discourse, figure.* Paris: Klincksieck.

Lyotard, J.-F. (1984). *The postmodern condition: A report on knowledge* (G. Bennington & B. Massumi, Trans.). Minneapolis: University of Minnesota Press.

Lyotard, J.-F. (1986–1987). Rules and paradoxes and svelte appendix. *Cultural Critique, 5,* 209–210.

Lyotard, J.-F. (1988). *The differend: Phrases in dispute* (G. Van Den Abbeele, Trans.,Vol. 46). Minneapolis: University of Minnesota Press.

Lyotard, J.-F. (1989). *The Lyotard reader.* London: Basil Blackwell.

Lyotard, J.-F. (1992). Answering the question: What is postmodernism? In C. Jencks (Ed.), *The postmodern reader* (pp. 138–150). London: Academy Editions.

Lyotard, J.-F. (1993a). *Libidinal economy.* Bloomington: University of Indiana Press.

Lyotard, J.-F. (1993b). Note on the meaning of 'post-'. In T. Docherty (Ed.), *Postmodernism: A reader* (pp. 47–50). New York: Columbia.

Lyotard, J.-F., & Thébaud, J. L. (1985). *Just gaming* (W. Godzich, Trans.). Minneapolis: University of Minnesota Press.

Macdonnel, D. (1986). *Theories of discourse. An introduction.* New York: Basil Blackwell Inc.

McGee, M. C. (1980). The "ideograph": A link between rhetoric and ideology. *The Quarterly Journal of Speech, 66,* 1–17.

McKie, D. (2001). Updating public relations. New science, research paradigms, and uneven developments. In R. L. Heath (Ed.), *Handbook of public relations* (pp. 75–104). Thousand Oaks, CA: Sage.

McKie, D., & Munshi, D. (2009). Theoretical black holes: A partial A to Z of missing critical thought in public relations. In R. L. Heath & E. Toth (Eds.), *Rhetorical and critical approaches to public relations II* (pp. 61–75). New York: Routledge.

McKinnon, C. (1987). *Feminism unmodified; Discourses on life and law.* Cambridge, MA: Harvard University Press.

McLennan, G. (1984). History and theory. *Literature and History, 10*(2), 139–164.

McNiff, J. (2007). My story is my living education theory. In D. J. Clandinin (Ed.), *Handbook of narrative inquiry. Mapping a methodology* (pp. 308–329). Thousand Oaks, CA: Sage.

McNutt, M. (2011). *Kern apologizes for comments on miniorities and women: NAACP says it is not enough.* News OK. Retrieved May 5, 2011 from http://www.newsok.com/article/3562835

Malpas, S. (2003). *Jean-François Lyotard.* New York: Routledge.

Mansur, S. (2007, December 29). Theologian finds peace path. *The Toronto Sun,* p. 20.

Marquand, R. (2007, July 18). A church's assertive shift toward tradition. *Christian Science Monitor,* p. 1.

May, T. (2006). Michel Foucault's guide to living. *Angelaki, 11*(3), 173–184.

Mickey, T. J. (1995). *Sociodrama: an interpretive theory for the practice of public relations.* Lanham, MD: University Press of America.

Mickey, T. J. (1997). A postmodern view of public relations: Sign and reality. *Public Relations Review, 23,* 271–285.

Mickey, T. J. (2003). *Deconstructing public relations. Public relations criticism.* Mahwah, NJ: Lawrence Erlbaum Associates.

Miller, G. J. (2005). The political evolution of principal-agent models. *Annual Review of Political Science, 8,* 203–225.

Miller, K. (1999). *Organizational communication. Approaches and processes.* Belmont, CA: Wadsworth.

Mink, O. (1992). Creating new organizational paradigms for change. *International Journal of Quality & Reliability Management, 9,* 21–23.

Mintzberg, H. (1979). *The structure of organizations.* Englewood Cliffs, NJ: Prentice-Hall.

Mintzberg, H. (1990). The design school: Reconsidering the basic premises of strategic management. *Strategic Management Journal, 11,* 171–195.

Monge, P. R., & Miller, K. I. (1988). Participative processes in organizations. In G. M. Goldhaber & G. A. Barnett (Eds.), *Handbook of organizational communication* (pp. 213–229). Norwood, NJ: Ablex Publishing Corporation.

Moravec, M. (1994). The 21st century employer-employee partnership: Professionally speaking. *HR Magazine, January,* 128–132.

Morgan, S. (2006). Writing feminist history: Theoretical debates and critical practices. In S. Morgan (Ed.), *The feminist history reader.* London: Routledge.

Morgan-Fleming, B., Riegle, S., & Fryer, W. (2007). Narrative inquiry in archival work. In D. J. Clandinin (Ed.), *Handbook of narrative inquiry. Mapping a methodology* (pp. 81-98). Thousand Oaks, CA: Sage.

Mumby, D. K. (1996). Feminism, postmodernism, and organizational communication studies. A critical reading. *Management Communication Quarterly, 9*(3), 259–295.

Mumby, D. K. (1997). Modernism, postmodernism, and communication studies: A rereading of an ongoing debate. *Communication Theory, 7,* 1–28.

Mumby, D. K., & Putnam, L. (1992). The politics of emotion: A feminist reading of bounded rationality. *Academy of Management Review, 17,* 465–486.

Murphy, P. (2000). Symmetry, contingency, complexity: Accommodating uncertainty in public relations theory. *Public Relations Review, 26*(4), 447–462.

Murphy, P. (1994). Postmodern perspectives and justice. In A. Patterson (Ed.), *Postmodernism and the law* (Vol. 14). New York: New York University Press.

Murphy, P. (2007). Coping with an uncertain world. In E. L. Toth (Ed.), *The future of excellence in public relations and communication management* (pp. 119–134). Mahwah, NJ: Lawrence Erlbaum.

Nilakant, V., & Rao, H. (1994). Agency theory and uncertainty in organizations: An evaluation. *Organization Studies, 15,* 649–672.

Northouse, P. G. (2007). *Leadership theory and practice.* Thousand Oaks, CA: Sage Publications.

Nunemaker-Bynum, L. (2002). *Corporate strategic philanthropy in conjunction with strategic public relations is more effective for the organization when measured through relationship outcomes.* Unpublished master's thesis, University of South Florida, Tampa.

O'Docherty, D., & Willmott, H. (2000–2001). The question of subjectivity and the labour process. *International Studies of Management & Organization, 30*(4), 112–132.

O'Sullivan, T., Hartley, J., Saunders, D., & Fiske, J. (1989). *Key concepts in communication* (3rd ed.). London: Routledge.

Pasadeos, Y., Berger, B. K., & Renfro, R. B. (2010). Public relations as a maturing discipline: An update on research networks. *Journal of Public Relations Research, 22*(2), 136–158.

Patterson, D. (Ed.). (1994). *Postmodernism and law* (Vol. 14). New York: New York University Press.

Pearson, R. (1989a). Beyond ethical relativism in public relations: Coorientation, rules, and the idea of communication symmetry. In J. E. Grunig & L. A. Grunig (Eds.), *Public relations research annual* (Vol. 1, pp. 67–86). Hillsdale, NJ: Lawrence Erlbaum Associates, Inc.

Pearson, R. (1989b). *A theory of public relations ethics.* Unpublished doctoral dissertation. Ohio University.

Pêcheux, M. (1982). *Language, semantics and ideology: Stating the obvious* (H. Nagpal, Trans.). London: Macmillan.

Pfeffer, J. (1997). *New directions for organization theory. Problems and prospects.* New York: Oxford University Press.

Pfeffer, J., & Salancik, G. R. (1978). *The external control of organizations: A resource dependence perspective.* New York: Harper & Row.

Pieczka, M., & L'Etang, J. (2001). Public relations and the question of professionalism. In R. L. Heath (Ed.), *Handbook of public relations* (pp. 213–235). Thousand Oaks, CA: Sage.

Pinnegar, S., & Daynes, J. G. (2007). Locating narrative inquiry historically. Thematics in the turn to narrative. In D. J. Clandinin (Ed.), *Handbook of narrative inquiry* (pp. 3–34). Thousand Oaks, CA: Sage.

Plumb, J. H. (2004). *The death of the past.* New York: Palgrave Macmillan.

Pompper, D. (2004). Linking ethnic diversity & two-way symmetry: Modeling female African American practitioners' roles. *Journal of Public Relations Research, 16*(3), 269–299.

Poniewozik, J. (2007, April 23). The Imus fallout: Who can say what? *Time, 169,* 32–38.

Poole, M. (1986). Participation through representation: A review of constraints and conflicting pressures. In R. N. Stem & S. McCarthy (Eds.), *International yearbook of organizational democracy. The organizational practice of democracy* (Vol. III). New York, NY: John Wiley & Sons.

Porter, M. (1985). *Competitive advantage: Creating and sustaining superior performance.* New York: Free Press.

Poster, M., & Aronowitz, S. (2001). *The information subject.* New York: Routledge.

Potter, W. (2009a). Commentary: How insurance firms drive debate. Retrieved August 17, 2009, from http://www.cnn.com/2009/POLITICS/08/17/potter.health.insurance/index.html

Potter, W. (2009b). GOP fear tactic from health insurance companies. Retrieved August 17, 2009, from http://www.ireport.com/docs/DOC-315401

PRSA. (2008). Independent practitioners alliance. Retrieved February 8, 2008, from http://prsa.org/networking/sections/ipa

Pyrch, T., & Castillo, M. T. (2001). The sight and sounds of indigenous knowledge. In P. Reason & H. Bradbury (Eds.), *Handbook of action research. Participative inquiry and practice* (pp. 379–385). Thousand Oaks, CA: Sage.

Quinn, J. E., Mintzberg, H., & James, R. M. (1991). *The strategy process: Concepts, contexts, and cases.* Englewood Cliffs, NJ: Prentice Hall.

Raab, J., & Kenis, P. (2009). Heading toward a society of networks. Empirical developments and theoretical challenges. *Journal of Management Inquiry, 18*(3), 198–210.

Rabine, L. (1990). The unhappy hymen between feminism and deconstruction. In J. F. MacCannell (Ed.), *The other perspective in gender and culture* (pp.20–38). New York: Columbia University Press.

Rabinow, P. (1984). Introduction. In P. Rabinow (Ed.), *The Foucault reader.* New York: Pantheon Books.

Racevskis, K. (2002). Michel Foucault. In H. Bertens & J. Natoli (Eds.), *Postmodernism: The key figues* (1st ed., pp. 136–140). Malden, MA: Blackwell.

Rahman, Z., & Bhattachryya, S. K. (2002). Virtual organisation: A stratagem. *Singapore Management Review, 24*(2), 29–46.

Reason, P., & Bradbury, H. (2001). Introduction: Inquiry and participation in search of a world worthy of human aspiration. In P. Reason & H. Bradbury (Eds.), *Handbook of action research. Participative inquiry and practice* (pp. 1–14). Thousand Oaks, CA: Sage.

Riessman, C. K., & Speedy, J. (2007). Narrative inquiry in th psychotherapy professions. In D. J. Clandinin (Ed.), *Handbook of narrative inquiry. Mapping a methodology* (pp. 426–456). Thousand Oaks, CA: Sage.

Roper, J. (2005). Symmetrical communication: Excellent public relations or a strategy for hegemony? *Journal of Public Relations Research, 17*(1), 69–86.

Rorty, R. (1984). Habermas and Lyotard on post-modernity. *Praxis International, 4*(1), 32–44.

Rosenau, P. M. (1992). *Post-modernism and the social sciences: Insights, inroads, and intrusions.* Princeton, NJ: Princeton University Press.

Ross, J. D. (2007). Offended by hip-hop? The rap's on me. *The Tulsa World,* p. G3.

Ruf, H. L. (2005). *Postmodern rationality, social criticism, and religion.* St. Paul, MN: Paragon House.

Rughase, O. G. (2006). *Identity and strategy.* Cheltenham, U.K.: Edward Elgar Publishing, Inc.

Samuels, R. (1992). Reading the signs II. *History Workshop Journal, 33,* 220–251.

Sarup, M. (1993). *An introductory guide to post-structuralism and postmodernism* (Vol. 2). Athens, GA: University of Georgia Press.

Sashkin, M. (1984). Participative management is an ethical imperative. *Organizational Dynamics, Spring,* 5–22.

Scherer, M. (2010). The new sheriffs of Wall Street. *Time, 175 (20),* 22–30.

Schiffrin, D. (1987). *Discourse markers.* Cambridge, UK: Cambridge University Press.

Schultz, P. (1996). The morally accountable corporation: A postmodern approach to organizational responsibility. *Journal of Business Communication, 33,* 163–183.

Seabright, M. A., & Kurke, L. B. (1997). Organizational ontology and the moral status of the corporation. *Business Ethics Quarterly, 7,* 91–108.

Seib, S., & Fitzpatrick, K. (1995). *Public relations ethics.* Fort Worth, TX: Harcourt Brace College Publishers.

Seidman, S. (1997). The end of sociological theory. In S. Seidman (Ed.), *The postmodern turn. New perspectives on social theory* (4th ed.). Cambridge, U.K.: Cambridge University Press.

Self, C. (2009). *Hegel, Habermas, and community: The public in the new media era.* Paper presented at the International Communication Association.

Sellars, J. (2006). An ethics of the event. Deleuze's stoicism. *Angelaki, 11*(3), 157–171.

Shapiro, S. P. (2005). Agency theory. *Annual Review of Sociology, 31,* 263–284.

Sharpe, J. (2001). History from below. In P. Burke (Ed.), *New perspectives on historical writing* (pp. 25–42). University Park: Pennsylvania State University Press.

Sim, G. B. (1996). *Nietzsche, Heidegger and the transition to modernity.* Chicago: University of Chicago Press.

Sim, S. (1999a). *Derrida and the end of history.* Duxford, U.K.: Icon Books.

Sim, S. (Ed.). (1999b). *The Routledge critical dictionary of postmodern thought.* New York: Routledge.

Simkin, J. (n.d.). Emily Hobhouse. Retrieved January 6, 2009, from http://www.spartacus.schoolnet.co.uk/Whobhouse.htm

Sloan, J. (2006). *Learning to think strategically.* Burlington, MA: Elsevier.

Smith, M. F., & Ferguson, D. P. (2001). Activism. In R. L. Heath (Ed.), *Handbook of public relations* (pp. 291–300). Thousand Oaks, CA: Sage.

Southgate, B. (2000). *Why bother with history?* New York: Longman.

Southgate, B. (2005). *What is history for?* New York: Routledge.

Spicer, C. (1997). *Organizational public relations: A political perspective.* Mahwah, NJ: Lawrence Erlbaum Associates.

Spicer, C. (2007). Collaborative advocacy and the creation of trust: Toward an understanding of stakeholder claims and risks. In E. L. Toth (Ed.), *The future of excellence in public relations and communication management. Challenges for the next generation* (pp. 27–40). Mahwah, NJ: Lawrence Erlbaum Associates.

Sriramesh, K., & Verčič, D. (Eds.). (2003). *The global public relations handbook.* Mahwah, NJ: Lawrence Erlbaum.

Stacks, D. W. (2002). *Primer of public relations research.* New York: Guilford.

Stappers, J. G. (1986). General discussion of political discourse. In T. Ensink, A. van Essen, & T. van der Geest (Eds.), *Discourse analysis and public life* (pp. 379–384). Dordrecht: Foris Publications.

Stauber, J., & Rampton, S. (1995). *Toxic sludge is good for you! Lies, damn lies and the public relations industry.* Monroe, ME: Common Courage.

Steedman, C. (2001). *Dust.* Manchester, U.K.: Manchester University Press.

Steyn, B. (2007). Contribution of public relations to organizational strategy formulation. In E. L.

Toth (Ed.), *The future of excellence in public relations and communication management* (pp. 137–172). Mahwah, NJ: Lawrence Erlbaum Associates.

Stokes, A. (2005). *A study in the relationship between organizational structures and public relations practitioner roles*. Unpublished thesis. University of South Florida, Tampa.

Strauss, G. (1982). Workers participation in management: An international perspective. *Research in Organizational Behavior, 4*, 173–265.

Strauss, G., & Rosenstein, E. (1970). Worker's participation: A critical point of view. *Industrial Relations, 9*, 197–214.

Ströh, U. (2005). *An experimental study of organisational change and communication management*. Unpublished doctoral dissertation. University of Pretoria, South Africa.

Ströh, U. (2007). Relationships and participation: A complexity science approach to change communication. *International Journal of Strategic Communication, 1*(2), 123–137.

Taylor, D., & Snell, M. W. (1986). The post office experiment: An analysis of industrial democracy meetings. In R. N. Stem & S. McCarthy (Eds.), *International yearbook of organizational democracy. The organizational practice of democracy* (Vol. III). New York, NY: John Wiley & Sons.

Taylor, S. (2007, April 11). The wit and wisdom of Snoop Dogg. Retrieved July 2, 2010 from http://poliblogblog.blogspot.com

Taylor, V. E., & Winquist, C. E. (Eds.). (2001). *Encyclopedia of postmodernism*. New York: Routledge.

Thompson, J. B. (1990). *Ideology in modern culture. Critical social theory and the era of mass communication*. Stanford, CA: Stanford University Press.

Thornham, S. (1999). Postmodernism and feminism (or; Repairing our own cars). In S. Sim (Ed.), *The Routledge critical dictionary of postmodern thought* (pp. 41–52). New York: Routledge.

Toth, E. L. (2002). Postmodernism for modernist public relations: the cash value and application of critical research in public relations. *Public Relations Review, 28*(3), 243–250.

Toth, E. L., Serini, S., Wright, D. K., & Emig, A. G. (1998). Trends in public relations roles: 1990–1995. *Public Relations Review, 24*, 145–164.

Tracey, J., & Hinkin, T. (1998). Transformational leadership or effective managerial practices? *Group & Organization Management, 23*, 220–236.

Tsekeris, C., & Katrivesis, N. (2009). Ethical reflexivity and epistomological weakness. *Tamara. Journal of Critical Postmodern Organization Science, 7*(3), 26–31.

Tucker, C. (2007, April 23). Viewpoint: Who are the hos here? *Time, 169*, 38.

Tucker, K. H. (1998). *Anthony Giddens and modern social theory*. London: Sage Publications.

Tulloch, S. (Ed.) (1993). *Reader's Digest Oxford complete wordfinder*. London: Reader's Digest Association Limited.

Tushman, M., & O'Reilly, C. (1997). *Winning through innovation: A practical guide to leading organizational change and renewal*. Cambridge, MA: Harvard Business School Press.

van Ruler, B., & Verčič, D. (2004). Overview of public relations and communication management in Europe. In B. van Ruler & D. Verčič (Eds.), *Public relations and communication management in Europe* (pp. 1–11). Berlin: Mouton de Gruyter.

Vattimo, G. (1988). *The end of modernity: Nihilism and hermeneutics in post-modern culture*. Cambridge, UK: Polity Press.

Venturelli, S. (1998). *Liberalizing the European media: Politics, regulation, and the public sphere*. Oxford, UK: Clarendon Press.

Verbeke, A., Schulz, R., Greidanus, N., & Hambley, L. (2008). *Growing the virtual workplace: The integrative value proposition for telework*. Northampton, MA: Edward Elgar Publishing.

Vickers, M. H. (2005). Illness, work and organization: Postmodern perspectives, antenarratives and chaos narratives for the reinstatement of voice. *Tamara. Journal of Critical Postmodern Organization Science, 3*(2), 74–87.

Walia, S. (2001). *Edward Said and the writing of history*. Duxford, U.K.: Icon Books.

Walker, O. C. J. (1997). The adaptability of network organizations: Some unexplored questions. *Journal of the Academy of Marketing Science, 25*(1), 75–83.

Webster's new collegiate dictionary. (1975). Springfield, MA: G. & C. Merrian Company.

Weick, K. E. (2001). *Making sense of the organization.* Oxford, U.K.: Blackwell.

Werder, K. G. P., & Holtzhausen, D. R. (2008). *The emergence of the communication strategist: An examination of practitioner roles, department leadership style, and message strategy use in organizations.* Paper presented at the Association for Education in Journalism and Mass Communication.

Werder, K. G. P., & Holtzhausen, D. R. (2009). An analysis of the influence of public relations department leadership style on public relations strategy use and effectiveness. *Journal of Public Relations Research, 21*(4), 404–427.

West, C. (1997). The new cultural politics of difference. In S. Seidman (Ed.), *The postmodern turn. A new perspective on social theory* (pp. 65–81). Cambridge, U.K.: Cambridge University Press.

Westwood, R., & Clegg, S. (2003). The discourse of organization studies: Dissensus, politics, and paradigms. In R. Westwood & S. Clegg (Eds.), *Debating organization: Point-counterpoint in organization studies* (pp. 1–42). Malden, MA: Blackwell Publishing Inc.

White, R., & Lippitt, R. (1960). *Autocracy and democracy: An experimental inquiry.* New York: Harper & Brothers.

Wilcox, D. L., & Cameron, G. T. (2006). *Public relations strategies and tactics* (8th ed.). Boston, MA: Pearson/Allyn & Bacon.

Williams, J. (1998). *Lyotard. Towards a postmodern philosophy.* Malden, MA: Blackwell.

Williamson, O. E. (1963). Managerial discretion and business behavior. *American Economic Review, 53,* 1032–1047.

Williamson, O. E. (1975). *Markets and hierarchy: Analysis and antitrust implications.* New York: Free Press.

Wilmot, H. (1994). Bringing agency (back) into organizational analysis: Responding to the crisis of (post)modernity. In J. Hassard & M. Parker (Eds.), *Towards a new theory of organization* (pp. 87–130). London & New York: Routledge.

Wilson, N. J. (1999). *History in crisis? Recent directions in historiography.* Upper Saddle River, NJ: Prentice Hall.

Wiseman, R. M., & Gomez-Mejia, L. R. (1998). A behavioral agency model of managerial risk-taking. *Academy of Management Review, 23*(1), 133–153.

Wittington, R. (1994). Sociological pluralims, institution and managerial agency. In J. Hassard & M. Parker (Eds.), *Towards a new theory of organization* (pp. 53–74). London & New York: Routledge.

Wright, P., Mukherjib, A., & Kroll, M. (2001). A reexamination of agency theory assumptions: Extensions and extrapolations. *The Journal of Socio-Economics., 30*(5), 413–417.

Yammarino, F. J., Spangler, W. D., & Dubinsky, A. J. (1998). Transformational and contingent reward leadership: Individual, dyad, and group levels of analysis. *The Leadership Quarterly, 9*(1), 27–54.

Zerfass, A. E. (2009). Institutionalization of strategic communication—theoretical analysis and empirical evidence. *International Journal of Strategic Communication, 3*(2).

Zerfass, A., Tench, R., Verhoeven, P., Verčič, D., & Moreno, A. (2010). *European communciation monitor 2010. Status quo and challenges for public relations in Europe. Results of an empirical survey in 46 countries.* Brussels: European Public Relations Education and Research Association.

Ziarek, E. P. (2001). *An ethics of dissensus.* Stanford, CA: Stanford University Press.

INDEX

An environmentally friendly book printed and bound in England by www.printondemand-worldwide.com

PEFC Certified

This product is
from sustainably
managed forests
and controlled
sources

www.pefc.org

PEFC/16-33-415

®

FSC

www.fsc.org

MIX

Paper from
responsible sources

FSC® C004959

This book is made entirely of sustainable materials; FSC paper for the cover and PEFC paper for the text pages.

#0135 - 040613 - C0 - 229/152/15 [17] - CB